C000001293

Published by Macmillan in ι
London School of Economics ι

THE NATIONALISATION OF BRITISH TRANSPORT
Michael R. Bonavia

LIVES, LIBERTIES AND THE PUBLIC GOOD
George Feaver and Frederick Rosen (editors)

PEASANTS AND GOVERNMENT IN THE RUSSIAN
REVOLUTION
Graeme J. Gill

THE ARMY AND THE CROWD IN MID-GEORGIAN
ENGLAND
Tony Hayter

PARLIAMENT, PARTY AND THE ART OF POLITICS IN
BRITAIN, 1855–59
Angus Hawkins

OIL AND EMPIRE: BRITISH POLICY AND
MESOPOTAMIAN OIL, 1900–1920
Marian Kent

ECONOMIC CRIME IN EUROPE
L. H. Leigh

MEN AND CITIZENS IN THE THEORY OF
INTERNATIONAL RELATIONS
Andrew Linklater

NESTOR MAKHNO IN THE RUSSIAN CIVIL WAR
Michael Malet

THE NATURE OF INTERNATIONAL SOCIETY
C. A. W. Manning

GRAHAM WALLAS AND THE GREAT SOCIETY
OPINION CONTROL IN THE DEMOCRACIES
Terence H. Qualter

THORSTEIN VEBLEN AND THE INSTITUTIONALISTS
David Seckler

THE DIPLOMACY OF BIOLOGICAL DISARMAMENT
Nicholas A. Sims

ARISTOTLE ON EQUALITY AND JUSTICE
HOBBES AND LOCKE
W. von Leyden

THE ORIGIN OF
THE
COMMUNIST AUTOCRACY

POLITICAL OPPOSITION
IN THE SOVIET STATE

FIRST PHASE · 1917–1922

LEONARD SCHAPIRO

*Remota itaque justitia quid sunt regna nisi
magna latrocinia?*
Saint Aúgustine

Second Edition

in association with
Palgrave Macmillan

TO THE MEMORY OF MY FATHER

First edition (published by G. Bell and Sons Ltd
and the London School of Economics
and Political Science) 1955

Reprinted 1956, 1966
Second Edition 1977
Reprinted 1987

Published by
THE MACMILLAN PRESS LTD
Houndmills, Basingstoke, Hampshire RG21 2XS
and London
Companies and representatives
throughout the world

British Library Cataloguing in Publication Data
Schapiro, Leonard
The origin of the Communist autocracy:
political opposition in the Soviet state:
first phase 1917–1922.—2nd ed.
1. Soviet Union—Politics and
government—1917–1936
I. Title
322.4'2'0947   DK265
ISBN 978-0-333-44140-4   ISBN 978-1-349-09509-4 (eBook)
DOI 10.1007/978-1-349-09509-4

PREFACE TO THE FIRST EDITION

This is the story of how a group of determined men seized power for themselves in Russia in 1917, and kept others from sharing it; and of the consequences which ensued both for themselves and for their political rivals when it became evident that they enjoyed but little popular support. These are the bare bones. The flesh and blood of the story are to be found in the passions which animated the actors in the drama. For all of those who figure in my narrative were revolutionaries. I have scarcely touched on the opponents of the Bolsheviks in the battlefield whose aim was to restore the overthrown monarchical régime, but have confined myself to political opposition during the active years of Lenin's life after the revolution.

The Bolsheviks believed passionately, though I think erroneously, that they were carrying into effect a revolution of the kind which had been written of by Marx. The Mensheviks, marxists of a different kind, believed the Bolsheviks' reading of the sacred books to be wrong, and their action accordingly premature. The Socialist Revolutionaries, not being marxists at all, were inspired by doctrines derived from an entirely different tradition. Among the Bolsheviks, different groups at different times challenged the particular lines along which Lenin strove to guide the policy of the party. But, I repeat, all were revolutionaries. Hence, the struggle between the various groups and individuals never took the form of a straightforward struggle by force of arms in which the stronger, or more popular, or more skilful, or more righteous side won. That is what makes the story one of particular human interest, and also gives it its true quality of tragedy.

It is strange that the story of political opposition to Lenin has never before, so far as I am aware, been told in detail or as a whole—there are several good short accounts of aspects of it, incidental to more general histories of the Russian revolution and civil war. Perhaps the reason lies in the fact that we have all been inclined to accept the bolshevik revolution as a marxist revolution in character and pattern. Hence, those who accept marxist doctrine as true tend to dismiss the elimination

v

of the Bolsheviks' political opponents as an inevitable step in the victory of the party of the proletariat, and not therefore of outstanding interest.   But even those who reject marxism, or keep an open mind about its dogmas, have tended, I believe, to accept, however much they may disapprove, the elimination of all political opponents as an inevitable consequence of trying to put marxism into practice—and therefore once again as not of particular interest.   I think there are at least two very good reasons for trying to examine the story of political opposition to the Bolsheviks as far as possible outside the framework of marxist categories and terminology.   First, because the difference of doctrine between Lenin in practice and Marx in theory is at any rate sufficient to raise serious doubt whether the political doctrines of the two men were really one and the same.   For example, Marx does not say, so far as I am aware, that one revolutionary party should eliminate and destroy all other workers' and peasants' parties and establish itself in sole power.   Again (as Mr. John Plamenatz has recently pointed out) to make a 'proletarian' revolution first and then to set about creating an industrial society afterwards, makes nonsense of historical materialism.   Secondly, whether it was marxist or not, there seems no doubt to me that Lenin's doctrine of action also had deep roots in Russian revolutionary tradition and Russian history.   Of course, Lenin believed himself to be a marxist.   No doubt he believed, and certainly was able to persuade his own followers, that the developments of his policy, with all the empirical changes and inconsistencies, were all fully justified by the principles enunciated in this or that work of Marx or Engels.   But I have been repeatedly struck with the peculiarly Russian character not only of Lenin's doctrines, or policies, but often also of his opponents' reactions to them.   There is nothing surprising or novel about this.   It is only one further demonstration of the chimaera of economic determinism in its extreme form, which supposes that all men will everywhere react in the same way at a given stage of economic development.   But it seemed to me a very good reason to try to see the political events of the early years of communist rule in Russia untrammelled by any kind of marxist assumptions or idiom.

I have indeed often been impressed by the dissonance which

the use of marxist categories sets up when applied to Russian conditions, in accounts of the Russian Revolution.   In what sense, for example, were the Mensheviks a 'bourgeois' party, as, of course, they are by definition in Leninist jargon? They drew their support mainly from trade unionists, and not very prosperous trade unionists at that.   There was nothing more 'bourgeois' about their supporters than there was about their leaders, who were of the purest 'intelligentsia'—that peculiar Russian social phenomenon, which transcended all class divisions, and provided the leadership for all but the most right-wing political parties:— liberal, radical, socialist, or communist. Again 'kulak' is quite intelligible as a term of abuse, to be applied to any peasant, rich or poor, who does not like communism.   It is however somewhat misleading to identify the peasant supporters of the Socialist Revolutionaries with the 'kulaks'.   Of course, these peasants disliked the communist régime.   But to identify their political outlook with the class background implied in the term 'kulak' (and even non-marxist writers occasionally sin in this respect) is to fly in the face of facts.   For even the 'medium' peasants, who supported the Socialist Revolutionaries, at most owned a few acres and one horse (if they were lucky); and the Socialist Revolutionaries were generally as much, if not more, hostile than the Bolsheviks to the few really rich exploiter peasants— the 'kulaks' in the true sense of this term.

I have therefore attempted to study the history of the Bolsheviks and their opponents without the distorting marxist framework—in short, to look at the principal characters concerned as human beings, and not as exponents of this or that theory, or as-representatives of this or that class interest.   I have tried, without, I hope, ignoring economic and social factors not to let them obliterate what is after all the key to any historical situation—the men who thought or acted in this way or that.   Lenin's policy of eliminating his political opponents naturally involved a good deal of cruelty and injustice.   This I have thought it right to assess and describe. Again, if a political party which does not enjoy the support of the majority of the population wishes to keep in power, it is forced to take certain liberties with its own doctrines, and to enforce the strictest discipline on its members.   I have tried to assess the impact of these developments on the ranks of the Bolsheviks. Finally, no minority can keep power by force alone, without the aid of other factors. One such factor which I have tried to assess was the effect of the hesitation, doubts, and scruples of Lenin's opponents.

I hope I shall not be reproached for not writing a history of the Russian Revolution. For this I have not attempted to do. I have tried to cover some new ground, and have therefore had to resist the temptation of going outside my own selected subject more than was barely necessary to make my material intelligible. Economic and social history of the period, foreign policy, nationality problems, or the development of institutions are only touched on to the extent necessary, as it seemed to me, to illuminate the main conflicts with which I am concerned. Those who are primarily interested in these aspects of the history of the U.S.S.R. must look elsewhere, in the several excellent works which have been devoted to them. My own Cinderella has not hitherto occupied the stage by herself. She is entitled for once not to be crowded out by the other more familiar performers.

The difficulty which besets the writing of any contemporary history is that it is not easy at so short a distance of time to see facts uncoloured by the living political issues which affect our daily lives. The position of the historian becomes even harder when he has to deal with a revolution which has had a deep, emotional impact on his own generation. No one of my generation will readily forget that impact in our universities, and in public, literary, and political life, nor the hopes which were raised among so many by what appeared to them at first to be a new and more just form of society. This was a good, even a noble, reaction. So, I think, was the no less emotional reaction against some of the tyrannies and cruelties of the Soviet régime on the part of those who did not believe in the new society with quite so naïve a faith. But all this was very bad for historical truth. It is not the deliberate pro- or anti-communist distortions which matter— they can usually be spotted and discounted by anyone at all familiar with the subject. More serious are the unconscious effects which the emotional impact of Russian communism has had on quite a number of historians. I think four schools of writers on Soviet history (outside the Soviet Union, of course) can be distinguished. There is first the 'no alternative' school. This school accepts as a fact that, however regrettable it may have been, there was no possible alternative to Lenin and the Bolsheviks—except, perhaps chaos. (There was chaos enough under Lenin, in all truth!) This view is coloured by the realization that for centuries the Russians had lived under an autocracy and had had no experience of free government. It may, for all I know, be quite a correct view—my quarrel with it is that it is an unverifiable assumption which has tended more than any other to distort the proper study of opposition to Lenin. For what, after all, upon such an assumption, did opposition matter, except possibly as a symptom of weariness, or of the natural disillusionment of all revolutionaries after the revolution has been accomplished? I have tried to make no such assumption. There are very good reasons why the Bolsheviks succeeded, and I have tried to analyse them. But I do not think that either historical necessity, or some fatality which predestines Russians to live forever under totalitarian rule, need be invoked.

Another school of historians of Soviet Russia is what might be called the 'things were different under Lenin' school. Their view has been widely encouraged by the vast literature by and around Trotsky. The facts do not, I think, bear it out very far. But my conclusions must speak for themselves. The third school, which owes much to the influence of marxism, tends to portray Soviet society as having issued, like Minerva, fully armed from Lenin's forehead, with no earlier pedigree. This is a view much encouraged by Soviet writers, of course, but it has not been without influence on some non-Russian historians. I have tried to remain true to my determination not to be circumscribed by marxist categories. I have therefore tried to see the two Russian revolutions as phases in Russian history, not as a new epoch built entirely afresh on the ruins of the old.

Finally there is the school which sees Soviet society from its inception purely in terms of power—seizing power, and keeping it. It is quite a useful corrective to the other schools, but it is nonetheless wrong. I should guess that there probably

comes a time in the history of every dictatorship when staying
in power becomes so all absorbing a problem that it tends to
colour or obscure every other motive or action. Possibly
something of the kind happened to the Bolsheviks at some
stage during the period with which I am concerned. But to
ignore the passion for justice, for the ultimate liberation of
mankind, for the utopia of the future, which animated most
if not all of the bolshevik leaders, is to do equal violence to
truth. I take the view that their passion for justice was bound
to lead to disaster when once they failed to see the need for
reconciling all the conflicting interests which will always exist
in practice in every state (whatever Marx and Engels may have
said on the subject) in a form of stable legal order. Without
the restraining *ne plus ultra* of law and independent judges it
is very tempting for any government to sacrifice first the
majority to a minority, then to-day to to-morrow, and finally
one generation to future generations. This is what Lenin
and his successors seem to have done. But they acted as
they did, at any rate when they first set out, because they
believed that in so doing they were serving the cause of justice.
I think they failed, because justice cannot thrive without
order—'a good disposition of discrepant parts, each in the
fittest place'. Lenin apparently believed that if you went on
long enough eliminating the discrepant parts, justice would
flourish in the monolithic rump that was left. Events did not
work out like that. However, it may be that justice can
never wholly disappear as a force in any human society—
those who are familiar with the context of the quotation which
I have chosen as an epigraph will recall that the great African
philosopher and saint meant something of this kind. In
Lenin's society the task of keeping the human passion for
justice alive fell mainly, though perhaps not entirely, to the
political opponents of the Bolsheviks—as I stressed, they were
all revolutionaries, even if their brand of revolution was not
the one which was victorious in October 1917. I do not
share the predisposition of some contemporary historians,
upon whom the hand of Hegel still lies somewhat heavily,
in favour of the seemingly victorious side in history. Who
are the victors, after all, and who the vanquished? Was
Cromwell victor or vanquished? Was Napoleon victor or

vanquished? It would perhaps be wiser for the present to suspend the verdict as between Lenin and say Martov, or Plekhanov, or Chernov—or Struve, or even Stolypin. The only really vanquished in history are, perhaps, those who cannot see anything beyond the apparent reality of immediate facts. All I hope is that I have succeeded in my aim of holding the balance equally between all the contending parties and factions, and not pleading the cause of any one of them.

I do not pretend to conceal my own predilection for a society based on an established legal order, in which varying and conflicting interests both of individuals and of the state are reconciled with the aid of a minimum of government compulsion. Nor can I disguise the fact that I view much of the analysis of history and society, and all the messianic promises of marxism with very considerable scepticism. It is not the historian's function to judge, so much as to analyse and describe. But in so far as judgment has been unavoidable, this was my criterion of individual actions. They say you cannot make an omelette without breaking eggs. So far as Lenin's cookery is concerned, perhaps the time has not yet come to judge the result. But since some leading gastronomes have already thrown doubt on the quality of the dish, I do not apologize for devoting some study to the eggs. It is all too easy a matter to accept with equanimity 'experiments in social engineering'—especially if one is not oneself called upon to live through them. 'Nous avons tous assez de force pour supporter les maux d'autrui.' But the stuff of history in the end is not an abstraction called society, but living and suffering man.

The problem of the historian of Soviet society is further complicated by the so called 'cold war', in the course of which the somewhat belated discovery of some of the elementary facts about Soviet life by Western politicians is being put to diplomatic and counter-propaganda uses. The academic nose, on this side of the Atlantic at all events, wrinkles all too readily at the thought that any work on Soviet history might be pressed into service by the politician for his mundane purposes, however serious the work, if it should contain any conclusions adverse to the communists' picture of themselves.

Unhappily, distortion both by the Bolsheviks and by their opponents of their own and others' actions and motives is as much an historical fact as the size of Napoleon's hat. To ignore the existence of such distortions by the Bolsheviks, for fear of talk of 'cold war', and not to attempt to probe for the truth behind the welter of lies and half truths by all parties would be merely to mislead. Nothing is farther from my mind than to decry academic aloofness from the current political conflicts. But, unfortunately, if one is hazardous enough to select Soviet history as one's subject, considerable caution is required lest, for fear of the dust from the political arena, one should fall a victim to the distortions of their own history spread abroad by Soviet politicians. As I turn the pages of a number of standard, reputable works on aspects of Soviet history published in this country in recent years, I find quite a few examples which served as a warning to me that he who has no stomach to probe the assertions made by the communists about themselves and their past is liable to be strangely deceived. Thus, one such recent work tells me that Bukharin plotted in 1918 with the Left Socialist Revolutionaries to arrest Lenin. Another tells me that it was never inherent in the Bolsheviks' programme to exclude others from government. A third, that Lenin's socialist opponents were merely striving to replace his dictatorship by one of their own. Those who trouble to read the facts which I have assembled will be able to assess the validity of these and similar assertions. I therefore make no apology for having dwelt in detail on different facets of opposition, both within and without the bolshevik party, in the hope that my work may help to dispel some current misapprehensions. I have accordingly tried to give as full a background of facts, especially where they are new, or little known, as is consistent with clarity of narrative. Above all, I have striven to make my selection of facts (and all historical writing consists of selection of facts) as fair and as objective as I could.

I was faced from the outset with the problem of presentation. The strictly chronological order seemed at first sight the most logical, and the most economical of space. For example, if one were writing the history of the British Labour Party before the First World War it would be the obvious order to choose. But to adopt it for the conditions of early Soviet society seemed to me, on reflection, to run the risk of falsifying the whole story. It would have meant sketching the development of bolshevik policy from the beginning to the end of my period, and showing at each stage the opposition, both within the bolshevik party and by the socialist parties, to a particular policy. But the attitude of the socialist parties to the Bolsheviks, at any rate after 1918, was not opposition in the ordinary, Western political sense of that term at all; it was a struggle for survival. These parties did not oppose the Bolsheviks merely because they disagreed with their policy—in many respects at different periods they fully supported it. It therefore seemed to me essential to treat each important opposition party separately, as I have done in the second part of my book, in order to show the struggle for survival and its outcome in the case of each individual party. This has involved some, though I hope not very much, repetition and cross reference. But I trust that any inconvenience or lack of clarity that may be caused by this method of treatment will be compensated by the greater historical accuracy which I am certain has resulted.

There is no lack of sources on this early period of Soviet history. A great deal of primary source material has been published by the Soviet authorities. I have found no reason to suppose that any of it, in publications before about 1928, has been falsified. The position is perhaps rather different in the case of materials published after that date, which sometimes tend to be tainted with signs of Stalin's conflict with Trotsky. Secondary sources,—the press, memoirs, reports of trials, etc.—are frankly polemic, and great discretion is needed in extracting the truth from them. Since some of this material is little known, I have appended a fairly detailed bibliography. It is not, of course, a complete record of all that I have read. But I have tried to list first, all publications from which I have actually quoted; and secondly, some of the many works which I have found illuminating or helpful on some aspects of my subject.

Translations, unless otherwise indicated, are my own, from the original languages. As regards the vexed question of transliteration of Russian, I have followed the system adopted by the *Slavonic and East European Review*, with some minor modifications which sacrifice accuracy to simplicity.

The search for material has taken me to many libraries of Europe. It has not been possible for me to visit the rich collections in the libraries of the United States, but in some instances I was fortunate in being able to obtain microfilm or photostatic reproductions of books not available in Europe. I am glad of this opportunity of expressing my gratitude to the staffs of all the libraries in which I have worked for their unfailing helpfulness, kindly interest, and assistance. If I single out for particular mention the staff of the Reading Room of the British Museum it is only because most of my research was in fact done on the magnificent collection of early Soviet publications contained in this delightful library.

The manuscript of this book was virtually completed in 1950, but publication was delayed through circumstances beyond my control. The delay has been of advantage in enabling me to avail myself of the kindness of a number of experts who were willing to comment on my work. Mr. E. H. Carr read the manuscript at a very early stage of its existence, and made a number of comments on points of detail which I was glad to adopt, and for which I am most grateful to him. I regret that I was not able to adopt some other suggestions which he was kind enough to make, because our interpretations of the facts diverged too fundamentally. Mr. Isaiah Berlin, Mr. R. N. Carew Hunt, Miss Violet Conolly, Dr. George Katkov, and Mr. Alec Nove have read the manuscript and made many valuable comments and corrections. Dr. V. Leontowitsch read and commented on the first chapter, and placed his unrivalled knowledge of the history of Russian liberalism at my disposal. Mr. David Footman read the book in proof, and made some most helpful suggestions. To all the above I wish to express my deep gratitude. I need hardly add that the responsibility for the text is entirely my own. I should also like to express my gratitude to many friends, some of them participants in the events I have described, with whom I have been able to discuss some of the questions raised by this difficult period of Russian history.

The greatest debt of gratitude I owe to my wife. She has

subjected the manuscript to repeated and critical scrutiny, and her balanced and mature judgment of men and events has on innumerable occasions provided a necessary corrective to my own judgment. I am conscious of the many faults of this book. But it would have been a great deal worse but for my wife.

Highgate
July, 1954

PREFACE TO THE SECOND EDITION

Twenty-two years have passed since the writing of this book was completed. Every author hopes, when a work of his which has gone out of print is once again made available, that it will still be of some interest to some readers. It is therefore incumbent upon him to ask himself: what has changed since I wrote this book? And if I were writing it today would it be very different?

Now, of course, in twenty-two years, especially in the past twenty-two years when there has been a considerable expansion in the study of the history of the Soviet Union, much new evidence has been uncovered by research. I can think of many details which I should like to change in the light of this research in several fields. We know a good deal more about the Kronstadt rising, for example—though I am bound to say the new knowledge has not affected the fundamental assessment of that event which is still a living influence in left-wing thought today. There has been new work on the left socialist revolutionary revolt of July 1918 which, if I were writing the book today, I should have to take into account. To take another example—and I am only citing a few examples—much work has been done on the basis of which I could now give a much fuller and probably more accurate picture of the early history of the Cheka than I was able to do at the time in an investigation of the sources available to me for the writing of what was only a minor section of the whole work. Even so, I think I was able to establish that concentration camps and arbitrary illegality long preceded Stalin, and were in fact a legacy from Lenin.

So far as new material is concerned, a great number of memoirs, pamphlets, documents and the like on Menshevism have been amassed since I wrote the book. Professor Radkey's definitive history of the Socialist Revolutionaries in two volumes also appeared after my book. His history is based on extensive study of the archives of the party and on much material and information made available to him by Victor Chernov. I have no doubt that if I were writing this book today my chapters on the Mensheviks and Socialist Revolutionaries would look very different. Many details omitted by me would be added and, no doubt, many errors corrected. But nothing which I have seen in the past twenty years has led me to alter my conviction that it was the Mensheviks' confused and muddled idealism and—in some, but by no means all—cases a betrayal of their principles which did much to help the Bolsheviks to seize power, and to cling precariously to it. There was, of course, a good deal of courageous opposition too by the Mensheviks—but it came too late to be effective, because the bolshevik apparatus of illegality had already been long set up, and was well able to resist 'constitutional' opposition. And this was all which the Mensheviks believed it right to advance. It is incidentally an ironical reflection that these strictures on menshevik illusions which figure in the book, and which, much to my regret, caused distress to some of my friends among the surviving former menshevik leaders, have passed unnoticed by Soviet critics of my book. They have repeatedly, for reasons best known to themselves, branded me as a Menshevik, or pro-Menshevik—when not describing me as something very much worse.

The principal change in the past twenty-two years has been the change in political attitude to Soviet history—and one cannot escape the fact, regrettable as it may be, that all students of contemporary or very recent history are affected by political climate. In 1954, when this book was completed, nearly two years were still to elapse before Khrushchev's shattering exposure of Stalin put an end to any lingering doubts that the evidence about his régime accumulating in the West may have been exaggerated. In spite of these doubts (exemplified usually by the occasional scholarly or quasi-scholarly study which preferred to leave the question of Stalin's brutal tyranny open for lack of firm evidence) there were few illusions left among scholars—and I exclude blatant fellow-travellers or communist party propagandists masquerading as scholars—about Stalin's régime by 1954. Much had been done to expose this era of Russian history in its true colours by Trotsky before his death, and by Trotsky's followers thereafter. It may be that because so much criticism of Stalin had emanated from Trotsky that, possibly unconsciously, the legend grew up that all had been well under Lenin. There had been full democracy inside the Communist party—so went the legend; while such unpleasant things as secret police, terror and hounding of political opponents could be explained as temporary aberrations brought about by the civil war, allied intervention and the like. If my book achieved anything that hadn't already been achieved by others it was the exposure of the shallowness of this view. What I tried to show was that the arbitrary illegality was inherent in the very nature of the régime created and maintained by Lenin—a small band of zealots, convinced of their own infallibility and of their divine right to rule alone, and ruling in defiance of their own law (or what there was of it). The fact that the scale was much smaller under Lenin is certainly important; but it does not destroy the continuity between Lenin and Stalin. Lenin's concentration camps were tiny when compared to Ezhov's or Beria's slave empires under Stalin. But the principle behind them—that you could exploit the labour of alleged or suspected enemies, without trial, under the guise of punishment—was the same. Solzhenitsyn's *Gulag Archipelago* has made this point much more effectively than I could ever hope to do. But I did at the time, in a climate which was not (at any rate in this country) propitious for any serious blaming of Lenin for the nature of the Soviet régime, put some of the record straight.

Equally important, in my view, in this context, is the lasting importance of the Tenth Congress of the Communist Party in 1921—the last Congress which Lenin, still in full possession of his faculties, was able to dominate and direct. This was the Congress which saw the introduction of the New Economic

Policy (N.E.P.)—which Stalin was to destroy only eight or nine years later. But it was also the occasion when Lenin was at long last able to put into effect the kind of monolithic régime in the party which—contrary to what Trotsky would later affirm—it was always his intention to effect. The entire conduct by Lenin of the control over his bolshevik faction between 1903 and 1917 proves this beyond doubt—and, indeed, it was Trotsky who at the time was most vocal in his criticism of what, in exile later, he would conveniently forget. The monolithic régime of 1921 which has prevailed in the Soviet Communist party—and indeed all other Communist parties—ever since, included the prohibition of all groups or factions in the party; severe inhibition of debate, for fear of giving comfort to the party's enemies; and strict, central discipline over all members. These were the main instruments, my book concludes, which Stalin used to set up his régime of terror.

I did not pose the hypothetical question: would Lenin, had he survived, have pursued a different policy from Stalin, or essentially the same policy? Perhaps, in the perspective of a further twenty years' distance from Lenin and Stalin the question is worth asking whether Lenin, who certainly forged the instruments which Stalin was able to use, would, had he survived, have used them in the same way as Stalin. Two arguments can be advanced against the view that he would have done so. The first is what we know about Lenin's views on future policy both from his own last writings and from the policy pursued after Lenin's death by Bukharin, who was in close touch with the leader during his last lucid months and who certainly claimed to be regarded himself as Lenin's disciple. This policy can best be described in the modern term 'communism with a human face'—that is reconciliation rather than conflict between town and country, and to a certain extent between classes, and consequently a considerable relaxation of terrorist and repressive methods, reform of penal policy in a more liberal direction, more intellectual freedom—and the like. It can certainly be argued that had Lenin lived it would have been such a policy that he would have tried to put through. And secondly, it can be urged that, tough and ruthless as he undoubtedly was, nevertheless Lenin still belonged to some extent—in a way that Stalin did not—to the European social democratic tradition, and would therefore have been reluctant to unleash the kind of mass terror on the country that Stalin perpetrated without hesitation. Perhaps a more realistic way of putting the same argument is as follows: one of the main reasons for Stalin's mass brutality was his paranoid fear of potential opponents; this fear was largely generated by the fact that Stalin knew only too well that he enjoyed no moral authority in the party, and therefore had to appeal either to the selfish motives of those who followed him, or to fear. Lenin—so the argument can be put—enjoyed enormous moral authority and ascendancy far and wide in the party and therefore would have had no need to use force on the same scale as Stalin, even if, like Stalin, he decided to reverse N.E.P. and enforce collectivization.

As against these rather hypothetical arguments stands the inexorable logic of events. If once a minority, with no claim whatever to legitimacy, embarks on a policy of coercion and arbitrary violence, the momentum of coercion and violence is bound to increase as opposition increases. The Bolsheviks were such a minority—their voting strength in the country, at its height, in 1917, was barely 25 per cent, and was probably a very great deal lower by 1921; while the theoretical claims to rule elaborated by Lenin could, at best, have persuaded his followers—and not all his followers at that, as the Kronstadt revolt showed. There are many examples in the history of the last fifty years alone to show that where a minority seeks to impose its will, in the profound conviction that it alone has possession of the truth, and the historic right to enforce it in defiance of all the legal and moral rights of those over whom it rules, the amount of violence which it employs will steadily and inexorably increase. Moral restraint on the part of those who are called upon to be the instruments of that violence will certainly be of little effect—as the example of National Socialist Germany clearly showed. The doing of evil can become a habit in the course of which normal moral judgment is suspended—this is a law of totalitarian rule which Hannah Arendt aptly called 'the banality of evil'. A secret speech by Himmler has been preserved in which he praised his henchmen, who were called upon to do such terrible acts (he was referring to the murder of millions of Jews) for remaining so 'decent'—by which, no doubt, he meant that they remained good husbands and fathers, kind to animals and jolly beer-garden companions. No doubt Himmler was right. His praise of the 'decency' of his killers serves to underline the complete irrelevance of moral principles when it comes to carrying out orders, however monstrous, within a society which is governed not by law but by the 'higher law' of the party, and similar double-speak. And what was true of Himmler's henchmen was also true of most—not all—of the henchmen of the Cheka and the N.K.V.D. and of the bands of Communists who hounded millions of peasants to their death. It is therefore doubtful if Lenin, whose contempt for law knew no bounds, could have avoided this logical advance of terror in the face of growing opposition had he once decided to put an end to the popular N.E.P. (popular in the country, that is, not in the party). Of course, Lenin may have been sincere and truthful when he spoke of N.E.P. as a system which would last for generations, but not centuries, and renounced all intention of using force to impose socialism on the peasants. This would, indeed, have been a very different Lenin from the one who founded the bolshevik party and led it up to 1921. But it is a development which, hypothetically, it is not impossible to contemplate—Bukharin certainly believed that such had been Lenin's intention. In the end the question I posed (though not in the book) must remain an open one. All I attempted in the book was to show how in the early stages of an arbitrary, unpopular minority régime terror and violence gather momentum if not automatically, then at any rate with great ease. Since bolshevik Russia under Lenin was by no means the last of the arbitrary, unpopular minority régimes which the world has had to, and no doubt will yet have to, endure, an account of this early experience may, I hope, still prove of some interest to readers.

I have spent the past twenty years, and more, in the study of totalitarian systems. Nothing has led me to alter the opinion which I formed as the result of work on this book that the key to a society is its attitude to law. (Hence the epigraph which I chose—though St. Augustine was inclined to the view, which I am not sure I can share, that all societies, even bands of brigands, are necessarily governed by some kind of law.)

The whole point about a modern, totalitarian society is that it is not just a more elaborate kind of tyranny, with harsher laws, and more of them. It is, on the contrary, a system of arbitrary rule which has discovered a convenient formula in order to ensure that law and the judges can be utilized as instruments for that arbitrary rule; and can never act as a barrier against such rule. (This was so under Lenin, who virtually destroyed law during his period of ascendancy—it is not perhaps entirely true of the Soviet Union today.) So the German National Socialists invented the 'higher law of the party', while Lenin operated with the marxist 'class consciousness' or the quasi-marxist 'revolutionary conscience' which were supposed to have greater authority than mere 'lawyers' tricks' ('Juristisch also falsch'—as Marx remarked in one of his less lucid moments). If once law, by means of one or other of these, or similar, tricks is turned into an instrument of arbitrary rule (and therefore destroyed) the position of the individual is beyond hope. In this respect, at all events, there was no difference between Lenin and Stalin.

L.S.

London School of Economics and Political Science
July, 1976

CONTENTS

xxiii

PART I

THE BOLSHEVIK COUP D'ETAT

CHAPTER I

THE POLITICAL BACKGROUND

On 22 January 1917 Lenin addressed a gathering of working youth in Zurich. Europe, he told them, was 'pregnant with revolution'. Popular risings, led by the proletariat and ending with the ultimate victory of socialism, would come about in the 'next few years'. But 'we older men may not live to see the decisive battles of this imminent revolution'. However, within eight months the Bolsheviks, headed by Lenin, had swept their political opponents from the field and were in sole if precarious possession of power in Russia. It was to take them several years to eliminate rival parties, and to lay the foundations of unity within their own. But the story of their struggle, which is the subject of this book, cannot be understood without a glance at the origins and faiths of the political parties mainly concerned.

Much of the social thought in nineteenth-century Russia was shaped by the liberation of the serfs which took place in 1861. The hopes and disappointments engendered by this momentous event continued to influence the course of politics, even after the rise of an industrial proletariat had shown that the society of the future would have to take account of this new class as much as of the peasants. Herzen, from his exile in London, had dominated progressive thought through the medium of his paper, *Kolokol* (*The Bell*). Bitterly disappointed in the results of the European revolutions of 1848, and repelled by the drab smugness and inhumanity which he saw in the West, Herzen turned with new hope to the Russian peasant society in which he believed the future salvation of Russia lay. He was convinced that the Russian village organization, unspoiled by the corruption of capitalism, and traditionally

1

accustomed to communal life and work, would make it possible for Russia to by-pass the capitalist phase of Western Europe. Russia, he believed, would follow a separate path, which would lead it straight 'by way of socialism to freedom', aided by this instinctive socialism of its vast peasantry, which did not exist in the Western countries.   His personal influence with the younger generation did not survive the disappointment which followed the much hoped for liberation, when it became apparent that, in the circumscribed form in which it was enacted, it was only going to prove of very limited benefit to the peasant.   The first secret revolutionary organization, *Zemlya i Volya*, (*Land and Liberty*), was founded in the year of the liberation.   Its activities culminated five years later in an attempt on the life of the Emperor—an act of violence which Herzen bitterly condemned.   Such acts of terrorism, while they palliated the sense of impotence of a generation, which longed for reforms which the autocracy was unwilling or unable to put into effect, did little to bridge the vast gulf between the revolutionary intellectuals who sacrificed their lives, and the peasantry on whose behalf they did so.   Thus, Karakozov's attempt on the Emperor's life in 1866 was followed by rioting in the villages.   This was because the peasants regarded the attempt as a plot by the landlords against their own special protector, the Tsar, and not because they approved of it.

The generation of revolutionaries which grew up after the liberation (the *Narodniki*)[1] was much preoccupied with this gulf between the peasants and the intellectuals, and also with the futility of individual acts of terror.   One writer who influenced them was Bakunin, who drew much of his faith and inspiration from the latent anarchical violence which always lies smouldering in the generally docile and submissive Russian peasant.   Russian history records a number of instances of blind and wild peasant risings, senseless, pitiless, and without result.   Bakunin believed that the function of the revolutionary was to harness this latent violence towards the destruction of the old order.   He believed that a better society would inevitably arise out of this destruction, though he had little to say on the form which this new society would take.

[1] From the Russian word for 'people', *narod*.

'Die Lust der Zerstörung ist zugleich eine schaffende Lust,' he once wrote. The Russian people, which he believed was 'socialist by instinct and revolutionary by nature', would of itself create the new forms. Another influence on the revolutionaries of the generation which followed the liberation of the serfs was Tkachev. A figure intellectually inferior to Bakunin, he is remarkable because of the parallel between his ideas and Lenin's practice, if not his theory. Tkachev believed that the transformation of Russian society should be achieved not by acts of terror, but by an immediate seizure of power by a small, disciplined élite, which would then effect from above the necessary economic transformation.

> The revolutionary minority [he wrote], having freed the people from the fear and terror which oppresses it . . . thus opens up to the people the possibility of displaying its destructive revolutionary force. Supporting itself on this destructive force, the minority skilfully directs it towards the annihilation of the immediate enemies of the revolution, and thereby destroys their strongholds and deprives them of all means of opposition and resistance. Thereafter, using its strength and authority, the revolutionary minority introduces new progressive, communist elements into the conditions of national life.'

The common denominator of such different thinkers as Herzen, Bakunin, and Tkachev was the faith that Russia could pass straight to socialism without travelling the path of capitalist development upon which the countries of Western Europe were embarked. Exactly the same faith formed part of the doctrine of two very influential thinkers of the eighteen-seventies and eighteen-eighties, Mikhailovsky and Lavrov, whose ideas were however far removed from those of Bakunin or Tkachev. Mikhailovsky, much more a sociologist and a publicist than a revolutionary, provided a scientific basis for the faith in the 'separate path'. Russia, according to him, belonged to a higher *type* of society, although it was on a lower *phase* of development than Western society. If these arrears of development were caught up with, Russia could pass straight to the higher type of society, without being forced to borrow from Western Europe any of its less desirable features. To give an impetus to this development, the intellectuals must accept it as their mission to educate the peasant for his future rôle. More influential yet on his generation was Lavrov, an exile like Herzen, who had been forced to leave Russia (on very slender evidence) soon after the attempt on the life of the Emperor in 1866. Lavrov was in many ways typical of the 'conscience-stricken nobleman' familiar in Russian late nineteenth-century society. The gist of his doctrine is that it is the duty of the 'critically thinking personality' to pay his debt to the people, at whose expense he has gained his opportunity to think. Lavrov was influenced by marxism and accepted much of its analysis of society. It is significant, for example, that he developed the marxist theory of the origin of society and of the state sixteen years before Engels' famous theory was first published. But Lavrov's emphasis on the rôle and moral responsibility of the individual, as the only vehicle of social progress—defined by him as 'the embodiment in social form of truth and justice'—distinguished his way of thought from that of the Marxists. He was also the very antithesis of Tkachev, believing that the revolution must be the work of the people themselves, and not that seizure of power must be the first aim. The mere replacement of one government by another would solve nothing. The immediate task which he preached was the preparation of the people by education and propaganda for their historic task.

The three main political parties of twentieth-century Russia —the Socialist Revolutionaries, the *Kadety*, and the Social Democrats—all owed much to these early ideas. The Socialist Revolutionary party, when it came into existence at the beginning of the twentieth century, claimed to be the heir to the beliefs expounded by the *Narodniki*. But these doctrines were already largely bankrupt. The faith that it was Russia's destiny to follow a separate path from Western Europe by virtue of the instinctive socialism inherent in the traditional peasant commune became less realistic as industrialization rapidly advanced, and the peasant commune equally rapidly disintegrated. The attempt to educate the peasant for his historic mission had met with no response. Terrorism had brought even less result in spite of the fanatical heroism which inspired it. The assassination of the Emperor Alexander II in 1881 had been followed by repressions and steady reaction. It had not been a signal for a general peasant rising, nor had it brought any reforms in its train. Outwardly, at all events, the Socialist Revolutionaries came into being in response to the aspirations of the nineteenth-century *narodnik* revolutionaries to create a political party on Western European lines. The very choice of the European term Socialist in the name of the new party indicated as much, and in 1903 at the Amsterdam Congress of the Second International the new Russian party was admitted as a member. The programme and statute of the party were adopted at its first congress in 1906. The somewhat utopian maximum programme envisaged a completely socialized society. The more concrete minimum programme demanded the convocation of a Constituent Assembly; the setting up of a federal republic with self-determination for the various nationalities of which Russia was composed; the separation of church and state; full political liberty with appropriate constitutional guarantees; and progressive labour and social legislation, including the eight-hour day and state assistance for poor litigants. So far as the land was concerned, the programme demanded expropriation of all privately owned land without compensation. Thereafter the land was to be managed by municipal democratic bodies and divided up in such a way as to ensure to everyone enough land to give him and his family a living. Dealing in land was to be prohibited, and special benefits enjoyed by individuals, such as better quality of soil or proximity to a river, were to be taxed for the general welfare. The new party did not renounce terrorism, believing that social progress might require the 'intervention of conscious warriors for truth and justice'. But such terrorism was to be confined to acts approved by the highest party authority. Local acts of spontaneous violence in village or factory were condemned, for fear that they would grow into wild popular anarchy which the party would be unable to control. The Congress recognized that a 'revolutionary dictatorship' might prove necessary before the maximum programme of full socialism could be realized. But it was careful to emphasize that this would be temporary only, and would be succeeded as soon as possible by a state founded on law. Even so, nearly one quarter of those present at the 1906 Congress voted against this part of the Programme.

The new Socialist Revolutionary party relied for its support on the very large number of peasant owners of small holdings, particularly those who remained linked to the surviving village communes. To these peasants, and to the landless peasants as well, the Socialist Revolutionary became the champion of their urgent land hunger. He got to know the peasant through the rapidly expanding agricultural co-operatives and through the local government services, in which Socialist Revolutionaries worked in large numbers. The Socialist Revolutionaries retained this support right up to 1917, as their outstanding victory in the elections to the Constituent Assembly showed. But their following, though large, was politically immature. The peasant's political vision extended little beyond his own holding. Of the form of central government and of political programmes he knew little, and cared less. Nor, in the political conditions of Russia in the decade before the revolution of 1917 was there much opportunity for any socialist party to learn the practical business of politics within the existing constitutional framework. The Socialist Revolutionaries had thirty-four deputies in the Second Duma. By the time of the Third Duma, the electoral law of 1907 had succeeded in manipulating the franchise so as to make the election of Socialist Revolutionaries by their peasant electors virtually impossible. A handful of them, however, succeeded in voicing the socialist revolutionary view in the Third and Fourth Dumas, camouflaged as *Trudoviki* (Labourists). The conditions in which the Socialist Revolutionaries had to operate on the margin between legal and illegal existence, made of them a party in which extremism, over-indulgence in theorizing, conspiracy, impatience, and frustration predominated. There was little unity, and less discipline, within the party as a whole, which sheltered the most divergent types and temperaments— patriotic, individualist terrorists such as Savinkov, moderate constitutionalists such as Avksentiev or Zenzinov, idealistic conspirators like Gershuni, masters of political inconsistency such as Chernov, or utopian absolutists such as Spiridonova.

Liberalism is a term little capable of exact definition and the application of the term to Russian conditions is fraught with peculiar difficulty. There did, however, exist in Russian nineteenth-century political society an important section of public opinion which stood for moderate and gradual reform, and which looked to the constitutionalism of Western Europe as the model for such reform. Had the autocracy possessed the political wisdom to trust and support the reformers who abounded in nineteenth-century Russia, social progress might perhaps have taken place without violent upheaval. But would-be reformers were often snubbed, ignored, or even exiled. Disappointment when the extensive reforms of Alexander II were halted drove many moderates into the revolutionary organizations. The violence and, be it said, the absurdity of some of the nineteenth-century revolutionaries drove many more moderates to reaction. Indeed, it is remarkable that so many and so vigorous political thinkers on constitutional lines retained the balance of mind to survive as such without falling into one extreme or the other. The gulf which separated the nineteenth-century liberal reformer from *narodnik* revolutionary thinkers, even those such as Herzen, Mikhailovsky, or Lavrov who did not preach violence, was their rejection of the doctrine that Russia could travel by a separate path from the rest of Europe. Turgenev, for example, warned Herzen that the instinctive socialism of the Russian peasant on which Herzen pinned his faith was a myth, that what the peasant wanted was to obtain his coveted land and then become a bourgeois. And in 1862 Turgenev wrote to Herzen: 'I am beginning to think that the so often repeated antithesis—the West, beautiful externally and hideous within, and the East, hideous externally and beautiful within—is false.' Neither Herzen nor Lavrov ever saw that this antithesis was false. Lavrov refused to admit that the parliamentary order of the Western European states could ever provide any model for Russia. It is true that he rejected dictatorship of any party, even the best, which might seek to rule 'by fear of the knout'; but equally he rejected the 'rotten liberalism' of Western Europe, branding as the direct enemy of progress a 'Russian constitutional party on the European model'. Russia must follow a path of her own.

The idea of a party of constitutionalists began to take root at the beginning of the twentieth century among several progressive groups of the intelligentsia and of the landed proprietors. The most important of these were *Osvobozhdenie* (Liberation), so named after a paper published from 1902 onwards by Peter Struve in Stuttgart; and the union of the local government, or *Zemstva*, representatives. Within these groups, which included in their number almost the entire liberal professions, there could be discerned both a right wing, whose demands were limited in the main to representative government, political freedom and greater autonomy for the *Zemstva*; and a left wing, which also demanded such reforms as the eight-hour day and the confiscation of privately owned land, with compensation to the owners. In 1905, after the revolution of that year had wrung a constitution from the reluctant autocracy, the party of National Freedom or Constitutional Democrats (abbreviated to *Kadet*) was formed by Milyukov, Petrunkevich, Nabokov, and the two Princes Dolgorukov, among others. The left wing did not stay long in the *Kadet* party. Its members either remained outside party allegiance, as was the case with Kuskova and Prokopovich, or eventually formed the small party of Populist Socialists, somewhat to the right of the Socialist Revolutionaries. Among the latter were Peter Chaykovsky and Peshekhonov. But although the *Kadety* were to lose their left wing at an early date, in 1905, under the impact of the revolution to which they had given whole-hearted support, their policy was more radical than it had been in 1902, when *Osvobozhdenie* first appeared. Speakers at their foundation congress associated themselves with the traditions of the liberal intelligentsia of the nineteenth century, with the Decembrists, with Herzen and the later revolutionary fighters. Thus, though the *Narodniki* had rejected the Constitutionalists, the Constitutionalists did not reject the *Narodniki*. In fact, now that the Socialist Revolutionaries had put political freedom in the forefront of their programme and had ostensibly abandoned the *narodnik* doctrine of the separate, non-Western path for Russia, the main division between them and the *Kadety* was that the Socialist Revolutionaries, unlike the *Kadety*, rejected private property. The *Kadet* programme called for an extension and widening of the Manifesto of 17 October 1905 in which the new constitution had been granted. It demanded a complete constitutional system safeguarded by the rule of law, a universal franchise, and freedom of speech and person guaranteed by an independent judiciary. The programme also included abolition of the death penalty, cultural autonomy for nationalities, home rule for Finland and Poland, liberal labour legislation including the eight hour day, full freedom for the formation of trade unions, and a system of social security against illness and old age, as well as universal compulsory primary education and the emancipation of education from both state and church control. The *Kadet* agricultural policy was based on confiscation of private estates upon payment of fair compensation to the owners, and on a wide system of state aid to the peasants.

The *Kadety* continued to attract and hold most of the best intellects and leaders of the universities and liberal professions. But, in the absence in Russia of a substantial middle-class upon which to lean for support, their political success depended upon one of two conditions, if not both: either support from the autocracy to help to build orderly freedom from above, or the support of the socialist parties behind whom stood some of the peasantry and proletariat. The repeated failure of the Russian autocracy to support and make use of the many tens of thousands of moderate reformers who were longing to serve it prevented the creation in Russia of a system of progressive reform within a stable order, and thus helped to create the conditions in which the victory of the Bolsheviks became possible. It was, however, also true that the *Kadety* were often intransigent and uncompromising, and lacked restraint and tact. They won a great victory in the elections to the First Duma, which returned 177 of their party. Before long they had precipitated a crisis, for which they were at any rate in some measure to blame. With more courage than wisdom they issued a revolutionary appeal to the nation against the autocracy, drawing upon themselves severe police repressions. The tone for the future was set by this first unhappy clash. If the autocracy was determined to circumvent even the modest concessions of the new constitution, the *Kadety* could never forget that they too were the heirs of the revolutionaries and viewed any compromise with the autocracy with suspicion. The gulf between the two is illustrated by the relationship between Struve and Stolypin during the period of the Third Duma, as described by Struve in his fragmentary memoirs. Struve had achieved an informal contact with the Prime Minister, Stolypin, and used to visit him on occasion in a vain endeavour to influence him to complement his important agrarian reforms by equally far-reaching political reforms. The visits had to take place in secret, and at dead of night—in the interests of both. Stolypin's position with the Tsar and his circle would have been endangered had his contacts with the liberal, Struve, become known. But Struve's reputation in the *Kadet* party would equally have suffered had he been suspected of any friendly contacts with the Tsar's Minister. Yet for all this, the last years before the outbreak of war in 1914 showed a marked improvement on the political scene. In the Duma, now based on a truncated franchise, the *Kadety*, reduced to 58, were playing a useful, if limited, part. Their relations with the socialists, particularly with the menshevik wing of the Social Democrats, were improving. The autocracy in turn was showing some signs of beginning to realize that a policy of concession was a better safeguard against revolution than police repressions. Hangings and imprisonment of revolutionaries continued, but at the same time some kind of constitutional order was taking shape. The *Zemstva* were doing valuable work in the fields of education and health, censorship was relaxed, the administration of justice was improving, and lawful activity in the trade unions was at last becoming possible. Had the revolution happened, say, in 1912, it is at the least improbable that it would have led to a victory of the Bolsheviks. The war put an end to this incipient stability in the Russian political scene.

To be seen in proportion, the development of social democracy, and of Bolshevism in particular, must be looked at against this background. In 1879 Plekhanov, then a *Narodnik*, had headed a split in this movement and had become leader of a separate wing. He had opposed the demand for an intensification of terrorist activity, believing then, as he thereafter believed all his life, that revolution must be the work not of a few chosen champions, but of the people themselves. But Plekhanov diverged from the *Narodniki* not only on the issue of terror, but because under the influence of marxism he rejected the doctrine that Russia could follow a separate path of its own and avoid the stage of capitalist development which was taking place in Western Europe. It is significant that it was Engels, whom he knew personally, who was the main influence on Plekhanov. Marx had to some extent lent the weight of his authority in support of the *narodnik* faith in Russia's separate path, both in 1875 in a letter to Mikhailovsky, and in 1882 in the Preface to the Russian edition of the Communist Manifesto, which Engels also signed. But Engels had from the first taken a firm stand against a premature coup d'état. In open dispute with Tkachev in 1875 he had ridiculed the theory expounded by Lenin's predecessor that a well organized party of professional revolutionaries should seize control and proceed to impose socialism from above. Plekhanov's conversion to marxism was signalized by attacks on Tkachev. Quotations from Engels on the disasters which would attend seizure of power if it should take place before the proletariat was experienced enough to know what to do with it, abound in his writings. Plekhanov's continued opposition to Lenin after 1903 was similarly due to his refusal to accept Lenin's views on the need for a disciplined party organization even at the expense of mass participation in the work of building the foundations of socialism, quite as much as to his revulsion from Lenin's political methods.

It was therefore as a movement Western in its character and orientations that Russian marxism came into being in 1883, when Plekhanov, together with Vera Zasulich, Deutsch, and Axelrod founded the Group for the Liberation of Labour, from which the Russian Social Democratic Labour Party evolved. By 1903 the impulse of the young Lenin's dynamic personality had split Russian Social Democracy into two wings, the Mensheviks and the Bolsheviks. This split, so eventful for the future history of Russia,[2] was certainly not at the outset a division between those marxists who believed in the necessity of a revolution and those marxists who did not. It was not therefore comparable to the division between the revolutionary and the reformist marxists which was taking place in Western Europe. All Russian Social Democrats,

[2] There is a lucid account of the tangled story of this split in *Carr* I, pp. 26–69, but much important supplementary material will be found in *Wolfe, passim*. Full titles of publications will not normally be used in footnotes. They will be found in the Bibliography (Appendix D, p. 369). The abbreviation used is either the author's name, as here, when only one work by a given author is quoted in the Bibliography, or a shortened form of the title, which will be found in its corresponding alphabetical order in the Bibliography.

including particularly Plekhanov, accepted the necessity for the revolution. They had combined to oppose, at the end of the nineteenth century, the 'Legal Marxists', of whom Struve, the future *Kadet*, was at the time the leading theorist, and the so-called 'Economists', of whom Kuskova was the intellectual leader, who both opposed evolution to revolution. The programme of the Russian social democratic party, approved in 1903 by Bolsheviks and Mensheviks alike, envisaged as a first stage a bourgeois, democratic revolution, but thereafter the 'dictatorship of the proletariat' as the essential condition of the next stage, the social revolution, or in other words 'the conquest by the proletariat of such political power as will permit it to suppress all opposition of the exploiters'. It was in fact the only socialist party programme which contained such a provision. Nor was the split between Bolsheviks and Mensheviks based on any fundamental difference of opinion on the nature of the political liberty which the revolution would achieve. The Programme was silent on the precise state forms which the ultimate socialist revolution would bring forth. But no Social Democrat ever imagined that it would entail a curtailment of the extensive liberties which the Programme proclaimed for the first phase of the revolution, the democratic phase; or that it would take the form which it did take, the curtailment of liberty for all except the party in power. Not one word, at any rate in public, nor one line of Lenin's before October 1917 had ever implied this. Finally, the division between the two wings of Russian social democracy was certainly not based on a difference of view as to the two phases through which, in the progress towards the social revolution, Russia would have to pass. In the West the democratic revolution with its consequent political liberties had already happened, and therefore only the final historical phase, the proletarian or socialist revolution, still remained to be achieved. In Russia the democratic revolution had not yet taken place, and therefore, as the Programme clearly acknowledged, the immediate aim was such a democratic revolution, bringing in its train full political liberties and a Constituent Assembly based on universal suffrage. At no time before April 1917 did Lenin publicly envisage any other course for Russia.

The primary cause for the disunity in Russian social democracy did not thus lie in questions of theory. The fact alone that the same Programme served until 1919 as the accepted plan of action for so many different groups and individuals goes a long way to prove this. This does not mean that there were not quite serious theoretical divergences of view. The most significant dissensions followed upon the revolution of 1905, which took the leaders of the Russian Social Democratic party, engaged in interminable arguments in exile, by surprise. The only outstanding Social Democrat to take part in the short-lived Petersburg Soviet which emerged after the revolution was Trotsky, then, as until 1917, neither of the bolshevik nor the menshevik faction. From the interpretation of the revolution of 1905 there emerged three fairly distinct political theories. The Mensheviks were reinforced in their conviction that the first phase of the revolution, the democratic phase, must be the work of the middle-class parties. In no circumstances must Social Democrats participate in the democratic government which might emerge from this revolution, or attempt to force the pace of the next phase, the social revolution. There must be no jump in the proper working out of the dialectical laws of history. Trotsky, intoxicated by the achievements, as they seemed to him, of the Petersburg Soviet, drew the conclusion that, given support from revolutions in the rest of Europe, the democratic and socialist phases could as it were be telescoped into one, so that the socialist phase could begin to grow simultaneously with the democratic phase. But Russia was a peasant country, and the overwhelming majority of peasants were not socialist but bourgeois by instinct. To overcome the reactionary nature of the peasantry the proletariat would have to assume leadership over them. The Bolsheviks, or more exactly Lenin, accepted neither of these views. On the one hand Lenin rejected as 'semi-anarchist' Trotsky's view that the socialist revolution could be telescoped into the democratic. Nor did he accept Trotsky's contention that the peasantry were bourgeois by instinct. On the other hand, Lenin in opposition to the Mensheviks urged that participation of the Social Democrats in the bourgeois, democratic government was essential. For the form which this coalition would take he coined the phrase, of which the meaning was never clearly defined, 'revolutionary-democratic dictatorship of the proletariat and the peasantry'. How little these theoretical debates of 1905 really mattered was revealed in 1917 when none of the three views was in the event adhered to by its exponents. The Mensheviks, who had preached non-participation in the democratic government, entered into coalition in the Provisional Government; the Bolsheviks, who had urged such participation, now resolutely rejected it and did their best to wreck the democratic government. Lenin now accepted Trotsky's view that the socialist revolution could be brought into being although the democratic phase had hardly begun, let alone ended, and put into practice what Trotsky had in 1905 somewhat euphemistically called the leadership of the proletariat over the peasantry. In the last resort, bolshevism proved to be less a doctrine, than a technique of action for the seizing and holding of power by the bolshevik party. Nor was 1917 the last occasion on which Lenin put into practice the views of the somewhat more outspoken Trotsky, in spite of having derided them when first put forward.

But if Lenin thus accepted in 1917 the 'semi-anarchist' views of Trotsky, Trotsky no less readily accepted in 1917 Lenin's views on the organization of the party, which he had quite as forcibly criticized in the past. Nor had Trotsky been alone in this criticism. From 1903 onwards Lenin's views on the party as a small disciplined élite which would lead the proletariat and would save it from its natural propensity to content itself with progressive reforms while ignoring the main object, revolution, had aroused staunch menshevik opposition. It was perhaps a view for which little solid authority could be found in the writings of Marx and Engels, even though it was close in spirit and temperament to Marx's outlook. But quite apart from the questions of marxist doctrine, Lenin's conception of the party as trained and geared to one end alone, revolution, was completely alien to very many Social Democrats of the menshevik wing. Like Plekhanov, they primarily saw in marxism a way to lead Russia along Western lines of democratic development. True, somewhere in the remote future, a social revolution would, as theory demanded, succeed the democratic revolution, which the middle-class parties would achieve. But it was upon political freedom, trade-union freedom, and the development of legal activity that their practical attention was mainly fixed. They believed with Lavrov and Plekhanov that the liberation of the workers could only be achieved on a sound basis if it were accomplished by the workers themselves. In the last resort the differences which kept Bolsheviks and Mensheviks apart were differences of temperament much more than of theory.[3]

This difference of temperament was particularly evident in the last years before the outbreak of war, years of bitter and confused conflict not only between Bolsheviks and Mensheviks, but between groups within each of the two wings of Russian social democracy. The Mensheviks, led by Martov, rallied in angry and excited protest against Lenin's methods of raising funds for his supporters by armed robbery. Lenin, for his part, was campaigning against the so-called 'liquidators'. This was the name applied to the majority of the Mensheviks who, in view of the increased opportunities for legal activity in the Duma and in the trade unions, believed that the time had come to disband the illegal underground party organizations. Lenin was supported in this campaign by Plekhanov, but, as Plekhanov later explained, this was due to motives quite different from Lenin's. He feared that a party decision to disband all underground organizations would only have the effect of leaving the field to the Bolsheviks, who, unlike the Mensheviks, would not comply with the decision. The rank and file of the party, inside Russia, indifferent to the wrangles of their mainly exiled leaders, were above all anxious for the union of all social democracy. The Bolshevik members of the Fourth Duma were elected on a specific mandate to bring this unification about. Lenin struggled to prevent it and was supported in his struggle by agents of the Tsarist

[3] Professor G. J. Renier in his analysis of the division of the seventeenth-century Dutch Calvinists into remonstrants and counter-remonstrants comes to a conclusion which offers a striking historical parallel to the Bolshevik-Menshevik split. The difference of doctrine between the groups was slight, yet 'it marked the difference between two temperaments, and temperament is the mother of conviction'. This difference of temperament produced, as in Russia, 'the parting of the ways for the two political parties that were, henceforth, going to fight for mastery in the Dutch Republic'. See *The Dutch Nation, an Historical Study* (London, 1944), pp. 41–50 at p. 49.

police who had penetrated the social democratic organizations. Nevertheless, the combined efforts of Lenin and of the Tsar's police agents came very near to failure. In 1912 Lenin executed a coup d'état. He convened at Prague a social democratic party conference at which all but two delegates were Bolsheviks. The Conference proclaimed itself an All Russian Party Conference, elected an all Bolshevik Central Committee, and proceeded to expel the great majority of Social Democrats, as 'liquidators'. The existence of the Bolsheviks as a separate party, as distinct from a wing or group, can be dated from this Conference. The effect of this move was to create greater unity among the opponents of Lenin than had hitherto proved possible. Aided by the powerful moral authority of the Second International, in the person of Vandervelde, the Mensheviks now began to make a more serious effort to unite among themselves. On the eve of the war, at Brussels in July 1914, almost all shades of social democratic opinion agreed in defiance of the Bolsheviks (Lenin had sent Inessa Armand as his delegate with instructions to oppose unification) on unification in principle and on 'the necessity for unity in the face of the splitting tactics of the Bolsheviks'. Details were to be worked out at a further conference in August. But the war came and the conference never met.

CHAPTER II

THE FEBRUARY REVOLUTION

In 1914 the great majority of the socialist parties of the belligerent countries, faced with actual hostilities, proved incapable of putting into practice the resolutions against war which they had adopted while war still remained a question of theory. When put to the test by the outbreak of hostilities, international socialism suffered a blow from which it never recovered. With the exception of the representatives of two parties, the Russian and the Serbian, the socialists in the parliaments of the belligerent countries voted, on the grounds of self-defence, to support their governments' war measures. In Russia, both the bolshevik and the menshevik deputies in the state Duma left the chamber and refused to vote the credits for the war. They were supported by the *Trudoviki*, the socialist revolutionary group in the Duma. Yet before long the Russian socialist parties proved to be far from united on the issue of defence. The Socialist Revolutionaries became, in the main, supporters of the war effort, with some exceptions such as Natanson (Bobrov), who had long been on the extreme left of his party, and Victor Chernov (Gardenin). Among the Mensheviks several trends appeared: the right wing became 'defensist'; the left wing, which included Martov and Larin, preached various degrees of internationalism. Alexandra Kollontay, who was then among the most extreme internationalists of the menshevik party, co-operated throughout the war with the Bolsheviks, and formally joined them in 1917. The founder of Russian marxism, Plekhanov, and his small group which included Vera Zasulich and Deutsch, were no longer organizationally linked either with the Mensheviks or the Bolsheviks. They advocated victory over Germany.[1]

[1] Plekhanov's attitude was not a change of front as the result of patriotic fervour. As far back as 1893 he had opposed in the Second International, as entirely contrary to marxism, the proposal of the anarcho-syndicalist Domela Nieuwenhuis that the socialists should, in the event of war, declare a general strike and practise fraternization. Then, as now, he argued that fraternization at the front, and demoralization of the army by the advocacy of steps purporting to lead to an immediate peace, merely played into the hands of less scrupulous aggressors.

The war cut right across the new movement towards unity which Lenin's tactics had helped to bring about in Russian social democracy. Those Mensheviks, who like the leader of the party, Julius Martov, went furthest in their opposition to the war, found themselves, though not without misgivings, closer to the Bolsheviks, usually the most resolute opponents of the war, than to their fellow Mensheviks who had become 'defensists'. In the same way, the small left wing of the Socialist Revolutionaries grew closer to the Bolsheviks on the issue of the war, and more estranged from the majority of their party. The war also destroyed the incipient co-operation between liberals and socialists. The *Kadety* supported the national war effort, without hesitation or qualification. This created a wide gulf between the two parties.

The Bolsheviks, though no more united on general doctrine than the Mensheviks, were however to a greater extent agreed on their opposition to the war, if not on the tactics to be pursued to that end. When Lenin and Zinoviev arrived in Switzerland from Austria in September 1914 there was virtually no bolshevik party organization in existence inside Russia. The opposition of the party to the war had drawn upon it severe police repressions. But even among the leaders scattered in exile the disunity inherited from the past years remained. Their dissensions were exacerbated, both by Lenin's ceaseless polemics,[2] and by the isolation which lack of contacts with the party inside Russia enforced on them. The future bolshevik leaders who were in Switzerland during the war included Zinoviev, Lenin's closest supporter throughout on all major issues of policy; Bukharin (then still in his twenties), until his departure for Sweden and then for the United States; Ryazanov; and, among others, Inessa Armand, G. Pyatakov, Sokol'nikov, Radek, and Manuilsky. Close contact was also maintained by Lenin with Alexandra Kollontay, who was in Sweden. Trotsky, who spent most of the war in the United States, participated in 1915 in the Zimmerwald Conference. Although he was more to the left than even the most radical of the Mensheviks, his refusal to break with the 'defensists'

---

[2] Years later, Lenin claimed that the war-time disputes, which had appeared to the short-sighted as chaotic, had in reality weaned the 'real socialists' from the 'bourgeois lackeys', such as Lieber, Dan, and Martov. *Lenin*, Vol. XXII, p. 530.

and his continuous efforts to achieve unity of all elements of Russian social democracy kept him and Lenin wide apart.[3]

For three years Lenin pursued a ceaseless struggle simultaneously with his own party colleagues and with international socialism. Yet in spite of the bitter terms which characterized Lenin when engaged in party disputes, both in Switzerland and later he remained as anxious to avoid a break with Bukharin as Bukharin was to avoid a break with him.[4] His quarrels with the socialist parties over the policy to be adopted towards the war led him to the conclusion that it was necessary for the revolutionary parties to break finally with the Second Socialist International and to found a Third Communist International. The effects of this decision on bolshevik policy towards the Russian socialist parties in 1917 were to be momentous. During the war, at the two international conferences of opposition groups of European socialists, at Zimmerwald in September 1915 and at Kienthal in April 1916, Lenin and Zinoviev led the small left minority group, which became known as the 'Zimmerwald Left'. The Zimmerwald Left voted in support of the manifesto of the Zimmerwald conference which called upon the workers of the world to unite in a fight for peace without territorial annexations or war indemnities. But at the same time they issued a call to the labouring masses to struggle against their capitalist governments in order to seize 'that political power which is necessary for a socialist organization of society'. By the time of the

[3] On 10 February 1916, Lenin wrote to Safarov: 'The helpless diplomats, or the "swamp" like Kautsky in Germany, Longuet in France, Martov and Trotsky in Russia, are doing tremendous harm to the labour movement, by defending the *fiction* of unity, and thereby *interfering* with the fully matured and urgent unification of the *oppositions* in all countries. and with the creation of the "Third International"' (*G. & F.*, p. 573). And to Kollontay on 17 February 1917: 'What a swine that Trotsky—left phrases, yet a bloc with the Rights against the aims of the Lefts!!' (*ibid.*, p. 576).

[4] His controversies with Bukharin in particular are relevant because they contained the germ of the conflict which arose in 1918 between Lenin and the Left Communists, of whom Bukharin became the leader. In one sense the differences between Lenin and Bukharin in Switzerland were the result of a collision between Lenin's revolutionary tactics, to which he was at all times prepared to subordinate theory, and Bukharin's more exact interpretation of the canon of Marx and Engels. See Lenin's letter to Shlyapnikov before Bukharin's departure for U.S.A. in 1916 (*Lenin*, Vol. XIX, pp. 273–6) ; and Bukharin's letter to Lenin (*Bol'shevik*, no. 22, 30 November 1932, p. 88), both quoted in *G. & F.*, pp. 253, 217. The controversies with Bukharin are dealt with in *G. & F. passim*.

Kienthal Conference the majority of the socialist delegates present had moved to the left, and were prepared to call for more concrete action: the workers were now enjoined to demand immediate opening of peace negotiations; while a lasting peace, it was asserted, could only be achieved by the seizure of political power and the abolition of capitalist power. But Lenin had irrevocably decided to break completely with the socialist parties of the Second International.   Accordingly, under his leadership, the Zimmerwald Left now demanded an even more radical call to the workers, incidentally one much more radical in its terms than Lenin ever raised in Russia in 1917.   Their draft resolution now ended with the following appeal: 'Lay down your weapons!   You should turn them only against the common foe—the capitalist governments.'[5]

The debates of the exiles were suddenly interrupted by the turn of events inside Russia.   On 8 March 1917 strikes and bread riots began in Petrograd which culminated within a few days in the collapse of the Romanov dynasty and in the victory of the unplanned and anonymous February revolution.[6] No political party could claim credit for its success.[7]   But they all, from right to left, rallied immediately to its support.   The *Kadety*, hitherto constitutional monarchists, became republicans overnight.   They joined with the progressive right-wing Duma members to form a Provisional Government.   For the socialist parties, somewhat stunned by these unexpected events, it seemed the dawn of a new era.[8]   In the country as a whole the monarchy could look nowhere for any serious support. But behind this apparent unity there was a dangerous cleavage.   For to the middle-class parties, including the now

---

[5] The Zimmerwald and Kienthal manifestos and resolutions and the draft resolutions of the Zimmerwald Left are reprinted in *G. & F.*, pp. 329–33, 349–53, 418–26.

[6] All dates are given in the current calendar, which was not introduced in Russia until February 1918.   Where necessary, the 'old style' date, which is thirteen days behind the current calendar, is shown in parenthesis.

[7] A report of the Tsarist secret police a few months before the February revolution stressed that popular discontent was growing far stronger than anything in 1905, but that 'revolutionary organizations as such are almost non-existent'— see *Grave*, pp. 136–9.

[8] The early reactions both of the *Kadety* and of the two socialist parties can best be studied in the flood of pamphlets on every conceivable political question which began to appear immediately.   There are excellent collections of these in the Preussische Staats-bibliotek (now in Marburg) and in the Library of the Institute of Social History in Amsterdam.

republican *Kadety*, the revolution meant an end to the corruption and muddle which had hindered the efficient conduct of the war. Now that the autocracy had fallen, they looked forward to a renewal of Russia's military strength and will to win. But to the mass of the peasants in soldier's uniforms and to many of the workers the revolution symbolized the very reverse—an end to the war, to discipline, law, and order. The socialist parties, whatever their particular theories, became to a greater or lesser extent, willingly or unwillingly, the spokesmen of these passions of the crowd. This circumstance alone doomed any prospect of coalition between liberals and socialists to failure and made a stable goverment in Russia between March and November 1917 almost an impossibility. It also ensured the victory of that party which was least afraid of anarchy, and least scrupulous in its promises of an immediate peace, the Bolsheviks.

Some five weeks passed after the February Revolution before Lenin succeeded in reaching Petrograd. During those weeks the pattern of the new order took shape. Side by side with the Provisional Government there arose Councils, or Soviets, both in the capital and in the provinces. These improvised organs of self-expression came into being largely as the result of the peculiar Russian genius for spontaneous organization. On 12 March a Soviet of Workers' and Peasants' Deputies was already in session in the Tauride Palace in Petrograd. Its predominant political composition was socialist revolutionary and menshevik, though it included some forty Bolsheviks. But the Bolsheviks did not consider it necessary, in view of their small number, to form a separate party organization, or 'fraction', within the Soviet.[9] For the time being the Bolsheviks shared with the Mensheviks the view that it was not the function of the socialist parties to govern, but to act as a pressure group upon the middle-class parties which had assumed office. Marxists, both menshevik and bolshevik, were agreed that the revolution which had been brought about by the combined pressure of the proletariat and the peasantry was a middle-class democratic revolution and that such it would have to continue for a long time to come. During this, the first stage, the function of the socialist parties was to

[9] *Shlyapnikov*, Vol. I, p. 119.

help to consolidate the middle-class revolution, to defend the rights of the workers and peasantry, and also to prepare for the next stage, the dictatorship of the proletariat, which would herald the transition to socialism. Some hotheads in the rank and file of the bolshevik party, possibly less troubled with questions of marxist orthodoxy than their leaders, were already on 14 March advocating seizure of power by the Petrograd Soviet, but they found little support from their party leaders.[10] A small minority of the Mensheviks in the Soviet, in common with some of the Socialist Revolutionaries, favoured a coalition with the middle-class parties. It soon became apparent that effective power, both in the capital and in the provinces, rested with the Soviets, and that the Provisional Government was in the position of enjoying responsibility without authority.[11] The mass of the population seemed ready to support the rapidly and roughly composed Soviets. The army, though weary of the war, was still willing to contain itself in patience, in the hope that the new government would somehow bring the fighting to a speedy conclusion. The uprising of the land hungry peasantry had not yet begun in earnest.

Though the Mensheviks, the smaller of the two main parties in the Petrograd Soviet, had for the most part accepted the Zimmerwald policy, the majority of them soon became reconciled to the policy of national defence pursued by the Provisional Government, which they now regarded as a struggle for the defence of the revolution. Chkheidze, for example, the leading Menshevik who in 1917 supported national defence, had publicly accepted the Zimmerwald programme in the Duma in February 1916. A small menshevik internationalist left wing, of which Martov assumed the leadership when he returned to Petrograd on 22 May 1917, continued resolutely to oppose the policy of the majority of their party, while avoiding both a split from their own party and defection

---

[10] See for example a resolution of the Vyborg Bolsheviks in *Shlyapnikov*, Vol. I, p. 186.

[11] On 22 March already, the Minister of War, Guchkov, wrote to General Alekseev : 'I beg you to believe that the true position is the following: the Provisional Government has no real power at its disposal, and its ordinances are carried out only to such extent as the Soviet of Workers' and Soldiers' Deputies permits. The Soviet controls the most important elements of real power such as the troops, the railways, the posts, and the telegraph.' Quoted in *Shlyapnikov*, Vol. II, p. 236,

to the Bolsheviks.[12] The larger party in the Soviet, the Socialist Revolutionaries, were still in favour of prosecuting the war to victory, though a small anti-war and internationalist wing, the germ of the future Left Socialist Revolutionary Party, was beginning to form around Natanson. Thus outwardly in March 1917 a coalition did not seem impossible, if once the Mensheviks overcame their scruples as orthodox marxists against a coalition with the government of the democratic phase. With the exception of small minorities in each, the major socialist parties agreed with the middle-class parties on the need for national defence. But the agreement was more apparent than real. The socialist parties, whatever their particular doctrines, were forced to express the mood of the soldiers, peasants, and workers whose spokesmen they were in the Soviets. Hence they supported defence, but in their own way. There must be no more strict military discipline, no repressive measures against anti-militarist agitators, and immediate efforts must be made to reach a democratic peace with the least delay, peace without annexations or indemnities, in accordance with the Zimmerwald formula. Their first object, the destruction of military discipline, was achieved with the famous Order Number One, which the Petrograd Soviet issued and the Provisional Government was forced to adopt. This Order abolished many of the outward marks of discipline and introduced the election of officers and unit committees. Indirectly, it had the more sinister effect of leading to the wholesale murder of officers. It was obvious that the sudden removal of discipline coupled with universal talk of peace would destroy any army as a fighting force, let alone an army weary and exasperated after years of defeats and mismanagement. The final disintegration of the Russian army did not come about until the last months of the Provisional Government, under the influence of bolshevik propaganda. But the Bolsheviks only helped on a process which began long before their influence became effective.

---

[12] *Sukhanov*, Vol. IV, pp. 22–38; Trotsky, *History*, P, pp. 241–42. Trotsky's remark that Martov opposed a rapprochement between the left Mensheviks and the Bolsheviks is a misleading half-truth. It is true that Martov was unwilling that he and his group should split off from their party, and join the Bolsheviks, but it is untrue to imply that the Bolsheviks ever offered or considered coalition on terms of equality, as distinct from absorption.

This disintegration of the army, which in turn brought in its train a rising tide of agricultural disturbances caused by deserters returning to their villages, cut the ground from under the Provisional Government. For it antagonized the only element in the country upon which they could ultimately hope to rely to keep order—the officers, and the few troops who retained their discipline amidst the growing chaos. It also made the successive attempts at coalition between the *Kadety* and the Socialists, after the latter had accepted the principle of coalition, more and more unlikely to succeed. The growing disorder in the country alarmed the *Kadety* and they veered away from the Socialists whom they blamed for it. The Socialists in turn veered to the left and their opposition to the war increased. After May 1917 both Martov's Internationalists and the left wing of the Socialist Revolutionaries grew rapidly. Their growth served to help the Bolsheviks, who alone had the resolution to carry their policy to its logical conclusion, and did not hesitate either to encourage popular anarchy or to make bold promises. The Provisional Government might have saved the country from chaos by calling on the loyal remnants of the army in time, though possibly at the cost of sacrificing its own rather nebulous authority. Perhaps it was some such idea that Kerensky had in mind in August 1917 when he first opened negotiations with General Kornilov, only to recoil when he saw that constitutional government might not survive if the military took charge. It is usual to find General Kornilov's attempt in September 1917 to march on Petrograd referred to as counter-revolution and indeed Kerensky's reaction at the time laid the foundation for the charge. If by counter-revolution was meant an attempt to restore the monarchy, it was certainly nothing of the sort, though it is possible that, had Kornilov succeeded, he would have paved the way for such a restoration. Monarchism in Russia revived as a political force only after the victory of the Bolsheviks and the collapse of the Provisional Government. There is nothing to suggest that Kornilov had anything more in mind in August 1917 than a military dictatorship which would save something of the revolution from the wreckage and put an end to the menace of a Bolshevik coup d'état. When his attempt failed the Provisional Government was doomed.

The bolshevik party had little influence in March 1917. During the war its leadership inside Russia had been seriously impaired by the banishment of such figures as Kamenev, Sverdlov, Rykov, and Stalin. The most prominent of the three Bolsheviks who in March 1917 formed the Petrograd Bureau of the Bolshevik Central Committee was Shlyapnikov, an honest, courageous, self-educated workman, but incapable either as a theoretician or as a tactician of leading a revolution. The other two were Molotov, then only twenty-seven, and Zalutsky, a figure of little significance. The revolution had taken them by surprise. Although many Bolsheviks had played an active part in the strikes and demonstrations, their leaders had not foreseen how far these apparently small beginnings were to lead. When faced with the event they made some efforts to restrain the spontaneous impulse of some of their more extreme followers to immediate disorganized violence, but they had no ready policy and no plan for the future.[13] Shlyapnikov had been able to maintain periodic contact with Lenin during the war, but had not received from him any instructions for the contingencies of March 1917, which Lenin himself had not foreseen. Lenin had been struggling for years to prevent union of bolshevik and men-shevik organizations. Yet, in spite of Shlyapnikov's efforts during these difficult years to carry out Lenin's policy, in March 1917 Bolsheviks and Mensheviks still retained joint organizations in a number of important industrial centres.[14] As for the workers, of whom the Bolsheviks, like the Mensheviks, were largely composed, their spontaneous move-ment was towards the unification of both wings of the party.[15]

For the first few weeks after the revolution the bolshevik party remained under the direction of Shlyapnikov and Molotov. But on 25 March Kamenev and Stalin returned to Petrograd from Siberia and took over control of the bolshevik

[13] A. Shlyapnikov, 'Fevral'skie dni v Peterburge', in *Proletarskaya revolyutsiya*, no. 13 (1923), at p. 82. cf. *Antonov-Saratovsky*, p. 88; and *Shlyapnikov*, Vol. I, pp. 56–7. Shlyapnikov had, however, in a letter to the Central Committee on 24 February 1917, foreseen that a 'revolutionary hurricane' might spring up 'any day'—*ibid.*, p. 52.

[14] e.g., in Baku, the Urals, the Donets Basin, and in Siberia—*Proletarskaya revolyutsiya*, no. 4 (63), 1927, p. 17.

[15] *Shlyapnikov*, Vol. III, p. 193.

party and of the party organ, *Pravda*, by virtue of their seniority. (*Pravda*, which had been suppressed during the war, had reappeared immediately after the February revolution under the editorship of the young Molotov.) The friction which undoubtedly arose in the bolshevik party leadership after the arrival of Stalin and Kamenev has been subsequently somewhat exaggerated by Trotsky and Shlyapnikov, into a right wing coup d'état.[16] It did not amount to this, but the policy of Stalin and Kamenev was in some respects more moderate than that of Shlyapnikov or Molotov, especially on the question of war. The Petrograd Bolshevik Bureau had in the first weeks after the revolution shown itself rather more determined in its attitude against the war. On 23 March, before the arrival of Kamenev and Stalin, it had passed a resolution demanding fraternization and negotiations between the proletariat of the warring countries for immediate cessation of the war, in order to turn the imperialist war against the capitalist oppressors.[17] Both the newly arrived leaders expressed themselves in *Pravda*. According to Kamenev, bolshevik policy in regard to the war should be 'pressure on the Provisional Government . . . compelling it to come out immediately . . . with an attempt to induce all the warring countries immediately to open up negotiations about means of stopping the world war. And until that time everyone remains at his fighting post.'[18] While, according to Stalin, 'the basic slogan "down with the war" is completely useless . . . Our proper course is pressure on the Provisional Government, to demand that it should declare its consent to open immediate peace negotiations.'[19] The change in bolshevik policy after the arrival of Stalin and Kamenev is reflected in a resolution of the Petrograd Bureau of 8 April which now merely contented itself with a demand for pressure on the Provisional Government to offer immediate and just peace terms.[17] With regard to other questions of bolshevik policy, an article by Stalin in *Pravda* on 31 March which foreshadowed the transformation 'at the necessary moment' of the Soviets as an organ of struggle into the Soviets as an organ of power reflected the generally

[16] Trotsky, *History*, Vol. I, pp. 302–5; *Shlyapnikov*, Vol. II, pp. 179–85.
[17] Quoted in *Proletarskaya revolyutsiya*, no. 4 (63), 1927, pp. 50–2, from *Pravda*.
[18] *Pravda*, 28 March, quoted in *Chamberlin*, I, p. 115.
[19] *Pravda*, 29 March; *Stalin*, Vol. III, pp. 4–8.

accepted view at the time,[20] while Stalin's opinion that unification was desirable between the Bolsheviks and those Mensheviks who accepted the Zimmerwald and Kienthal programmes also corresponded to the view widely expressed among the Bolsheviks in Russia.[21]

For three weeks before Lenin's arrival in Petrograd Stalin rather than Kamenev was the leader of the party—leading it, as he later admitted, along the wrong lines.[22] During his short reign two bolshevik party conferences were held, the first between 11 and 14 April, a conference of the Petrograd party, the other immediately after, an All Russian Party Conference, representing no less than 58 bolshevik party organizations. Of the Petrograd Conference the only surviving report is a short account by Milyutin in a provincial party paper.[23] The All Russian Conference Protocols were destroyed during the street disturbances in July 1917 (not suppressed by the communists, as is sometimes asserted), and all that survives of them is an account based on notes made at the time, which has been published by Trotsky.[24] In so far as it is possible to distinguish the alignment of opinion at these conferences, there appear to have been three groups: the main or centre, group, to which Stalin and Kamenev belonged, was supported by the Moscow City Bolshevik Party organization, and also enjoyed a large following in the Petrograd organization. Rykov and Nogin, two of the more moderate party leaders, now returned from exile, also belonged to this centre group. The Moscow *Oblast'* Bureau (the bolshevik party organization for an area consisting of thirteen *gubernii*, or counties, centred on Moscow) reflected the temper of the more radically-minded provinces. This organization ranged itself with Shlyapnikov, Molotov, and Zalutsky of the Petrograd Bureau of the Bolshevik Central Committee to form a left wing. It was reinforced by Alexandra Kollontay, lately

[20] *ibid.*, Vol. III, pp. 11–15.

[21] See for example the views of the Petrograd Bolshevik Committee in *Pervyy Leg. Komitet.*, p. 55.

[22] In 1924, in the Preface to *The Road to October*. See Stalin's *Na putiakh k oktyabryu*, p. ix. Soviet historians now deny that Stalin erred in 1917, maintaining that both he and Molotov actively upheld the Leninist line against Shlyapnikov and Kamenev—see e.g. *Moskalev*, pp. 233, 242–3, where, however, no evidence is adduced.

[23] *Shlyapnikov*, Vol. III, pp. 206–10.

[24] Trotsky, *Stalinskaya shkola*, pp. 225–90.

returned from Norway (bombarded before her return by Lenin with letters and telegrams of advice on tactics). No doubt she and Shlyapnikov were urging what they believed to be Lenin's views. It does not, however, appear that they had yet succeeded in grasping them, nor is this to be wondered at, since they had as yet not been fully developed by Lenin. Finally, there was a right wing, for which Voytinsky, Avilov, and Gol'denberg were the spokesmen, which was mainly anxious for organizational union with the Mensheviks.

On the question of relations with the Provisional Government, Stalin's proposals, after initial opposition, won almost universal support at both conferences. These proposals were based upon the assumption which no one questioned, that a long period of middle-class democratic government was now beginning, which would only eventually be crowned by the next phase, the socialist revolution. When one spokesman, and only one, attempted to raise the question of the 'realization of the dictatorship of the proletariat', he was stopped by the chairman, Nogin, with a reminder that the subject of the conference was 'present-day political steps'. No one questioned Nogin's ruling. The resolution accepted at both conferences (unanimously at the Petrograd Conference) called for 'vigilant control over the activities of the Provisional Government at the centre and in the provinces' and for support of the Petrograd Soviet as the 'beginning of a revolutionary power', alone capable of defending the revolution. But there was considerably stronger disagreement on the question of the war, on which Stalin and Kamenev advocated the moderate policy which had been laid down after their return in the columns of *Pravda*. The left wing now demanded that the war should be turned into a civil war against the capitalist exploiters— though no one appears to have had any practical suggestions as to how this was to be achieved. In the end the views of Stalin and Kamenev were accepted by a majority of both Conferences. There was also opposition to Stalin's thesis that organizational union with the Mensheviks was possible on the basis of acceptance of the Zimmerwald-Kienthal lines; it was, however, unanimously agreed at the All Russian Conference to take part in an informal joint meeting between representatives of both parties which had been arranged, provided it was understood that the meeting was for the purpose of information and exploration only. Stalin's more concrete proposal, that the Bolshevik Central Committee should approach the leaders of the menshevik internationalist wing on the question of arranging a joint conference, was only adopted by one vote. It seems probable that this proposal met with opposition not only from the left, but also from the right wing of the party. Too concrete for the left wing, which did not strongly favour union with the Mensheviks, it was suspect to the right-wing Bolsheviks, who hoped that the Russian social democratic party would be reunited. They saw in Stalin's proposal an attempt to undermine the Mensheviks, by persuading their internationalist followers to split off from their party and join the Bolsheviks.

Meanwhile Lenin had been chafing impatiently in Switzerland, casting around for some way to get back to Russia. The February Revolution had taken him by surprise. His main activity since 1914 had been his struggle with the Socialist International on the policy to be adopted towards the war, and theoretical controversy with his own colleagues. It was characteristic of Lenin to think more in terms of action than of theory, and to develop his thought in relation to the tactics which he considered necessary to achieve his aims. If his actions appeared to his followers to run counter to marxism, he could usually rely on his mastery of marxist theory to justify himself and to prove his followers wrong. In an article of reminiscences on the October revolution which he wrote towards the end of his life he quotes a saying of Napoleon: 'On s'engage, et puis . . . on voit.' Much of Lenin's policy between April and November 1917 can be summed up in these words.

But the consequence was that his tactical policy often outstripped the comprehension of his followers. Thus, that his momentous decision to break finally with the socialist parties of the Second International would lead in Russia to a final break between the Bolsheviks and the Mensheviks does not appear to have been grasped by the Bolsheviks before Lenin's arrival in Petrograd. It is true that during the war his ideas could hardly have come to the knowledge of exiles in Siberia like Stalin. But even Shlyapnikov, who had last been in contact with Lenin towards the end of 1916 and must have been better informed than others of the new policy, had maintained desultory (and abortive) conversations on unification with the Mensheviks for some months before the February Revolution.[25] Nor does *Pravda* during the short period of its existence under his direction appear to have so much as mentioned the Zimmerwald Left.

Lenin had never openly rejected the orthodox marxist law of revolution—from autocracy to middle-class democracy, and only thereafter to the next stage, the proletarian, socialist revolution. But the possibility that a party, if sufficiently well organized, could seize power at once was never far from his mind. In 1914, in an article on Marx inspired by the newly published correspondence of Marx and Engels, Lenin had argued that marxism justified the view that in some situations it was better for the proletariat to attempt to seize power, and fail, than to risk demoralization by a refusal to give battle.[26] One letter, which he quotes, had particularly impressed him. In this letter of 16 April 1865 Marx had written, with reference to events in Germany, that everything would depend on whether it proved possible 'to back the Proletarian Revolution by some second edition of the Peasants' War'.[27] This letter may well have been fresh in Lenin's mind during those irksome weeks of waiting for an opportunity to return to Petrograd, since he quotes it again in the article of reminiscences already referred to. It did not require acute political foresight to realize that the dormant peasant land hunger in Russia would before long break out into a raging storm, which the weak Provisional Government could, or would, do little to lull.

Lenin's plan of action for the bolshevik party took shape in a series of letters which he wrote while still in Switzerland. First and foremost, there was to be no coalition with socialist parties. In a telegram to Kollontay and others on their departure from Christiania towards the end of March he said: 'Our tactics: absolute mistrust, no support of new govern-

---

[25] *Shlyapnikov*, Vol. I, p. 43.
[26] *Lenin*, Vol. XVIII, pp. 30–1.
[27] *Lenin*, Vol. XXVII, pp. 398–401 ; *Der Briefwechsel zwischen Friedrich Engels und Karl Marx*, Vol. II, pp. 106–8. The sentence quoted is in English in the original.

ment. Kerensky particularly suspect; to arm proletariat only guarantee; . . . *no rapprochement with other parties.* The last is a *conditio sine qua non.* We do not trust Chkheidze.'[28] On 16 March he had written to Alexandra Kollontay, then still in Norway:

> This first stage of the first of the revolutions (brought about by the war) will be neither the last, nor confined to Russia . . . the most important thing now is the press, the organization of the workers into a *revolutionary* social democratic party . . . On no account must we again tread the path of the Second International.[29]

He did not, while in Switzerland, propound the doctrine that the middle-class phase of the revolution should be cut short at birth and that the proletariat should immediately attempt to seize power and thus bring about the next phase, the socialist phase. On the contrary, on the very eve of his departure for Petrograd he wrote:

> Russia is a peasant country, one of the most backward countries in Europe. Socialism cannot conquer there *directly* and *at the moment.* But the peasant character of the country *can,* by reason of the immense extent of the domains of the landed nobility, lend formidable dimensions to the bourgeois democratic revolution in Russia and make of our revolution the *prologue* to the Socialist Revolution, a *little step* towards it.[30]

But in his *Letters from Afar,* written between 20 and 26 March,[31] there is constant emphasis on the instruction, organization, and arming of the widest masses of the people in order to ensure the full victory of the next phase of the revolution; above all—no coalitions. The same views were set out in theses on policy prepared jointly by Lenin and Zinoviev on 17 March.[32] Thus what Lenin visualized was ultimate seizure of power by the proletariat, identified in his mind with its armed vanguard, the bolshevik party. There is nothing in his writings during the weeks of waiting in Switzerland to

[28] *Lenin,* Vol. XXIX, p. 343, quoted in a letter of 25 March 1917. Emphasis here (and throughout in quotations from Lenin) as in the original.
[29] *Lenin,* Vol. XX, p. 5.
[30] *ibid.,* pp. 65–70, 'Farewell Letter to the Swiss Workers', written on 8 April 1917.
[31] *ibid.,* pp. 13–47. [32] *ibid.,* pp. 9–12.

suggest that the Soviets as opposed to the armed proletariat should seize power. In one of his *Letters from Afar* he writes that what he had written of the Soviets in 1905 as 'organs of revolutionary power' now requires reconsideration. Power must be conquered by the armed people 'fusing the police, the army and the bureaucracy with the people armed to a man'.[33] In contrast, perhaps, in this respect to Trotsky, Lenin treated the Soviets merely as a tactical means to power, to be abandoned or taken up as circumstances directed. But to most of his followers the bolshevik revolution signified seizure of power by the Soviets—bodies in which, as it happened, the Bolsheviks had secured majorities by November 1917, but which nevertheless comprised substantial representation of the other socialist parties. This was to be the issue on which the first major crisis in the party arose.

Lenin arrived in Petrograd on 16 April 1917 in the middle of the All Russian Party Conference. He was met at the Finland station by a delegation headed by the Menshevik Chkheidze, one of the leaders of the Petrograd Soviet. Chkheidze, in a speech of cautious welcome, emphasized the need for unity between all socialists. Lenin ignored him and turned and addressed the crowd: 'Dear comrades, soldiers, sailors, and workers.' He spoke of the robber imperialist war as the 'beginning of civil war in all Europe' which might bring European imperialism to an end 'any day'. He ended his speech: 'Long live the world socialist revolution!' The same evening, for two hours, he addressed a bolshevik party gathering at the palace which now served the party for headquarters. 'I hear that there is a tendency for unification with the defensists abroad and in Russia,' he said in the course of his speech. 'That is nothing but the betrayal of socialism.' For the first time Lenin raised the question of the passing of power to the Soviets. Perhaps in the few hours since his arrival in Russia he had realized the enormous confidence enjoyed by the Soviets among the masses of the people, of which he may not have been aware in Switzerland. 'So long as we are in a minority,' he told the All Russian Party Conference that evening, 'our work must consist in criticizing and exposing mistakes, preach-

[33] *Lenin*, Vol. XX, pp. 34–5. And see Chapter III, note 38, for Lenin's views on the 1905 Soviet.

ing at the same time the necessity for the passing of all state power to the Soviet of Workers' Deputies.'[34]   There was no discussion of his speech that night.   But the following day it became apparent that Lenin's ideas had found very little support in his startled party.

Lenin attended and addressed the joint meeting of bolshevik and menshevik representatives which had been convened, on Stalin's proposal, as a part of the All Russian Bolshevik Party Conference.   He was received sceptically, even with hostility. His closest followers, with the notable exception of Alexandra Kollontay, hesitated to support him openly in what appeared to be wild, anarchist ideas.   So far as unification with the Mensheviks was concerned, Sukhanov, the extreme left menshevik ('Quarter Bolshevik' as Lenin called him) chronicler of the two revolutions, observes: 'the tenor of his speech . . . amounted to a first class funeral of the whole idea of unification'.[35]   The meeting decided, in spite of Lenin and against the opposition of the Bolshevik Central Committee representatives, to set up a joint Bolshevik-Menshevik Bureau to prepare for a conference on union.   At least twenty Bolsheviks voted for this proposal in defiance of their Central Committee, and the principal figures of the bolshevik right wing, Voytinsky and Gol'denberg, entered the Bureau which was formed.[36] The Bolsheviks also refused to adopt Lenin's proposal to change the name of the party from Social Democratic Labour Party (Bolshevik) to Communist, a change which he had designed to emphasize the final break with social democracy.

The doctrine which had most startled even the left wing members of Lenin's following was the proposal that the Soviets should become the governing power in the country, that is to say, that steps should be taken towards the setting up of a socialist society in the almost immediate future.   Lenin had, according to his usual practice, embodied his ideas in a series of theses.   These, which became known as the April Theses, were printed in *Pravda* within a day or two of his arrival.   They called for 'No support for the Provisional

[34] *Lenin*, Vol. XX, p. 79.   The speech is lost and only a short note of the very similar speech delivered the following day is printed in Lenin's works.
[35] See *Sukhanov*, Vol. III, pp. 14–50, for the account of Lenin's arrival and its impact: and cf. Tolstov in *Krasnaya letopis'*, no. 3 (18), 1926, pp. 70–5.
[36] *Avdeev*, Vol. II, pp. 10–11.

Government' . . . and demanded 'not a parliamentary republic, but a republic of soviets of workers' soldiers' and peasants' deputies in the whole country . . . confiscation of all landlords' estates, nationalization of all land . . . a single, national bank . . . elimination of the army and police'. They also stated that 'the war cannot be ended in a genuinely democratic peace . . . without the overthrow of capitalism', and urged 'the widest propaganda of this view in the army in the field' and 'fraternization'.[37] Kamenev immediately disowned Lenin's view in *Pravda* as 'unacceptable in that it starts from the assumption that the bourgeois democratic revolution is ended, and counts upon an immediate transformation of this revolution into a socialist revolution'.[38] He was voicing the general view of the responsible leaders of the party. Yet within a very short time Lenin won round almost the entire bolshevik party. Shlyapnikov, who was knocked out of action by a tramcar about this time, came out of hospital a few weeks later to find to his astonishment that the party was now solidly behind Lenin. Some of the older Bolsheviks, notably Krasin, stood aloof from party activity, and took no part in the struggles of the ensuing months. There were a few, but only a few defections.

The germs of the future rifts were inherent in the very circumstance of Lenin's rapid ascendancy over the party. First and foremost among the reasons for this rapid conversion was the personality of Lenin, his ability to decide without hesitation on a course of action and to convince, batter, or ridicule his opponents off the field. He enjoyed an almost legendary, and well merited, reputation in the party for intellectual superiority, and moreover possessed the rare gift of guiding the interminable theoretical discussions to which it was particularly prone to a concrete and practical resolution. A bolshevik party without Lenin's leadership was at that date unthinkable. Moreover, there were few among the leading Bolsheviks who had the political education or training which would have enabled them to meet the formidable arguments from the canons of marxism with which Lenin invariably bolstered proposals which

---

[37] *Pravda*, 20 April 1917; *Lenin*, Vol. XX, p. 88.
[38] Quoted in Trotsky, *History*, I, p. 325. And cf. a similar article by him on 25 April in *Pravda*.

appeared to run directly counter to marxism. The indecision which had prevailed in the party before Lenin's arrival made the Bolsheviks all the readier to follow a firm lead. Perhaps the most important single factor was his skill, after the shock caused by the April Theses, in unfolding his plan with a sufficient gradualness, a sufficient appearance of compromise with hesitations and dissensions inside the party to lead it to the main issue at which he aimed, while seeming in the process to be yielding to the doubts or scruples of his followers. Hence, the results of a policy seemed to them to flow more from circumstances beyond control than from that policy. It is for this reason that the more serious dissensions in the party came after the October Revolution rather than before it, when the full results of a course of action which had not been clearly foreseen at first were revealed. It is for this reason too that the dissensions were now the more easily overcome, because those who dissented from the result were forced to realize that they had all along been committed to it by their acceptance of the policy which had inevitably led to it. This process is most clearly illustrated in the events which led to the peace of Brest-Litovsk, but it played an important part in the questions which were to be debated between April and November of 1917.

Thus on the vital question of the forcible seizure of power, the fears and reluctance of many of the party leaders were overcome, to a great extent, because the full implications of Lenin's policy did not become apparent until after the seizure had been accomplished. It was only then that his intention to keep power for the Bolsheviks alone, in defiance of the majority in the country which supported the other socialist parties, was fully grasped. The first shock of this revelation caused a crisis in the bolshevik party. It was short-lived because, having followed Lenin thus far, there was no longer any possibility of drawing back. Lenin since 1902 had held the view that, if left to its own spontaneous action, the proletariat would remain subordinate to the ideology of the bourgeoisie, contenting itself with the satisfaction of immediate, secondary demands. To him it seemed incontrovertible that the bolshevik party, as the vanguard of the proletariat, should have the right to act in the name of the proletariat, without the formal support of an electoral mandate, a majority. Writing over two years after the October Revolution, he summed up his tactics for seizing power in the following words:

> Now it is this dialectic which the traitors, numbskulls, and pedants of the Second International could never grasp: the proletariat cannot conquer without winning over to its side the majority of the population. But to limit this winning over of the population to, or to make it conditional on, 'acquiring' a majority of votes in an election, *while the bourgeoisie is in power* is impracticable imbecility, or simply cheating the workers. In order to win over the majority of the population to its side the proletariat must first overthrow the bourgeoisie, and seize state power into its own hands; secondly it must introduce Soviet power, having smashed to bits the old state apparatus, whereby it immediately undermines the dominion, authority, and influence of the bourgeoisie and of the petty bourgeois compromisers among the non-proletarian labouring masses. It must, thirdly, *complete the destruction* of the influence of the bourgeoisie and the petty bourgeois compromisers among the majority of the non-proletarian labouring masses by the *revolutionary* fulfilment of *their* economic needs, *at the expense of the exploiters.*[39]

Commonplace by the time they were written, these ideas were not yet obvious in 1917. To many of Lenin's followers who had, after the first shock, accepted the possibility of the jump from middle-class democracy to socialism, the form of the future socialist power still appeared in the simpler terms of organs expressing the actual will of the entire people, the Soviets. Many of them, perhaps without realizing it, were closer in their views to Martov, the leader of the menshevik left wing, and a no less learned marxist than Lenin. Martov saw the solution of the crisis of the Russia of 1917 in a quasi-parliamentary régime, backed by a 'popular front' of the main socialist parties, governing through the Soviets. In November 1917 there were still many leading Bolsheviks who believed that Lenin's aim in seizing power had been to create just such a régime.

[39] *Lenin*, Vol. XXIV, p. 641.

CHAPTER III

THE BOLSHEVIKS IN ACTION

On his arrival in Russia, Lenin adopted, for tactical reasons, the doctrine that it was the Soviets which must seize power. To have acted otherwise would have been to risk alienating mass support, since the confidence of the masses in the Soviets grew daily. But, Lenin had at the same time to curb the growing impulse which his own rank and file was showing, against the views of its leaders, to seize power at once: such a premature attempt must either have given power to the Soviets with their non-bolshevik majorities, or have precipitated strong counter-measures by the Provisional Government. He discerned the danger of premature action early in May 1917. A note on Russian War Aims which the *Kadet* Foreign Minister, Milyukov, had dispatched to the Allied powers on 1 May provoked angry demonstrations in Petrograd from workers who thought it showed a determination to carry on the war to victory. Owing to the impulsiveness of rank and file Bolsheviks, these demonstrations had assumed a more extreme form than Lenin had intended. The slogan of the demonstrators 'Down with the Provisional Government', evoked a reprimand to the Petrograd Bolshevik Committee from Lenin and a reminder that the proper policy was to wait until the masses had been won over to the Bolsheviks by the bankruptcy of the Provisional Government.[1] There was certainly no doubt where the sympathies of the Petrograd crowd in the May demonstrations lay or of the authority which it recognized, for it had obediently yielded to the request of the non-bolshevik Petrograd Soviet to disperse.[2] Meanwhile Lenin took advantage of the opportunity to moderate the policy which in its extreme form had so startled his own party a fortnight before. A series of party resolutions in the early part of May achieved the double purpose of allaying the fears of the upper ranks of the Bolsheviks

[1] *Protokoly VII Konf.*, pp. 56, 97. Cf. the Moscow City Committee which on 5 May pased a resolution which included the slogan 'Down with the Government'. *Avdeev*, Vol. II, pp. 60-1.

[2] *Sukhanov*, Vol. III, pp. 293-5.

that Lenin intended to seize power by hook or by crook, and of moderating the dangerous enthusiasm of the impetuous rank and file in the factories.   The slogan 'Down with the Provisional Government' was wrong, according to one of them, until a bolshevik majority had been won in the Soviets; and power must only pass to the Soviets when 'they come over to our political view and wish to take power themselves'.[3]   Party agitators must everywhere denounce the 'vile lie' of the capitalists that the bolshevik party was threatening civil war, ran another.[4]   Before power could pass to the Soviets, stated a third, 'prolonged work' inside the Soviets would be required in order to strengthen them and in order to 'clarify the proletarian class consciousness'.[5]

It was therefore without very much difficulty that Lenin succeeded at the Seventh All Russian Party Conference of 7–12 May in uniting the party behind him in a way that Stalin had failed to do some weeks before.   There was little opposition to the main resolutions proposed by Lenin.[6]   A moderate resolution on relations with the Provisional Government, which linked the passage of power to the Soviets with the winning of a majority by the Bolsheviks in the Soviets, pacified the right wing of the party;[7] while a carefully worded but at the same time vigorous resolution against the war conciliated the left wing.   Kamenev and a number of the Moscow Bolsheviks opposed Lenin with a demand for a policy of 'control': they argued that as the middle-class revolution was not yet completed, the masses must be given concrete tasks, and these should take the form of vigilant control over the activities of the government—in short, the view proposed by Stalin in his resolution some weeks before. Lenin ridiculed control; he was warmly supported by Stalin,

---

[3] Resolution of the Central Committee of the Bolsheviks on 5 May 1917, reprinted in *Protokoly VII Konf.*, p. 258.

[4] Resolution of the Central Committee of 4 May 1917, *ibid.*, pp. 256–7.

[5] Resolution of the Petrograd Party Conference of 27 April to 5 May, adopted by 33 votes to 6, with two abstentions—*ibid.*, pp. 29, 242–3.

[6] There was most opposition on the general resolution 'On the current moment', which, while rejecting the immediate realization of socialism as impossible, called for nationalization of the land and for various forms of state control over undertakings.   Thirty-nine voted against it, seventy-one in favour, and eight abstained.   See *VKP(b) v rez.*, pp. 256–8 ; and *Protokoly VII Konf.*, pp. 52–98, for the debates on Lenin's proposed resolution.

[7] *VKP(b) v rez.*, pp. 259–60.   It was adopted with only three dissenting votes and eight abstentions, by some 130 delegates, representing 80,000 party members.

who otherwise took little part in the conference, except for a report on the nationalities question, his special subject. The partnership between Stalin and Kamenev was at an end. Kamenev was by now in open disagreement with Lenin;[8] but Stalin fully accepted his leadership. In an article published in *Soldatskaya Pravda*, he ranged himself behind Lenin and emphasized the importance of unity in the party, since 'only a united party can lead the people to victory'.[9] The Seventh All Russian Conference proved less tractable on the question of coalition with the Mensheviks. The resolution on coalition which was adopted unanimously (though with ten abstentions), rejected as impossible union with parties which supported the war, but recognized as 'essential' union with internationalist groups and parties— 'upon the basis that they break with the policy of petty bourgeois treason to socialism'.[10] But the conference refused to follow a proposal by Lenin which would have signified a final break with the Second International. This proposal, which did not receive a single vote, was that the Bolsheviks should remain in the Zimmerwald bloc as observers only, in order to put an end to the illusion that this bloc could ever serve as a foundation for the new International.[11] The conference accepted instead a resolution put forward by Zinoviev that 'our party remains within the Zimmerwald bloc, while making it its task to propagate there the tactics of the Zimmerwald Left, and to take part in the forthcoming Conference of adherents to the Zimmerwald line'.

Lenin had, however, drawn other conclusions from the May demonstrations than would appear from the resolutions of the Conference alone:—that it was necessary to create in each district, sub-district, and factory an organization 'capable of acting as one man' and bound to the Central Committee by strong ties.[12] As Lenin's notes for the Seventh Party

---

[8] At the Petrograd Bolshevik Conference which preceded the May All Russian Conference he had put forward an alternative resolution, which that conference had rejected, warning against the slogan 'Down with the Government', as one which could 'hamper the lengthy task of educating and organizing the masses, at present the fundamental aim of the Party'. *Protokoly VII Konf.*, pp. 29 and 64–73.

[9] Reprinted *ibid.*, pp. ix–x.   [10] *VKP(b) v rez.*, p. 262.

[11] *Protokoly VII Konf.*, p. 215; *Yaroslavsky*, Vol. IV, p. 251.

[12] 'Neumnoe zloradstvo', Lenin, Vol. XX, p. 234.

Conference show, what was already uppermost in his mind was not action through, or in, the Soviets, but directly among his followers, 'to prepare for a revolution a thousand times stronger than that of February'.[13] The party resolutions of this period invariably called for the transfer of all power to the Soviets. But Lenin was preparing the means by which power could be seized independently of the Soviets. By June the factory and shop committees were organized and under the control of the Bolshevik Central Committee and they provided it with powerful support. (Unlike the trade unions, where the Bolsheviks were a minority.) Lenin appears to have regarded these committees as possible organs of power in preference to the Soviets.[14] There was force behind these factory committees as well, for it was in the factories that the bolshevik military Red Guard began to be organized, the armed force by means of which the subsequent seizure of power was mainly accomplished. The Executive Committee of the Petrograd Soviet, on which the Bolsheviks were still a small minority, voted against the maintenance of this armed force. The Bolsheviks disregarded this, and the Executive Committee seem to have forgotten their resolution. By July the Red Guard in Petrograd numbered some ten thousand.[15] The factory committees also enabled the Bolsheviks in Petrograd to compete with the Petrograd Soviet for control over the city masses. At the same time they were developing their party organization in the army both in Petrograd and at the front and rear.[16] In the capital the rising temper and discontent of the workers and soldiers were outgrowing control by either the Soviet or the Bolshevik Central Committee. But in the competition for control the bolshevik influence grew. In May the demonstrating workers had obeyed the orders of the Petrograd Soviet to disperse. By June it was the Bolshevik Central Committee which appeared to control the demonstrators. The bolshevik party leaders had decided to call a demonstration for 23 June,

[13] *Leninskiy sbornik*, Vol. IV, p. 290.
[14] *Yaroslavsky*, Vol. IV, p. 168—to the consternation of Ordzhonikidze, when Lenin first told him of his idea—*Izbrannye stat'i i rechi*, p. 214.
[15] *Fedotoff-White*, p. 17. About twenty thousand Red Guards were available on the eve of the seizure of power—see *Chamberlin*, I, p. 307.
[16] At a conference of bolshevik military organizations held from 29 June to 6 July over a hundred delegates represented 26,000 bolshevik party members from sixty army organizations. *VKP(b) v rez.*, p. 274.

in spite of the opposition of some of them, notably Zinoviev, Kamenev, and Nogin. Lenin himself was uncertain about the wisdom of calling the demonstration, but yielded to the insistent demand from the rank and file, especially from the party's military and factory organizations. On 22 June the First All Russian Congress of Soviets, then in session, passed a resolution forbidding the demonstration. This caused hesitation among the bolshevik members of the Petrograd Soviet; they demanded the abandonment of the demonstration, and the Bolshevik Central Committee acceded to this view at the last minute, and called it off. With some difficulty party emissaries persuaded the workers and soldiers to go back. Thus, this time it was not the Soviet, but the Bolshevik Central Committee which had stopped the crowds,[17] an indication which Lenin carefully noted. 'We must not give them a pretext to attack us, let them attack of their own accord', he said two days later, 'life is on our side'.[18] The influence of his party appeared to be overtaking the influence of the Soviet, at any rate so far as Petrograd was concerned.

On 5 July the Bolshevik Central Committee decided that, in spite of the mood of the soldiers and the masses 'the moment is disadvantageous for accepting battle'.[19] But on 16 and 17 July crowds of workers and soldiers in Petrograd broke out in the streets into an angry and disorderly demonstration which Lenin characterized as 'something considerably more than a demonstration and less than a revolution'. The Bolsheviks had not planned the outbreak, though they were not unnaturally accused of having done so. They had of course in large measure contributed towards it by the unrest which their incessant propaganda fanned. It was under the slogan 'All power to the Soviets' that the demonstrators came out into the streets, and the leaflets issued by the Bolshevik Central and Petrograd Committees proclaimed this as the object. It was with the promise that this would remain the bolshevik slogan that the

---

[17] For the June demonstration see *Chamberlin*, Vol. I, pp. 160–2; *Trotsky, History*, Vol. I, pp. 450–4 ; *Yaroslavsky*, Vol. IV, pp. 139–41. The agitation was particularly strong in the bolshevik army organization ; on 29 June at a conference of the bolshevik party military organization a part of the Petrograd garrison agitated loudly that the conference should lead a rising—see N. I. Podvoysky, in *Krasnaya letopis'*, no. 6, 1923, p. 77.

[18] *Pervyy Leg. Komitet*, p. 154.

[19] *Proletarskaya revolyutsiya*, no. 5(17) 1923, p. 111.

demonstrators were urged to return to their posts.[20]   According to Zinoviev, Lenin, at the height of the disturbances, toyed with the idea of seizing power immediately.   But he decided against this course, fearing that the Provisional Government still retained sufficient support in the army outside the capital to overthrow the Bolsheviks.[21]

Thus the July demonstrators were pacified once again by the bolshevik party, though with greater difficulty than in June.   There had been several hundred casualties during the July demonstrations and the Provisional Government decided at last to take steps to repress the Bolsheviks.   In this move they had the support of the great majority of the members of the socialist parties in the Petrograd Soviet, whose representatives had by now entered the Provisional Government in coalition with the middle-class parties.   Two factors helped to overcome the scruples of the Socialist Revolutionaries and of most of the Mensheviks against the use of forcible measures to restrain political opponents.   One was panic following on defeat at the front.   The other was the revival, on allegedly new evidence, of the charge that the bolshevik leaders were agents in German pay, a suspicion which had never entirely died out of popular currency since the arrival of Lenin and Zinoviev in Petrograd by arrangement with the Germans.[22] But the measures adopted, though they drove a part of the bolshevik leadership underground, were indecisive, because the government either would not or could not destroy the growing bolshevik machine—the Red Guard,[23] the factory

[20] *Vladimirova*, Vol. III, pp. 148, 153.   A strange mood dominated the angry crowds, determined to force power on the Petrograd Soviet although they no longer wholly trusted it.   This mood is well summed up in the scene noted by Milyukov, when an angry worker shook his fist at Chernov, the socialist revolutionary leader who had entered the coalition Provisional Government in May as Minister of Agriculture, and shouted: 'Take power, you son of a bitch, when it's given you!'

[21] Zinoviev, *Lenin*, p. 39.   cf. also *Yaroslavsky*, Vol. IV, p. 151, for resolutions of confidence in the Central Executive Committee (of the non-bolshevik Soviet) passed at this date by various army units in the field, and *Chamberlin*, Vol. I, pp. 178–9, for the weak response evoked in the provinces by the outbreak in the capital.

[22] The slender evidence of the charge that Lenin was financed by the German General Staff has recently been reinvestigated by S. P. Mel'gunov, who considers that it was not entirely unfounded.   See his *Zolotoy nemetskiy klyuch*.   The question may perhaps be definitely answered some day on the basis of captured German archives.

[23] See *Trotsky, History*, Vol. III, pp. 185–8, for the development of the Red Guard after July.

organization, and the military organization. Lenin and Zinoviev went into hiding;[24] others, including Alexandra Kollontay, were arrested. The internationalist left wing of the Mensheviks, headed by Martov, strongly opposed these measures.

As Lenin had foreseen in Switzerland, the revolt of the land-hungry peasantry proved an all-important factor in the bolshevik conquest of power. Peasant disturbances, which had started in March, were spreading rapidly. In July recorded incidents of peasant violence were ten times more numerous than in March. Peasant unrest had at first taken the form of organized seizure of land under the control of local peasant committees. By October it had become a mass movement of unorganized violence,[25] swelled by the growing number of deserters from the disintegrating army. In view of the irresolution, not only of the Provisional Government, but of the two major socialist parties in formulating a policy on the land question, a party which seemed ready to champion the peasants' immediate demand for land was sure of a powerful ally. Yet it was obvious that what the peasant wanted was land, not socialism, and that his political progress would be from anarchical violence to get the land to support of an order which would safeguard his possession of it. He was therefore an ally of revolution, but an enemy of socialism. Lenin had assessed the value of the peasant as an ally immediately after the revolution of 1905, yet for years thereafter the Bolsheviks demanded the abolition of all private property in land.[26] In his April Theses Lenin still demanded 'nationalization of all land'. At the Seventh Bolshevik Party Conference in May

[24] Lenin remained in hiding until the October Revolution, first in Finland, then nearer Petrograd. There was some difference of view in the party whether he should stand his trial on the charge of being a German agent. Nogin, and a number of the Moscow City Committee members who were on the right wing of the party, favoured a trial and Nogin and Ordzhonikidze apparently negotiated tentatively with the Praesidium of the Central Executive Committee to see whether Lenin's safety could be effectively guaranteed, but without satisfaction. Stalin, and later Lunacharsky, resolutely urged that Lenin should remain in hiding, and Lenin, though hesitant, yielded. See Ordzhonikidze, *Izbrannye stat'i i rechi*, pp. 211–12.

[25] *Chamberlin*, Vol. I, pp. 211–52.

[26] The Mensheviks more realistically envisaged privately held small-holdings as a transition stage to ownership of the land by local self-governing communes. See the (majority) menshevik resolution at the Fourth Party Congress in Stockholm in 1906, *VKP(b) v rez.*, p. 85, and Lenin's draft resolution, *ibid.*, p. 67.

Lenin argued somewhat artificially that nationalization was what the peasant really wanted when he said that the land belongs to God.[27] He was only too well aware of the importance of winning over the peasantry to the Bolsheviks by championing their demand for land. Accordingly, while the resolution adopted by the Conference paid lip service to theory and still urged nationalization of all land, it also advised the peasants 'to take the land in an organized manner.'[28] It was the second half of the resolution which proved the more influential as a popular slogan. Before long bolshevik deputies in Soviets all over the country were advocating seizure of land. Lenin's speech and draft resolution on 4 June at the First All Russian Congress of Peasant Deputies, telling the peasants that the land was now theirs to take, not unnaturally made a deeper impression than the moderate socialist revolutionary resolution passed by the Congress, counselling patience until the Constituent Assembly could decide the question.[29] The repercussions in the country were felt immediately on the deputies' return to their villages.[30] The wave of land seizures and agrarian unrest which bolshevik propaganda helped to encourage played an important part in the downfall of the Provisional Government. Yet it was obvious that if once the peasants seized the coveted land, nationalization would remain a dead letter. In November, under guise of nationalization, the seizures of the past months were legalized. It was no exaggeration for Rosa Luxemburg to prophesy a year later that Lenin's agrarian reforms would create a 'new powerful class of enemies' for socialism whose resistance would prove even more dangerous than had been that of the former landowners.[31] There were some spokesmen in the bolshevik party in the summer of 1917 who foretold the consequences of the

---

[27] He was opposed by Angarsky who maintained that 'nationalization of the land presupposes the abolition of private ownership of land. But how are we to reconcile this with the peasant tendencies towards a purely proprietary basis?' Angarsky belonged to the Moscow City Bolshevik Committee, which advocated bolshevik support for peasant seizures of land so long as such seizures were of an organized nature. *Protokoly VII Konf.*, p. 173; cf. *Trotsky, Stalinskaya shkola*, p. 264; and *Avdeev*, Vol. II, p. 45.

[28] *VKP(b) v rez.*, p. 70.

[29] See *Avdeev*, Vol. II, p. 170, pp. 278–9, and pp. 293–5.

[30] See, for example, a report of a government land commissioner of 14 June 1917, printed in *Krasnyy arkhiv*, Vol. XIV, p. 225.

[31] *Die Russische Revolution*, pp. 85–7.

agricultural trend. One of them was Bukharin, who argued that while the land-hungry peasantry would support the revolution in its first phase, the sated peasantry would draw back in the second phase 'when only the proletarian elements within the country and the proletariat of Western Europe will support the Russian proletariat'.[32] If no one heeded this warning, it was because in 1917 no bolshevik leader seriously doubted that revolution in Western Europe was imminent, and that, without the support of revolution in Western Europe, the proletarian revolution in Russia was in any case inevitably doomed.

Throughout May, June, and July Lenin worked to build up that party of 'firmly welded revolutionaries' in which, since 1902, he had unswervingly believed as the only means for the proletariat to seize and hold power. With the growth of his authority in his party, it was not difficult for him to overcome the trend towards reunion with the Mensheviks, which had been evident on his arrival in Russia in April. When the joint conference with the Mensheviks, which had been arranged in defiance of the Bolshevik Central Committee the day after Lenin's arrival, took place on 15 June, it was foredoomed to failure. The results were inconclusive, and it was never resumed.[33] There were no more joint bolshevik-menshevik local party organizations after June, though a few survived, until that date.[34] The trend of events also made any question of union of the two wings of the social democratic party increasingly unlikely. The right Mensheviks, committed to coalition with the middle-class parties and to support of the prosecution of the war, no longer had anything in common with the Bolsheviks. They were also fast losing popular support. Martov's left group gained in strength, while that of the party as a whole declined. The opposition of this group, both to the war and to coalition with the Provisional Government, was voiced in Maxim Gorky's paper, *Novaya Zhizn'*. Martov's followers included many of the best marxist intellectuals who, consciously or unconsciously, clung to the European and international tradition of their years of struggle in exile.

[32] *Protokoly VI*, p. 134.
[33] There is a short account in *Vladimirova*, Vol. III, pp. 13–14. cf. also *Yaroslavsky*, Vol. IV, p. 137.
[34] *Trotsky, History*, Vol. I, p. 443.

They were repelled by the uncomprising extremism and demagogy which now increasingly characterized the Bolsheviks. Martov, indeed, had originally broken with Lenin on the very issue of party organization and had for years criticized in strong terms Lenin's methods of running the Russian Social Democratic party.[35] To him union with Lenin was unthinkable, though some of his close followers, notably Larin, were later tempted to join the Bolsheviks. Even when municipal elections proved beyond doubt that the Mensheviks were sinking into political insignificance, Martov rejected the tentative suggestion of Sukhanov and others that it was now time for some form of union between the left Mensheviks and the Bolsheviks. It was no longer any serious difference on marxist doctrine which held the menshevik internationalists apart from the Bolsheviks. Martov had after the events of July 1917 conceded that 'history demands that the proletariat in the person of the Soviets should seize power into its hands'.[36] But the tactics of the Bolsheviks in the past months had created a gulf between the two parties. 'The danger to the revolution is now from the left, and not from the right,' he replied to Sukhanov's suggestion.[37]

On 17 May Trotsky had arrived in Petrograd from New York. His reputation, oratory, and energy immediately made him a dominating figure in the Petrograd Soviet. There must have been many who still recalled the stirring part which he had played in an earlier Petersburg Soviet during its short existence in 1905. Lenin had then regarded the spontaneous and unorganized revolutionary Soviet, a conglomeration of all parties and of many non-party delegates, with some slight degree of scepticism. But to Trotsky it had been 'the natural organ of the proletariat in its . . . struggle for power', the 'democratic representative organ of the proletariat' and the 'focus of all revolutionary power in the country'.[38] It was

[35] 'The curse of "Nechaev" methods must be excised from the party organism' he had written in 1904 in one of his early controversies with Lenin. See *Ob odnom nedostoynom postupke*, p. 10; and cf. the account of Martov's fight over Lenin's method of raising party funds by armed hold-ups in *Wolfe*, pp. 371–81.
[36] In the Central Executive Committee on 17 July—see *Vladimirova*, Vol. III, p. 143. He was also supported by the left wing of the Socialist Revolutionaries. And cf. Martov's views at the Menshevik Party Conference on 28 July, *ibid.*, p. 186.
[37] *Sukhanov*, Vol. VI, pp. 196–7.
[38] *Trotsky, 1905*, pp. 225–30; contrast *Lenin*, Vol. VIII, pp. 400–1, 409–11. However, in the draft of an article written in November 1905, but first published

inevitable that to Trotsky the seizure of power should have been bound up with the Soviets. He was not, in May 1917, either a member of the bolshevik party or committed to its doctrines. Soon after his arrival, he reconstituted the little group of *Mezhdurayontsy* which had been formed in 1912, and which occupied a position half way between the Bolsheviks and the Mensheviks. But Trotsky and his followers showed no immediate anxiety to fuse with the Bolsheviks. 'You cannot demand that we should recognize bolshevism,' Trotsky had declared at the very first joint discussion between the Bolsheviks and his group.[39] Some of his speeches soon after his arrival certainly suggested a degree of moderation and a recognition that salvation need not lie with one party alone which were in marked contrast to the uncomprising speeches of the bolshevik leaders at the time.[40] For two months Trotsky maintained his independence, publishing a weekly organ, *Vpered*, in conjunction with Lunacharsky, of which the policy was avowed to be that of 'uniting all shades of internationalism'. By mid-July, without yet finally joining the Bolsheviks, Trotsky had cast in his lot with them. On 15 July he published a letter in *Pravda* stressing that there were no differences between his group and the Bolsheviks, 'either on principles or on tactics' and that union was therefore desirable.[41] When, after the disturbances of July, Trotsky was omitted from the order for the arrest of the bolshevik leaders issued by the Provisional Government, he went out of his way to express publicly his solidarity with Lenin, Kamenev, and Zinoviev, and to emphasize that if he was not yet a member of their party it was due to historical reasons which had 'lost all significance'. He demanded that the charge of being a German agent be extended to him as well.[42] He was arrested some weeks later. The formal union of the *Mezhdurayontsy* with the Bolsheviks did not take place until the Sixth Bolshevik Party

only in 1940, Lenin expressed the view that the Soviet should aim to include all workers' parties and to proclaim itself the provisional revolutionary government —see *Lenin* (4), Vol. X, pp. 3–11.

[39] *Leninskiy sbornik*, Vol. IV, p. 303.

[40] See, for example, his speech in the First Soviet Congress in June; *Trotsky, Sochineniya*, Vol. III (i), pp. 113–22; and cf. *Sukhanov*, Vol. III, pp. 441–2, Vol. IV, pp. 237–40.

[41] *Trotsky, Sochineniya*, Vol. III (i), p. 149.

[42] See his letter to the Provisional Government of 26 July, *Sochineniya*, Vol. III (i), pp. 165–6, and his letters from prison, *ibid.*, pp. 201–2.

Congress on 8 August. The delay was due partly to the misgivings of the men who formed his group, in the face of 'the habits and methods of the bolshevik côterie' as Trotsky put it,[43] and partly to their agreement with the bolshevik leaders to use the intervening weeks for an endeavour to bring into the bolshevik party the entire menshevik internationalist wing. They explained their failure by these Mensheviks' 'old fractional fear of being eaten alive by the Bolsheviks'.[44] The union with the *Mezhdurayontsy* brought to the ranks of the Bolsheviks a number of individualists most of whom were eventually to realize that their misgivings had not been unfounded. They included Ioffe, Lunacharsky, Yurenev, and Ryazanov. They retained no identity as a group. So far as Trotsky was concerned, his acceptance of Lenin's leadership in July 1917 was complete and unreserved, as Lenin more than once emphasized.

By the end of July, Lenin had reached the conclusion that the bolshevik party must take power by force. The Soviets, he now argued, could have taken power before July, and in this way the proletarian revolution could have been accomplished in a peaceful manner. He may have been right. The Soviets with their socialist majorities had enjoyed the confidence of the mass of the people and of the army. Had they decided to wrest power from the Provisional Government they might well have succeeded with little or no bloodshed. Had they been able, further, to consolidate their government by bringing the war to a speedy end and by satisfying the peasants' demands, some workable system of moderate socialism might have come into being and stayed in power. Whether the Bolsheviks would in such case have been content to sit and wait, as Lenin now wrote, until the petty bourgeois tendencies of the socialist parties had 'been worked out of their system in the course of practice' is a matter of speculation. But now, he continued, the socialists had missed their opportunity. He hinted not only that the Bolsheviks intended to seize power, but that they intended to seize power for themselves alone. Only the 'revolutionary masses of the people' can take power, turning away from the socialist parties who have betrayed

---

[43] *Trotsky, Sochineniya,* Vol. III (i), pp. 145–6.
[44] See Yurenev's account at the Sixth Party Congress, *Protokoly VI,* pp. 47–8.

the revolution and who have supported a government 'which must now be overthrown'.[45]   Moreover, Lenin now discarded the Soviets as the organs of the forthcoming proletarian power. In his view they had become organs of reaction.   The Petrograd Soviet had supported the reprisals against the Bolsheviks. Therefore, power must be seized by the 'revolutionary masses' themselves.   This view of revolution without the Soviets was very close to Lenin's first plan in Switzerland, before he reached Petrograd.   After his arrival in Russia he had, for tactical reasons, adopted the slogan 'All Power to the Soviets'. Now it was to be discarded.   To Lenin revolution without the Soviets meant seizure of power by the bolshevik party, the vanguard of the proletariat, through the Red Guards and the factory and army party organizations.   But it is unlikely that this view was either understood or accepted by a good many of his followers.   To them the idea of government by the mass of the workers, which the socialist revolution was intended to bring about, still retained some of its original meaning.   It had not yet acquired the meaning which Lenin attached to it, of government by the bolshevik party, with the support of, but without control or indeed participation by, the masses.   Lenin's followers therefore saw the future proletarian government as inextricably bound up with the Soviets— with a bolshevik majority in each, no doubt—but nevertheless Soviets, in which each party which could get some delegates returned would have a voice.

Thus, at the end of July, Lenin abandoned the slogan 'All power to the Soviets' without indicating to his bewildered party what would take the place of the Soviets as organs of government.   On 8 August the Sixth Bolshevik Party Congress met in Petrograd.   Lenin and Zinoviev were in hiding and did not attend it.   The task of putting Lenin's new ideas over at the Congress fell to Stalin.   He was not yet equal to it. Somewhat casually he put forward a resolution: The familiar slogan 'All power to the Soviets' was now out of date.   The Bolsheviks were to take on the rôle of 'front rank fighters against counter-revolution', and without being tempted into a 'premature battle' were to prepare for the ultimate seizure

[45] See an article written at the end of July, 'K lozungam', *Lenin*, Vol. XXI, pp. 33–8.   cf. 'Uroki revolyutsii', *ibid.*, pp. 69–77.

of power by the 'revolutionary classes'.[46] There was no indication in the resolution of what organs would take the place of the Soviets, and many members of the congress were profoundly disturbed by this obvious difficulty. Stalin's efforts to explain it away did little to clarify the problem. Nevertheless there was no serious opposition to the resolution, which was vague enough not to arouse too much misgiving. The discussion however revealed some disunity on doctrine in the party. Those most to the right, such as Nogin and Angarsky of the Moscow City Bolshevik Committee, were not yet reconciled to an interpretation of marxism which considered that the time was already ripe to 'step over the bourgeois revolution to the socialist revolution'. They did not agree that the country had made such a jump forward in so short a time that it was 'already prepared for socialism'. Many, among them Manuilsky, Volodarsky, and the newly-joined Yurenev, were unwilling to throw over the Soviets, and were not satisfied with Stalin's explanation that the change of slogan did not in fact mean that the Soviets were to be jettisoned. Sokol'nikov, of the radical-minded Moscow *Oblast'* Bureau, fully supported Stalin, as also did Molotov— now apparently reconciled with him after the disagreements which followed Stalin's return to Petrograd from Siberia. Only Bubnov perceived that the 'differences of opinion are much deeper than the comrades seem to think'. But the differences did not appear in the voting, since the resolution was adopted unanimously with four abstentions.[47] However, the fact that no vote was cast against the resolution did not mean that the party leadership as a whole was ready to support an immediate armed rising. Few opposed it on principle —perhaps four in the Central Committee of twenty-one, and a few more in the important committees outside. But while in the rank and file of the party there appeared to be widespread support for an armed rising, many of the leaders were only too ready to put off the decisive day for as long as possible. Volodarsky probably expressed a fairly general view when he said in the Petrograd Bolshevik Party Committee at the end of October: 'We must realize that when we take power we shall have to lower wages . . . we shall have to introduce terror

[46] *VKP(b) v rez.*, pp. 291–3.   [47] *Protokoly VI*, pp. 110–41, and 234.

. . . We have no right to refuse to adopt these means, but neither is there any need to rush towards them.'[48]   It is for this reason that for the last two months before the seizure of power Lenin had to struggle with the other party leaders to galvanize them into action at the moment which he perceived to be the right one.   He feared that if the Bolsheviks let slip the decisive moment, the deadlock in the dyarchy of Provisional Government and Soviets might be resolved, and long delayed measures be taken on the burning questions of the day, which would cut the ground from under his feet.   He may also have feared (Lenin never underestimated his opponents) that before long the Provisional Government, or some more determined government which might replace it, would at last take effective measures against the handful of Bolsheviks and the skeleton of their organization in whose hands the future revolution lay.

[48] *Pervyy Leg. Komitet*, p. 296.

CHAPTER IV

THE OCTOBER REVOLUTION

Trotsky had accepted Lenin's leadership in July. After his release from prison on bail on 17 September, his ascendancy over the Petrograd Soviet grew. Probably Trotsky could have made the October Revolution without Lenin, at any rate in Petrograd. But it is doubtful whether without the control which Lenin gained over his party in the weeks before and after the seizure of power the revolution would have had any chance of surviving. Soviet historians of the revolution (and not only Soviet historians), with little regard for the very full published documentation which is available, have often falsified the story of the rising until it bears little relation to the known facts.[1] One such falsification for example is the assertion that Trotsky had 'boastingly blurted out' the date fixed for the revolution, namely 7 November (25 October), with the result that it had to be hastily changed to 6 November.[2] But while there is no truth in this and similar absurdities, there was in the last weeks before the rising a difference of opinion on tactics between Lenin and Trotsky. Lenin thought in terms of seizure of power by the 'proletariat', which he identified with the bolshevik party, its Red Guard, its factory committees, and its organizations in the army. He had discarded the Soviets as organs of power. Trotsky believed that it was vital that the seizure of power by the Bolsheviks should be crowned with a popular symbol, the Soviets. He feared that otherwise the revolution would not command sufficient popular support. During the critical weeks in which the rising was planned and executed, Lenin was in hiding, controlling his party by letters and messengers. Trotsky was in Petrograd at the centre of events. Lenin struggled to build up the united party organization which could at the right moment seize the vital points

---

[1] An analysis by Trotsky of some of these distortions will be found in his *History*, Vol. III, pp. 345–68. It may be observed that Trotsky's *History of the Revolution* though it contains judgments which are not acceptable to non-marxist readers, does not apparently attempt to falsify facts.

[2] *Istoriya VKP(b)*, p. 198.

throughout the country. Trotsky, in addition to directing insurrection in Petrograd, worked to create the belief that the revolution was an assumption of power by an organ rightfully claiming to speak in the name of the masses, the Congress of Soviets. The tactics of both leaders were necessary for the success of the revolution and complemented each other. Without Lenin's organization the seizure of power outside the capital could not have been ensured. Without Trotsky's stage management the coup d'état might have failed to win the popular support, or at any rate to ensure the neutrality of the workers and soldiers in and near the capital, upon which its success depended.

It was therefore thanks to Trotsky that the October Revolution developed along the line in which the seizure of power was cloaked under a cover of democratic action. This corresponded to the views of the not inconsiderable section of the bolshevik leadership which still visualized the socialist revolution in semi-parliamentary terms. It also corresponded to the mood of the bolshevik rank and file, and to that of wide sections of the population for whom the Soviets represented the only tangible symbol of authority. But the capital was not the whole country. 'Our point of view was the point of view of Petrograd', Trotsky said five years later, recalling the days of the rising, 'but Lenin was looking at the rising not only from the point of view of Petrograd, but of the whole country.'[3] The success of the revolution required something more— agitation, organization, co-ordination throughout the country and at the front. Without a determined party machine this could not have been accomplished. The creation of this machine was the work of Lenin, whose conception of revolution was totally devoid of the quasi-parliamentary illusions of some of his lieutenants, which Trotsky skilfully exploited, if he did not himself share them.

Viewing the events from the Petrograd Soviet which Trotsky dominated, the final phases of the seizure of power present a picture of virtually open preparations for insurrection, thinly, if at all, disguised as defensive moves against a threat of counter-revolution, all culminating in the assumption of power by the Second All-Russian Congress of Soviets. The failure in early

[3] *Proletarskaya revolyutsiya*, no. 10 (1922), p. 58.

September of General Kornilov's attempted coup d'état had had immediate repercussions in the elections to the Soviets which followed it. By 13 September the Bolsheviks had secured a majority in the Petrograd Soviet, of which Trotsky was elected chairman on 8 October. This was followed by equal Bolshevik successes in Moscow and in a number of industrial centres in the provinces.[4] The Socialist Revolutionaries still retained the traditional support of the peasants in elections, but the peasantry was moving rapidly towards complete anarchy. Bolshevik preparations for the day which was to prove fatal to the Provisional Government unfolded before the eyes of that government without any apparent efforts on its part to hinder them. The government was quite aware of the imminent attempt at a coup d'état. But it remained confident that this attempt would spell ruin for the bolshevik party. It was also hamstrung by the circumstances in which it had to try to govern. The dyarchy of the government and of the Petrograd Soviet had not been resolved by the coalition of Socialist Revolutionaries, Mensheviks, and *Kadety* and the government was as a result weak and incapable of decisive action. Yet either of two methods could alone have averted the threat of a bolshevik coup d'état: either the effective destruction of their organization, or the stealing of their thunder by an immediate resolute policy on peace and on land. Neither of these drastic courses was in the circumstances possible. Neither liberals nor socialists were prepared, only a few months after the February Revolution had brought delivery from despotism, to use the methods of despots against political opponents, however violent. Nor were they prepared, as Lenin was, to end the war by signing a separate peace; or to satisfy the land hunger of the peasants by giving legal form to their forcible seizures of the land. But the Provisional Government's misappreciation of the potential strength of the Bolsheviks is perhaps easier to understand when one recollects that it was shared by such prominent Bolsheviks as Kamenev and Zinoviev. Besides, the assessment of the extent of popular support for the Bolsheviks was not an easy matter, as the following reports on 28 October

[4] *Chamberlin*, Vol. I, pp. 278–9. The swing in opinion did not affect regional strongholds of menshevism, such as Georgia.

from local bolshevik delegates to the Petrograd Committee show.

> Krasnoe Selo . . . Out of (our organization of) 5000, 500 will come here, the rest will remain in Krasnoe Selo, to see what happens. In Kronstadt, morale has dropped considerably . . . Among the postal and telegraph workers . . . we have few sympathizers. In Vasil'evsky Ostrov . . . there is no mood for insurrection . . . In the Vyborg region . . . the masses will support us . . . Telegrams received from Finland protesting against the bolshevik insurrection . . . Second City district: morale is better than before 16–18 July . . . Moscow district: the masses will come out at the bidding of the Soviet, but few at the bidding of our party. Narva district: in general . . . no urge to insurrection. Obukhov factory: a decisive change in our favour. Okhta district: there is no mood for insurrection among the workers . . . Schlüsselburg district: the masses will rise at the bidding of the Soviet. Lettish district: the comrades will come out at the bidding of the Petersburg Bolshevik Committee, but not of the Soviet . . . Estonia: the same. Trade Unions: in case of a counter-revolutionary attack, the masses will resist, but they will not come out of their own accord. If the Petrograd Soviet calls for an insurrection, the masses will follow the Soviet. Finland district: the quicker the better.[5]

The only general conclusion that can be drawn from a report of this nature ten days before the vital day is that, with the exception of a few bolshevik strongholds, the workers were neutral, rather than straining for the fight; and that their loyalty was, in general, to the Petrograd Soviet rather than to the bolshevik party.

Logically, the acceptance in August by the Sixth Bolshevik Party Congress of the principle that power must be seized irrespectively of the Soviets should have prepared the party for Lenin's next move. But perhaps the issues debated at the congress appeared neither as imminent nor as clear to the participants as they did to Lenin. Certainly, Lenin's utterances in the following months did not help to solve the dilemma of the average party member which Stalin had failed to solve at the Sixth Party Congress: if not the Soviets, who was to govern? While in hiding, Lenin was clarifying his ideas on

[5] *Pervyy Leg. Komitet*, pp. 312–15.

the subject and writing his *State and Revolution*, but this was not to be published until 1918.[6] For a fleeting period, after the rout of Kornilov's move early in September, Lenin seems to have toyed with the idea that a majority could now be won by the Bolsheviks in the Soviets, and that bolshevik seizure of power independently of the Soviets might be unnecessary. In an article published about the middle of September he proposed what he called a 'compromise': that in return for full freedom of agitation (i.e. the repeal of all measures passed against them) the Bolsheviks would re-assume their slogan 'All power to the Soviets'. It was not a very convincing peace offer. A postscript to the article discarded the proffered 'compromise' as belated,[7] and on 28 September a series of pungent and direct calls to action from Lenin reached the astonished Central Committee of the bolshevik party.

The Bolsheviks were at that date participating as a left wing of opposition in the so-called 'Democratic Conference', a loose assembly of representatives of the Soviets, municipal authorities, trade unions, and co-operatives, one of Kerensky's last attempts to find a solution for the crisis of government power. For the first time the party was faced with a demand by Lenin, from his hiding place in Finland, for immediate insurrection, not in the indeterminate future, but here and now. They

[6] In February 1918. The importance which Lenin attached to this work is evident from his directions to Kamenev after the events of July to publish his notes and drafts on the question of the state, prepared in exile, should they 'bump me off'—*Leninskiy sbornik*, Vol. XIV, pp. 204–385. An article published by him on 27 September sketched the central idea of this work, that with the seizure of power the old state machine must be smashed, with the corollary that the workers and peasants will 'quickly learn in the doing of it, how to run the state economy, without elaborate machinery'—an utopian ideal soon to be shattered in practice. For this article see *Lenin*, Vol. XXI, pp. 142–8. Presumably at this date Lenin still retained his belief, enunciated in April 1917, that with the arming of the entire people, no police would be necessary in the new state—see *Lenin*, Vol. XX, pp. 121 and 139.

[7] *Lenin*, Vol. XXI, pp. 132–6. The article ('O kompromissakh') was written between 14 and 16 September. Kerensky's order of 15 September, calling for an end to political agitation in the army and for an 'immediate stop to the formation of independent detachments under the pretext of struggle against counter-revolutionary risings' may have influenced Lenin's change of mind; for the text of this order see *Vladimirova*, Vol. IV, p. 155. Lenin's article was later to be much pressed into service, to taunt the socialist parties for their 'indignant rejection' of his offer e.g., by Zinoviev, in December, 1917, Zinoviev, *Sochineniya*, Vol. VII, (i), p. 454. It is unlikely that it was taken very seriously by anyone. Even Sukhanov, at that time on the verge of joining the Bolsheviks, ridiculed the suggestion—and indeed no one could have had much illusion as to what would happen to the Mensheviks and Socialist Revolutionaries when the Bolsheviks did win their majority. See *Sukhanov*, Vol. VI, p. 44.

were to leave the conference and go to the factories, organize a staff to lead the revolutionary detachments, arrest the government, and so forth. Lenin's demand found no supporters in the bolshevik Central Committee. There was even strong feeling that all records of his suggestion should be destroyed, since it seemed to disregard the danger that seizure of power in the capital would not guarantee success in the provinces. It was only by a vote of six to four, with six abstentions, that one copy of Lenin's proposals was preserved for posterity and the committee resolved to take measures to see that no outbreaks should take place in the factories and barracks.[8] Indeed the bolshevik party was at this time still firmly committed to 'parliamentary illusions'. The Council of the Republic (the so-called 'Pre-Parliament'), another constitutional improvization designed by the Provisional Government to resolve the deadlock caused by the failure of coalition, was due to meet in some three weeks' time, on 20 October. The Bolsheviks could only form a minority on this body, which included the middle-class parties. Yet even Trotsky, in conjunction with Kamenev, urged (in the bolshevik 'fraction' of the Petrograd Soviet) that all effort should be directed to force the forthcoming Council of the Republic 'to take power into its hands; this will be the first stage for the transfer of power into the hands of the Soviets'. Shortly afterwards the bolshevik 'fraction' resolved by a vote of 72 to 50 to participate in the Council of the Republic.[9] However, within a few days Trotsky had changed his views, probably on the insistence of Lenin, who urged that the Bolsheviks should boycott the Council of the Republic. On 4 October, at a meeting of the same bolshevik 'fraction', Trotsky now demanded that the Bolsheviks should decide to participate in the Council only in order to walk out of it as a gesture, at the very start of the proceedings. Opinion was evenly divided at this meeting.

[8] For Lenin's plan, see *Lenin*, Vol. XXI, pp. 193–4, and pp. 197–9. The first letter, 'Bol' sheviki dolzhny vzyat' vlast', which asserts that 'to wait for a formal Bolshevik majority is naive', was sent to the Petrograd and Moscow Committees, over the heads of the Central Committee. For the meeting see Bukharin in *Proletarskaya revolyutsiya*, no. 10, 1922, p. 316 and *ibid.*, no. 10 (69), 1927, pp. 246–7, for the protocol of this meeting.

[9] *Sukhanov*, Vol. VI, pp. 110–11. Trotsky does not deal with these 'fraction' meetings (at which Sukhanov was present), but says that the decision of the 'fraction' to participate was 'ratified by many local committees, if not a majority of them'—*History*, Vol. III, p. 145.

The right wing, led by Kamenev and Ryazanov, proposed that the Bolsheviks should not decide to walk out of the forthcoming Council meeting until some justification arose, since otherwise their conduct might not be intelligible to the masses.   In the end, Trotsky won by a few votes.   Ryazanov announced the bolshevik decision to the Democratic Conference: they would attend the forthcoming Council in order to 'unfurl in this stronghold of compromise the banner of the proletariat and make it easier for the Soviets to create a truly revolutionary power'.[10]

But, while Trotsky thus modified his tactics to conform to Lenin's views, Lenin likewise seems at last to have realized that he had gone too far in disregarding the strong feeling in his party when he discarded the Soviets as organs of popular government.   In the next few weeks the force of his exhortations overcame the scruples inside his party, and thus made possible the final determined effort on which seizure of power depended.   But at the same time he found it necessary to make some concessions to the widespread faith in the Soviets. The Second All Russian Congress of Soviets was due to meet on 2 November.   In a series of articles written between 10 and 21 October Lenin now outlined the form which the revolution was to take.   Power must be seized independently of the Soviets.   The strength of the party must be directed to the factories.   Above all, power must be seized.   'It is necessary to fight the constitutional illusions and hopes based on the forthcoming Congress of Soviets.'   But, at the same time, Lenin no longer entirely dismissed the Soviets as organs of government.   There must be re-elections to the Soviets, he wrote, and the new proletarian government must be responsible to them.   But the party must realize that without an armed insurrection the mere assumption of power by the Congress of Soviets could not create a proletarian government.   On 21 October he revived the old slogan 'All Power to the Soviets'.   But it now acquired a new meaning.   'The slogan 'All Power to the Soviets' is a slogan of insurrection. He who uses this slogan without understanding this fact,

[10] See *Lenin*, Vol. XXI, p. 219.   The wavering in the upper ranks of the party 'may ruin the whole enterprise', he wrote; and see *Sukhanov*, Vol. VI, pp. 157, 168, and pp. 247–8.

without realizing it, has only himself to blame. . . . To delay means death.' Once again Lenin urged the Central Committee to take immediate action, and to move the Baltic Fleet and the Finnish troops of Reval and Kronstadt against the troops of General Kornilov, stationed near Petrograd.[11]

Lenin's agitation in the party, not only within the Central Committee but far and wide outside it, had its effect. Among a large section of the Bolshevik rank and file, or in the radical Moscow *Oblast'* Committee, he was sure of immediate response, a fact which probably influenced the final decision of the Central Committee.[12] On 23 October in the bolshevik Central Committee, after a stormy meeting attended secretly by Lenin and Zinoviev, still in hiding, Lenin's resolution recognizing that 'an armed uprising is inevitable and the time perfectly ripe' and proposing that 'all the organizations of the party should act accordingly' was passed against the dissenting votes of only Kamenev and Zinoviev.[13] Nine members of the Central Committee of twenty-one elected at the Sixth Congress, were not, however, present at the meeting, among them Nogin and Rykov, both of the moderate and right-wing Moscow City Committee, and Milyutin, also an opponent of insurrection. A vote of the full committee would probably have revealed an opposition approaching a quarter of those present. Trotsky, Stalin, and Kollontay were among those who voted for the resolution.

The opposition of Kamenev, and subsequently of Nogin and Rykov, presents no problem. None of them had accepted Lenin's doctrine that the time was ripe to jump from the bourgeois democratic to the socialist revolution. Kamenev had continued to oppose Lenin's views for some time after April. On 19 August he had openly supported a menshevik proposal to participate in a forthcoming international socialist conference at Stockholm (which in fact never took place) in

[11] See *Lenin*, Vol. XXI, pp. 221–8, 'Zadachi revolyutsii', 9 and 10 October, 'Krizis nazrel', 11 October; in the latter Lenin tendered his resignation from the Central Committee in order to leave him free to agitate in the lower ranks of the party and complained that the Central Committee had ignored his demands and cut passages out of his articles—*ibid.* pp. 235–41; and Theses for a Conference on 21 October of the Petrograd Organization *ibid.* pp. 287–9.

[12] See *Trotsky, History*, Vol. III, pp. 145–6, and pp. 137–8.

[13] *B. & F.*, pp. 56–8. For Trotsky's account of this historic meeting in Sukhanov's flat (in Sukhanov's absence) see *Proletarskaya revolyutsiya*, no. 10 (1922), pp. 57–8.

defiance of a decision of the bolshevik party congress. As late as 18 October he had voted against the final decision of the Bolsheviks in the Council of the Republic to make their demonstrative withdrawal from that body. Nogin had argued at the Sixth Bolshevik Party Congress in August that the time was not nearly ripe for the jump from middle-class democracy, not many months old in Russia, to socialism. But Zinoviev's attitude is more puzzling. He was Lenin's closest collaborator both in exile[14] and after the return to Petrograd. A powerful orator and demagogue, he was one of the major factors in kindling the blaze of class war in Petrograd. There had been nothing to indicate that he shared the doubts of orthodox marxists like Kamenev or Nogin. After the October Revolution Zinoviev was to follow Lenin without faltering, through all his changes of policy, and prove himself an able lieutenant in tasks requiring cunning—his enemies, and he had many, would say intrigue. But courage was not one of his qualities, and he was apt to lose his nerve in moments of crisis. It was possibly to panic that his hesitation on 23 October was due. Meanwhile, in conjunction with Kamenev, he justified his view in a long private letter, addressed to the principal bolshevik party committees and organizations. In essentials, the views expressed in this letter were the same as the views which Kamenev had already advanced against Lenin's April Theses. To stake everything on an armed revolt now was to gamble with the fate of 'both the Russian and the international revolution'. The chances of the Bolsheviks in the elections to the Constituent Assembly were 'excellent'—they might win as many as a third of the votes—and then either 'our opponents will have to yield to us at every step, or we shall form "a governing bloc" together with the Left Socialist Revolutionaries and non-party peasants to carry out our programme.'[15] It was a parliamentary and not a revolutionary victory which Kamenev and Zinoviev envisaged. Lenin's

[14] Lenin's solidarity with Zinoviev during this period is well demonstrated by some of his letters to Inessa Armand, written between November 1916 and February 1917 and recently published for the first time, with the avowed object *inter alia* of proving the contrary. They reveal to anyone familiar with Lenin's style of controversy nothing but insignificant minor friction over Zinoviev's attitude to Lenin's denunciation of Radek—see 'Neopublikovannye dokumenty V.I. Lenina' in *Bol'shevik* no. 1, 15 January 1949, pp. 39–53.

[15] Text in Zinoviev, *Sochineniya*, Vol. VII (i), pp. 547–51.

accusation, frequently repeated since,[16] that Zinoviev and Kamenev deliberately carried their inner-party controversy outside the bounds of the party and thus revealed the party's plan for an insurrection, was not true, nor was the letter itself published till 1925. But their views were widely gossiped about on the fringes of the party, and on 30 October an article by Bazarov in the left menshevik *Novaya Zhizn'* referred to the Zinoviev-Kamenev letter, which was circulating among the Bolsheviks in manuscript. There is no evidence to suggest that this disclosure by Bazarov (who was a menshevik internationalist), was made with the approval of Zinoviev or Kamenev. On the contrary, on the very next day, a letter from Zinoviev and Kamenev appeared in *Novaya Zhizn'*. It stated that there were many Bolsheviks, in addition to the signatories of the letter, who were of the opinion 'that initiation of an armed rising . . . independently of and a few days before the Congress of the Soviets' would be a disastrous step for the future of the revolution. It then went on to deny that any day had been fixed by the Bolsheviks for a rising. It is even likely that the form of this letter was intended to camouflage the dissensions inside the bolshevik Central Committee which Bazarov had revealed. There was a persistent rumour at that time in Petrograd that the Bolsheviks had fixed 2 November (20 October) as the day of the rising—a rumour which was true to the extent that the Bolsheviks had at one time decided to start an industrial strike on this date. It was also the date originally fixed for the opening of the Congress of Soviets. Public declarations by bolshevik leaders about this time indignantly denying that the Bolsheviks intended to start an insurrection were a familiar feature in the press.[17] But Lenin was incensed at Bazarov's revelations which he read on the day of publication in his Vyborg retreat. He immediately carried the campaign into the open by denouncing the waverers in a series of three articles which appeared in the first days of November. He further demanded their expulsion from the Central Committee, but the majority of the committee, including Stalin, opposed him. It was not surprising that

---

[16] e.g. *Deutscher*, p. 164; *Carr, I*, pp. 96–7.
[17] See *Novaya zhizn'* for 17 and 18 October (old style); on the incident see *Lenin*, Vol. XXI, pp. 348, 350–6, 536. And see note 21.

Lenin should immediately have carried the split within the party into the open. Years before he had laid down his principles for dealing with a split. The first of these was to wrest the masses away from the leaders of a dissident section of the party and to conduct against these leaders 'a fight of extermination'.[18] There was, in this instance, in view of the radical temper of many of the rank and file of the party, every prospect of wresting mass support in the party from Zinoviev and Kamenev.

Meanwhile a meeting on 29 October of the bolshevik Central Committee, together with representatives of the Petrograd Committee, of the military organization, trade unions, and factory committees showed that opposition to an immediate rising among the bolshevik leaders was not confined to Zinoviev and Kamenev. At this larger meeting of 29 October Zinoviev and Kamenev were once again the only two to cast their votes against the resolution adopted on 23 October when it was put forward for reaffirmation. But a compromise alternative resolution proposed by Zinoviev that no action should be taken until the bolshevik delegates to the impending All Russian Congress of Soviets had been consulted, received no less than six votes as against fifteen, with three abstentions. Kamenev resigned from the Central Committee and his resignation was accepted a few days later, and further public utterances against the decision on the insurrection were prohibited by the Central Committee.[19] Both Kamenev and Zinoviev attempted to cover up in the public eye the split in the party which had been revealed. When Trotsky on 31 October declared in the Petrograd Soviet that no armed rising had been ordered by the Bolsheviks, but that the forthcoming Congress of Soviets would be defended against all counter-revolutionary attempts, Kamenev subscribed to this declaration, as he put it, 'with both hands'.[20] Zinoviev on 2 November in *Pravda* also publicly associated himself with Trotsky's declaration, renouncing 'for the time being' his reply to Lenin. Stalin aroused Lenin's anger by adding an editorial

---

[18] See two interesting quotations dating from 1906 in *Wolfe*, pp. 355–6.
[19] See *Proletarskaya revolyutsiya*, no. 10 (69), pp. 272–86, 287–9. In spite of his resignation, Kamenev seems to have continued to participate in Central Committee meetings, including the vital meeting on 6 November—*ibid.*, pp. 296–8.
[20] *Ryabinsky*, p. 119.

note that the party discussions could now be regarded as closed.[21] Stalin also opposed the acceptance of Kamenev's resignation from the Central Committee. It is not clear whether his conduct was reinsurance against a possible defeat, as Trotsky suggests,[22] or whether he was trying to undo the effect of Lenin's over-violent quarrels with valuable revolutionary leaders of whom there were not too many. Be that as it may, there is no doubt that Stalin himself supported the rising, and had opposed Zinoviev and Kamenev in debate on 29 October.[23]

According to Trotsky, though he is unsupported by any of the published documents, the rising was originally fixed for 'not later than' 28 (15) October, thus preceding the Congress which was originally fixed for 2 November (20 October).[24] On 31 October the Congress was postponed until 7 November.[25] But whether or not Trotsky is right about the fixing of the date, the evidence suggests that much of the preparation for the final stage of the insurrection was only completed a short time before the Congress met.

The bolshevik majority in the Petrograd Soviet skilfully exploited an opportunity presented them by the Mensheviks in order to create a general staff of the revolution. They seized on a menshevik proposal to create some organ for co-operation between the Soviet and the Petrograd garrison troops. In the teeth of vain protests from the Mensheviks, who now realized what the bolshevik object was, the Petrograd Soviet voted on 22 October to set up a Military Revolutionary Committee. Trotsky became chairman of this body, which won rapid ascendancy over the garrison troops. The troops were united to a man in their determination to resist any proposal to send them to the front. By 3 November, when the

[21] *Oldenbourg*, p. 91. [22] Trotsky, *History*, Vol. III, pp. 163–4.
[23] *Stalin*, Vol. III, pp. 381–2.
[24] The assertion was first made by Trotsky in 1922 at an evening devoted to reminiscences on the revolution—see *Proletarskaya revolyutsiya*, no. 10, 1922, p. 59. See also *Trotsky, History*, Vol. III, p. 156. This, together with the difference of opinion between Trotsky and Lenin on the wisdom of Trotsky's open assertions that the Congress would seize power, was skilfully utilized by Stalin in later years in controversy with Trotsky, designed to discredit the latter's part in the rising. See *ibid.*, Appendix I, for this rather barren dispute, where the sources of the accusation that Trotsky's indiscretion led to the date of the rising having to be advanced by a day are also to be found.
[25] *B. & F.*, p. 67. By the Central Executive Committee appointed at the First All Russian Soviet Congress in June. The Bolsheviks were in a minority on it.

Commander of the Northern Front and Kerensky attempted to transfer some troops from Petrograd, a series of conferences of units of the Petrograd garrison passed resolutions recognizing the Petrograd Soviet as the only authority which had power to issue orders to the troops.   It seemed scarcely an exaggeration to say that the 'Provisional Government was on that date already overthrown', at any rate in Petrograd.[26]   One of these conferences also resolved that the 'All-Russian Congress of Soviets must take power into its hands, and guarantee the people peace, land, and bread'.

These moves, however, while preparing the way for the assumption of power by the Congress of Soviets, did not satisfy Lenin.   As late as the evening of 6 November Lenin was still urging that to delay was death, and stressing with all his power that it would be 'disaster or formalism to wait for the uncertain voting' in the Congress.   'The people', he wrote, 'have a right and duty to decide such questions not by voting but by force'. . . .   The main thing was to seize power, 'not against the Soviets, but for them'; the political object would be 'clarified after the seizure'.[27]   The practical details of the rising were only worked out by the Central Committee on the same date at a meeting in which Kamenev (in spite of his resignation) took part, but which Lenin, still in hiding, did not attend.[28]   The vital decision of the Petrograd Bolshevik Party Committee to 'pass to the attack without the slightest delay' was also only taken on 6 November.[29]   Nevertheless, by the evening of the 6th the Military Revolutionary Committee was in virtual control of the capital, and the situation appeared so serious to the Provisional Government that the existence of insurrection in Petrograd was declared in the Pre-Parliament.[30]   By 7 November, before the Second All Russian Congress of Soviets opened, the Provisional Government was under arrest, and the bol-

---

[26] *Sukhanov*, Vol. VII, pp. 94–7.   [27] *Lenin*, Vol. XXI, pp. 362–3.

[28] *Proletarskaya revolyutsiya*, no. 10 (69), 1927, pp. 296–8.

[29] *Pervyy Leg. Komitet*, p. 326.

[30] All this had happened before Lenin's arrival in Petrograd, from his hiding place in Vyborg, in the early hours of 7 November.   Exaggerated accounts by such writers as, for example, Podvoysky, which paint a picture of complete indecision and disorganization in the Military Revolutionary Committee before the arrival of Lenin, must be treated with caution.   They are part of the intensive campaign to discredit Trotsky's part in the revolution.   On the other hand, there is no reason to doubt that the arrival of Lenin on the scene did much to increase the tempo of effort—it usually did.

shevik Red Guards were in control of all vital points in the capital. Similar action was taken about the same time in many provincial centres.

The socialist parties in the Pre-Parliament, relying on the widely known differences among the bolshevik leaders on the question of insurrection, believed on the evening of 6 November that if concrete steps on peace and land were taken immediately a compromise could be reached with the more moderate elements within the bolshevik party against the extremists headed by Lenin.[31] They were right in their assessment of the strength of the dissensions in the ranks of the bolshevik leadership, since the question of a coalition between Bolsheviks and socialists shortly led to a crisis in the party more serious than that produced by the decision to resort to armed seizure of power. But Kerensky would not be persuaded to attempt the compromise, and it is in any case unlikely that it would have been crowned with success.

The vote of the bolshevik Central Committee of 23 October had been an essential preliminary to the setting in motion of the machinery of the party in order to ensure seizure of power throughout the whole country, and to enable the Bolsheviks to counteract any attempt by the Provisional Government to move troops against the capital. In the capital the winning over of the garrison some days before the Congress of Soviets met dictated the pace of events almost irrespectively of party organization, and the meeting of the Soviet Congress merely confirmed an already accomplished fact. The coincidence in time of the seizure of power in Petrograd and of the opening of the Congress was in accordance with Trotsky's view of the tactical advantage of giving the revolution the legal cover of an assumption of power by the Soviets. But Lenin had never been entirely won over to this view.[32] It is not easy to determine to what extent the completion of the rising in Petrograd on the day fixed for the opening of the Congress was the result of chance or plan. But there is no doubt that it turned out fortunately for the Bolsheviks, since the cloak of legality which the opening of the Congress gave to the rising was of greatest assistance to them in retaining their precarious hold on power in the difficult days which followed.

The first phase of the revolution which had been accomplished by the Military Revolutionary Committee was over. But the main part of the revolution still lay ahead—the achievement of control over the Congress of Soviets by the bolshevik party.

The Second Congress of Soviets which opened at eleven o'clock at night on 7 November 1917 was little more than half the size of the First Congress which had met in June, and was to that extent less representative of the country. The Bolsheviks together with their supporters had a small majority. About 300 delegates out of some 650 were Bolsheviks, and in addition at least half of the Socialist Revolutionaries were of the left wing of their party which now supported the Bolsheviks. The remaining Socialist Revolutionaries, of the right and centre, numbered between seventy and eighty. The number of Mensheviks was about the same. The total bolshevik and pro-bolshevik strength was therefore some 370 or 380 out of 650.[33] At the opening of the Congress the question of the nature of the new government which was to be formed arose. Neither Lenin nor Trotsky had the slightest intention of setting up a coalition rule of Bolsheviks and socialists, if it could be avoided. But Lenin had refrained from stressing his intentions to his party, while Trotsky had used every endeavour to make the seizure of power appear as an assumption of power by the Congress of Soviets. Almost the entire bolshevik party, therefore, took it for granted that the slogan 'All Power to the Soviets' would now be implemented and that the government formed would reflect the party composition of the Soviet Congress. In a referendum on the question of the form of government which was taken among the delegates of the Second Congress of Soviets, the great majority declared themselves for 'All Power to the Soviets', while quite a few specified more precisely what was really the same view, that 'Government must be a coalition', or a 'coalition of all parties without the *Kadety*.'[34] The immediate proposal on behalf of the Bolsheviks (by Avanesov) was to elect a praesidium com-

[33] For figures of the composition of the Congress, see *Vs. syezd II*, p. 171.
[34] *Vs. syezd II*, p. 107.

THE OCTOBER REVOLUTION   67

posed in proportion to party strengths. The two major
socialist parties refused to take part in the elections to the
praesidium for fear that this would be interpreted as condona-
tion of the military coup d'état. Martov then proposed to
deal in the first instance with the question of the formation of a
united democratic government of all socialist parties in order
to avert bloodshed. His suggestion was immediately welcomed
on behalf of the bolshevik fraction by Lunacharsky, and was
adopted unanimously.[35] But the next move by the Mensheviks and Socialist Revolutionaries played right into Trotsky's
hands and gave him the opportunity for which he was waiting.
Representatives of each of these parties now declared that their
party refused to be associated with an armed conspiracy
which was a violation of Soviet democracy, and which threatened civil war. By way of protest, they stated, they would
leave the Congress. Erlich, on behalf of the *Bund* (the
Jewish Social Democratic Party), made a similar declaration,
and ended: 'It may be that our leaving will make the madmen
or criminals come to their senses.'[36] The socialists thereupon
left, followed by catcalls from the congress hall. The result
was to cut the ground from under Martov's feet. He and
his group of internationalists did not follow the rest of the
Mensheviks out of the Congress. Immediately after their
departure he put forward a resolution, which embodied his
proposals for a government. This called on the Congress to
appoint a delegation for the purpose of forming a coalition
government composed of all socialist parties and of representatives of all democratic organs. He did not render his resolution more acceptable to the excited Congress by its opening
sentences. These referred to the 'coup d'état . . . which
gave power to the Military Revolutionary Committee . . . by
a pure military conspiracy'. Trotsky was not slow to exploit
the advantage which the inept move of the socialist parties
offered. Were the Bolsheviks, he asked, whose rising had
been victorious, to conclude an agreement with 'mere broken

[35] *Vs. syezd II*, pp. 32, 34. *Sukhanov*, Vol. VII, p. 199, noted that Martov's
proposal was followed by loud applause, since 'evidently many, many Bolsheviks
had not absorbed the teaching of Lenin and Trotsky and would be glad to follow
this path'.
[36] *Vs. syezd II*, pp. 37–48. Erlich was put to death by the Soviet authorities
in 1941. For details of this judicial murder see J. Braunthal in *Socialist International Information*, Vol. I, No. 4, 24 November 1951.

fragments, miserable bankrupts, whose part is ended and who are destined for where they belong,—the waste-paper basket of history'? The resolution which he put forward branded the departure of the socialist parties as a 'hopeless and criminal attempt' to break up the Congress, and proposed that the Congress should continue with its work. The departure of the socialist delegates also produced a change in the temper of the Bolsheviks in the Congress. Lunacharsky, who not many minutes before had welcomed Martov's suggestion, now enthusiastically supported Trotsky's resolution. The Left Socialist Revolutionaries, however, were anxious for a coalition of all socialist parties, and criticized Trotsky's language as too harsh.

Neither Trotsky's nor Martov's resolution appears to have been put to the vote. The events of that night were too dramatic in their rapid succession to allow for normal procedural forms. But at 5.30 a.m. the following morning the resolution of the truncated Congress to seize power into its hands was adopted with only two dissenting votes and twelve abstentions. It was an academic resolution, because power had already for some time been in the hands of the bolshevik party and its organization. But its significance as a symbol was immense. As Trotsky all along intended, it set the seal of legality on an armed insurrection. Moreover, it enabled the Bolsheviks to claim the right to wield popular power by themselves, in view of the departure from the Congress of the socialist parties, other than the Left Socialist Revolutionaries.

CHAPTER V

THE CONSOLIDATION OF POWER

The bolshevik seizure of power and the resolution of the Congress of Soviets still left the question of government undecided. By 8 November the position of the Bolsheviks in the Congress was further consolidated. The Left Socialist Revolutionaries, whose support of the rising had been somewhat hesitant, and who were strongly in favour of a coalition of all socialist parties, were finally won over to the bolshevik side by the bolshevik decision to adopt and to pass through the Congress their land decree. This complicated decree abolished private ownership for ever and re-distributed the land for the peasants' use in accordance with a formula designed to secure to all an adequate standard of living. A left socialist revolutionary measure in all its detail,[1] the decree ran counter to accepted bolshevik doctrines, in that it recognized that land would be held in usufruct for cultivation by individual peasants, and not as nationalized property by communal or collective bodies. But tactics demanded that the Bolsheviks should not appear to be taking power in complete isolation, and the support of the Left Socialist Revolutionaries was therefore essential to Lenin.[2] He unhesitatingly jettisoned his own land policy. In the new Central Executive Committee of the Soviet Congress (i.e. legislative committee between sessions of the Congress), the Left Socialist Revolutionaries were allocated 29 seats, to the bolshevik 67. Twenty seats were divided among minor groups, including six 'united internationalists', a menshevik left wing fragmentation. (Martov's group had by then left the Congress.) The Congress also set up a new government, the Council of People's Commissars. The Left Socialist Revolutionaries declined to join it. They believed that by remaining outside this organ they could more effectively mediate between the Bolsheviks and the

[1] See *B. & F*, pp. 128–32, for the text.
[2] In 1921 Lenin told the Third Congress of the Communist International that the Bolshevik adoption of the socialist revolutionary land programme ensured them victory.—See *Lenin*, Vol. XXV, p. 446.

socialist parties and promote a wider coalition.   The Congress approved by a large majority the exclusively bolshevik Council of People's Commissars, headed by Lenin.

The adherence of the Left Socialist Revolutionaries to the Bolsheviks was to prove an important factor in the consolidation of their power in the first weeks.   The Bolsheviks could now claim, with some semblance of truth, to have secured the support of the peasantry, of whom the representation in the Soviet Congress was no more than a token.   But it was neither the Left Socialist Revolutionaries, nor yet the parliamentary waverings within their own party which were to throw the Bolsheviks for the next few weeks into a fever of discussions on coalition.   It was the resolute action of the All-Russian Executive Committee of the Union of Railway Workers, the so-called *Vikzhel*.   The delegate of this body insisted on a hearing at the Soviet Congress, in spite of the attempt of Kamenev as chairman of the Congress to silence him.   This delegate declared the opposition of *Vikzhel* (which had a non-bolshevik majority) to the seizure of power by one party; demanded a government composed of all socialist parties; declared its intention to keep control of the railways; and threatened, in the event of reprisals on its members, to deprive Petrograd of food.[3]   In view of the fact that the railways were vital both for supporting the, as yet, unsuccessful rising in Moscow, and for preventing the movement of troops loyal to the Provisional Government to Petrograd, this was a serious threat.   In the protracted negotiations which followed, Lenin and Trotsky played for time; but to many of the other bolshevik leaders the negotiations appeared as an honest attempt to form a broader coalition, and thereby to avert civil war and minority rule by force.

On 11 November *Vikzhel* issued an ultimatum, demanding a coalition government of all socialist parties, under threat of a railway strike.   The position of the Bolsheviks was precarious.

[3] *Oldenbourg*, pp. 255–7.   *Vikzhel* was composed of three groups: a pro-bolshevik and an anti-bolshevik group, of about equal size, and a third non-party group, said to be pro-*Kadet*—*B. & F.*, p. 153, note 31.   The anti-bolshevik strength of *Vikzhel* was, however, considerably neutralized by the fact that, as events soon showed, it failed in many cases to enforce the decisions on the rank and file of railway workers—see *Pervyy Leg. Komitet*, p. 231, for a report on 11 November to the Petrograd Committee by the Railway Section of the bolshevik party.

In Moscow the rising was still far from victorious, and the insurgent Moscow Military Revolutionary Committee, influenced both by pressure from *Vikzhel* and by the more moderate Moscow Bolsheviks, had signed a two days' armistice. The outcome of Kerensky's attempt to move troops on Petrograd was not yet decided. However, at a meeting of the garrison troops of the capital attended by Lenin and Trotsky, nearly half the units had already offered their full support to the Bolsheviks.[4] At a meeting the same day, 11 November, the new Central Executive Committee of the Soviet Congress accepted without discussion Kamenev's proposal to send delegates to a conference of all socialist parties proposed by *Vikzhel* to discuss the formation of a coalition goverment. This conference, which took place later that day, revealed little ground for agreement, since the socialist parties all insisted that the new government should be formed without the Bolsheviks, whose resort to arms had put them outside the ranks of democracy. In spite of this unpromising beginning, the Bolsheviks, headed by Ryazanov, agreed to the formation of a commission to discuss *Vikzhel*'s compromise proposal for an all-socialist government, pledged to accept the bolshevik programme as already accepted by the Soviet Congress—immediate peace, and land to the peasants. Although it was not expressly so stated at the time, it became clear from the subsequent course of events that this proposed new government was not intended to include either Lenin or Trotsky, but was to be formed of more moderate elements of the bolshevik party. Kamenev was no doubt aware of this when he assured the conference that acceptance of the Soviet programme by this proposed new government was the important thing, and 'certainly not its proposed composition.'[5] During the abortive discussions which took place daily for the next few days, it became plain that the omission of Lenin and Trotsky from any proposed government was the

---

[4] Twenty-three units were represented at this conference, out of a total of fifty-one, *Lyubimov*, pp. 23, 45.

[5] *Lyubimov*, p. 22. cf. Krasin, in a letter to his wife on 14 November, with reference to the abortive negotiations for coalition then in progress: 'Lenin and Trotsky were to be sacrificed because, as it happens, they stand quite alone in their attitude to the Socialist Revolution.' L. Krassin, *Leonid Krassin*, p. 62. Krasin, an old Bolshevik who remained aloof from the revolution for some time, in common with the socialist parties expected the imminent collapse of the insurrection, if the Bolsheviks persisted in their determination to rule on their own.

only condition upon which the reluctance of the socialist parties to include the Bolsheviks at all could be overcome. Even so, the (Right) Socialist Revolutionaries resolved on 15 November 'that an agreement with the Bolsheviks is impossible'. But the Mensheviks, in spite of considerable dissension inside their party, expressed their readiness on the same day to resume negotiations, subject to agreement by the Bolsheviks to declare a truce; to free all political prisoners under arrest; and to stop what they described as political 'terror' by restoring freedom of press and speech.[6]

Since this allegation of 'terror' was to play an important part in the crisis in the bolshevik ranks a few days later, it is necessary to consider what was meant by 'terror' in the first days of the revolution. The actions of the Petrograd Military Revolutionary Committee during these days were necessarily somewhat rough and ready, and it is not easy to establish the exact position. The Provisional Government, which included several socialist ministers, had been arrested. The arrest of these socialists had led to violent protests from the peasant delegates at the Congress of Soviets, which have been graphically described by John Reed. The socialist ministers were in fact transferred to house arrest almost immediately and released within three days.[7] The *Kadet* ministers were to remain in prison for considerably longer, and some of them were never released.[8] Right-wing papers were suppressed in the first days, while the liberal press survived little longer, according to the ingenuity and courage of various papers in evading the attempts to close them. The leading socialist papers enjoyed no security from the start of the revolution and were repeatedly exposed to forcible and arbitrary suppressions by the Military Revolutionary Committee.

[6] *B. & F..* pp. 198–200.
[7] See a telegram of 10 November, quoted in *Kostomarov*, p. 198. There were also other arrests of socialists. For example, Burtsev, a leading Socialist Revolutionary, was arrested on the very day of the bolshevik revolution. He had not endeared himself by his activity for some months before it in exposing the alleged contacts of the bolshevik leaders with the Germans during the war and after their return to Russia. See V. L. Burtsev, *Prestupleniya i nakazanie bol'shevikov*, Paris n.d., p. 65.
[8] In November 1918, an order of the *Vecheka* (the All-Russian Extraordinary Commission for the Combating of Counter-Revolution and Speculation), permitted the liberation of those *Kadety* who had not been active members—quoted in *Latsis*, p. 54. The order for the arrest of all leading *Kadety* was made on 11 December 1917—see *Krasnyy arkhiv*, Vol. 10, p. 136.

In the uncertain conditions of 12 November, the bolshevik Central Committee (in the absence of Lenin and Trotsky, be it noted) unanimously recognized the need for broadening the base of the government by adding representatives of the socialist parties to the Central Executive Committee of the Soviet Congress.[9]   But events were moving in favour of the Bolsheviks.   By 14 November Kerensky was in flight, and the movement of troops on Petrograd from the front had foundered on the pro-bolshevik, or at any rate neutral, temper of these troops.   These new events were immediately reflected in the deliberations of the bolshevik party on the question of coalition. The *Vikzhel* conference had worked out a tentative plan for the new government, but again this plan insisted upon the exclusion of Lenin and Trotsky from any government formed.[10] However, on 14 November the Central Executive Committee, by 40 votes to 31, adopted a resolution which at any rate still left the negotiations open.[11]   At this point Lenin, who had hitherto taken no part in the discussions on coalition, intervened in the councils of his party.   Immediately after the Central Executive Committee had adopted its resolution, a meeting took place of the Central Committee, together with certain other party representatives, to hear the delegates Kamenev and Ryazanov report on the *Vikzhel* conferences. As appears from the short report of the speeches of Trotsky and Dzerzhinsky, there was considerable resentment by some of those present at the meeting that Kamenev and Ryazanov should even have considered the suggestion to omit Lenin and Trotsky from any proposed government.   Lenin came plainly to the point: Kamenev's policy should have been stopped from the start.   'The discussions should have been treated merely as diplomatic cover for military action', to give time to send troops to Moscow.   This drew from Rykov the protest that there appeared to have been a misunderstanding: he had taken the discussions seriously.   Sverdlov (who until his early death in 1919 was henceforward to be Lenin's right hand man in the Central Committee) possibly voiced the views of Lenin and his supporters, when he proposed that a few members of *Vikzhel* should be arrested.   But this view did not command

[9] *Lyubimov*, p. 21.   [10] *B. & F.*, pp. 190–1.
[11] Text in *Pravda*, 15 November 1917, reprinted in *Pervyy Leg. Komitet*, p. 344.

the support of the majority of the Central Committee. Many, like Kamenev and Ryazanov, were still prepared, if need be, to sacrifice Lenin and Trotsky in order to make a coalition government possible. They viewed with apprehension the prospect of a small minority of Bolsheviks continuing to govern in the teeth of opposition, not only from the middle-classes, but from the many workers and peasants who supported the Mensheviks and the Socialist Revolutionaries. Lenin's proposal to break off discussions immediately was defeated by ten votes to four, and a resolution permitting members of the party to take part in a 'last attempt' to form a 'so-called coalition government' was adopted by nine votes to four, with one abstention.[12] Lenin continued his diatribes at a meeting held the same day, 14 November, of the Petrograd Bolshevik Committee, which opened ominously with his proposal to expel Lunacharsky. The proposal was rejected. It is not certain what had occasioned Lenin's move but he had considerable suspicion of all the ex-*Mezhdurayontsy* (except Trotsky) and Lunacharsky was neither steady nor reliable from the bolshevik point of view.[13] Lenin's main attack was directed against Zinoviev and Kamenev, whom he accused of treason, and of causing a split. 'If there is to be a split—let it be so', said Lenin. 'If you have a majority, take power . . . and we shall go to the sailors.' The coalition talks must be broken off at once. When Lunacharsky observed that the result of such tactics would be 'that one man would be left in the party—the dictator' he was greeted with applause, which Trotsky, probably rightly, interpreted as an expression of the feeling inside the committee against Lenin and himself.[14] In Moscow, too,

[12] *Proletarskaya revolyutsiya*, no. 10 (1922), pp. 465–70. And cf. Molotov's report the following day in the Petrograd Committee: 'In our party only some of our comrades attached importance to these discussions' (on coalition)—*Pervyy Leg. Komitet*, pp. 339–42.

[13] He resigned his post as People's Commissar for Education in 15 November, in a somewhat hysterical letter on the strength of a rumour that the Kremlin had been bombarded but withdrew his resignation the following day.

[14] The protocol of this meeting was omitted when the collected protocols of the Petrograd Committee for 1917 were published in 1927. The proof sheet immediately reached Trotsky from one of his supporters and he later published it in facsimile in *Byulleten' oppozitsii*, no. 7 (1929), pp. 30–2, and reprinted it in his *Stalinskaya shkola*, pp. 116–31. Comparison of the type with that of the published edition leaves little doubt that it is genuine. The facsimile bears a large fat question mark against a passage in Lenin's speech which refers with praise to Trotsky's attitude on coalition. In the same pencil is noted in the corner of the proof sheet 'scrap'.

opinion on coalition was strongly divided. In the Military Revolutionary Committee, where moderate elements prevailed from the start, the majority favoured coalition against the stubborn opposition of the two future left communists, Stukov and Lomov. The radical Moscow *Oblast'* Bureau, on the other hand, was less favourable to compromise, though even this Bureau as late as 20 November adopted unanimously a resolution accepting a coalition of 'all Soviet parties' provided the Bolsheviks had an assured majority.[15]

The split in the bolshevik party widened. On 15 November, in the Central Executive Committee, Zinoviev, Kamenev, Rykov, Nogin, Ryazanov, and possibly other Bolsheviks voted against the bolshevik resolution on the coalition negotiations, which asserted that the inclusion of Lenin and Trotsky in any government must be insisted upon. On the following day, Lenin drew up a declaration embodying the views of the majority of the Central Committee against coalition and summoned the available members one by one to demand their signatures. The declaration demanded submission by the minority, coupled with a threat of expulsion. Better an honest split than sabotage from within.[16] The following signed: Lenin, Trotsky, Stalin, Sverdlov, Uritsky, Dzerzhinsky, Ioffe, Bubnov, Sokol'nikov, and Muranov. Zinoviev, Kamenev, Milyutin, Nogin, and Rykov did not sign. Bukharin was in Moscow, and a number of others, such as Kollontay, Shaumyan, Berzin, and Smilga, were probably also absent from Petrograd at the time and would otherwise have signed with Lenin.

However, the desire inside the bolshevik party for a coalition with the other left-wing parties was not the only cause of dissension at this date. It was evident that the suppression let alone of the socialist, but even of the liberal, papers was from the outset a matter which troubled some sections of the bolshevik party. It had never been an avowed object of bolshevik party policy. Lenin, whatever may have been his private intentions, had, in his rare utterances on the subject before

---

[15] *Proletarskaya revolyutsiya*, no. 10 (1922), p. 476. On Moscow generally, see I. Stukov in *Oktyabr'skie dni v Moskve i rayonakh*, pp. 18, 22; and *Dokumenty velikoy proletarskoy revolyutsii*, Vol. I, pp. 140–1. The Moscow City Committee (which was generally right wing and included Rykov and Nogin) supported the Kamenev-Zinoviev view—see *Krasnyy arkhiv*, Vols. LIV–LV, 1932, pp. 151, 130. They sent Ignatov as delegate to Petrograd to support their view.

[16] *Lenin*, Vol. XXII, pp. 38–9, 580; *Lenin v pervye mesyatsy*, p. 46.

November, laid down as the bolshevik policy with regard to
the press the nationalization of printing presses and paper and
the re-allocation of these resources to all parties in proportion
to their popular strength.

> The first claim [he wrote on 28 September 1917] would be
> that of the government, representing the interests of the majority
> of the people.   Secondly—that of the larger parties, those which
> have mustered, shall we say, a hundred or two hundred thousand
> votes in both capitals.   Thirdly—that of the smaller parties, and
> after them any group of citizens which comprises a certain
> number, or which can muster so-many signatures.

This just distribution, he added, would be 'quite easily
achieved when power is in the hands of the Soviets'.   A
decree on the press of 10 November, which conferred upon the
bolshevik authorities the right to close down newspapers which
'call for open opposition' to the government, or 'sow sedition
by a frankly slanderous perversion of facts' was carefully
stated to be of a temporary nature, to last only so long as
abnormal conditions prevailed.[17]   In Moscow the Military
Revolutionary Committee as late as 19 November passed a
decree which allowed complete freedom to the press of all
parties without exception.   The only grounds for confiscation
and prosecution were to be incitement to insurrection against
the Soviets.[18]

Matters came to a head in Petrograd on 17 November following a meeting of the Central Executive Committee to debate a
Bolshevik proposal to confiscate all newspaper presses.   This
was intended to give more effective control over their publication.   Lenin had originally drawn up for this meeting a draft
resolution which, while providing for the nationalization of all
presses and paper, also provided for the equal right of 'each
group of citizens over (say) ten thousand in number to paper
and printing facilities for the expression of their views'.[19]   But
the resolution as actually proposed to the meeting by Avanesov
went a good deal further.   It conferred upon the government
the additional power of suspending the liberal papers.   Every
one knew that in practice the socialist newspapers were little

[17] *Lenin* (4), Vol. XXV, p. 352; *B. & F.*, p. 220.
[18] *Krasnyy arkhiv*, Vol. XXIII, pp. 127–8.
[19] *Leninskiy sbornik*, Vol. XXI, pp. 101–2.

more secure from suspension than the liberal papers. But there were many Bolsheviks who, though prepared to tolerate violations of the freedom of the press as an emergency measure during the first days of the revolution, were not prepared to see government control of the press enshrined in a legislative act of the Central Executive Committee. In the debates of 17 November the main criticism came from Larin, a recent convert to bolshevism from menshevism: now that the struggle was over, 'the press must be free, the only limitation should be that it does not incite to revolt'. He was supported by the left socialist revolutionary Karelin in an impassioned speech.[20] Lenin defended the right to suspend the bourgeois papers. He made no reference to what, as everyone recognized, was the main object of the proposed resolution, the control of all the press, including the socialist papers. Larin's resolution in opposition to the bolshevik resolution secured 22 votes against 31; the Bolsheviks secured 34 votes in favour of theirs against 24, the latter vote comprising the Left Socialist Revolutionaries, and the Bolsheviks Ryazanov and Lozovsky.[21] There followed a spate of resignations. Kamenev, Rykov, Milyutin, Zinoviev, and Nogin presented a letter of resignation to the bolshevik Central Committee, justifying their action by their 'consciousness of duty before the socialist proletariat'. A declaration was then presented by Nogin on behalf of a number of People's Commissars, which repudiated the 'preservation in power of a purely bolshevik government by means of terror'. The following handed in their resignations from the various offices held by them: Nogin (People's Commissar of Commerce and Industry), Rykov (People's Commissar of Interior), Milyutin (People's Commissar of Agriculture), Teodorovich (People's Commissar of Food), Ryazanov, Derbyshev, Arbuzov, Fedorov, and Larin. Shlyapnikov (People's Commissar of Labour) and Yurenev associated themselves with the declaration, without however resigning from their appointments. Lozovsky the bolshevik secretary of the All Russian Council of Trade Unions, on the following day published in *Novaya Zhizn'* a somewhat lyrical letter explaining

[20] The avowed aim of this party at this period was to isolate Lenin, while maintaining support of bolshevism in general—see *Lyubimov*, p. 83, quoting a press interview with Karelin.

[21] *Oldenbourg*, pp. 398–406.

why 'I cannot be silent in the name of party discipline', and reciting at length the misdeeds of the Bolsheviks.[22] It will be seen that, although coincident with the debates on the control of the press, the revolt was expressly upon the wider issue of bolshevik dictatorship by force, and the form which it was assuming. Both letters of resignation state as their main reason the refusal of the bolshevik leaders to form a government of all socialist parties. But there may also have been a certain amount of feeling on the suppression of the liberal papers, particularly in view of the impending elections to the Constituent Assembly. There were many Bolsheviks who felt that all parties should be given full freedom to put their views before the electors so that the Assembly should be truly representative. Apart from this substantial revolt within the bolshevik party, there was also the not unimportant opposition of the Left Socialist Revolutionaries, who now resigned from all Soviet organs, such as the Military Revolutionary Committee on which they had several representatives, remaining however in the Central Executive Committee.

But there was neither organization, coherence, nor for that matter, determination, behind the revolt. The dissident Bolsheviks were too far removed in their traditions from the agrarian Socialist Revolutionaries for any solid co-operation with them. None of the dissident Bolsheviks had the capacity for leadership or the courage to assume it at so critical a moment. Had there been such a leader, prepared to defy Lenin, he would have been sure of a wide following in the upper ranks of the bolshevik party. Whether he could have resisted Lenin's 'going to the sailors', in other words appealing to the semi-anarchist rank-and-file extremists (whom Lenin would later suppress), is another matter. But the greatest weakness of the opposition lay in the fact that, having supported thus far a policy of insurrection without foreseeing its full implications, they felt it was too late for them to withdraw. When the meeting of the Central Executive Committee was resumed after the interruption caused by the resignations, Lenin dismissed the incident as the splitting away of 'isolated intellectuals' whom the workers would not follow. The revolt

[22] All these documents are reprinted in *Lyubimov*, pp. 423-30, together with the subsequent documents in the dispute. See also *B. & F.*, pp. 202-6.

did not last long. The bolshevik Central Committee demanded that the rebels should recant and threatened them with expulsion.[23] Zinoviev recanted on the 21 November, and was readmitted to the Central Committee. The others resisted a little longer, until 12 December, when Kamenev, Milyutin, Nogin, and Rykov submitted. Lenin was less lenient with them, however, and they were not reinstated until some time later. Lozovsky continued for a while to agitate inside the trade unions against bolshevik methods of government and was eventually expelled from the party.[24] Meanwhile for some days the conference arranged by *Vikzhel* continued in session to the accompaniment of some acrimonious argument between the Central Executive Committee and the menshevik Central Committee. The conference ended in complete failure at a session on 20 November, which the Bolsheviks did not even trouble to attend.

The political problem was not however solved. While the Mensheviks could be ignored, since they carried little popular support, the Socialist Revolutionaries could not. The vast peasantry was behind them. Although a coalition between the Bolsheviks and the Socialist Revolutionaries was by now inconceivable, Lenin was anxious not to lose the alliance of the pro-bolshevik Left Socialist Revolutionaries, whose leaders had some following among the peasants. Before long he succeeded in forming a coalition with the Left Socialist Revolutionaries, to the satisfaction of the simple-minded *Vikzhel*. This was achieved at the Second Congress of Peasant Deputies which met on 9 December. This Congress was divided about equally between the right and the left, and promptly split into two sessions, deliberating separately. The dilemma was easily solved. The bolshevik and left socialist revolutionary half proclaimed itself unanimously the only plenipotentiary congress and elected a new Peasant Executive. The right half was finally silenced by exclusion from its dormitories and forcible deprivation of its rations.[25] Thereupon eight Left Socialist Revolutionaries entered the Council of People's Commissars. It was to prove a shortlived and uneasy coalition;[26]

[23] *Lenin*, Vol. XXII, p. 57.
[24] After a short period in the wilderness, he eventually returned to a career of exemplary obedience—see Chapter XII.
[25] See *Rakitnikova*, pp. 25–6.   [26] See Chapter VII.

but it pacified *Vikzhel*, gave the Bolsheviks the appearance of peasant support, and no doubt also served to allay dormant apprehensions among the recent dissidents within the bolshevik party.

There was a faint echo of the coalition crisis two months later, when Lenin decided to disperse the Constituent Assembly. The dispersal of this body had been no part of official bolshevik policy. The summoning of a Constituent Assembly figured largely in the programme of the social democratic party, to which the Bolsheviks still nominally adhered. Before the October Revolution they had constantly insisted on the summoning of the Assembly, and delay in doing so was one of the frequent bolshevik charges against the Provisional Government. It is unlikely that Lenin made up his mind on the question until faced with the problem—though, if Sukhanov is right, he had already in Switzerland, in private conversation, dismissed the Constituent Assembly as a 'liberal pleasantry'. In his writings between March and November 1917 he did not have much to say on the Constituent Assembly, beyond his reiterated promises that the Bolsheviks, and only the Bolsheviks, would ensure that it was summoned without delay. In the popular imagination, and more particularly that of the peasants and of the socialist revolutionary following in general, the Constituent Assembly stood for the crown and apex of the revolution and of liberty. The Bolsheviks, after seizing power, were careful to make it plain that the authority of the Congress of Soviets to legislate on such a fundamental matter as the land, for example, was provisional only. The final decision would rest with the Constituent Assembly. 'Even if the peasants should return a socialist revolutionary majority to the Constituent Assembly,' said Lenin, 'we shall say, so be it. . . . We must leave full creative freedom to the popular masses.'[27] It is, to say the least, unlikely that this represented Lenin's intention at the time. A few weeks later, in the Central Executive Committee, Lenin spoke in support of a decree which conferred on the voters in the elections to the Assembly the right of recalling delegates and electing others in their place. He supported the decree on the grounds that it would ensure that 'the transfer of power from one party to

[27] *Vs. syezd II*, p. 57.

another will proceed in a peaceful manner, by way of mere election'.[28] There was little in bolshevik policy in 1917 to indicate that this party ever had any intention of peacefully surrendering its power to another party in the event of an adverse vote in an election. And there was not the remotest chance of a bolshevik or pro-bolshevik majority in the Constituent Assembly. Zinoviev and Kamenev had not been far wrong in forecasting a third as the maximum the Bolsheviks could hope for. The Mensheviks and the *Kadety* were not likely to achieve serious successes, and could be discounted. The crux of the problem was the certainty that in any free election throughout Russia the majority of the votes would go to the anti-bolshevik Socialist Revolutionaries. The left wing of this party only became a separate entity after 19 November when its first congress met, less than a week before the date fixed for the elections to the Constituent Assembly. The lists of candidates for the elections had been prepared some time before the party had split. Moreover, such indications as there are do not suggest that the new Left Socialist Revolutionaries, would have won many votes from the main socialist revolutionary party.[29] The majority of the peasants would certainly vote for the socialist revolutionary party leaders whom they by tradition regarded as their own. The Bolsheviks, by encouraging land seizures, had won some support among the peasants. But there was no possible chance of a majority. The dilemma with which the Bolsheviks were faced, therefore, was on the one hand the popular demand that the long awaited Assembly should meet and on the other, the certainty that if elections were held on the appointed day, 25 November, an anti-bolshevik majority would be returned. Lenin at one time considered postponing the elections until such time as the voting age could be lowered and the *Kadet* party outlawed, but was dissuaded on the grounds that the

---

[28] *Lenin*, Vol. XXII, pp. 96–7.
[29] The fact that the Socialist Revolutionaries' lists had been made up before November, and hence before the splitting of the party, was used by Lenin as his main justification for dispersing the Constituent Assembly, with its socialist revolutionary majority. In fact, in some instances, the Left Socialist Revolutionaries did succeed in putting forward separate lists in competition with the Right—with disastrous results to themselves. See Svyatitsky in *Bol'sheviki u vlasti*, p. 119, and cf. *Radkey*, p. 72, note 6. But it may be true that the Left Socialist Revolutionaries had more support in the country than was represented by the 40 members of their party returned to the Assembly.

Bolsheviks were still too weak to flout the popular demand.[30]
Thus it came about that the elections to the Constituent
Assembly took place without the Bolsheviks being able to do
very much to prevent the electorate from voting freely for the
candidates of their choice.   A recent survey of all available
evidence on the elections concludes that 'although a good
many voters were subjected to intimidation in one form or
another, the vast majority of the electorate freely exercised
the right of suffrage. . . .   It was far from being a model
election; but it certainly was not a farce.'[31]   As the opening
of the Assembly approached there was uncertainty among
bolshevik leaders.   Those who still retained the 'parliamentary illusions' which the November crisis had revealed in their
midst, could ill reconcile themselves to open flouting of an
electoral majority.   Yet their hesitations were necessarily
tempered by the reflection that to submit to that electoral
majority was to place their fate in the hands of a party which
had openly declared itself against them from the moment of
the seizure of power.   Some Bolsheviks cherished the hope,
as the opening date of the Assembly approached, that the
Gordian knot would be cut in some manner which preserved
the semblance of constitutional legality.   Among such were
the young Bukharin, Zinoviev, Ryazanov, Lozovsky (not yet
expelled from the party), and a good number of others.   But
no one got nearer to a practical solution of the dilemma than
Bukharin, who proposed on 12 December that when the
Assembly met the left pro-bolshevik delegates should expel the
right wing delegates, and that thereupon the left wing should
declare itself a 'revolutionary convention'.[32]   Among the Left
Socialist Revolutionaries opinion was similarly uncertain.
They could not lightly abandon the crowning symbol of the
revolution, the Constituent Assembly, which had been the
traditional *Narodnik* demand for over a generation.   Natanson, the veteran socialist revolutionary, who with Maria
Spiridonova had assumed leadership of the Left Socialist
Revolutionaries, had exacted a promise from Lenin when the
coalition with the Bolsheviks was formed in December that the

[30] *Trotsky, Lenin*, pp. 119–20.
[31] *Radkey*, pp. 46–7, 50.
[32] In the bolshevik Central Committee.   He was opposed by Stalin—*Lyubimov*,
p. 233.

Constituent Assembly would open on 18 January 1918.[33] Yet the Left Socialist Revolutionaries also had no concrete solution for their dilemma, which differed little from that of the Bolsheviks.   For a time they hoped to save both themselves and the Constituent Assembly by forming, together with the Bolsheviks and the centre group of the Socialist Revolutionaries, a majority bloc in the Assembly.   But the centre on which they placed their hopes was already virtually non-existent.[34]   Many of the Left Socialist Revolutionaries realized that a compromise was unlikely.   But if it failed, their view was that above all the people must be taught to see for themselves the reactionary character of the Assembly, and its opposition to the popular will as expressed through the Soviets.[35]   On 11 December 1917 a Party Congress of the Left Socialist Revolutionaries resolved that the Constituent Assembly could only receive their support if it 'puts into effect the power of the workers and peasants, as laid down at the Second Congress of Soviets'; a little later, Spiridonova maintained that there had never been anything finer than the Soviets, and that one must not flinch from dispersing the Assembly.[36]   By the middle of December the results of the voting left no doubt of the overwhelmingly anti-bolshevik composition of the Assembly.

But Lenin was solving the problem in his own way.   Before the results were known, while the bolshevik press indignantly denied that there was any intention of frustrating the Constituent Assembly, clear hints were dropped in party circles that force might be required as a corrective to the ballot box.   On 21 November Volodarsky spoke in the Petrograd Bolshevik Committee of the possibility of a 'third revolution' if the majority in the Constituent Assembly should prove to be anti-bolshevik.[37]   When, after the middle of December, the bolshevik delegates began to arrive in the capital, they were immediately assigned, under Sverdlov's directions, to factory

[33] Steinberg, *Als ich Volkskommissar war*, pp. 61–2.
[34] V. M. Chernov, *The Great Russian Revolution*, p. 398.
[35] See an interview by Karelin in *Novaya zhizn'* of 2 January 1918 reprinted in *B. & F.*, pp. 366–7.
[36] *Lyubimov*, pp. 225, 384.   According to Natanson 'Some of us are wavering, but I think in the end they will agree to it (dispersal)'.   *Trotsky, Stalin*, p. 342.
[37] For Lenin's views on the subject in private conversation early in December, see *Solomon*, Vol. I, p. 17.

and garrison units to work for the 'supplementary revolution'.[38]
On 11 December, the *Kadety* were accused of preparing a
counter-revolutionary coup d'état at the time of the Assembly,
and the arrest of all the leading members of the party was
ordered.[39] Having eliminated the *Kadety* (in face of some
opposition from the Left Socialist Revolutionaries, who were,
in general, more prepared to accept results than to support
the means necessary for obtaining them), Lenin still appears to
have hoped to secure a pro-bolshevik majority in the Assembly
by persuading the electors to recall the delegates to the
Assembly and to elect pro-bolsheviks in their place. He
seems to have believed it possible that the peasants could be
persuaded to replace right Socialist Revolutionaries by the
members of the new left party.[40]

There was, however, little vocal opposition within the bolshevik party when it became plain that forcible dispersal
of the Constituent Assembly was being contemplated. One
incident is of interest, not so much in itself, but because it
involved, somewhat surprisingly, Stalin. Stalin, together
with Milyutin, Larin, Kamenev, Ryazanov, Sapronov, and
others, had been elected on 15 December to the Bureau, or
Steering Committee, of the bolshevik 'fraction' of the Constituent Assembly. This Bureau immediately fell foul of the
bolshevik Central Committee, which found that it was 'dominated by right-wing views'. Evidently the Bureau did not
immediately accept the Central Committee's views on the
course of action to be pursued in regard to the Assembly.
On 24 December, on Lenin's proposal, the whole of the Bureau
was dismissed, and Bukharin and Sokol'nikov were appointed
to take charge of the bolshevik fraction of the Assembly.
Lenin also prepared for the guidance of the 'fraction' and for
publication in *Pravda* a series of Theses on the Constituent
Assembly. The Theses were unanimously adopted by the

[38] *Trotsky, Lenin*, p. 122; The Moscow *Oblast'* Bureau on 18 December voted
by a majority that the Assembly was 'unnecessary and harmful'. *Yaroslavsky*,
Vol. IV, p. 283.
[39] *B. & F.*, pp. 357–59.
[40] See a decree of 6 December 1917, on re-election of delegates to the Assembly,
B. & F., p. 348; Draft proclamation to the peasants of 18 December, *Lenin*,
Vol. XXII, pp. 116–20; and *Leninskiy sbornik*, Vol. IV, pp. 353–66, for the subsequent fate of this draft which did not meet with the full approval of the Left
Socialist Revolutionaries.

'fraction' a few days after the removal of its intractable Bureau.[41] They did not expressly threaten armed dispersal of the Assembly, but left little doubt that this was the intention. 'Any attempt to . . . consider the question of the Constituent Assembly from a formal, legalistic point of view . . .', ran the Theses, 'is a betrayal of the cause of the proletariat.' Soviet sources are now naturally reticent about Stalin's membership of the unruly Bureau of the bolshevik fraction of the Constituent Assembly. It is very unlikely that he had either any illusions about the authority of the Assembly, or scruples about dispersing it. But his tactical skill seems on this occasion to have fallen short of Lenin's.

Yet, in January 1918, it was no easy task to estimate the amount of force which the Assembly could rally to its side if threatened by the Bolsheviks. Should it succeed in defending itself, Lenin and Trotsky would inevitably be swept aside. But some of the more moderate party leaders may have hoped that in such an event they could still take their place in an all-party coalition, much as they had planned to do in November. Though the Petrograd garrison was not likely to oppose the Bolsheviks,[42] the temper of the provinces was an uncertain factor.

When the Assembly opened on 18 January 1918 the Bolsheviks had prepared a long Declaration of the Rights of the Toiling and Exploited Peoples, embodying the legislation of the All Russian Congress of Soviets on land, workers' control of industry, and peace. One point of this Declaration was that the Assembly 'admits that it has no powers beyond working out some of the fundamental problems of reorganizing society on a socialistic basis'. When, by a vote of 237 to 136, the Assembly rejected this act of abdication, the Bolsheviks withdrew, followed by the Left Socialist Revolutionaries.[43] In the

---

[41] *Lyubimov*, pp. 257, 322–3; *Yaroslavsky*, Vol. IV, p. 283; cf. Uritsky in the Petrograd Committee on 25 December in *Pervyy Leg. Komitet*, p. 374. Some of the modern accounts pretend, without a shadow of foundation, that Trotsky was among the dissident fraction—see e.g., *Rubinshtein*, p. 70. For the Theses, see *Lenin*, Vol. XXII, pp. 131–4. See *ibid.*, p. 593, for an account of this incident of the unruly Bureau—an account, however, which modestly conceals Stalin's membership of this Bureau as 'Kamenev, Larin, Milyutin, Nogin, Rykov, Ryazanov, and others'.

[42] A garrison meeting on 27 December adopted a resolution that the slogan 'All Power to the Constituent Assembly' was a slogan of counter-revolution, with only three dissenting votes. *Lyubimov*, p. 346.

[43] *B. & F.*, pp. 372–7.

Council of People's Commissars, the Bolsheviks now urged immediate dissolution of the Assembly. The Left Socialist Revolutionaries still clung to constitutional forms and urged that there should either be new elections, or that a revolutionary convention consisting of the left elements of the Assembly should be formed. The question was referred to the Central Executive Committee. There the small group of Martov's menshevik internationalists (who had returned to the Central Executive Committee after the coalition with the Left Social Revolutionaries had taken place in December) made a courageous attempt to protest against the bolshevik resolution. One of them, Stroev, who spoke (with reference to the dispersal of a workers' demonstration) of 'Socialist banners reddened with proletarian blood' was shouted down, and not allowed to finish his speech. Of the Bolsheviks, only Ryazanov and Lozovsky voted against the dispersal.[44] On 19 January the Red Guards refused to admit the delegates to the adjourned session of the Assembly, and the meeting did not take place.

It was the end of the Constituent Assembly. Its dispersal by the Bolsheviks caused little stir in the country. The attempts by some Socialist Revolutionaries in Petrograd and by officers of the garrison in Moscow to organize armed defence of the Assembly foundered completely, In Petrograd a mass demonstration in favour of the Assembly, mainly by workers, was easily scattered, with a number of casualties, by the rifles of the Red Guards.[45] There was very little opposition in the rank and file of the bolshevik party, or of the left socialist revolutionary party. At the Third Soviet Congress which met soon after, 'to pass sentence on the Constituent Assembly', as Zinoviev expressed it, the Bolsheviks and Left Socialist Revolutionaries had assured themselves an overwhelming majority. In a referendum on the question of the withdrawal of the Bolsheviks and the Left Socialist Revolutionaries from the Assembly, 377 out of 419 voted their approval.[46]

[44] For an abbreviated account see B. & F., pp. 380–4, based on fuller accounts in *Novaya zhizn'*, 22 January 1918; *Izvestiya*, 20 January 1918, and *Pravda*, 24 January 1918.

[45] On this demonstration see Gorky's bitter article in *Novaya zhizn'*, 22 January 1918. In the army the news was received with 'utter indifference'—*ibid.*, 14 February 1918.

[46] *Rubinshtein*, p. 110.

According to his widow, Lenin found justification for his decision to disperse the Assembly in a speech by Plekhanov at the Second Russian Social Democratic Party Congress in 1903, which contained a passage to the effect that the well-being of the revolution is the supreme law, to which in the early stages of revolutionary ardour even the ideal of universal franchise must yield.[47] It is unlikely that Lenin even gave a passing thought to any question of principle, where 'parliamentary cretinism' (he was fond of quoting this phrase of Marx) was involved. But his peculiar genius in the tactics of power was revealed in his assessment, based on very inadequate information, of the strength of the opposition with which he might have been faced. He realized that a weary and bewildered population, with no experience of democratic institutions, would not rally to defend the Constituent Assembly. Even Spiridonova had been willing to disperse the Assembly if it did not happen to agree with the Soviets. There were very many among both the bolshevik and the left socialist revolutionary following who shared this point of view. 'Men from another World' was the title of an unfinished article on the Assembly, which Lenin wrote about this time. So fast had events moved since November that to anyone who had lived through the first months of the October Revolution in Petrograd, these words did not appear an exaggerated description of those who had hoped that the Assembly would bring constitutional government to Soviet Russia.

In the elections to the Constituent Assembly, the Bolsheviks polled under one quarter of the forty-one million votes recorded. The remaining votes, excluding some two million *Kadet* votes, some two million unclassified, and some seven and a half million votes cast for various national minority parties, went to socialists of all kinds. The Socialist Revolutionaries secured over fifteen million votes. Three-quarters of the country did not vote for the Bolsheviks. Half the country

---

[47] *Krupskaya*, Vol. I, p. 98. For Plekhanov's speech at the Second Congress see *Vtoroy ocherednoy syezd*, p. 169: 'If, carried away by the impulse of revolutionary ardour, the people should elect a very good parliament . . . then we ought to try to make it a long parliament; but if these elections should turn out to be unsuccessful, then we should have to try to disperse this parliament, and not in a year or two years' time, but in a fortnight.' In the last article which he wrote Plekhanov referred to this speech, but denied that it could be used to justify Lenin's action. See *God na rodine*, Vol. II, pp. 257–68.

voted for socialism, but against bolshevism.[48]   Of the 707 delegates elected, 175 were Bolsheviks, 370 Socialist Revolutionaries, 40 Left Socialist Revolutionaries, 16 Mensheviks, and 17 *Kadety*.[49]   The Bolsheviks had a majority in the industrial centres, and polled about half the votes in the army. They were supported by some of the peasants in uniform, but not by those who remained in the villages.[50]   Some years after the dispersal of the Assembly, Lenin analysed the more detailed results of the elections which had only then become available; his analysis revealed how well founded his instinctive assessment of opposition had been in January 1918.   The decisive factor in Lenin's view was that in those sections of the army which were closest to the two capitals, the bolshevik vote had been more than double the socialist revolutionary vote.[51]   The strategic guns had been behind the Bolsheviks.

[48] For the figures of the voting based on all available, though incomplete, information, see *Radkey*, p. 80.

[49] *Mal'chevsky*, p. 115.   The remainder were delegates elected by the various national groups.

[50] *Radkey*, pp. 57–8, and Chapter V, *passim*.

[51] *Lenin*, Vol. XXIV, pp. 631–49, at p. 638.

CHAPTER VI

THE PEACE OF BREST-LITOVSK

In April 1916 Lenin had called upon the workers in the belligerent armies to lay down their arms. This raised the question of what would happen if one side did lay down its arms, but the other side did not follow the example. To this Lenin had in part already given the answer in an article published on 13 October 1915. Should revolution place the proletariat at the helm in Russia, he stated, the government of the proletariat would immediately offer peace to all the belligerents on condition that all colonial and dependent peoples be liberated. Neither the Central Powers nor the Entente would, under their present governments, accept this. 'If so, we should have to prepare and lead a revolutionary war' and 'systematically arouse to insurrection' the socialist proletariat of Europe and the oppressed peoples of Asia, for which revolution in Russia would provide 'unusually favourable conditions'.[1] This idea continued to dominate official bolshevik doctrine as it developed between April and November 1917. On the eve of his departure for Petrograd, Lenin reaffirmed that, if need be, a revolutionary war would be waged in the interests of international socialism.[2] In his April Theses, on his arrival in Russia, he laid down the conditions upon which the 'class-conscious proletariat' could accept a 'revolutionary war, which really justifies revolutionary defensism', namely, the passing of power to the proletariat, renunciation of all annexationist ambitions, and complete breach with all capitalist interests. Propaganda to this end should be organized in the army. The hastily drafted paragraph ended with the isolated word 'fraternization', which called forth particular scorn from Plekhanov. 'What does this mean?' he asked. 'What does it amount to but a separate peace?' It was a pertinent question. At the All-Russian

---

[1] 'Neskol'ko tezisov', published in *Sotsial demokrat*, 13 October 1915. *Lenin*, Vol. XVIII, pp. 311–13.
[2] 'Farewell Letter to Swiss Workers', *Lenin*, Vol. XX, pp. 65–70.

Bolshevik Party Conference in May 1917, Lenin dismissed Plekhanov with a phrase—his criticism was 'just trickery, and not a serious agrument'.[3] Lenin's resolution adopted with no dissenting vote and with only seven abstentions, stressed that 'the war cannot be ended by the refusal of the soldiers on one side to continue it. . . . The conference protests again and again against the low slander, spread against our party by the capitalists, that we are in favour of a separate peace with Germany.'[4] There was little discussion of the possibility of revolutionary war, though Lenin reminded the Conference that 'we are not pacifists and cannot renounce revolutionary war'. There is, however, an interesting omission in the resolution as adopted. The original draft contained the extract from Lenin's article of 13 October 1915 quoted above, on the necessity for a revolutionary war in the event of a refusal of the Russian offer of a democratic peace by the Western belligerents and the assertion that the conference 'fully confirms this declaration'.[5] This passage did not appear in the resolution when it was put to the vote, nor do the debates reveal how it came to be omitted, since there seems to have been no discussion of this part of the draft.[6] For months the Bolsheviks continued to preach as their doctrine 'not a separate peace, but a just, democratic peace'. On 22 June a bolshevik proclamation ended with the words: 'An end to the war! Let the Soviet declare just conditions of peace! Neither a separate peace with Wilhelm, nor secret treaties with the French and English capitalists! Bread! Peace! Freedom!'.[7] On the same day Lenin told the First All-Russian Congress of Soviets that 'in certain conditions a revolutionary war is unavoidable and no class of revolutionaries can shrink from revolutionary war'.[8] At the Sixth Bolshevik Party Congress in August, where there was little discussion of, and no dissension

---

[3] *Protokoly VII Konf.*, p. 157.   [4] *VKP(b) v rez.*, pp. 266–9.
[5] *Protokoly VII Konf.*, p. 46.
[6] The abstentions in the voting on the resolution are not to be explained by any doubts on the question of revolutionary war. They were more probably a reflection of the views of a minority of the conference, headed by Kamenev, which called for agitation among the masses to demand publication of the secret treaties. This would demonstrate to them the imperialist nature of the Provisional Government and that there could be no 'revolutionary policy in the international sphere' without power passing to the Soviets. *ibid.*, pp. 71; and cf. Nogin's speech at p. 89.
[7] *Vladimirova*, III, p. 269.   [8] *Vs. syezd. I*, Vol. I, pp. 322–33.

on, the question of war, it was once more reasserted that 'the only way of putting an end to the war in a democratic way is for the international proletariat to conquer power'.[9] As late as September Lenin was still proclaiming that 'war cannot be ended by the decision of one side'. In one of his many dramatic appeals to his party on the eve of the rising, he deals with a question which was obviously troubling some of his followers: what if our efforts at democratic peace fail, and the soldiers refuse to carry on a revolutionary war? His answer is characteristic in its appeal to emotion when faced with a difficult argument. 'This reasoning reminds one of the saying: one fool can ask ten times more questions than ten wise men can answer. We never denied the difficulties which would beset power. . . . Are we to renounce it when the moment for action has come?'[10] In another such appeal Lenin skilfully utilized the current rumours that the Provisional Government intended to conclude a separate peace. 'Only our party,' he wrote, 'after victorious insurrection, *can* save Petrograd; for if our offer of peace is rejected . . . *we* shall become determined supporters of national defence, . . . we shall become *the most "military"* party, we shall wage war in a truly revolutionary fashion.'[11]

The Bolsheviks thus continued simultaneously in their propaganda, to demand an end to the war, to denounce a separate peace, and to promise revolutionary war. As far as the weary soldiers were concerned, only the first, 'An end to the war!' had any meaning. It must indeed have been obvious that it was impossible to preach both 'peace' and 'revolutionary war' at one and the same time. In their letter of protest against the decision of the Central Committee to resort to insurrection, Zinoviev and Kamenev used this inconsistency as one of their arguments. On the one hand, they said, a seizure of power by the Soviets must inevitably lead on to a revolutionary war; but, on the other hand, the waging of such a revolutionary war would alienate the soldiers. 'The very delegates from the front who are now . . . agitating against the war openly ask our speakers not to mention

---

[9] *VKP(b) v rez.*, I, pp. 289–91.
[10] Written on 29 and 30 October; see *Lenin*, Vol. XXI, p. 344.
[11] *Lenin*, Vol. XXI, p. 197; cf. *ibid.*, p. 224.

revolutionary war, since this repels the soldiers.'[12]   Even if Lenin had realized the effect of his party's propaganda and had decided to face the consequences when they arose, he did not share his views with his party.

The Russian army, in spite of the extreme privations to which it was subjected, was at first comparatively little influenced by the insistent bolshevik peace propaganda.   For a time the suspicion that Lenin and Zinoviev were German agents and the belief that they were advocating a separate peace with the Germans antagonized the naturally patriotic sense of the Russian soldier.   Up to the summer, at any rate, the army still remained a fighting force for purposes of defence, in spite of its weariness and longing for peace, and in spite of the effect of Order No. One.[13]   It was even still possible to agitate with some hope of success for an offensive.   Kerensky, in his rapid propaganda tours of the front, achieved astonishing response.[14]   Although by July the bolshevik military organizations became much more influential, both in Petrograd and at the front, yet Lenin was sufficiently apprehensive of the attitude of the army to dismiss the idea of attempting to seize power during the disturbances of that month.   More effective than bolshevik peace propaganda, was the work of the bolshevik military organizations in advocating 'democratization' of the army, with the object of undermining the army as an effective striking force which could be used against themselves.[15]   The

[12] Zinoviev, *Sochineniya*, Vol. VII (i), pp. 547–51.
[13] See Chapter II; and see *Fedotoff-White*, pp. 13–14, for the text.
[14] *Sukhanov*, III, pp. 367–8; IV, p. 70.
[15] General Brusilov has left, in his memoirs, a picture of army morale in the middle of 1917, which, incidentally shows that the propaganda which caused the disintegration was menshevik and socialist revolutionary as much as bolshevik, at any rate in the early stages.   'The officer corps, which understood nothing of politics, and which had in the past been strictly forbidden even to think about such things was in the hands of the soldier masses, over whom the officers had no influence whatever.   At the head of this mass there were various emissaries and agents of the socialist parties, who had been sent out by the Soviet of Workers' and Soldiers' deputies to preach "peace without annexations or indemnities".   The soldier did not wish to fight any longer, and was of the opinion that, since peace must be concluded without any annexations and without any indemnities, and since the principle of self determination for all nations had been proclaimed, there was no further point in bloodshed, and it should be stopped.   This was, as it were, the official reason for not wanting to fight.   Unofficially, however, the slogans "Down with the war," "Immediate peace at any price," and "Immediate confiscation of the landowners' land" had taken possession.   The basis of the demand for the land was that the landlords had accumulated their riches over centuries at the price of the peasants' suffering and that their ill gotten gains must be taken away from them as soon as possible.   The officer immediately became

Bolshevik N.I. Podvoysky in his report to a conference of delegates of the bolshevik party military organization in June[16] admitted that this was the intention of the party. Quite apart from the activity of the Bolsheviks, there were other factors at work which led to the collapse of the army in the last weeks before the October Revolution:—the delay of the Provisional Government in dealing either with peace, or with what was equally important to a peasant army, with land; General Kornilov's bid for power; and the defeat of the Russian counter-offensive at the front which came soon after it. By October, the vast army was disintegrating. At a secret session on 2 November the Minister of War of the Provisional Government described the catastrophic state of the army. There were two million deserters, and supplies were falling disastrously.[17] For the fall in supplies bolshevik propaganda was in part responsible, since their advocacy of workers' control had helped powerfully to produce chaos in industry. But the evidence suggests that their peace propaganda at the front did not begin to tell until late September or October.[18] It was disorganization and lack of supplies, rather than loss of morale, which caused the Russian defeat in early September, when the Germans captured Riga.[19] By the time the Bolsheviks seized power, all these cumulative causes had done their work in the army. It was plain that the vast Russian army would not fight again as an army. But it was not by

an enemy in the soldiers' eyes, because he demanded continuation of the war. He became a landlord in uniform so far as the soldier was concerned.' Brusilov goes on to describe his efforts to counteract the disintegration of the army which was being produced not only by the undermining of discipline as a result of Order No. One, but also by all the various local army soviets, who continued to undermine the authority of the army commanders under the pretext of meeting a completely imaginary and non-existent threat of counter-revolution. See *Brusilov*, pp. 209–12. Brusilov was one of the most left-wing generals in the army and eventually joined the Bolsheviks.

[16] *Fedotoff-White*, p. 21. And see the resolution on 'democratization' of the army (election of officers, self-government, initiative from below) adopted at this conference, in *VKP(b) v rez.*, pp. 278–80. Although election of officers was not formally decreed until 29 December 1917, in many instances where the bolshevik organizations had established control, they had succeeded in putting the finishing touches to the army by anticipating the decree, and putting through election of officers some time before this date—see F. Rtyshchev in *Bol'sheviki u vlasti*, pp. 79–83.

[17] *Oldenbourg*, pp. 92–109. cf. other estimates quoted in *Fedotoff-White*. p. 10.

[18] See, for example, *Kakurin*, for contrasting reports on the effectiveness of bolshevik agitation in the Second Army for 7 September and 11 October, pp. 118, 151–2.

[19] See reports quoted in *Sukhanov*, Vol. V, pp. 201–5.

any means solidly pro-bolshevik. Out of the entire army, only some thirty to fifty thousand were ready actively to support the Bolsheviks.[20] Of the remainder the majority were intent only on getting home, away from the war, or were at very best 'neutral', that is to say determined to remain out of any fighting that might be going on. The units which preserved their morale were for the most part anti-bolshevik. It should have been obvious to anyone in November 1917 that there would be little prospect of fighting a successful 'revolutionary war' under bolshevik leadership if the necessity arose. But for months to come the idea continued to exercise a powerful effect on very many Bolsheviks.

When on 7 November Lenin emerged from hiding and appeared in the Petrograd Soviet, he did not promise immediate peace. 'The new power would do everything', he said, to stop the war. 'But we do not say that we can finish the war simply by sticking our bayonets into the ground . . . we do not say that we shall make peace to-day or to-morrow.' This passage was omitted from the reports in the bolshevik papers, possibly for fear of alarming the soldiers.[21] The following day, the Second All-Russian Congress of Soviets adopted the Declaration of Peace, which proposed to all belligerents 'a just democratic . . . immediate peace, without annexations and without indemnities'. Lenin ended his speech: 'We do not now close, nor have we ever closed our eyes, to the difficulties. Wars cannot be ended by a refusal to fight, they cannot be ended by one side alone. We are proposing an armistice for three months—though we do not reject a shorter period—so as to give the suffering army a breathing space.'[22] But, though doctrine was thus faithfully observed, the evidence was inescapable that to hold out to the Russian army the prospect of an immediate armistice would put an end to even such remnants of morale as still survived in some parts of it. Yet to destroy the army led straight to that very separate peace which the party had so steadfastly

---

[20] *Grazhdanskaya voyna*, Vol. II, p. 50. These included the Lettish Rifle regiment and armoured car detachments, which retained their identity after the revolution.

[21] See *Oldenbourg*, pp. 169–70, 173–4. It was also omitted from the main menshevik paper.

[22] *Vs. syezd II*, p. 62.

disclaimed. It was not likely that the belligerent powers would accept an invitation to an armistice from a handful of adventurers whom even their closest supporters (and a fair proportion of their own number) did not expect to survive in power for more than a few days. It is difficult to believe that Lenin had not foreseen this consequence of his policy. But the great majority of his party were so hypnotized by phrases that they failed to see that to capture an army by promises of immediate peace effectively destroyed that army as an instrument for 'revolutionary war'. With the tactical skill which characterized his leadership of his party, Lenin had not attempted to disillusion his followers. It was only some ten days before the seizure of power that the Petrograd Bolshevik Committee awoke to the fact that the

> mood of the soldiers, reaching the point of complete despair, is quickly developing into a demand for 'peace at any price', which can in its own way be exploited by imperialism in order to conclude an anti-democratic, imperialist peace. The absence of immediate decisive steps towards peace threatens complete disorganization at the front, leading to mass desertion of soldiers from their posts, and by this means creates an enormous threat to the possibility of organized struggle for democratic peace.[23]

Yet this same Petrograd Committee had for some months been working towards that very disorganization in the army which had now finally been brought about.

The offer of a general armistice remained unanswered, and on 21 November the Commander in Chief of the Russian Army, General Dukhonin, was ordered to address himself directly to the enemy armies with the proposal for an immediate armistice. Dukhonin refused, and was promptly dismissed and replaced by Krylenko, a lawyer with some slight military experience, who later became the first Chief Prosecutor in the Soviet State. On the following day Lenin broadcast to the soldiers: 'The question of peace is in your hands. Do not let the counter-revolutionary generals wreck the great cause of peace.' Krylenko issued similar appeals.[24] It was plain that the effect of appealing directly to the ranks against their officers would be very demoralising. Lenin, however, when charged in the Central Executive Committee with weakening

[23] *Pervyy Leg. Komitet*, pp. 326-8.   [24] See *B. & F.*, pp. 236-7, 240.

the army's resistance against the Germans, dismissed the suggestion as 'grotesque'.[25] The time had not yet come for him to join issue squarely with those leaders both of his own party and of the Left Socialist Revolutionaries to whom a 'revolutionary war' still appeared inevitable, should the attempts at a democratic peace fail. On 3 December armistice negotiations were opened with the Germans and an armistice was signed on 15 December. Before entering into negotiations, the Bolsheviks had taken possession of the field headquarters of the army, in the course of which the former Commander in Chief, Dukhonin, was lynched by sailors in the presence of Krylenko. The Germans refused a Russian proposal that a joint appeal be issued to all the belligerent nations not represented at the armistice talks inviting them to take part. Trotsky called upon the Allied Powers in the press and by radio to join in the armistice negotiations and to state their conditions, blaming them on 13 December for the fact that in their absence 'the armistice is thus assuming the character of a separate agreement'.[26] These appeals evoked no response from the Allied Powers, except at first from the United States. But the latter yielded to the objections of Britain and France and suspended all direct contact with the Bolsheviks.[27] On 22 December negotiations with the Germans, which had been suspended on 15 December, were resumed. The Russian delegation, headed by Ioffe and Kamenev, insisted in their proposals on the principle of self-determination, to be realized by means of a referendum for 'nationalities which did not enjoy political independence before the war'. This principle, applying in particular to the Baltic States and to Poland (other events complicated the question of the Ukraine, which had proclaimed its independence on 20 November) was the dominant issue in the peace negotiations in bolshevik eyes. Self-determination was the minimum foundation upon which the peace could be

[25] *Lenin* (1), Vol. XV, p. 36; for a picture of the rapid disintegration of the XII Army (on the Petrograd front) during November and December, see F. Rtyshchev in *Bol'sheviki u vlasti*, pp. 79–83. The bolshevik leaders may have feared, with reason, that the army, impatient of the delay in the armistice, might be goaded into action against the Bolsheviks' precarious power—see documents printed in *Krasnyy arkhiv*, Vol. XXIII, pp. 196–248. A report for 28 November–13 December on the overall morale in the army shows that the 'masses of the soldiers are definitely in sympathy with the new order'—(*ibid.*, p. 248), but this could not last indefinitely if peace were not concluded.

[26] *U.S. Foreign Relations*, Vol. I, p. 260.   [27] *ibid.*, pp. 279, 289.

regarded as 'democratic'. In insisting upon these rights for Poland and the Baltic States, the Bolsheviks were defending neither Russian self-interest, nor their own, but (possibly for the first and last time in their foreign policy) a question of principle. No referendum at that date could possibly have resulted in a majority in favour of union with Russia in any one of these states. The Central Powers were willing to accept the principle of self-determination publicly, but with private reservations. In their reply they agreed to conclude a general peace 'without forcible annexations or indemnities', but on condition that all the belligerents should pledge themselves to accept these conditions for a general peace within a certain time. General Hoffman of the German delegation, however, explained in private to the staggered Ioffe that 'self-determination' in the German conception of the term did not extend either to the Baltic territories or to Poland. These states had already withdrawn from Russia, and should they choose to unite with Germany, that would not in the German view be annexation.

The supposed success of bolshevik diplomacy was celebrated by a demonstration in Petrograd, and Trotsky promised support to the workers of any country who should 'rise against the imperialists of their own nations'. Meanwhile in a joint session of the Central Executive Committee, the Petrograd Soviet, and army representatives, a left socialist revolutionary resolution was adopted condemning German aggressive intentions, and a further appeal was launched to the peoples of the Allied Powers calling upon them to prevent an imperialist war against revolutionary Russia. On 2 January a Russian note was dispatched to the Central Powers condemning their peace proposals as contrary to the principles of national self-determination. The Central Powers replied that since the allies of Russia had failed to join in the peace negotiations, their original terms were now withdrawn. Negotiations were taking a critical turn. The only hopes that remained were either that an outbreak of revolutions in Western Europe, and particularly in Germany, would remove the menace of continued war; or, that if hostilities were renewed allied aid would still be available to Russia. No one at this stage publicly envisaged the solution of the dilemma by the acceptance of German annexationist terms. But Lenin's decision probably began to be formed at an All-Army Congress on Demobilization, which took place in the second fortnight in December. The delegates to this congress were searchingly questioned by Lenin both verbally and in written questionnaires. The results were never published; but subsequent accounts show that the unpalatable fact emerged that the units which were still in fighting trim were generally anti-bolshevik.[28] It was obvious that if they were put into the field to fight the Germans they would before long rally round any new government which might attempt to overthrow the Bolsheviks. Meantime, Trotsky was despatched to Brest-Litovsk, in place of Ioffe, with instructions from Lenin to drag out negotiations to the utmost. At the same time, secret negotiations were begun with unofficial allied representatives in Russia in an endeavour to secure from them the promise of military aid. These negotiations came to nothing.[29] But the startling idea that a revolutionary government could even enter into such negotiations with imperialists was a contributory factor in the subsequent rift among the party leaders.

The negotiations at Brest-Litovsk were resumed on 9 January. There was no longer any common ground for agreement, but Trotsky carried out brilliantly his instructions to delay the proceedings. But there were limits to the delay which even Trotsky's fireworks could impose on the negotiations, and Lenin may well have guessed that the Germans would before long decide to resume their offensive with the intention of bringing bolshevik rule to an end, and in the belief that any other

[28] See M. Kedrov, in *Proletarskaya revolyutsiya*, no. 1 (60), 1927, p. 53. V. Rakhmetov, who has examined the origins of Lenin's decision to sign a separate peace, comes to the conclusion that the idea may have been in Lenin's mind from the start, but concealed 'for tactical or for some other reasons'; the actual decision to sign a separate peace on any terms he places between 5 and 10 January —see *Proletarskaya revolyutsiya*, no. 5 (88), 1929, pp. 3–16.

[29] The United States unofficial contact with the Bolsheviks, Colonel Robins, believed as late as 5 March, that Lenin was prepared to go back on the Brest-Litovsk treaty in the event of allied aid being assured—see *Hard*, pp. 151–2, 138–9. cf. N. A. Kornatovsky in *Krasnaya letopis'*, no. 3 (36), 1930, at p. 9, for the Russian version of the interview with Lenin described by Robins. Such documents as there are do not suggest that the Russians ever went further than sounding allied intentions against the event of the German advance being resumed for whatever reason. Bruce Lockhart apparently on the same day also still expected, on the basis of Trotsky's assurances, that such action would be taken at the Congress 'as will make a declaration of war on Germany's front inevitable' —see a document said to be his dispatch to the Foreign Office of this date reprinted in Cumming and Pettit, *Russian-American Relations*, pp. 82–4.

government would be forced to sign peace.[30] On 14 January
Lenin's car was shot at, apparently from an ambush, and the
Vecheka claimed to have frustrated an officers' plot to kidnap
him fixed for 18 January. The United States' Ambassador's
conjecture in a dispatch to his government that the (Right)
Socialist Revolutionaries were behind these attempts, and that
the Germans had entered into a compact with them in an
endeavour to overthrow the Bolsheviks and set up a more
pliant government to negotiate the peace may have been
somewhat fanciful.[31] But for all that, the possibility of a
German-sponsored coup d'état could not be ignored. On
18 January Trotsky returned to Petrograd and negotiations
were interrupted. The final decision could not now be long
delayed.

By 20 January Lenin had formulated his views in a series
of Theses on Peace. He began by enunciating a doctrine
which has now become a communist commonplace. He
asserted that now that a socialist government had been
victorious in one country, Russia, all questions must henceforth
be decided 'exclusively from the point of view of the best
conditions for the developing and strengthening of the socialist
revolution which has already begun.' He denied that the
Bolsheviks had ever promised a revolutionary war. They had
preached the need to prepare and lead such a war, in order
to 'combat abstract pacifism . . . and the purely selfish interests
of a part of the soldiery'. The great mass of the peasantry
would beyond doubt vote even for an annexationist peace.
If war were now to be renewed, the infuriated peasants would
overthrow the socialist government in a week. His conclusion
was that the German terms should be accepted notwithstanding their demand for annexations. Such acceptance would
be the price of purchasing a short period of peaceful reconstruction to tide over the delay until revolution in the West
came to Russia's aid.[32] Lenin had at that date greater

[30] They did in fact so decide on 25 January. *Ludendorff*, p. 443.
[31] *U.S. Foreign Relations*, Vol. I, pp. 480, 350, 352. For the plot see *Izvestiya*
26 January 1918. The attempt on Lenin's life may have been the work of some
right wing Socialist Revolutionaries—see B. Sokolov in *Arkhiv russkoy revolyutsii*,
Vol. XIII, p. 48.
[32] *Lenin* (1), Vol. XV, pp. 63–9. (The first edition of Lenin's works provides
the fullest annotation on the Brest-Litovsk period.) Most of the relevant documents are also reprinted in *Protokoly VII*.

confidence in the imminent outbreak of the revolution in the West than, for example, Stalin. 'There is no sign of a revolutionary movement in the West . . .' Stalin said on 24 January, 'only a possibility. We cannot build on a possibility.'[33] But these views did not prevent Stalin from staunchly supporting Lenin's peace policy in the following weeks.

Lenin's views met with immediate opposition. So far as the mass of the population was concerned, it was true that more peasants were in favour of peace than of any form of renewed warfare. But it is doubtful whether the peasant majority in favour of peace was quite as overwhelming as Lenin chose to portray it to his party. A referendum of the views of two hundred soviets was held during February. Of these a majority—one hundred and five as against ninety-five —voted for war against the Germans. In the industrial city soviets the majority in favour of war was overwhelming. Of the provincial and village soviets, which expressed the peasant view, eighty-eight voted for peace as against eighty for war. It is hardly surprising that the full results of this referendum were not published until eleven years later.[34]

Wide sections of the bolshevik party including the great majority of the Petrograd Committee and of the Moscow *Oblast'* Bureau, were in favour of a revolutionary war, which in practice now meant the same thing as continuation of the war against Germany. The views of many of the rank and file could be summed up in the phrase used by Obolensky, one of the members of the Moscow *Oblast'* Bureau: 'I stand for Lenin's old position', meaning by that 'the revolutionary war', which Lenin had, in spite of his denials, promised again and again. Lenin, in turn, taunted the 'obstinate Muscovites' with refusal to see that an entirely new situation had now arisen.[35] Trotsky at no time supported 'revolutionary war'. 'It is as clear as day that if we wage revolutionary war, we

[33] *Stalin*, Vol. IV, p. 87, at a meeting of the Central Committee. For Lenin's views at this meeting see *Lenin*, Vol. XXII, p. 202.

[34] See *Leninskiy sbornik*, Vol. XI, pp. 59–60, published in 1929. See also the list in *Yaroslavsky*, Vol. IV, p. 306. cf. *Trotsky*, *Ma Vie*, Vol. III, pp. 73–4 and Steinberg, *Als ich Volkskommissar war*, p. 249. In a speech, after the signing of the peace, on 4 March 1918, Sverdlov stated that of the peasant soviets, seventy-two had voted for peace and sixty against. See his *Izbrannye stat'i i rechi*, p. 46.

[35] See an unfinished postscript to his Theses which Lenin wrote about this time, in *Leninskiy sbornik*, Vol. XI, pp. 46-7.

shall be overthrown'—he told the party on 21 January.[36] But he doubted whether the Germans were in a position to resume their advance. He was in favour of a plan which he had evolved about the time that Lenin was preparing his Theses on Peace. This was that Russia, as a gesture, should declare war at an end, but at the same time refuse to sign the annexationist peace proposed by the Germans. The proposal raised considerable doubts in Lenin's mind.[37] But it was one which, by holding out some hope of staving off the evil moment, corresponded to the mood of indecision of a large number in the bolshevik Central Committee. For the Central Committee was at this date far less ready to decide on an immediate 'revolutionary war' than were the active party workers lower down the scale of the hierarchy. Thus, when Lenin's Theses were discussed at a meeting of active party workers on 21 January, at which much wider sections of the party were represented than in the Central Committee, fifteen votes were cast for immediate peace; thirty-two for a revolutionary war; and sixteen for Trotsky's formula, 'no war, no peace'.[38] By contrast, at a meeting of the Central Committee the following day, only two, Lomov and Krestinsky, supported revolutionary war. The 'no war, no peace' formula was approved by nine votes to seven.[39]

In the last week of January the Third All-Russian Congress of Soviets authorized all steps 'directed towards the achievement of a democratic peace'. Negotiations at Brest-Litovsk were resumed on 30 January. Meanwhile, the Petrograd Committee of the bolshevik party and a group of Moscow Bolsheviks now to be known as the Left Communists—including Bukharin, Lomov, Obolensky (Osinsky), Yakovleva, V. M. Smirnov, G. Pyatakov, and Preobrazhensky—demanded that the Central Committee should call a special representative party conference on the question of peace. The Central Committee agreed and at the same time fixed the Seventh Bolshevik Party Congress for 6 March. The special party

---

[36] *ibid.*, p. 42. In Lenin's note of this speech by Trotsky made at this meeting, this passage is heavily sidelined.

[37] See Trotsky *Ma Vie*, III, pp. 71–2; and see his *Stalin*, pp. 248–9, for a slightly different version.   [38] *Lenin* (1), Vol. XV, p. 621; *Trotsky, Ma Vie*, III, p. 73.

[39] *Trotsky, Ma Vie*, III, p. 74; *B. & F.*, p. 499. A policy of 'no peace—no war' was also approved on 25 January in a joint session of the bolshevik and left socialist revolutionary Central Committees—*Sorin*, p. 16.

conference took place on 3 February. Although only an analysis of the voting is preserved, it is sufficient to show that at this date there was as yet neither coherence nor decision among those who could not bring themselves to accept the drastic course proposed by Lenin of peace at any price. The indecision may possibly be explained by the fact that Bukharin, who was the ideological leader of Left Communism, was only present for a part of the time and left before the voting. All those present at the meeting, with the exception of the hot-headed Stukov, were opposed to breaking off discussions with the Germans immediately, though only the staunch supporters of peace—Lenin, Zinoviev, and Stalin—were prepared to sign an annexationist peace at once. All, except Stukov and Obolensky, agreed that in principle peace treaties were permissible between socialist and imperialist states; and that in particular an annexationist peace was permissible with Germany if the talks were broken off and followed by a German ultimatum. Yet, when the decisive question 'should the peace be signed in such a case?' was put to the vote, the great majority of those present abstained.[40] This was the last meeting of the party leaders, so far as is known, before 10 February, the date on which Trotsky broke off negotiations with the Central Powers in a statement in which Russia refused to sign an annexationist peace, but at the same time declared the war at an end. It was a useless gesture, an 'international political demonstration', as Lenin called it. But, in the light of the indecisive voting of the meetings described, it cannot be said, as Stalin and Zinoviev were first to assert seven years later, that Trotsky acted against the will of the party. In fact the Russian declaration at Brest-Litovsk probably corresponded most closely to the mood of indecision of the party leaders other than Lenin, Stalin, Sverdlov, and Zinoviev.[41] There was to be a good deal of acrimonious debate on Trotsky's action at the Seventh Party Congress, but the majority refused

[40] *Lenin* (1), Vol. XV, p. 626.

[41] Even Stalin, after the German advance had been resumed, advocated at one time that the German conditions of peace should not be signed,—at a Central Committee meeting on 23 February—see *Proletarskaya revolyutsiya*, no. 2 (73), 1928, pp. 149–50. Trotsky's own evidence that Lenin was for a time converted to his point of view is not entirely convincing—see *Ma Vie*, III, pp. 77–8. If Karakhan's account as told to Louis Fischer is correct, Stalin gave his approval before the declaration—see *The Soviets in World Affairs*, Vol. I, p. 57.

to pass a resolution, proposed by Trotsky himself, censuring his conduct.[42]

On 17 February, before the Germans resumed their attack, the Central Committee once again discussed the question of peace, and specific questions were put to the vote. The question whether or not a revolutionary war should be waged was for the first time put squarely before the Central Committee. All voted against war, except Bukharin, Lomov, and Ioffe, who refused to vote on the question in the unqualified form in which it was put. Lenin, Stalin, Sverdlov, Sokol'nikov, and Smilga were in favour of offering to sign an immediate peace; Bukharin, Lomov, Trotsky, Uritsky, Ioffe, and Krestinsky voted to wait for the reopening of hostilities before making the offer, so as to allow time to gauge the effect of this move on the European workers' movement. But on the crucial question: if the Germans advance, and there is no revolution in Germany, do we sign peace? only one, Ioffe, voted against. Trotsky voted with Lenin and his supporters: Bukharin, Lomov, Uritsky, and Krestinsky abstained.[43] On 18 February the Germans resumed their attack.

The Central Committee met again. Lenin's proposal to send an immediate offer of peace was defeated by seven votes to six. Trotsky voted against it. There was still some doubt whether an offer of peace would be accepted by the Germans. Lenin made it plain to the Central Committee that, if it should become evident that the object of the German advance was the overthrow of the Bolsheviks, it would then be necessary to fight. The masses would understand 'a revolutionary war for the socialization of land'.[44] In the course of the day the

[42] *Sed'moy syezd*, p. 158. Trotsky's proposal evoked a spiteful comment from Zinoviev, who accused him of trying to cause a party split, an accusation which was quite unjustified. This appears to have been the first public instance of the personal animosity between Zinoviev and Trotsky which a few years later became a marked feature of party controversies.

[43] See *Lenin* (1), Vol. XV, p. 625; cf. *Lenin*, Vol. XXII, p. 557, and *Proletarskaya revolyutsiya*, no. 2 (73), 1928, pp. 132–3, which gives the same version. At the height of the campaign against Trotsky in 1928 a reprint of this document was apparently altered to show Trotsky abstaining on this question—*B. & F.*, p. 512, note 63. Trotsky states that about this time he was approached by Uritsky, Radek, and possibly Obolensky to form a 'united front', but that he rejected the suggestion (*Ma Vie*, III, p. 79).

[44] *Proletarskaya revolyutsiya*, no. 2 (73), 1928, pp. 134–6. The Germans had issued a proclamation at the start of the offensive explaining that their advance was undertaken against the Bolshevik government in the interests of civilization

military news swayed Trotsky to Lenin's side. The Germans had captured Dvinsk, and were advancing into the Ukraine, and apparently meeting with no resistance. In the evening, in the Central Committee, the voting on sending an immediate offer of peace was now seven to six in favour.[45] But the decision had to be confirmed in the Council of People's Commissars, where the seven votes of the Left Socialist Revolutionaries could have defeated it. In the emotional deliberations of the night there was wavering among the seven left socialist revolutionary commissars, and hesitation to break with the Bolsheviks. They did not know at the time, however, the narrow majority by which the decision of the Bolsheviks had been taken (the Bolsheviks had held their deliberations apart). When the two groups of commissars met for the final decision, four out of the seven Left Socialist Revolutionaries voted with the bolshevik majority.[46] Their action was repudiated the following morning by the left socialist revolutionary 'fraction' in the Central Executive Committee, but the telegram with the offer of peace to the Germans had already been sent. The Germans continued their advance. In spite of acute party disagreements all now joined in preparations for defence. There was as yet no army to replace the one which had melted away. The formation of a volunteer army had been decreed on 28 January, but it made no progress. Yet the events of those few days when military preparations were at long last set afoot may well have given the opponents of the peace some grounds for believing that the obstacles in the way of a revolutionary war had been exaggerated by Lenin and his faction. The response to a proclamation by the Council of People's Commissars, 'The Socialist Fatherland is in Danger' was not that of a completely demoralized nation. In Petrograd, in a few days, over ten thousand volunteered.[47] Near Pskov, the infuriated peasants were rising to defend their

---

(*B. & F.*, p. 512, quoting *Pravda* of 2 March 1918). According to Trotsky (*Ma Vie*, III, p. 80), all, including Lenin, then believed that the Germans in agreement with the Allies intended to destroy Bolshevism and make peace at the expense of Russia.

[45] *Proletarskaya revolyutsiya*, *loc. cit.*, pp. 136, 142. Lenin, Smilga, Stalin, Sverdlov, Sokol'nikov, Zinoviev, and Trotsky voted in favour: Uritsky, Ioffe, Lomov, Bukharin, Krestinsky, and Dzerzhinsky against.

[46] Steinberg, *Als ich Volkskommissar war*, pp. 203–14.

[47] G. S. Pukhov, *Kak vooruzhalsya Petrograd*, pp. 12–14.

farmsteads against German expropriation.[48] If Radek was right, expert military opinion was agreed that, if Petrograd were abandoned, military cadres could be built up in depth within three months.[49] Krylenko and Raskol'nikov painted a dramatically exaggerated picture of the disintegration of the army and the navy in their reports to the Central Executive Committee on 23 February, but many no doubt dismissed this as a piece of special pleading arranged by Lenin.[50] Some of the bolshevik leaders doubtless wondered why, in spite of the fact that on 31 December the Council of People's Commissars had decided on immediate measures for reorganization of the army, so as to make it fit for defensive purposes on a reduced scale, nothing had been done for nearly two months.[51] But all these were military considerations, which left the vital political question out of account. Lenin and his supporters saw much more clearly than their opponents that a war of defence against an invader would rally and strengthen the anti-bolshevik forces in the country, who had hitherto failed to agree among themselves. All parties, including the *Kadety* and the (Right) Socialist Revolutionaries, would unite against Germany. In the remnants of the army, as the demobilization conference had revealed at the end of December, it was the anti-bolshevik units which retained their morale. In a war of defence the Bolsheviks would quickly lose the ascendancy which they had acquired through their peace propaganda. New political leaders, with the armed forces behind them, would speedily overthrow a handful of adventurers who had broken their promise to end the war. 'To wage war', Lenin wrote on 24 February, 'means in effect to yield to the provocation of the Russian bourgeoisie . . . the bourgeoisie wants war since it wants the overthrow of Soviet power and agreement with the German bourgeoisie.'[52] The main chance of bolshevik survival lay in the disunity of their internal enemies. Nothing was more likely to unite these enemies than a war of defence.

[48] *Sed'moy syezd*, p. 75. [49] *ibid.*, p. 72.
[50] See Steinberg, *op. cit.*, p. 228; and an article by L. Stupochenko quoted in *Wollenberg*, pp. 11–12, for an account of this meeting and the impression produced by these reports.
[51] *Leninskiy sbornik* Vol. XI pp. 17–18.
[52] *Lenin*, Vol. XXII, p. 295. See also *Fedotoff-White*, pp. 29–32, for other facts and quotations in support of the view that this was the decisive argument.

Four anxious days passed before the receipt of the German reply on 22 February to the Russian peace offer. It was followed by a revolt in the bolshevik party. When the severe German terms became known both the Petrograd Committee and the Moscow *Oblast'* Bureau combined to oppose Lenin's peace policy. On 23 February, the following jointly offered their resignations from all responsible posts held by them, and reserved their right of 'freely agitating both within the party and outside it': Lomov, V. M. Smirnov, Bukharin, G. Pyatakov, Bubnov, and Yakovleva, of Moscow; Uritsky of Petrograd. On the same day the Central Committee received another declaration from the same members of the party in similar terms. (Lomov, Bukharin, Bubnov, and Uritsky were members of the Central Committee.) But the second declaration no longer reserved the right to agitate outside the party. Several members of the Moscow *Oblast'* Bureau, not members of the Central Committee, including Stukov and Pokrovsky, and Spunde of Petrograd now also appended their signatures. Both the declarations characterized Lenin's decision to sign an annexationist peace as 'a blow at the international proletariat, especially severe at the moment of a revolutionary crisis in the West'. It was a capitulation to the petty bourgeois element in the country, contrary to the interests of the proletariat and to the mood of the bolshevik party. The signatories of the second declaration therefore claimed the right, 'without violating unity of organization' of widespread agitation within party circles in preparation for the forthcoming party congress, which had been fixed for 6 March.[53] Ioffe, Krestinsky, and Dzerzhinsky had also signed this declaration. But a threat by Lenin to resign had caused these three to hesitate. They accordingly stated that in their view a split in the party directed against Lenin would be more dangerous to the revolution than signing the peace, and that they therefore renounced the right of agitation even within the party.[54] They kept their promise, and took no further part in left communist activities. This attitude was in substance also Trotsky's, though he did not sign either of the two declarations.

On the same day, 23 February, the Central Committee

[53] *Sorin*, pp. 19–20. [54] *Proletarskaya revolyutsiya*, no. 2 (73), 1928, pp. 145–7.

discussed the German terms, which had been received the day before. Bukharin, Lomov, Bubnov, and Uritsky were still present, in spite of their resignations. Since there is no army, Lenin stated, the terms must be accepted and he threatened resignation; otherwise 'you will be signing the death sentence of Soviet power in three weeks from now'. He secured six votes in support of the peace: Stasova, Zinoviev, Sverdlov, Stalin, Sokol'nikov, and Smilga; Trotsky, together with Krestinsky, Dzerhinsky, and Ioffe abstained; Bukharin, Bubnov, Lomov, and Uritsky cast their votes against signing the treaty. The majority in the Central Committee was therefore seven to four in favour of signing the peace, with four abstentions. This time Lenin, in contrast to his policy in October and November 1917, was anxious at all costs to prevent a split inside the party. Conditions were no longer the same. Whereas in October the rank and file were straining for immediate seizure of power, and in November were indifferent to a break with the socialist parties, and would have upheld Lenin against the waverers, the position now was very different. They might not so readily follow him. Stalin failed to appreciate the balance of political forces. A supporter of conciliation of the rebels in October, when he opposed the expulsion of Kamenev and Zinoviev, he now attempted to force a split by suggesting that the resignations from responsible positions should be considered as resignation from the party. He was silenced by Lenin. To Lomov's question whether free agitation against the peace was permitted, Lenin replied in the affirmative. As a concession to feeling in the Central Committee, a resolution in favour of preparation for an immediate revolutionary war was adopted unanimously.[55] A party circular appealed for unity in spite of disagreements.[56]

Lenin's conciliatory tactics in the Central Committee were effective on all except Bukharin. On 24 February three resolutions were adopted: Lenin's, which requested the four members of the Central Committee concerned to postpone their decision to resign until the Party Congress, and reaffirmed their right openly to put forward their point of view; and two

[55] *Proletarskaya revolyutsiya, loc. cit.*, pp. 148–59. It is not clear why Stasova, who was not yet a member of the Central Committee, should have had a vote.
[56] *Lenin* (1), Vol. XV, p. 634.

resolutions, in very similar terms, by Trotsky and Krestinsky.[57] Lomov, Bubnov, and Uritsky then withdrew their resignations; Ioffe, who had not resigned, agreed in the name of party unity to submit to the decision of the Central Committee and to participate as consultant in the Soviet delegation to Brest-Litovsk.[58]

Bukharin, however, was not to be placated, nor to be persuaded to defer his resignation, but broke with the Central Committee. He had been outraged by its decision to accept aid from the allied powers in the event of Russian resistance to the Germans.[59] Moreover, his theoretical differences with Lenin were more clearly formulated than the more emotional dissent of the rank and file of the party, whom men like Uritsky represented. Before long he was to find a close ally on questions of doctrine in Obolensky (Osinsky), an economist of noble origins, and at one time leader of the Moscow University left wing student movement. In the Moscow *Oblast'* Bureau, (which it will be recalled covered a much wider area of party organizations than Moscow) Bukharin found immediate support. On 24 February (in the absence of Bukharin, then in Petrograd), the Bureau adopted unanimously a resolution of no confidence in the Central Committee. In an explanatory text appended to the resolution, it expressed the view that a split in the party in the near future was 'hardly to be avoided'; and set itself the task of uniting all revolutionary communists for the struggle against the supporters of a 'separate peace' and against opportunism in general. 'In the interests of international revolution,' wrote the Bureau, 'we consider it incumbent upon us to accept as a possibility the collapse of Soviet power, which has now become a pure formality.'[60]

---

[57] *Proletarskaya revolyutsiya, loc. cit.,* pp. 159–69.

[58] *Lenin* (1), Vol. XV, p. 635.

[59] The day before, Trotsky had announced in the Central Committee a proposal by the French to lend support to Russian resistance against the Germans. The proposal was adopted by six votes to five. Lenin, not present at the meeting at the time of the vote, had sent his vote in writing, in favour of 'accepting food and weapons from the bandits of Anglo-French imperialism'. 'We are turning the party into a dung-hill' was Bukharin's comment. *Lenin,* Vol. XXII, p. 607; *Trotsky, Ma Vie,* Vol. III, pp. 81–2.

[60] This Bureau, of which Yakovleva was the secretary, included at the beginning of 1918, Lomov, Stukov, Maksimovsky, Kizel'shtein, Mantsev, Safonov, T. B. Sapronov, and Z. P. Solov'ev. Bukharin had been a member since 1917. See *Lenin* (1), Vol. XIV (ii), p. 513. (But cf. Vol. XXII, p. 609 of the 2nd-3rd edn., edited by Bukharin, first printed in 1928, in which Bukharin is omitted from the

There is no doubt that the rank and file of the party and some of its more prominent figures too were inspired with the ideal of leading an immediate 'revolutionary war'—come what might—a war against any odds, which by its heroic example would kindle the flame of revolution all over the world. 'And if our Soviet Republic should perish', Alexandra Kollontay ended her speech at the Seventh Party Congress, 'others will carry the banner forward!'[61] Certainly this expressed the emotional faith of the ordinary party member that the almost impossible could be achieved, or if not, that death was better than dishonour.[62] Lenin neither understood this idealism, nor apparently gave a thought to the principle of socialist internationalism involved. 'What is better,' he wrote in his draft jottings for the Theses of 20 January, 'to lose Poland *plus* Lithuania *plus* Courland *plus* etc, or to lose the socialist revolution in Russia?'[63] It was not the loss of Poland which disturbed the Left Communists, but the connivance by socialist Russia at imperialist aggression, implicit in the signing of the peace treaty with Germany. Moreover, along with the emotional demand for 'revolutionary war', there was also dissatisfaction among a number of bolshevik intellectuals with the whole trend of Lenin's policy. But the identification in the popular mind of the policy of Lenin's opponents inside the party with a 'holy war'—the advocacy of which, after the peace had been signed, became increasingly unrealistic—suited Lenin well. He himself never failed, when opportunity presented itself, to describe their programme in such terms. Bukharin and his group were nicknamed the 'holy men' in the party. This over-simplification of left communism served the purpose of diverting attention from the more fundamental parts of their criticism. Meanwhile, however, the differences within the party were not debated outside party circles. In the Central Executive Committee on the night of 23/24 February acceptance of the onerous German terms was voted by 116 to 84, with 26 abstentions. On 3 March 1918, the Treaty of Brest-Litovsk was signed. Under it Russia lost 27 per cent of her

list of members!) For the resolution, which Lenin attacked in his article 'The Strange and the Monstrous,' see *Lenin* (1), Vol. XV, pp. 109–10.
    [61] *Sed'moy syezd*, p. 105.
    [62] See, for example, Lenin's note of Yakovleva's speech in *Leninskiy sbornik*, Vol. XI, p. 43.   [63] *ibid.*, p. 38.

sown area, 26 per cent of her population, a third of her average crops, three quarters of her iron and coal, and 26 per cent of her railway network.[64]   Lenin thus achieved his main object, the peace.   But serious dissension inside the party still lay ahead.

[64] From official calculations made somewhat later, quoted in *Dennis*, p. 40.

PART II

THE FATE OF THE OPPOSITION PARTIES

CHAPTER VII

THE LEFT SOCIALIST REVOLUTIONARIES

At the time of the bolshevik revolution the left wing of the Socialist Revolutionaries offered its support to the Bolsheviks and soon after set itself up as a separate political party. In December 1917 its members formed a coalition with the new ruling party; on 6 July of the following year they were fighting the Bolsheviks in the streets of Moscow and Petrograd. These Socialist Revolutionaries had been won over to the Bolsheviks by their resolute policies on peace and on the land question. The gulf between the non-marxist Socialist Revolutionaries and the Bolsheviks was in reality far greater than that between the marxist internationalist Mensheviks and the Bolsheviks. Yet, carried away by enthusiasm in which emotion predominated over reason, the more extreme Socialist Revolutionaries attempted a union which the greater foresight of Martov's left menshevik group realized was impossible.

The Left Socialist Revolutionaries originated during the war when a small number of Socialist Revolutionaries revolted against the support of national defence which the majority of their party advocated. The veteran Natanson and Victor Chernov had been very close to the Zimmerwald Left. Soon after the February Revolution dissatisfaction with the policy of their party leaders led to the growth of a vocal, and ever increasing, socialist revolutionary left wing, which at times spoke the same language as the Bolsheviks. Natanson, the peasant leader with the face of a rabbi, headed this left wing and became one of the founders of the new party.[1]   Chernov,

---

[1] Natanson had been for years on the left wing of his party, and was one of the oldest, as well as the most outstanding, socialist revolutionary figures. *Wolfe* (p. 389) suggests that the way for a coalition between the Left Socialist Revolutionaries and the Bolsheviks may already have been paved by co-operation

however, disappointed the expectations of the left by taking office in the Provisional Goverment on his return from exile to Petrograd, and by vainly endeavouring to maintain within his party a rapidly diminishing centre. Another left leader was Maria Spiridonova, who had captured popular imagination in 1906 when as a young girl she had assassinated a provincial governor responsible for the suppression of peasant revolts. Her popularity among the peasants was almost legendary. Among the younger left leaders were Boris Kamkov (Katz) and V. A. Karelin.

At the Third Congress of the Socialist Revolutionaries in Moscow, on 18 May 1917, the left wing, including Spiridinova, Natanson, Kamkov, Proshyan, and Steinberg, demanded a programme of no coalition with the bourgeois parties, an all-socialist government, an immediate peace, and socialization of land. Early in July they published a declaration that the official policy of their party was calculated to alienate the masses, and would tend to 'transfer the centre of party support to that part of the population which, by reason of its class composition, cannot stimulate a policy of real, revolutionary socialism'.[2] When the Provisional Government after July reintroduced the death penalty at the front, the left wing of the Socialist Revolutionaries drew even closer to the Bolsheviks, who at that time in common with all Russian socialist parties were still opposed to the death penalty.[3] By August the socialist revolutionary left wing could command well over a third of the votes at a party conference, and the Petrograd organization of Socialist Revolutionaries went over in its entirety to the left. The first open revolt of the socialist revolutionary left wing took place on 28 October, in the Council of the Republic (Pre-Parliament). Its members declared that

between the more extreme members of the socialist revolutionary party and the fighting groups for expropriation and hold-ups which Lenin secretly maintained. Natanson spent some years after 1905 in Baku, the centre of this activity, and may therefore have had the opportunity of co-operating in these exploits with the Bolshevik Krasin, who was the brain behind them.

[2] See a manuscript essay by Miss A. Steinberg, 'The Left Social Revolutionaries', in the British Library of Political and Economic Science, at p. 36.

[3] They opposed it throughout up to the seizure of power, and one of the first acts of the Second Soviet Congress was to repeal Kerensky's reimposition of it. If Trotsky is right, Lenin regarded the repeal as madness, and only yielded to the persuasion of Kamenev and Trotsky in view of public feeling, and on the understanding that shooting would nevertheless be resorted to 'when there is no other way'. See his *Lenin*, pp. 133–4.

they would not obey the directions of their party to vote in support of national defence and walked out in a body.[4]   The part played by the Left Socialist Revolutionaries in the October Revolution is difficult to assess.   Eight of their number joined the Military Revolutionary Committee when it was formed on 29 October.   But this committee was ostensibly formed not as the staff of insurrection which it became, but as a link between the Petrograd Soviet and the city garrison.   The presence upon it of non-bolshevik members was of value to the Bolsheviks as camouflage.   Only two days before the Military Revolutionary Committee was formed, the Left Socialist Revolutionaries voted in the Central Executive Committee, together with the right members of their party and with the Mensheviks, for the Menshevik Dan's resolution that 'an insurrection is at the present moment completely inadmissible'.[5]   The bolshevik Central Committee resolved only as late as 6 November to 'enter into conversations and political contact with' the Left Socialist Revolutionaries,[6] and on this same date the Petrograd Left Socialist Revolutionaries were sending out telephone messages to their local organizations warning them not to take part in demonstrations without sanction from Petrograd.[7]   It is possible that there was informal co-operation during the seizure of power,[8] but no bolshevik source has ever admitted it.

The final break between the left wing and the main socialist revolutionary party came on 7 November 1917 when the former refused to leave the Second All-Russian Soviet Congress and decided to throw in their lot with the Bolsheviks.   The left rebels were expelled from the socialist revolutionary party and held their first independent conference, at which 99 local organizations were represented, from 19 to 28 November.   In a somewhat romantic resolution, they proclaimed that as a party they were independent of the Bolsheviks; asserted that 'if the Constituent Assembly will not go with the people it will pass away by itself'; and renounced terror: 'In the Russian Republic a dictatorship, which is a dictatorship of the

---

[4] Steinberg, *Spiridonova*, pp. 172, 178–9.
[5] *Ryabinsky*, p. 99.
[6] *Proletarskaya revolyutsiya*, no. 10 (69), 1927, pp. 296–8.
[7] *Ryabinsky*, p. 170.
[8] Miss Steinberg, *op. cit.* p. 60, suggests that there was such informal co-operation between Natanson and Trotsky.

overwhelming majority of the population, does not shrink from taking repressive measures against the enemies of the Republic. No need exists, however, for a system of terror; and the party rejects it as a threat to the sovereign power of revolutionary democracy.'[9] They were echoing Lavrov, who had visualized the new order as 'sufficiently rational not to need to defend itself by compulsion'.[10]

The alliance of the Left Socialist Revolutionaries with the Bolsheviks, though based on an apparent temporary identity of policy, was founded on sand. The Left Socialist Revolutionaries wanted a broad coalition, the Bolsheviks did not. It was only after all hope was lost of winning over the right wing of their party and the Bolsheviks to form a joint government (without Lenin) that the Left Socialist Revolutionaries finally agreed to enter the bolshevik government.[11] On the peasant question, foundations for co-operation seemed to have been laid when the Bolsheviks, of their own accord,[12] adopted the socialist revolutionary land law. But unlike the Bolsheviks the Left Socialist Revolutionaries were thinking of an equal partnership between the overwhelming majority of peasants (75–80 per cent) and the minority of industrial workers (3–5 per cent), founded on a free exchange of food for goods. Moreover, it seemed obvious to them that peasant support of the Bolsheviks would last no longer than the few months which would be needed to divide up the land. Thereafter, when a 'new life will have to be built on foundations of love and altruism, the Bolsheviks will show themselves bankrupt'. It was for the leading rôle in this new life that Spiridonova cast her party.[13] It was not destined to play it.

Faced, immediately on the assumption of power, with the simultaneous collapse of industry and a catastrophic drop in grain supplies to the towns,[14] the Bolsheviks declared a crusade

---

[9] Quoted from the Protocols of the Conference by Miss Steinberg, *op. cit.*, pp. 63–6.

[10] P. Lavrov, *Gosudarstvennyy element v budushchem obshchestve* (1876), p. 175 of the edition published in Petrograd in 1920.

[11] See Chapter V.

[12] According to Lenin. Kamkov (*Kto takie levye s-r-y-*, p. 8) claims that it was only adopted under pressure from his party.

[13] Steinberg, *Spiridonova*, pp. 184–5.

[14] Supplies of grain to the state-purveying institutions dropped from 641,000 tons in November 1917 to 136,000 in December, and to 46,000 in January 1918 (*Prokopovicz*, p. 88).

of compulsory confiscation against the peasants, and relentless war against the illegal private trade which sprang up between the towns and villages. The excesses and cruelties committed in the execution of this policy created in the first few months such a gulf between the Bolsheviks and the Left Socialist Revolutionaries as would alone have sufficed to make co-operation between them impossible.[15] Nor was there ever complete accord between the two parties on the question of the use of force generally. The Left Socialist Revolutionaries insisted, apparently against Lenin's opposition, on having their representatives on the *Vecheka*, in order to exercise some control over its activities.[16] They therefore shared the responsibility for the excesses of that body, though they did—to the growing exasperation of Lenin—endeavour to moderate some of them.[17] Relations between the two parties were already near breaking point by 26 February 1918 when, as the results of the efforts of the left socialist revolutionary Commissar of Justice, Steinberg, an inquiry into charges of corruption against two members of the *Vecheka* was set afoot. The two were cleared, because of difficulty in obtaining evidence, and the Council of People's Commissars passed a resolution denouncing Steinberg's inquiry as part of the 'campaign of lying and slander by the agents of the bourgeoisie against the Soviet Government'.[18] However, the Left Socialist Revolutionaries had the doubtful satisfaction of knowing that the death penalty did not officially exist during the short time in which they shared the responsibility for government. Its official restoration on 16 June 1918, followed by the first death sentence pronounced by a Revolutionary Tribunal on 21 June 1918 (on Admiral Shchastny), met with

[15] For the left socialist revolutionary criticism of bolshevik policy on the land see extracts from Spiridonova's speech at the Fifth Congress of Soviets on 5 July 1918, reprinted in *Bunyan*, pp. 205 ff.; and Kamkov's vigorous pamphlet *Organicheskiy nedug* (written in 1919). The Bolsheviks found it convenient (as communist and pro-communist historians have found it since) to allege, without any justification in fact, that socialist revolutionary criticism of bolshevik land policy was motivated by a desire to champion the richer peasants.

[16] Steinberg, *Als ich Volkskommissar war*, pp. 91–2. Aleksandrovich was appointed.

[17] If they can be blamed for not resisting more actively the ever-increasing bolshevik lawlessness at a time when they were still in a position to do so, it is to their credit that one of their few leaders to escape, Steinberg, later admitted this failure in moral courage. See *Nravstvennyy lik revolyutsii*, p. 31 (1923).

[18] Steinberg *Als ich Volkskommissar war*, p. 136; *Leninskiy sbornik*, Vol. XXI, pp. 116–17.

violent opposition from them.[19] Lenin, not unnaturally, taunted them with the fact that, having for some time past condoned the 'shootings in Dzerzhinsky's commission' (the *Vecheka*) they were now objecting to an open sentence by a court.[20] But it was characteristic of this quixotic party that it could accept as a temporary evil political terror against the 'enemies of the revolution', while rejecting any revival of the trappings of the tyrant state.

The break between the two parties came over the peace with Germany. The wide gulf which separated the Left Socialist Revolutionaries from even the Left Communists was evident from the policy which each adopted towards the peace when once it had been signed. The Left Communists went no further than to claim the right to voice their disapproval of it inside the communist party, as an opposition group. The Left Socialist Revolutionaries bitterly reproached them for this 'sacrifice, in the name of party unity, of the very reason for the party's existence'.[21] At the Fourth All-Russian Soviet Congress, which met in March 1918 to ratify the peace treaty, the Left Communists, some 68 in all, merely abstained from the vote.[22] The Left Socialist Revolutionaries in contrast voted against the peace. It was the end of their short and precarious coalition with the Communists. On 19 March they resigned from the Council of People's Commissars in order not to be parties to the ratification of the treaty. Henceforward they saw their mission as a return to the people 'to continue among them the struggle which was now destined not to cease, but to take on a new and grimmer form'.[23] When once the peace had been signed and ratified, the Left Communists' demand for a 'revolutionary war' very soon subsided.[24] The Left Socialist Revolutionaries, on the contrary grew even louder in their clamour for it. But to them, rooted in the peasant tradition, it meant something quite different from what it meant to Bukharin and his followers. The Left Communists were thinking of a battle in which the flower of the revolutionary proletariat would go forth to resist the imperialist aggressor, or die in the attempt. The Left Socialist Revolu-

---

[19] And from Martov—see his *Doloy smertnuyu kazn'* written after the sentence.
[20] *Lenin*, Vol. XXIII, p. 124.   [21] *La Russie socialiste*, p. 28.
[22] *ibid.*, p. 24; they also published a declaration in *Kommunist* of 19 March 1918.
[23] Steinberg, *Als ich Volkskommissar war*, p. 250.   [24] See Chapter VIII.

tionaries demanded 'not a war but a rising', a spontaneous insurrection of the dark peasantry from beneath the feet of the conqueror; not nation against nation, but the infuriated peasant against the invader. 'Let the Germans advance, let them conquer all Russia—they will only conquer a hundred million rebels'.[25] There was a measure of Slav patriotism in their enthusiasm, not unmixed with memories of the *Narodnik* faith in the liberating mission of the revolt of the peasants. These feelings found expression in Blok's poem, 'The Scythians', which was first published in a left socialist revolutionary paper on 20 February, two days after the resumption of the German attack.[26] In this poem the Slav mission of world brotherhood is linked to a prophecy of the end that awaits the 'savage Hun'. Its language is very different from the reasoned marxism of Bukharin or Obolensky. Nevertheless for a short time the Left Socialist Revolutionaries seemed to have believed that a coalition between them and the Left Communists, headed by Pyatakov and Bukharin, could provide a basis for an alternative Soviet government to lead the revolutionary war. At the end of February and at the beginning of March they made tentative approaches to Pyatakov and Bukharin, and possibly to Radek, for the formation of such a coalition government. The suggestion was also made on one of these occasions that Lenin should be arrested for twenty-four hours while war was declared on Germany.[27]

[25] Steinberg, *Als ich Volkskommissar war*, p. 243. (The last eight words are a quotation from Hervé, the most uncompromising pacifist in the Second International).

[26] *Znamya truda*, 20 (7) February 1918. It was written on 29 and 30 January —see A. Blok, *Polnoe sobranie stikhotvoreniy*, Vol. I, p. 678. It was the last poem of importance which Blok wrote before his death in 1921. In addition to Blok, Andrey Bely, Esenin, Remizov, and Kluev contributed to the left socialist revolutionary papers. Together with R. Ivanov-Razumnik they formed in 1917 a literary group known as *Skify* ('the Scythians')—see the latter's *Pisatel'skie sud'by*, New York, 1951, p. 3.

[27] See a letter in *Pravda*, of 3 January 1924, signed by Pyatakov, Stukov, Radek, Yakovleva, V. M. Smirnov, Pokrovsky, Preobrazhensky, Sherudin, and Maksimovsky, all former Left Communists; and a letter by Bukharin in the same issue confirming their version as 'substantially correct'. It is unlikely that these approaches were treated seriously at the time by the Left Communists, who could have had few illusions on the prospect of coalition between Bolsheviks and Socialist Revolutionaries after the experience of the last few months. In any case the moment for such a coalition, if it was ever contemplated, had passed by the middle of March, at the latest, when the rank and file of the Bolsheviks were won over to support of the peace.

The foreign policy of the Communists after the peace had been signed played a big part in fanning the flame of left socialist revolutionary indignation. Secret diplomacy and the playing off of one adversary against the other were an inevitable consequence of Brest-Litovsk, even if in 1918 these violations of socialist principles could still be justified as a temporary expedient—until the international revolution 'inevitably comes to our aid', though this was happening 'immeasurably more slowly than we expected'.[28] But the plain fact was that in 1918, with their army gone, the Communists were at the mercy of the Germans. They manœuvred for survival accordingly. It fell to Trotsky, in his new capacity as Commissar for War, to conduct the tentative negotiations for Allied aid which continued even after the treaty of peace had been signed. That Trotsky was ready to go quite a long way in these efforts to secure Allied aid is attested by witnesses as different as Colonel Robins and Mr. (now Sir) R. H. Bruce Lockhart.[29] Thus, it was with the co-operation of the Communists that the first British landings in Murmansk were carried out in the spring of 1918. It is evident from Lenin's vote at the Central Committee meeting of 22 February that it was in no way inconsistent with his policy to accept the aid of one lot of 'brigands' against another. But this policy did not prove a success. It achieved little in terms of positive Allied help, it exasperated the Germans, and it risked rallying the local anti-communists to the Allies, and against the Communists, as indeed happened in Murmansk. The Germans were not slow to exploit their advantage. By the end of April their troops were advancing on Orel, Kursk, and Voronezh, in disregard of the treaty. The Communists approached the Germans to discover what their demands were.[30] One of the results of these talks was a radical change for the worse in relations with the forces of the Allied Powers who were then in

[28] See Lenin's speech to the Central Executive Committee on 14 May, *Protokoly VTSIK V*, p. 263.
[29] See a letter from Bruce Lockhart to Robins, dated 5 May 1918, quoted in *Hard*, pp. 202–03.
[30] See *Chicherin*, p. 9. The negotiations did not start until the end of May. Milyukov suggests, from private information, that the Germans had already concerted a plot with anti-Communists to seize Moscow, fixed for mid-June, and that the plan was suddenly called off on 18 June—see P. Milyukov, *Rossiya na perelome*, Vol. II, pp. 20–3.

Murmansk with Russian connivance.   As has so often happened
in the history of communist inner-party warfare, this reversal
of policy was later used to discredit Trotsky, who is now portrayed as having plotted behind Lenin's back to open up
Russia to Allied invasion.   Nevertheless, it is possible that
Trotsky, whose opposition to the peace was certainly stronger
than that of the diehard defeatists like Lenin, Stalin, Sverdlov,
or Zinoviev, may have had some friction with his colleagues at
the time on the question of accepting Allied aid.[31]   Another
consequence of the talks with the Germans and of the resulting
change in Russian policy was the negotiation with the Germans
on the fate of the Black Sea Fleet.   A flood of rumours and
suspicions soon began to sweep the country—some true, some
not—and fanned popular excitement.   There was widespread
belief that the full measure of Russian submission to the
Germans had not been made public, that there were secret
terms in the Brest-Litovsk treaty foreshadowing still greater
humiliation for Russia, and that the Communists were going
to hand over the fleet.   The attempt of the Communists to
quell these rumours by force only added to the belief that there
was some truth in them.   One of the charges on which Admiral
Shchastny of the Baltic Fleet was condemned to death on
21 June was that he had claimed to possess documents showing
a secret agreement between the Communists and the Germans
to hand over the Baltic Fleet.[32]   The true course of relations
between the Communists and the Germans in the few months
between the peace treaty and the German collapse is not easy
to determine with accuracy.   There is no evidence, and it is
certainly unlikely, that there were secret clauses to the main

[31] One document, if genuine, lends support to this view.   This is a record of
a telephone conversation between Stalin and Yur'ev of the Murmansk Soviet,
probably dated some time in mid 1918, when Stalin was urging a more vigorous
anti-allied policy.   Yur'ev then referred to Trotsky's original telegram in the
spring, which had urged full co-operation with the allied force.   Stalin's reply
is of interest: 'Trotsky's telegram has nothing to do with the case.   It won't help
matters and we are not proposing to look for scapegoats'—see *Kedrov*, p. 42.   See
ibid., p. 119, for another document of the period, published as part of the campaign against Trotsky, an angry note from Lenin, of early June, stressing that
Soviet policy is 'equally hostile to the British and to the Germans'.

[32] See the sentence reprinted in *Kozhevnikov*, pp. 54–5, and see *Izvestiya* of
16 June 1918 and 21 June 1918 for the indictment and report of the trial.
Admiral Shchastny was refused the right to call witnesses in his defence.   For
Trotsky's evidence against him, see his *Kak vooruzhalas' revolyutsiya*, Vol. I,
pp. 136–41.   Shchastny's revolt was undoubtedly motivated by the belief that
the Baltic Fleet was to be handed over to the Germans.   See *Fedotoff-White*, p. 72.

treaty of Brest-Litovsk of 3 March 1918. On the other hand, it is clear that every endeavour was made to keep some of the concessions made to the Germans after June 1918 secret, and there was undoubtedly a secret exchange of notes attached to the supplementary peace treaty of 27 August 1918. But while making concessions, the Communists at the same time made efforts to hoodwink the Germans, sometimes with success, as the case of the Black Sea Fleet reveals. At the end of April the fleet, then at Sebastopol, had been moved to Novorossiysk to evade capture by the Germans. The Germans demanded its return, claiming that the departure was a violation of article 5 of the treaty of Brest-Litovsk, and an ultimatum threatening a new military advance was issued on 10 June. Thereafter, according to the Communists, the fleet decided to return to Sebastopol, and was only dissuaded and induced to scuttle by the energies of Raskol'nikov who had been sent there to deal with the situation. But the version widely believed inside Russia at the time was that the communist commissars endeavoured to force the fleet to comply with the German demands, and that the patriotism of the sailors succeeded in defeating their efforts and in scuttling a part of it. Some documents relating to the Black Sea Fleet published later in Berlin, if genuine, show that the Communists did to some extent hoodwink the Germans, by sending orders in clear to the fleet to return to Sebastopol, and at the same time sending an order in secret cipher to scuttle. A part of the fleet was scuttled, and part returned to Sebastopol. However, the official announcement, on 22 June 1918, that the Russians had exacted a guarantee from the Germans that the vessels which had returned to Sebastopol would not be used 'by Germany or her allies during the war' was probably untrue. At any rate, in the secret Exchange of Notes appended to the supplementary peace treaty of 27 August 1918 it was provided with regard to these vessels that 'in case of war necessity they might also be used for military purposes.'[33]

---

[33] For the documents published in Berlin, of which the source is not indicated, see *Arkhiv russkoy revolyutsii*, Vol. XIV, pp. 151-221, especially at pp. 216-17. Chicherin's announcement is in *Izvestiya* of 22 June 1918. The secret exchange of notes was published, from the German archives, in 1926 in *Europäische Gespräche* at pp. 148-53. See also A.P. Platonov, *Fevral' i oktyabr' v chernomorskom flote*, Chapter XIV.

These events had a considerable impact on the Left Socialist Revolutionaries, who had a fairly large following both in the Baltic and Black Sea Fleets. Between May and July their temper rose rapidly. By the end of June they were openly calling for an armed rising against the Germans and for the expulsion of the German Ambassador, von Mirbach. They were also conducting intensive agitation inside the army. Passions were so high that even Spiridonova, who had for long opposed any final split with the Communists, was now converted to this step. On 24 June the left socialist revolutionary Central Committee resolved 'in the interest of the Russian and the international revolutions' to 'organize a series of terrorist acts against the leading representatives of German imperialism'. It was not a secret resolution. 'We regard our policy', the Central Committee stated, 'as an attack on the present policy of the Soviet government, not as an attack on the Bolsheviks themselves.' But since 'it is possible that the Bolsheviks may take aggressive counter-action against our party, we are determined in such an event to defend the position we have taken up by force of arms. In order to prevent our party in the event of such a clash from being exploited by counter-revolutionary elements, it is resolved to announce our new policy far and wide in our propaganda and to urge the need for a firm and consistent internationalist social-revolutionary policy in Soviet Russia.'[34] Quixotic to the end, this party fought its battles alone. No scrap of evidence has ever been adduced to show any contacts between the Left Socialist Revolutionaries and the Allied Powers.

When the Fifth All-Russian Congress of Soviets met on 4 July, the Left Socialist Revolutionaries, who formed about one-third of the Congress (and according to Spiridonova would, with genuine elections, have formed more) were on the verge of revolt.[35] On 6 July the German Ambassador was assassinated in his embassy by Blyumkin, a left socialist revolutionary member of the *Vecheka*, with the connivance of other Left Socialist Revolutionaries. The bolshevik members of the *Vecheka*, Dzerzhinsky, Latsis, and Smidovich, rushed to the

[34] *Krasnaya kniga Vecheka*, a rare publication by the *Vecheka* of its interrogations on the plots and risings of 1918, withdrawn soon after publication, pp. 197-9.
[35] There is a graphic account of the Congress in *Bruce Lockhart*, pp. 294-300; see also *Bunyan*, pp. 205-12.

Vecheka headquarters to deal with the situation and were kept under arrest by the Left Socialist Revolutionaries. Although the troops at the disposal of the latter only numbered a few hundred,[36] the Communists were quite unprepared, and had few forces in Moscow beyond their trusted Lettish riflemen to deal with the situation. But there was in truth no serious preparation and no real attempt at seizure of power. The few troops at the disposal of the Left Socialist Revolutionaries remained as a bodyguard for their Central Committee, though a detachment of fifteen soldiers led by Proshyan did succeed in seizing the telegraph office and sending off a few telegrams to the provinces calling on them to disregard orders signed by Lenin. No attempt was made to seize any other strategic point in the city. The revolt was put down in a few hours in both Moscow and Petrograd, with a few dozen casualties. Spiridonova denied that any rising had been planned and claimed that what happened was 'mainly a result of the excitement with which the Russian government rushed to the defence of the assassinated agent of German imperialism and of an attempt at self-defence' on the part of the Left Socialist Revolutionaries.[37] She immediately accepted responsibility for the assassination. The entire delegation of the Left Socialist Revolutionaries to the Soviet Congress was arrested, though some of its members were later released. The Communists also arrested all members of the left socialist revolutionary Central Committee who did not succeed in escaping, while the *Vecheka* shot Aleksandrovich, a left socialist revolutionary member of the *Vecheka*, and a number of sailors, who had supported the Left Socialist Revolutionaries, but not Blyumkin, who escaped. But these were apparently measures of panic. At all events no one else was shot for the time being, and for

---

[36] 600–800 according to the Left Socialist Revolutionaries. See *Krasnaya kniga Vecheka*, pp. 197 ff. According to Trotsky, quoting Vatsetis, who was responsible for putting down the rising, the L.S.R.'s had 800–2,000 men, 4–8 guns, and 60 machine-guns. A detachment of 300–400 on its way to Moscow from the Western front regions was also disarmed by the Communists (*O myatezhe levykh S-Rov*, pp. 34, 38).

[37] *Krasnaya kniga*, p. 321. An account of the event by A. Minichev in *krasnaya letopis'*, No. 1 (25), 1928, pp. 65–9, also confirms that there was no planned rising. In a private letter from prison later Spiridonova wrote: 'How is one to persuade them that there was no plot, no rising? . . . I am beginning to believe they have convinced themselves of it . . . and now believe it. After all they are maniacs.' See *Kreml' za reshetkoy*, p. 13. See also Steinberg, *Spiridonova*, pp. 214 ff., for an account of the July events.

some months thereafter the Germans kept complaining that the Communists had failed to take adequate measures against the guilty.[38] But if the Communists hesitated in July 1918 to provoke public temper by excessive reprisals for a popular assassination, the rising came opportunely to give them an excuse for putting an end to the Left Socialist Revolutionaries as a party. Their press was closed down and their delegates expelled from the All-Russian Congress of Soviets, though the party as a whole was not declared illegal. In the Central Executive Committee on 15 July 1918 a resolution was passed which permitted as representatives on this body (and consequently in the Soviets, since the Central Executive Committee was the apex of the constitutional pyramid) those members of the party who 'categorically renounced their solidarity with the assassination and with the revolt which followed it'.[39] Legally, therefore, those Left Socialist Revolutionaries, and there were very many, who repudiated the action of their Central Committee were after July still entitled to sit in the Soviets. In practice, however, their participation was rendered virtually impossible by the zeal with which they were hounded out of all local organs to which they had secured election. A private letter by Lenin written to the Communists of Elets shortly after the July revolt shows that this policy of the local Communists was not discouraged by the central authorities:

It is a pity [wrote Lenin in this letter] that you have not arrested them [the Left Socialist Revolutionaries of Elets] as is being done everywhere. It is essential to oust all Socialist Revolutionaries from responsible posts . . . we cannot, of course, give you written authorization to arrest Socialist Revolutionaries, but if you drive them out of Soviet organs, if you arrest them and expose them before the workers and peasants and destroy their influence among the peasantry (if they have any) you will be doing good revolutionary work, and we in the centre . . . will only praise you for it.[40]

[38] *Helfferich*, Vol. III, pp. 469–70; when Helfferich, Mirbach's successor, complained at the end of July to Chicherin, he was met with the reply that Russia was a revolutionary state where freedom of speech prevailed and the Soviet government was powerless to take any action (*ibid.*, p. 482). cf. *Lenin*, Vol, XXIII, pp. 257–8, for a German note of 5 November 1918.
[39] *Protokoly VTSIK V*, p. 7.
[40] Quoted in *Lenin*, Vol. XXIII, pp. 560–1, from the memoirs of one Grodner, a Bolshevik of Elets, who had come up to Moscow to explain to Lenin certain

There seems to have been little hesitation in following Lenin's advice, even where the Left Socialist Revolutionaries were in the majority, though in some instances, notably in the Petrograd Soviet, their delegates avoided expulsion for many months after July 1918.[41]

Four days after the shooting of von Mirbach, the left socialist revolutionary Commander-in-Chief on the Volga front declared war against the Germans. He was killed at a session of the local Soviet Executive Committee while endeavouring to win over the communist members to his side. In the course of the next few weeks the situation of the Communists became precarious. In the last week of July a rising broke out in Yaroslavl', and other local insurrections followed. Anti-communist forces were advancing into the heart of Russia. Allied troops had landed in Archangel and Siberia. On 30 August an attempt took place on Lenin's life, and Uritsky was assassinated. The Communists inaugurated the mass arrests and executions, accompanied by the suppression of practically all the surviving non-communist newspapers, which became known as the Red Terror. The left socialist revolutionary leaders, however, escaped further reprisals, for the time being. They were a popular party, particularly among the sailors, and public feeling was in too excited a state to risk rousing it further by unduly severe reprisals. Moreover there was good reason to hope that many members of the party might eventually join the Communists. Trotsky may not have been far wrong in his assertion that, in organizing the assassination of von Mirbach their Central Committee had 'acted behind the backs of nine-tenths of the members of the party'.[42] Whatever the reason for this comparative leniency, Natanson was allowed to go abroad, where shortly afterwards he died. When at last on 27 November 1918 a revolutionary tribunal tried the leading members of the left socialist

---

statements in the local press about a left socialist revolutionary meeting which Lenin had criticized, notably the assertion that they enjoyed communist support —and see *ibid.*, p. 172.

[41] For an account of events in Petrograd *guberniya* (province), see A. Kuzmin, in *Krasnaya letopis'*, no. 3 (27), 1928, at p. 246; for the Left Socialist Revolutionaries in the Petrograd Soviet see a spirited illegal leaflet, undated (but apparently after February 1919, in view of the reference to Spiridonova's recent re-arrest, which took place in February 1919), headed 'Otvet fraktsii levykh S-r Petrogradskomu Sovetu na zapros ot 14-go fevralya', in the British Museum.

[42] *Trotsky, KVR*, Vol. I, p. 277.

revolutionary Central Committee, including Kamkov, Karelin, Mayorov, Sablin, Spiridonova, and Blyumkin, the sentences imposed were mild. Three years imprisonment was the
sentence in each case, except for Spiridonova and Sablin, who
were sentenced to one year, but, in view of their services to the
revolution were amnestied a few days later.[43] It is not clear
whether any of the others served their sentences. Blyumkin,
then only eighteen years old, joined the Communists, fought
in the Civil War, and thereafter served under Trotsky, and
in the G.P.U.[44] Proshyan, who had been the most active in
what there was of the rising, died soon after, at liberty, and
Lenin wrote a generous obituary on him. So far as Maria
Spiridonova was concerned, there was good reason to avoid
any provocative action, as she was too popular among the
peasants.[45] After her trial she immediately threw herself
into a campaign of public meetings up and down the country
sometimes even debating with communist speakers.

The July revolt of the Left Socialist Revolutionaries caused a
break-up in their party. The more extreme leaders, including
Kamkov and Irina Kakhovskaya, formed an underground
terrorist group, which some time later successfully organized
the assassination by Boris Donskoy of Eichorn, the German
Commander in the Ukraine. Some other minor revolts were
also organized by extremists, especially inside the army and
navy, but they had been hastily improvised and were easily
put down. In October 1918 a demonstration of young sailors
of the Second Baltic Fleet, protesting against the peace with
Germany as well as against the terror, was dispersed without
difficulty, and achieved little more than to throw Zinoviev
into a panic. Later in the year a more serious attempted
military coup d'état near Kursk, involving tens of thousands of

---

[43] See *Krasnaya kniga Vecheka*, pp. 365–7. The date of the amnesty as shown
on p. 367 of the typescript copy of this work in the Hoover War Library, 29 November 1919, is an error for 29 November 1918. Sverdlov, whose signature appears
on it, was dead in November 1919. I have not been able to trace the date of
Blyumkin's arrest or surrender.

[44] He was shot in December 1929, without trial, one of the first victims of the
anti-Trotskyist reprisals.

[45] There is an account by Emma Goldman in *My Disillusionment in Russia*
(Chapter XVI) of her visit to Spiridonova, then in hiding, in the middle of 1920,
in which letters to her from the peasants are quoted. cf. a *Vecheka* circular
instruction of June 1920 which refers to Spiridonova as 'fairly popular' among the
peasant masses—*Sotsialisticheskiy vestnik*, 5 April 1921, pp. 12–13.

troops, was put down by one battalion of the Red Army. In 1919 an explosion at the Moscow Communist Headquarters, organized by extremist Left Socialist Revolutionaries (and some Anarchists) as a protest against communist terrorist methods, caused some casualties and succeeded in wounding Bukharin.[46] But such incidents were the work of a minority. The majority of the party repudiated von Mirbach's assassination and attempted to keep peace with the Communists. It was with this end in view that a number of prominent Left Socialist Revolutionaries helped to form the two splinter parties which came into existence after July 1918, and which will be described later.[47]

On 18 February 1919, Spiridonova was re-arrested together with a large number of Left Socialist Revolutionaries. The press carried the story of the discovery of a left socialist revolutionary plot. In the trial which followed Spiridonova was sentenced to be banished for one year from political and social life, and isolated in a sanatorium, where she was to be 'given an opportunity for healthy mental and physical work'. The conditions in the 'sanatorium' were such that it was only a successfully organized escape which saved her from dying of consumption. She then went into hiding until October 1920, when she was arrested for the last time, and nothing is now known of her fate.[48]

Deprived of their press and eventually of representation in the soviets, the Left Socialist Revolutionaries played virtually no part as a legal opposition during 1919. In the spring of 1920 a small group of the party including Steinberg, succeeded in acquiring legal status. They were allowed again for a short time to publish their periodical (*Znamya*) a privilege which had long been denied to almost every party other than the communist. Six issues appeared in 1920 and three up to May 1921. The tone of this last voice of left socialist revolutionary legal opposition was mild and academic. It looked forward to the withering away of the state,

---

[46] See *Voennoe delo*, no. 3 (32), 31 January 1919, p. 174; Il'in-Zhenevsky, *Bol'sheviki u vlasti*, pp. 145–6; and I. Flerovsky in *Proletarskaya revolyutsiya*, 1926, no. 55 (8), pp. 218 ff., for the revolt of the Baltic sailors; and for the Moscow explosion see M. M. Pokrovsky, *Oktyabr'skaya revolyutsiya*, pp. 362–8; *Krasnaya kniga Vecheka*, pp. 391 ff., and *Pravda*, 6 November 1919.

[47] See Chapter IX.

[48] Steinberg, *Spiridonova*, Part IV, Chapters III to VI.

and saw the practical solution of current problems in a federation of all productive forces controlled by the trade unions, including unions of the labouring peasantry, and in a system of distribution controlled by the co-operatives. There was also some cautious discussion of the 'limits of the use of violence in the revolutionary struggle'.[49] At the end of the year, in December 1920, Steinberg was summoned (with a 'consultative voice') to the Eighth Congress of Soviets to read a rather vapid declaration, calling on the peasants and workers to 'rise above the temporary and historically accidental difficulties of the present phase of the revolution' and look forward to the great future of the Russian and world revolutions.[50] However, this temporary reconciliation did not survive the Kronstadt rising, three months later. The mass arrests which took place at this time effectively put an end to this remnant of the party. Steinberg almost alone among the leaders of the party escaped arrest and eventually left Russia. Izmailovich, Kakhovskaya, and Mayorov were last heard of in exile in the Urals in the thirties. The ghosts of Kamkov and Karelin made a brief appearance at the trial of Bukharin in 1938.[51] As late as 1922 there were still isolated Left Socialist Revolutionaries in some soviets, including the Moscow Soviet, but the party had long ceased to be of any significance.

The Left Socialist Revolutionaries were thus forced out of existence, but they nevertheless escaped more lightly than the other opposition parties. The total of their leading members shot by the Communists up to 1921 was only 26, while four died in prison.[52] Perhaps this comparative tolerance was based on the belief that they could be attracted sooner or later into the communist fold. Certainly, many did join the communist party, and it appears that the *Vecheka* drew a number of its recruits from among them.[53] Perhaps it was due to this expectation of winning the younger members over to

[49] *Znamya*, no. 1 (3), April 1920. This periodical first reappeared legally early in 1919, but was closed down after two issues (see *Postnikov*, p. 392).
[50] *Vs. syezd VIII*, pp. 120–3.
[51] See Chapter VIII.
[52] *Kreml' za reshetkoy*, pp. 205–8, 214–16.
[53] The *Vecheka* instruction referred to in Note 45 directs that all Left Socialist Revolutionaries are to be sent to Moscow on arrest, in view of the fact that many of them can be recruited for work in the *Cheka*. The Left Socialist Revolutionaries formed the largest number of political inmates of the Moscow Butyrki prison in April 1920.

communism that, as late as June 1922, when the surviving leaders of their party were banished or imprisoned for life, a trial was held of seven young party members. The accused were all under 26, and the sentences imposed very light, in some cases even conditional, amounting to an immediate acquittal.[54] No doubt the Communists hoped by their display of leniency to attract the few remaining heirs of the *Narodniki* still at liberty into their party.

The political evolution of the Left Socialist Revolutionaries from November 1917 until July 1918 need not have surprised anyone. The Left Socialist Revolutionaries were romantic absolutists, but they were not marxists. They were a peasant party, and their intellectual tradition was that of Lavrov and Bakunin. They were drawn to the Bolsheviks because they promised a socialist utopia, a revolution which was apparently going to follow the separate path so dear to the *Narodniki*—one which would lead backward Russia straight to socialism without the intermediate Western capitalist phase. The gulf between marxists and non-marxists was bridged because the marxists in 1917 appeared to be following a line which was far removed from marxism. The Left Socialist Revolutionaries were of course internationalists like the Bolsheviks, but their internationalism was not unmixed with Slav patriotism. What attracted them in Lenin's internationalism was the 'revolutionary war', when (as they pictured it) the dark peasant masses would rise in a vast spontaneous and passionate revolt, perhaps not unlike that hoped for by Bakunin, and the example of the Slavs would light a torch of freedom for all the oppressed peoples of the world. They broke with Lenin in 1918 not because they had changed, but because the Lenin of 1918 bore little relationship in their eyes to the Lenin of 1917. And the Left Socialist Revolutionaries were before all else idealists. It was this quality which attracted to them many of the poets who had before the revolution attached themselves to left wing socialist revolutionary circles, without joining any political party, among them Alexander Blok and Sergey Esenin. The same idealism drew them on to bolshevism, and was in turn the cause of their revulsion from it. Blok saw the figure of Christ leading a detachment

[54] Steinberg, *Spiridonova*, pp. 275–80.

of Red Guards in his poem *The Twelve*, only to fall soon after the October Revolution into bitter, disillusioned silence for the remaining years of his life.   The peasant Esenin similarly drew very close to Bolshevik circles for a short time after the revolution.   The following lines from one of his best poems, written in 1918, typify the emotional attraction which bolshevism held for the more immature Socialist Revolutionaries:

> I do not want a heaven which has no way up to it
> I am ready today with hands firm as steel
> To overturn the whole world. . . .

Esenin, unlike Blok, did not remain silent.[55]   Lenin's bolshevik followers, for all their doubts and differences, supported Lenin in the end because they knew that without him they had no chance of survival in power.   The Left Socialist Revolutionaries were inconsistent, romantic, unrealistic, and politically naïve to the point of childishness.   But they did not sacrifice their principles to power.

[55] On Esenin see his *Stikhotvoreniya, 1910–1925*, Paris, n.d., pp. 5–19.   For a moving account of Blok's last years and his bitter remorse regarding *The Twelve*, see G. Ivanov, *Peterburgskie zimy*, New York, 1952, pp. 208–10.

CHAPTER VIII

LEFT COMMUNISM

The bolshevik opponents of Lenin's peace policy kept to their agreement with the Central Committee. They made no public pronouncements until after the treaty with Germany had been signed. But they opened their campaign as an opposition group inside the party at the Seventh Party Congress of the Bolsheviks, which met from 6 to 8 March 1918. Hastily convened, it represented less than half the total party membership. The strength of opposition within the party to the official peace policy was undoubtedly at that date considerably stronger than the final voting in favour of Lenin's resolution approving the peace indicated, thirty votes against eleven, with four abstentions.[1] Bukharin was the main spokesman for the left opposition, and the author of the minority resolution. This resolution called for a revolutionary war 'by flying partisan detachments' in the early stages, and gradually drawing to its side the proletariat and the poorer peasantry. Meanwhile, both intensive training of the new Red Army and the most active international propaganda should aim to draw the proletariat of the world to the side of Russia. Lenin's argument that the peace would provide a breathing space for peaceful reconstruction was an illusion, according to Bukharin. There could be no peaceful co-existence in any circumstances between the Soviet Republic and international capital: either Germany would crush Russia, or the capitalist states would partition her by agreement among themselves. The vanguard of the party was ready for the struggle, but the present peace policy was a capitulation to the lowest level of the demoralized

---

[1] Only 135,000 out of a total membership of 300,000 were represented. The 69 delegates of the Seventh Congress should be contrasted with the 264 of the Sixth, and the 403 of the Eighth. The percentage of workers among delegates was also remarkably low, 13–14 per cent in 1918, compared with 40 per cent and 35 per cent in 1917 and 1919—see *Bubnov*, pp. 512, 621. At a Moscow Party Conference on 4 March Pokrovsky's opposition resolution gathered 46 votes against Zinoviev's 64—see G. Zinoviev, *Sochineniya*, Vol. VII (ii), p. 282. It is perhaps significant that at this meeting Obolensky's resolution which not only opposed the peace, but went on to censure the Central Committee for its conduct, collected only 5 votes.

peasantry. Bukharin was supported by Kollontay (who appears to have been absent from all the crucial meetings of the Central Committee in February) by Ryazanov, Uritsky, Radek, and by several provincial delegates.[2] Again, as in the Central Committee, Lenin used every endeavour to avoid a split in the party, and this was the general feeling of the congress. Bukharin was re-elected to the Central Committee by a large vote, and Uritsky and Lomov were elected as candidates. They attempted to resign, but their resignations were not accepted. In the end the matter was left in abeyance. For some months to come they did not attend any meetings of the Central Committee. In a private memorandum to party members they stated that they did not want to cause a split in the party, but could not serve on the Central Committee and therefore did not consider themselves as members.[3] Trotsky also regarded party unity as the paramount consideration. He expressed his reluctant acceptance of the majority opinion of the congress in face of the possibility of a split in the party. He did not in any way participate in the left communist movement. Having already resigned his position as Commissar for Foreign Affairs before the congress, he was almost immediately appointed Commissar for War, and threw his energies into the building up of the Red Army. The following October, at a moment when revolution seemed imminent in Germany, and Lenin's policy thus appeared to have been justified in the interests of world revolution, his acknowledgement in the Central Executive Committee that at the time of the Brest-Litovsk negotiations he had been wrong and Lenin had been right was greeted with a prolonged ovation.[4]

On one question the congress proved united. Lenin's proposal to change the name of the party from Russian Social Democratic Labour Party (Bolshevik) to Russian Communist Party (Bolshevik), evoked no opposition. The change symbolized a complete break with the socialist parties of the Second International, and with the Russian Mensheviks in particular. In April 1917, Lenin's proposal to make this symbolic change had met with considerable resistance. But in March 1918

---

[2] *Sed'moy syezd*, p. 72.   For the minority resolution, see pp. 200–03; Bukharin's speech, *ibid.*, pp. 35–8, and reply, pp. 48–9.
[3] *Protokoly VII*, pp. 229–30.   [4] *Protokoly VTSIK V*, p. 248.

the break with the socialists was so complete, that in no section of the party were there any remnants of that desire for union of the two wings of social democracy which had still been strong after the February Revolution.

The Seventh Congress also dealt with the question of the party programme, though inconclusively. Lenin's proposal to make changes in it had aroused considerable differences of opinion at the All-Russian Bolshevik Party Conference in May 1917. In the course of 1917, before the October Revolution, the disagreements between Lenin on the one hand and a Moscow group consisting of Bukharin, Lomov, Sokol'nikov and V. M. Smirnov on the other, were developed in a series of pamphlets.[5] Although inconclusive, these early controversies on theoretical questions revealed a difference of outlook between Lenin and the 'Muscovites' which in part explained left communism. From the proposition that a new phase of imperialist wars had been reached in world capitalism, in which future military conflicts were inevitable, the more radical Moscow theorists drew the conclusion that the only solution lay in the victory of the proletariat on an international scale. Accordingly their proposals for the new programme stressed the need to work out one unified programme for the international proletarian party, rather than to concentrate upon the specific needs of the Russian party. The Moscow group were likewise anxious to abandon the division of the programme into a 'minimum' and 'maximum', an immediate and an ultimate part, on the grounds that, since the socialist revolution (as distinct from the middle-class democratic stage) was imminent, the minimum programme was no longer applicable. Lenin's arguments against this Moscow 'utopianism' show the evolution of his ideas, which reached their maturity at the time of the Brest-Litovsk treaty. On 19 October 1917 he wrote:

We do not know whether we shall be victorious tomorrow or a little later (I am personally inclined to think it will be to-

[5] See two collections entitled *Materialy po peresmotru partiynoy programmy*, one published by the Moscow *Oblast'* Bureau, the other in Petrograd with a preface by Lenin. The discussion was also conducted in two periodicals, in *Prosveshchenie*, of which only one issue was published, in Petrograd, and in *Spartak*, of which ten issues were published between June and November 1917 the Moscow by *Oblast'* Bureau.

morrow . . .) We do not know how soon after our victory the revolution in the West will come. . . . Therefore it is ludicrous to jettison the minimum programme, which is *essential* so long as we are living within the framework of the bourgeois order, so long as we have not yet destroyed this framework, and have laid the foundations for the passage to socialism by smashing and destroying the enemy, the bourgeoisie.

And again, in reply to the argument that the programme should be international: 'Until the proletarian revolution has conquered in one country at least' no full scale international conference to decide on a programme is conceivable.[6] A commission on the party programme, appointed on 18 October 1917 and consisting of Lenin, Bukharin, Trotsky, Kamenev, Sokol'nikov, and Kollontay had made no progress, and had been curtailed to Lenin, Bukharin, and Sokol'nikov on 6 February 1918. But divisions of opinion were too sharp for agreement on the programme at the Seventh Congress of the Party. The main doctrines of the Left Communists were developed after the congress and are dealt with below. But one interchange between Lenin and Bukharin in the desultory discussions which took place is of interest. Bukharin's proposal to amend the programme by including in it a reference to the withering away of the state drew a characteristic retort from Lenin: 'At present we are undoubtedly supporters of the state.' The realization of the principle 'from each according to his abilities, to each according to his needs' is still a long way off. 'One may well wonder when the state will begin to wither away. . . . To proclaim this withering away in advance is to violate historical perspective.'[7] A new commission on the party programme was appointed by the Seventh Congress, consisting of Lenin, Trotsky, Bukharin, Sokol'nikov, V. M. Smirnov, Zinoviev, and Stalin,—showing, incidentally, both the growth of Stalin's authority in the party, and the endeavours of the congress to prevent a split in party

---

[6] *Lenin*, Vol. XXI, pp. 311–17.

[7] *Lenin*, Vol. XXII, pp. 364–5. He had changed his mind. Only a month before in Chapter V of his *State and Revolution* (published in February 1918, though written in August and September 1917) he had proclaimed that the state would begin to wither away immediately after the proletarian revolution. Lenin had already crossed swords with Bukharin on this question in Switzerland. For a different interpretation of Lenin's attitude to the state at various times, see *Carr*, I, pp. 248–9.

leadership. A new party programme was finally adopted the following year at the Eighth Party Congress, in March 1919.

However, early in March 1918, the opposition inside the communist party to the peace was rather more extensive than Lenin's easy victory at the Seventh Party Congress might have suggested. A large number of the rank and file, probably a majority, and many leaders opposed it; and yet before long this opposition melted away. In Petrograd a very short period of intensive agitation and discussion inside the party brought about a considerable change in the temper of those party organizations which had largely supported the left wing on the issue of peace. To this conversion Zinoviev, who was an energetic and convincing debater, made an important contribution. Lenin had originally proposed that he should be sent with Ioffe as a delegate to Brest-Litovsk, but at Sverdlov's request he had been retained in Petrograd for the purpose of these party debates.[8] Zinoviev did not confine his activities to Petrograd. On 3 March, accompanied by Sverdlov, he harangued in debate with Pokrovsky, the historian, a vast party audience in the Zimniy Theatre in Moscow. The following day he collected sixty-four votes against forty-six at a party conference in favour of the peace,[9] for which shortly afterwards the committee of the Moscow *rayon* voted by a large majority.[10] On 5 March 1918 there appeared the first number of *Kommunist* published by the Petrograd District Committee of the party, and edited by Bukharin, Radek, and Uritsky. It appeared daily and was devoted to popular agitation for revolutionary war. By 7 March a Petrograd Party Conference had adopted by a large majority a resolution condemning the Left Communists and calling upon them to abandon their 'independent organizational existence'.[11] As a result of this resolution *Kommunist* was forced soon after to cease publication in Petrograd and was transferred to Moscow, where it re-appeared in April under the auspices of the Moscow *Oblast'* Bureau. It was not, of course, only the eloquence of Zinoviev and others which produced this conversion in the

[8] *Protokoly VII*, pp. 212–15.   [9] Zinoviev, *Sochineniya*, Vol. VII (2), p. 282.
[10] *Pravda*, 12 March 1918.
[11] Zinoviev, *Sochineniya*, Vol. VII (i), p. 521. The resolution was adopted by 57 votes to 7—see Yaroslavsky, *Kratkie ocherki*, Vol. II, p. 189.

party. The signing of the treaty and the halting of the German advance, with its promise of certain peace at long last, operated to sway many within the party over to Lenin's side. By 13 March it was already evident that opposition to the peace was on the decline. In the bolshevik 'fraction' meeting which preceded the Fourth All-Russian Congress of Soviets, 453 voted for Lenin's resolution in favour of ratification of the peace treaty, against 36, with 8 abstentions. At the congress, which met between 14 and 18 March, at which Lenin secured an overwhelming majority in favour of ratification of the treaty, the Left Communists merely abstained from voting.[12] On 15 May Lenin won another victory in the stronghold of Left Communism, the Moscow *Oblast'*, when after debate with Lomov at a party conference his resolution was passed by forty-two votes to nine.[13]

But the Left Communists' opposition to Lenin was not confined to the question of the peace of Brest-Litovsk. In the realm of doctrine, the Left Communists jettisoned revolutionary war as a practical policy, but continued for some months after to advocate, in the pages of *Kommunist* and in particular at the First Congress of Councils of National Economy, a more radical socialist policy. When *Kommunist* reappeared in Moscow (its spiritual home) on 20 April it was as a weekly, devoted to theoretical discussion of the foundations of left communism, in contrast to the more popular Petrograd daily. Its editorial board was reinforced by Obolensky and V. M. Smirnov. (Uritsky had remained in Petrograd.) Four numbers appeared in Moscow, between April and June 1918. The official theses of the group appeared in the first Moscow issue of *Kommunist*, over the signatures of the editorial board—Bukharin, Radek, Obolensky, and V. M. Smirnov.[14] Revolutionary war was now completely discarded. But, the Left Communists argued, since the signing of peace had been a capitulation to the less advanced and least revolutionary sections of the proletariat and peasantry, it therefore presented a threat to socialist principles. They saw signs of this threat in the policy which Lenin was now

[12] *Lenin*, Vol. XXII, p. 620. It seems that all the delegates had not yet arrived, for the 'fraction' meeting. See also *B. & F.*, pp. 529–33.
[13] *Lenin*, Vol. XXII, p. 537.
[14] Reprinted in full in *Lenin*, Vol. XXII, pp. 561–71.

advocating—industrial discipline in place of workers' control, the employment of non-communist specialists to build up enterprises brought to a standstill by the excesses of the early months of the revolution, and bargains with the capitalist owners of large-scale industrial enterprises in order to enlist their co-operation. To Lenin's policy of utilizing the breathing space provided by the peace in order to build up the ruined industrial strength of the country, they opposed a demand for radical socialist measures—extensive nationalization, workers' control of industry, no bargains with Russian or foreign capitalists. With some foresight, the left opposition sketched the future as they feared it, should the preservation of what remained of the Soviet state become the main aim of the communist party. The scarcely begun process of socialization would be arrested, 'with the nationalization of the banks incomplete, with a capitalist form of financing undertakings, with only partial nationalization of industrial undertakings, with the prevalence in the countryside of small holdings and properties, with the peasants striving to solve the land question by dividing up the land'. This course, they foretold, would be officially defended by the need to preserve at all costs for the sake of international revolution the power of the Soviet state.

'In such case, all efforts will be directed to the strengthening and development of productive power. . . . In foreign policy aggressive tactics of exposure of the imperialist powers will be replaced by a policy of diplomatic manœuvre by the Russian state amidst the imperialist powers. The Soviet republic will not only conclude trade agreements with them, but will also develop organic economic and political bonds with them, use their military and political support', and take loans from them. In the result, 'in conjunction with the policy of managing undertakings on the principle of the extensive participation of capitalists, and of bureaucratic centralization, there will quite naturally arise a policy towards the workers designed to restore discipline among them under the guise of so-called self-discipline, and the introduction of labour conscription. . . . The form of government must then develop in the direction of bureaucratic centralization, the rule of all manner of commissars, the loss of their independence by the local soviets and rejection in practice of government from below.'

In face of this danger the Left Communists advocated communal farming of the land,[15] and socialist measures in a nationalized industry. Their own future they visualized as a 'businesslike and responsible proletarian opposition'.

The Left Communists did not play this part for long. A fundamental weakness of the left position was the fact that they had to admit that their socialist utopia would be doomed if the revolution in Western Europe did not come to the aid of Russia pretty quickly. V. M. Smirnov in the same April issue of *Kommunist*, wrote of the 'efforts, foredoomed to failure, to build socialism in a side turning off the main highway of European socialism', and in the following issue an anonymous writer concluded that 'socialism cannot be put into operation in one country, and in a backward country at that'.[16] At the First Congress of Councils of National Economy in the following month Obolensky's opposition resolution admitted that the restoration of the normal industrial life of the country was 'unthinkable without co-ordinated support on an international scale'.[17] Yet, while faith in the coming revolution in the West was still strong in May 1918 among most leading Communists, few, if any, were so sanguine as to regard it as imminent. It was perhaps with some justification that Milyutin at the Congress of Councils of National Economy remarked that he had quite expected Obolensky to end his speech with the suggestion that 'we should procure a rope and hang ourselves'.[18]

Another weakness of left communism, which prevented its supporters from gathering around them any effective following against Lenin, was the demonstrable failure of the early

---

[15] There was no thought of communal farms or collectivization during the first months of feverish division of the land. But from the time of the Fundamental Land Law of 19 February 1918 onwards, the encouragement of state and collective farms was a constant aim of communist policy. For a variety of reasons very little advance was made in this field during the first few years. See *Prokopovicz*, pp. 65–75 for the best short account and figures. In July 1918, Bukharin, then in Germany, drew upon himself an attack by Lenin for publishing an article in the Copenhagen *Nachrichtendienst*, which, among other measures, advocated intensified collectivization of land holdings, though in reality the policy advocated by him differed little from the official line. See *Lenin*, Vol. XXIII, pp. 585, 402–3.

[16] Quoted in *Proletarskaya revolyutsiya*, no. 11 (194), 1929, p. 32, and in *Yaroslavsky*, IV, p. 310.

[17] *Trudy VSNKh*, I, p. 88.

[18] *ibid.*, pp. 84–5.

experiments in workers' control of industry.[19] There was point in Bukharin's criticism of Lenin: 'Comrade Lenin has written that in Russia every scullion will be taught to govern the country. It is a good thing to teach a scullion to govern a country. But what will be the result if you put a commissar over the scullion?'[20] Unfortunately every one knew the chaos which resulted if you did not put the commissar over the scullion, and sometimes even if you did. Bukharin and Obolensky further advanced the criticism that Lenin's policy amounted to nothing more nor less than state capitalism; and that unless the masses exercised economic dictatorship, their political dictatorship would inevitably disappear.[21] To this Lenin could reply that where the state embodied the interests and the will of the proletariat, economic control by the state meant economic control by the proletariat. Indeed in 1918 the communist dictatorship still appeared to the Russian proletarian minority as their own dictatorship, in the sense that (as Martov was to say years later) 'they entrusted to this handful of Bolsheviks the task of setting up a communist order which they did not know how to tackle themselves'. The criticism of the Left Communists might more aptly have been directed against the policy, which they had wholeheartedly and without exception supported, of seizing power alone and building socialism by force in a country which was not yet ready for it.

Control of industry by the workers which the Left Communists now demanded had been supported and advocated by the Bolsheviks between March and November 1917 as an effective method of disorganizing the industrial machine, and as a popular slogan to rally the proletariat behind them. It was introduced by the Bolsheviks in the first instance, as Lenin later explained to the Sixth Soviet Congress in 1919, to consolidate the faith of the workers in the revolution,

---

[19] For Lenin's arguments against the Left Communists see especially 'O levom rebyachestve i o melkoburzhuaznosti' ('Left wing childishness and the petty bourgeois outlook') published in *Pravda* on 9 and 11 May 1918, *Lenin*, Vol. XXII, pp. 505 ff.; and his speech on 29 April in the Central Executive Committee, *ibid.*, pp. 471–98.

[20] *Protokoly VTSIK IV*, pp. 233–4.

[21] See *Trudy VSNKh I*, pp. 64–5. cf. quotations from Bukharin's articles in *Kommunist* in an article by A. Sidorov in *Proletarskaya revolyutsiya*, no. 11, 1929, at pp. 46–8.

although, as Lenin admitted, the Bolsheviks well knew that the result could only be chaos.[22] There was no doubt about the chaos, now, in May 1918. The case of the railways will suffice as an illustration. After the seizure of power, the management of the railways remained in the hands of the committee of railwaymen, *Vikzhel*, which, though temporarily placated by the coalition with the Left Socialist Revolutionaries, remained hostile to the Bolsheviks. At an All-Russian Congress of Railwaymen held between 18 January and 12 February 1918, *Vikzhel* had managed to secure a small majority in favour of a resolution supporting the Constituent Assembly. The minority thereupon constituted itself an Extraordinary Russian Congress of Railwaymen, and formed a new Executive Committee, now renamed *Vikzhedor*, of twenty-five Bolsheviks, twelve Left Socialist Revolutionaries and three Menshevik Internationalists. To this committee the overall management of the railways was entrusted, and complete control by the workers decreed on 23 January 1918. Within a few months the railways were in a state of collapse. The 'complete and utter disorganization' was growing daily:

> The workers by present-day rules are guaranteed their pay. The worker turns up at his job . . . does his job, or not, as he pleases, no one can control him, because the [railway repair] shop committees are powerless. If the workshop committee attempts to exercise some control, it is immediately disbanded and another committee elected. In a word, things are in the hands of a crowd, which thanks to its lack of interest in and understanding of production is literally putting a brake on all work.

Ironically enough it fell to Shlyapnikov, the future leader of the Workers' Opposition and advocate of workers' control of industry, to paint this deplorable picture before the Central Executive Committee, and to demand the restoration of work discipline on the railways.[23] On 26 March the Council of People's Commissars centralized control of the railways under

[22] In November 1919, *Lenin*, Vol. XXIII, pp. 250–1. Zagorsky aptly compares the use of workers' control to disintegrate industry with the policy pursued in November and December of completing disintegration of the army. In each case reconstruction had to begin *de novo*, and in each case by methods of centralized discipline.—See *La République des Soviets*, p. 13.

[23] *Protokoly VTSIK IV*, pp. 43–8.

the Commissar of Communications, who was given complete dictatorial powers. Lenin drafted the decree. But the railways were only one instance out of many. The inescapable fact that workers' control had failed was Lenin's strongest argument in winning support for his industrial policy of work discipline, one-man management, and efficient methods of production.

The Left Communists' advocacy of greater initiative for the workers and of less interference by the bureaucracy appeared therefore in 1918 to be a counsel of perfection, but not practical politics. At the May Congress of Councils of National Economy the left were completely routed in the voting, their resolutions being defeated by overwhelming majorities. Their only success was in one of the committees. Smirnov and Obolensky, with the backing of many provincial delegates, especially from the Urals, put through an amendment on industrial management, which gave factory workers the right to elect one third of the technical personnel of the management. This 'stupidity', as Lenin called it, was 'put right' in the full meeting by ensuring to the central state economic organ, the Supreme Council of National Economy, a right of veto over all appointments.[24] The only resolution passed by the congress which could in any sense be regarded as a victory for the left point of view was one advocating nationalization of all branches of key industries—iron and steel and the chemical and textile industries. The Supreme Council of National Economy already possessed, since its creation at the end of 1917, the power of nationalization. But expropriation had proceeded anarchically, without any effective guidance or control by the central authorities, often as a result of spontaneous local action, and more often than not as a punitive measure against owners who attempted to oppose the excesses of workers' control.[25] Now it was intended to introduce more system into nationalization, a policy which the left welcomed, though not without some misgivings. Some time later, on 28 June 1918, a decree was hurriedly passed extending nationalization to all large scale industrial undertakings. To some extent this precipitous

---

[24] *Leninskiy sbornik*, Vol. XXI, pp. 130–1.
[25] Details in Milyutin's speech, *Trudy VSNKh I*, p. 54, and in his *Istoriya ekonomicheskogo razvitiya SSSR 1917 1927*, pp. 112-13.

measure was dictated by the inevitable necessity of extending nationalization, once embarked on, if any central control was to be achieved. But it would seem that the decree was dictated less by economic than by political considerations. It was certainly in no way a concession to the left. It had arisen from Larin's negotiations with the Germans at about this time. Under Articles 12 and 13 of a supplementary agreement to the Treaty of Brest-Litovsk, expropriated enterprises had to be returned to their foreign owners within a year of ratification. But where 'the properties expropriated have passed into the hands of the state, or of the local self-government and remain in their possession on the ground of legislative acts, obligatory for all the inhabitants of the country', compensation was payable instead of restoration. Larin's negotiations convinced him that there was a risk of a considerable part of Russian industry falling into German hands. He shrewdly suggested nationalization to Lenin as a means of avoiding this, and the decree of 28 June, hurriedly drawn up and passed, was the result.[26] No doubt with the object of making this decree appear more convincing to the Germans, a radiogram in clear informing him of the decree was dispatched to the Soviet Ambassador in Berlin in which the nationalization was described as being 'in accordance with the plan worked out long ago'.[27]

The decline of left communism was as rapid as its rise. During April and May the left communist strongholds were still from time to time passing resolutions in favour of revolutionary war at some of the numerous meetings which were held throughout the country. The left won a major temporary success in the Urals (where the metallurgical industry was one of the oldest bolshevik strongholds).[28] But by June, if not before, left communism was a spent force. The last number of *Kommunist* appeared during this month without the *imprimatur* of the Moscow *Oblast'* Bureau. A period of free

[26] For the text of the supplementary agreement, see *U.S. Foreign Relations*, Vol. I, p. 449. Larin's account is quoted in *Zagorsky* at p. 40. cf. Lomov's account in 'Kak my nachali stroit'', reprinted in *Lenin v pervye mesyatsy*, pp. 114–24, at p. 122.

[27] *Leninskiy sbornik*, Vol. XXXV (1945), pp. 27–8.

[28] After a period of agitation in this area, led by Preobrazhensky, a resolution was passed by a local party conference calling for a new all-Russian party congress. See *Kommunist*, no. 4, pp. 13–14.

debate within the communist party had had the result of rapidly eliminating serious conflict, and of obviating a split. Left communism had suffered from the weakness that it had from the first been linked with the advocacy of revolutionary war. In Bolshevik eyes, this policy was tainted by the fact that it was also the policy of the vociferous Left Socialist Revolutionaries. [29] Already on 20 April, when *Kommunist* first reappeared in Moscow, the Left Communists had been anxious to disassociate themselves from such unwelcome allies, and to jettison revolutionary war. 'It would be laughable', they wrote in their theses published on that date, 'to preach, like the Left Socialist Revolutionaries, the refusal on principle to accept this peace.'

Indeed, it was the open hostility of the Left Socialist Revolutionaries to the Communists which finally put an end to the Left Communists as a separate group. Many of them feared to be identified with a policy which by July 1918 had led straight to an armed rising. When the Fifth Congress of Soviets met on 4 July, Obolensky at the preliminary meeting of the communist delegates accepted in the name of the Left Communists Lenin's report on the political situation. [30] Left Communists, including Bukharin, took an active part in the suppression of the left socialist revolutionary rebellion. There is no evidence of any kind of solidarity between the two political groups in July or indeed at any time. The most that can be said is that in February and March they both opposed the peace. In the panic following on the assassination of the German Ambassador many Left Communists hurried to disavow in *Pravda* any connection between themselves and the treasonable ideas of the Left Socialist Revolutionaries. Yaroslavsky, henceforward to become one of the most reliable communist propagandists, was the first. Others followed in the course of July and August. Bukharin and Radek admitted

---

[29] And of the Mensheviks. The Mensheviks, headed by Martov, had in March at the Fourth All-Russian Congress of Soviets demanded that the treaty should not be ratified; they further called for the resignation of the Council of People's Commissars; the setting up of a commission 'to clarify all the circumstances which led to the final disorganisation of defence'; the recall of the Constituent Assembly in order to set up a democratic republic and a government enjoying the confidence of all democratic elements; and the arming of a people's rising against the advance of German imperialism. Quoted in *Vardin*, p. 70.

[30] *Lenin*, Vol. XXIII, p. 548.

their errors in the autumn.[31] The terror received full support from the Left Communists, many of whom, including Bukharin and Obolensky, took part in public campaigns in justification of it.[32]

But the tentative approach by the Left Socialist Revolutionaries to the Left Communists in February 1918, in itself of no importance, was destined to have dramatic consequences. It was first revealed by Bukharin at a party meeting at the end of 1923, with the object of discrediting the oppositionists of that date grouped round Trotsky. This group made a practice of referring to the early period of the revolution, with its freedom of discussion within the party such as the debates at the time of the Brest-Litovsk peace, as an illustration of what inner party democracy should be. Bukharin, then an opponent of Trotsky, chose the incident of the left socialist revolutionary approach to the Left Communists to point the moral that the existence of groups and factions within the party was fraught with grave danger to the state. His illustration of the dangers of party disunity was immediately seized on by Stalin and Zinoviev to discredit some of the oppositionists of the time who had once been Left Communists, such as G. Pyatakov and Preobrazhensky.[33] But Bukharin's reminiscences were also to be turned against him many years later, when he was on trial for his life in 1938. No fewer than five ghosts from the past were brought out of the prisons where they had been for many years, as witnesses against him: Yakovleva, Obolensky (Osinsky), and Mantsev, formerly of the Moscow *Oblast'* Bureau; and the Left Socialist Revolutionaries Karelin and Kamkov. It was important in 1938 to discredit Bukharin: his later policy of encouraging freedom of enterprise among the peasant small-holders was

[31] Yaroslavsky, *Kratkie ocherki*, Vol. II, pp. 190–2; *Popov*, II, p. 39. It is notable that the current charge of a political bloc between the Left Communists and the Left Socialist Revolutionaries did not appear until quite late in Soviet history. Contrast Yaroslavsky, *loc. cit.*, published in 1928, who only goes so far as to say that the Left Socialist Revolutionaries tried to exploit the split in the party (which is quite true), with e.g. *Bubnov*, p. 516, published in 1931, who already writes of 'the political bloc' between the two groups. (Bubnov was himself a Left Communist.)

[32] See e.g. *Pravda* of 6 and 8 September 1918.

[33] See *Pravda* of 15 December 1923, 16 December 1923, and 3 January 1924 for the letters relating to this incident by Zinoviev, Stalin, a group of former Left Communists, and Bukharin.

remembered with nostalgia during the rigours of Stalin's enforced collectivization. He was accordingly charged with having plotted in 1918 together with the Left Socialist Revolutionaries to arrest, and if necessary kill, Lenin, Stalin, and Sverdlov, and to form a new government of 'Bukharinites', 'Trotskyites', and Left Socialist Revolutionaries.[34] Of the unhappy broken spectres of the past, only Kamkov proved obdurate in giving evidence. A courageous militant terrorist of the party, he could not be induced even by Vyshinsky to confirm the existence of the 'plot' which the chief prosecutor was seeking to establish.[35] Karelin, so broken and altered that Bukharin had difficulty in recognizing him, recited his evidence without resistance, though even in his case Bukharin was able to show that what he had said outside the court at the preliminary interrogation had been different.[36] The three Left Communists told a grotesque story in which the open opposition of 1918 was now portrayed as a secret conspiracy. The resolution of the Moscow *Oblast'* Bureau of 24 February in opposition to Lenin's peace policy, became a secret resolution, the destruction of which had been ordered by Bukharin— although everyone who had access to the current edition of the works of Lenin could find it quoted *in extenso* in his article 'The Strange and the Monstrous'. (This article had been published by Lenin soon after he had received the offending resolution from the Moscow *Oblast'* Bureau.) The open conferences of the Left Communists after the signing of the peace now became conspiratorial meetings. Obolensky's evidence even went to the length of implicating Bukharin in the rising of the Left Socialist Revolutionaries which followed the assassination of von Mirbach. Bukharin's endeavours by questioning to establish that he had participated in the arrest of the Left Socialist Revolutionaries after the assassination of the German Ambassador, as well as his efforts to show that the Left Communists had numbered among their adherents such pillars of orthodoxy as Yaroslavsky and Kuybyshev, were

[34] *Report* (*Bukharin*, etc.), p. 29.
[35] *ibid.*, pp. 489–90, 491. 'We (the Left Socialist Revolutionaries and the Left Communists) did not make any joint decision.... I have already replied. There were no such meetings and discussions.'
[36] *ibid.*, p. 505. Karelin's evidence at the trial, for full measure, implicated Bukharin in the attempt on Lenin's life by Dora (Fanny) Kaplan, and in a joint plot with the Right Socialist Revolutionaries as well (p. 502).

frustrated by the court.[37] Bukharin, whom not even a year's imprisonment before his trial had been able to break on this issue, denied the fantastic charge to the end. His version of the incident was substantially the same as that originally disclosed by him in 1923.[38]

But while the modern Soviet portrayal of the Left Communists as a secret band of traitors from the first can be dismissed, it is true that the group of leading Left Communists included a number whose names were to recur in future years as members of this or that opposition tendency. Soviet writers are often at great pains to demonstrate, with scholastic ingenuity, the direct ideological line which leads from, say, Bukharin the Left Communist in 1918 to Bukharin the opponent of enforced collectivization after 1928. This is a barren pursuit. Men's ideas change though their temperaments may not. The Left Communists were united by a somewhat emotional faith in what they believed were true communist principles, perhaps also by inability to accept the logical result of the tactics which had led to the seizure of power, and which in turn derived from the policies which they had themselves approved. In this respect alone perhaps some kinship of outlook with their views in 1918 can be traced in the later history of some of the adherents of Left Communism.[39]

The May Congress of Councils of National Economy was the last occasion at which the Left Communists appeared as a more or less united opposition. But the views which they advocated remained alive inside the party. For the few years during which differences within the party could still be openly ventilated there was to be much friction over such questions as the control of industry, the employment of non-communist specialists, relations with the co-operatives, relations between the centre and local bodies, and above all, the trade unions. But the object of the Left Communists, to preserve a united opposition within the party, failed. It failed not because the oppositionists were suppressed or restricted in the advocacy of their views, but because, after the first shock of the signing of the peace, they could no longer draw on sufficient support from the rank and file of the party. For in truth, they stood

[37] *Report* (*Bukharin* etc.), pp. 454–5.   [38] *ibid.*, pp. 772–4.
[39] A list of the more important Left Communists will be found in Appendix B.

for a different outlook rather than for an alternative policy, and their idealistic theories could not stand up either before Lenin's argument, or before the even more devastating logic of events. Their fundamental inconsistency lay in the fact that though they were prepared to support the dictatorship of a minority over the majority, their somewhat scholastic temperament made them less ready than Lenin to approve the deviations from marxist theory by which alone it could be maintained.

CHAPTER IX

THE SOCIALIST REVOLUTIONARIES[1]

The Socialist Revolutionaries unlike the Mensheviks were not linked to the Bolsheviks by a common adherence to marxism. Moreover, when once their left wing had broken away to form the separate party of Left Socialist Revolutionaries, they were much more united than the Mensheviks in their support of national defence against the Germans. They therefore repudiated the bolshevik coup d'état without any of the hesitations which beset the Mensheviks, and, unlike them, were not even prepared to discuss a coalition with the Bolsheviks. Again, in contrast to the Mensheviks, they enjoyed in 1917 very considerable popular support. They had made little attempt before November to assert the political authority to which this support entitled them, because they believed that no decisive legislative step should be taken until the Constituent Assembly had met. Within a few weeks of the October Revolution they had won a definite majority of the delegates' seats in the elections to that Assembly. Yet they failed either at the time or later to exploit what would in normal political conditions have been a position of impregnable strength.

The first reason for this lay in the nature of the support on which they could rely. The elections to the Assembly were representative enough of opinion in the country, but any parallel between the significance of an election in politically inexperienced Russia, voting for the first time on a universal franchise, and its significance in a maturer democracy would be false. In a mature country the voters who support a political party do so with the intention that the members of

[1] Very little material is yet available upon which a history of the Socialist Revolutionaries between 1918 and 1921 can be written. Even the evidence at the trial of their leaders in 1922, which in any case is far from trustworthy, has not been published in full. The sketch which follows is based mainly upon Soviet materials, as supplemented and checked by such memoirs as have been published. While, therefore, it is far from complete, insofar as it deals with armed activity of the party against the Communists during the civil war, it errs, if anything on the side of overstating this activity.

this party should be returned as their chosen delegates to govern in their interests. The millions of peasants who voted for the socialist revolutionary lists in November 1917 had never had the chance of acquiring this political maturity. Their desires were simple—they wanted the land, and after that they wanted to be left alone. They had no idea for the most part that the election in which they were voting was in any way linked with any government which would be formed in the future. They had learnt over the years to regard the Socialist Revolutionaries as the men who championed their aspirations. They knew them as friends through the agricultural co-operatives and the local authorities (*Zemstva*), and, during the war, through the manifold activities of the vast voluntary Red Cross, welfare, and supply organization known as *Zemgor*. No doubt they had some mental picture of their own of the Constituent Assembly as something which would give them their land and safeguard their possession of it. But they had not the remotest conception of the simple fact that their interests were bound up with the form of government in Petrograd or Moscow, nor did they realize that their well-being depended on the extent to which they were prepared by their own action to support their own government in power. Hence, while they naturally voted for the Socialist Revolutionaries in November 1917, they equally naturally turned away from them a few months later, when the Socialist Revolutionaries began to make demands on them. The Socialist Revolutionary who promised them land was a friend. The same Socialist Revolutionary, when he endeavoured to enlist the peasant's aid to fight for a government which he was told would safeguard that land, was as much an enemy as any other government official. During the civil war the peasant was by inclination neutral—except in defence of his own plot of land. He was only driven to fight by compulsion, whether in the Red Army or against it in one of the anti-Soviet armies; or else by exasperation, in one of the thousands of guerrilla bands, against the Communists or against the White Armies, and often against both. As a conscious supporter of this or that political régime he hardly counted.

The second reason for the failure of the Socialist Revolutionaries lay in the nature of the party itself. The Socialist

Revolutionaries were in truth less a political party than a popular, national movement. Despite the veneer of a Western European left wing party which they acquired early in the twentieth century, they remained in essence the *Narodniki* of the nineteenth century—a conglomeration of idealists, theorists, intellectuals, terrorists of all types, with little experience of the Western form of parliamentary political action, and often less inclination for it. Unlike the Mensheviks, they had not even experienced the modernizing, westernizing aspects of marxism and trade unionism. The banner of their party sheltered a variety of individuals, united not so much by any political programme of action as by faith in the Russian people, its destiny, the ultimate rightness of its will. The Socialist Revolutionary saw his mission more in terms of constant readiness to place himself in the forefront of the people's fight for its rights, than in terms of political leadership. There was some truth in Trotsky's jibe that for the Socialist Revolutionaries nobility took the place of a programme. One consequence of all this was the total lack of party discipline, or even cohesion. In order to sketch the course of Socialist Revolutionary policy after the October Revolution one has to trace the policy of its leaders, of the Central Committee, and of the various groups which attempted to form themselves into anti-communist governments in the early phases of the civil war. Yet at the same time the lines of the sketch are blurred by the actions of countless individuals, who called themselves, or who were called, Socialist Revolutionaries, but whose policy, whether pro-communist or anti-communist, had often nothing to do with either the policy of the party leaders, or with that of any party organization. A second consequence of the peculiar tradition of the socialist revolutionary party was its lack of political skill. In their relations with the other anti-communist parties the Socialist Revolutionaries showed little tact or moderation. Above all, they had little ability to compromise over any of their political aims in order to achieve a united anti-communist front.

The decision of the socialist revolutionary deputies to leave the Second All-Russian Congress of Soviets on 7 November 1917 was immediately followed by a repudiation of the bolshevik coup d'état. On the day after they issued a proclamation:

the seizure of power by one party alone was a 'vile and criminal' betrayal. The only way to save the revolution was to create a new revolutionary government which all the country would recognize.[2] But the immediate efforts which they made towards this end came to nothing. After a period of conversations at the army field headquarters the socialist revolutionary leaders and the army commanders failed to reach agreement on the form which this new government should take, or on the military support which would instal it in power.[3] All their hopes were now centred upon the Constituent Assembly, which was due to meet in January 1918. At their Fourth Party Congress, which met some ten days after the October Revolution, the Socialist Revolutionaries had resolved that they must 'muster all their strength in order to concentrate around the Constituent Assembly and the defence of all its rights sufficient force to be able, in case of need, to join battle against any criminal attempt on the supreme will of the people'.[4] But they failed in this resolve, and their failure dealt a severe blow to their prestige. The garrison troops of Petrograd were for the most part 'neutral' —but if anything more prepared to fight for the Bolsheviks, than against them. Yet, on the eve of the opening day of the Assembly, 18 January 1918, the military committee of the Socialist Revolutionaries could count on two Guards regiments, and some armoured troops. These were ready to turn out in armed support of a workers' demonstration which the party had organized for the opening of the Assembly, in order to deter the Bolsheviks from dispersing it. Even a few thousand troops was quite a formidable force to oppose to the slender military resources of the Bolsheviks. But when the moment came the socialist revolutionary Central Committee refused to allow these troops to be called out. 'Not one drop of the people's blood must be spilt,' said Chernov. When the troops were told of this decision, and invited to parade without arms with the demonstrators their indignation was

[2] Quoted from *Delo naroda* in *Ryabinsky*, pp. 294–5.
[3] *Krasnyy arkhiv*, Vol. XXIII, pp. 230–1.
[4] *Obvinitel'noe zaklyuchenie*, pp. 6–7. The Bolsheviks ordered the arrest of the socialist revolutionary leaders on 31 December 1917. The order was not carried out partly owing to the intervention of the Left Socialist Revolutionaries and partly for fear of popular reaction.

unbounded. 'Do you think the Bolsheviks are children?' one of the soldiers asked. 'They will fire on us all right, if we are unarmed . . . or do you want us to scuttle, like rabbits?' The workers paraded without the soldiers, and unarmed. There were a hundred casualties from the rifles of the bolshevik Red Guards.[5]

So ended the defence of the Constituent Assembly. The troops which had been ready to follow the socialist revolutionary lead broke with the 'intellectuals' who had disappointed them. Of the two regiments principally concerned, one, the Preobrazhensky, allowed itself to be disarmed by the Communists; the other, the Semenovsky, hoodwinked them by a seemingly loyal resolution, and then deserted to the White Volunteer Army.[6] The dispersal of the Constituent Assembly left the Socialist Revolutionaries undecided, distracted, and disunited. For a short time they attempted to oppose the Communists by using the rapidly dwindling opportunities of lawful opposition. Their press was virtually closed down in January 1918. Isolated members of the party continued to find their way into local soviets and soviet congresses. Arrests and forcible expulsions soon reduced the numbers of such delegates to a handful. There were four Socialist Revolutionaries in the Central Executive Committee elected at the Fourth Soviet Congress, held between 14 and 18 March 1918. They repudiated from the outset the authority of this executive committee and refused to participate in elections to its praesidium.[7] During a few months they fought a losing battle for a hearing. For Sverdlov had on 21 November 1917 replaced the comparatively tolerant Kamenev as permanent chairman of the Central Executive Committee. He did not conceal his contempt for parliamentary forms and made no pretence of allowing any rights to minorities.

On 14 June 1918 the Central Executive Committee resolved to 'exclude from its number the representatives of the Socialist

---

[5] B. Sokolov, 'Zashchita uchreditel'nogo sobraniya', in *Arkhiv russkoy revolyutsii*, Vol. XIII, pp. 5–70; cf. *Obvinitel'noe zaklyuchenie*, pp. 1–14, which is based on the evidence of the renegades, Paevsky and Semenov, and is to much the same effect. For the demonstration, see *Rakitnikova*, pp. 40–2. And cf. V. Chernov, *Pered burey*, pp. 356–60.

[6] *Semenov*, pp. 22–3.

[7] *Protokoly VTSIK IV*, p. 38. The Communists (141) and Left Socialist Revolutionaries (48) had an overwhelming majority on this body.

Revolutionary Party (right and centre) and of the Mensheviks, and likewise to propose to all Soviets of Workers', Soldiers' and Peasants' deputies to banish representatives of these fractions from their midst.' The reasons assigned for this step were twofold. First that the evidence was conclusive that both the socialist revolutionary and menshevik leaders were engaged in fomenting risings throughout the country, in alliance with counter-revolutionaries on the Don, and with the Czech legionaries in Siberia; and secondly that 'the representation in Soviet organizations of the members of parties openly aiming at the overthrow and discrediting of Soviet power, is entirely inadmissible'. In a speech explaining the resolution the communist Sosnovsky argued that the socialist parties having lost all hope of winning over the masses in a constitutional way through Soviet elections, had now turned to open counter-revolution. The military work was being carried on by the Socialist Revolutionaries, while the Mensheviks were engaged more in the 'civilian tasks' of 'working up public opinion'. The Left Socialist Revolutionaries, though loud in their attacks on the other socialist parties, opposed the decree on the ground that the proper course was not expulsion, but a 'hard, straight, and clear line of Soviet policy'.[8]

The reason assigned for the expulsion of the two socialist parties, though unjustified so far as concerned the Mensheviks[9] (whom the Communists henceforward found it expedient always to bracket with the Socialist Revolutionaries), was to some extent true so far as the Socialist Revolutionaries were concerned. The peace of Brest-Litovsk had led to a radical change in the policy of their Central Committee on the question of forcible action against the Communists. In April 1918 it resolved that the Soviet government had 'betrayed democracy, Russia, the Revolution, and the International, and that it must be and shall be overthrown'. The Central Committee no longer, as hitherto, emphasized that the struggle must take an open, mass character, and must in no circumstances be in the form of an underground conspiracy.[10] At

---

[8] Lozovsky, who had been expelled from the communist party some months before and now headed a small group, the Socialist Labour Party of Internationalists, also protested in a vigorous speech. *Protokoly VTSIK IV*, pp. 422 *et seq.*
[9] See Chapter XI.   [10] *Obvinitel'noe zaklyuchenie*, pp. 15–17.

a party conference, held secretly, on 26 May 1918, the Socialist Revolutionaries further resolved to 'accept Allied assistance in the war against Germany . . . on condition that Russia's territorial integrity and political sovereignty will not be violated. . . .'[11] It is not clear what plan the party evolved in order to implement these decisions, but it would appear that their intentions were long term rather than short term, and centred on Siberia and on the Volga district, which were socialist revolutionary strongholds.[12] But whatever their plans may have been events which were happening while their May conference was in session decided their future action.

Thus the leaders of the socialist revolutionary party, who were not prepared to shed blood in a civil war in defence of the Constituent Assembly, were at last goaded into the decision to take up arms against the Communists by Lenin's capitulation to the Germans. There were many individuals who were, or who were said to be, Socialist Revolutionaries who endeavoured to pursue an active struggle against the Communists by such means as lay in their power, and turned their experience of conspiracy, terror, and underground war against the new tyranny. Throughout the civil war individual Socialist Revolutionaries were to be found participating in many of the plots, conspiracies, or other anti-communist activities within or outside Russia. It was to such free lance activity for example that the attempt on Lenin's life on 30 August 1918 by Dora (Fanny) Kaplan was due.[13] Another lone fighter was Boris

[11] *Bunyan*, pp. 185–7.

[12] See the evidence of Timofeev at the trial in 1922, *Pravda*, 28 June 1922, p. 3. The socialist revolutionary strength in Siberia is illustrated by the figures of returns in the elections to the Constituent Assembly which, though incomplete, show a socialist revolutionary vote of 1,706,357 as compared with 273,982 bolshevik votes—see *Radkey*, p. 79. And cf. Chernov, *op. cit.* pp. 368–73. The party rejected an approach by the Don Cossack army of General Kaledin.

[13] Lenin's assailant is invariably described by socialist revolutionary writers as Dora, and by the *Vecheka* as Fanny. At the trial of the Socialist Revolutionaries in 1922 their Central Committee was accused of complicity in this attempt, which it denied then, as at the time. The evidence of this complicity was mostly hearsay, and the evidence of renegades at that, and in parts a little fanciful—for example, that the bullets used had been treated with curare (arrow poison)—see *Obvinitel'noe zaklyuchenie*, pp. 91–7, for a summary. A fuller version of the evidence will be found in *Pravda*, 16 July, 20 July, and 21 July 1922 (pp. 4, 3, and 3, respectively); this version mostly omits the cross-examination by the defence. The curare story, incidentally, which is based on the evidence of the renegade Semenov at the trial, is not to be found in a book dealing with these events which was published by him a short time before the trial. It is possible that some members of the Central Committee may have known that plots of

Savinkov, who had already broken with the socialist revolutionary party before the revolution in September 1917, when he was expelled for his support of General Kornilov. Early in 1918 he set up a military organization of his own, the Union for the Defence of the Fatherland and Freedom. It included some extreme right wing socialists and the chief of staff was a monarchist. This organization, the forces of which never amounted to more than a few hundred, planned a number of risings in the summer of 1918, in Yaroslavl', Rybinsk, Murom, Kazan', Kaluga, and Vladimir. None of them achieved any success. Savinkov himself escaped from the Communists, first to Kazan', then to Paris, and threw his energies into enlisting Allied aid against the Soviet régime. An indomitable fighter, he continued the struggle against the Communists long after nearly everyone else had given it up. Up till June 1924 he conducted raids across the Soviet frontier by members of his Green movement, from his headquarters in Warsaw. After most of the leaders of this movement had been captured in 1924, Savinkov himself was apparently tricked across the borders of the U.S.S.R.; he was tried, convicted, and sentenced to imprisonment. At his trial he admitted that his struggle had been unjustified, and the mildness of the sentence may have been due to what the Communists regarded as the propaganda value of this admission from so stubborn an enemy. It is impossible to say whether his confession was extorted from him, or represented a genuine attempt to make his peace with the new Russia. A written confession in his own hand-writing, subsequently published in facsimile by the Communists, was ostensibly dated only a few days after his capture. Assuming that the date is genuine, it is unlikely that a few days would have been enough to break a man like Savinkov. Moreover at the end of the previous year, in Paris, he had published a novel full of bitter disillusionment with his struggle. He died in prison, allegedly by his own hand.[14]

assassination were afoot—see e.g. V. Zenzinov (ed.), *Gosudarstvennyy perevorot admirala Kolchaka*, pp. 152–3—but, since they could hardly have been expected to inform the *Vecheka* of them, it is difficult to see what they could do about them.

[14] See Savinkov, *Bor'ba s bol'shevikami*, and the Epilogue to his *Memoirs of a Terrorist*, by Joseph Shaplen. The novel, *Kon' voronoy* (the Black Horse of the Apocalypse) was published by him under the pseudonym Ropshin. For the stenogram of his trial see *Boris Savinkov etc.* There is also some information on

While the Socialist Revolutionaries were still engaged in conference in May 1918, the first shots were fired in the civil war which was to last for two and a half years. Hitherto there had been sporadic fighting against the Communists mainly by the Don Cossacks, who had been routed in March, and by the Germans in their resumed advance in the Ukraine in April and early May. From now on the campaign began in earnest. During the war against the Central Powers the leaders of the future Czechoslovakia had been allowed to recruit a legion of Czechs and Slovaks from among prisoners of war in Russia, in order to assist in the conquest of the territory of their future state. By the end of 1917 this legion numbered some 45,000 and was placed under French command. In the spring of 1918 it was stationed mainly in Siberia. Its relations with the Communists, friendly at first, were aggravated by mutual suspicions. In May 1918 the Czech Army Corps, as it was now called, intended to make its way to Vladivostok in order to get to France, and take part in the war against Germany. This led to friction with the Communists, which culminated in open revolt when the latter ordered the Czechs to disarm. The Communists were unprepared, and as yet virtually unarmed. The Czechs, on the other hand, were supported both by the local population and shortly after by some Russian volunteer units. With amazing rapidity they occupied a number of strategic points—Chelyabinsk on 26 May, Omsk on 7 June, Samara on the Volga on 8 June. A formidable force was now in existence astride the vital Trans-Siberian railway and this factor influenced the decision of the Allied Powers to intervene in Russia. The Czech Army Corps was now ordered to remain in Russia. Japanese troops had already been landed at Vladivostok early in April, but had taken no part in hostilities, and there was a small British force at Murmansk. On 2 August an Allied force occupied Archangel. Shortly after the Russian Volunteer Army, which had been forming in the first half of 1918 under General Denikin, captured Ekaterinodar and Novorossiysk.

the Union for the Defence of the Fatherland and Freedom in *Krasnaya kniga*, pp. 1 *et seq.* The communist counter-intelligence had apparently successfully penetrated Savinkov's organization in Warsaw for some time before his movement was routed in 1924—see an article entitled 'Trest' by R. Wraga, in *Vozrozhdenie*, Jan./Feb. 1950, at pp. 121–2.

The Czech offensive won the immediate support of the Socialist Revolutionaries. They had made no contact with Denikin's Russian Volunteer Army, nor indeed was there any possible ground of agreement between them. An army monarchist in outlook, and led by reactionary officers, was a force which most of them regarded as no better than the Communists, while some considered it a good deal worse. The officers, in turn, little trained in political niceties, viewed all Socialist Revolutionaries however moderate as no different from Communists. The Czechs, on the other hand, were democrats as well as fellow Slavs, and with them the Socialist Revolutionaries felt a close bond. They were also ready to co-operate with the Allied Powers, though not without misgivings at the thought of foreign troops on Russian soil. Hence whatever the Socialist Revolutionaries' plan of action may have been in May, the rapid Czech success led to its abandonment. When the Czechs occupied Samara, a socialist revolutionary Committee of Members of the Constituent Assembly (known as *Komuch*) proclaimed itself the government of the region and persuaded the Czechs to stay at Samara until it could organize a force of its own to fight the Communists. At Omsk, similarly, a largely socialist Siberian Revolutionary Commissariat was formed. At Archangel two months later, just before the Allied landing took place, a mixed populist socialist and socialist revolutionary government was set up, known as the Supreme Administration of the North. It was headed by the veteran populist socialist Peter Chaykovksy. In the Urals, at the end of July, after the capture of Ekaterinburg by Czech and Russian volunteer forces, the Socialist Revolutionaries joined in forming a coalition Regional Government of the Urals with the *Kadety*, the Populist Socialists, and some Mensheviks.

The Archangel government was isolated and depended for survival on the support of the Allied military force, which was insufficient to withstand the Red Army when it eventually passed over to the assault. The other governments controlled vital areas in the heart of Russia and disposed of a substantial military force, the nucleus of which, the Czech Army Corps, was reinforced by Russian units recruited in the areas occupied by them. But the democratic governments perished from internal dissensions and contradictions long before the entire territory held by them was reconquered by the Red Army. Of the three governments concerned, the only one in which Socialist Revolutionaries predominated was that at Samara. *Komuch* claimed to derive its authority from the Constituent Assembly elected in November 1917. Unquestioning acceptance of this Assembly as the fountain of all constitutional power of any future Russian government was the first plank of its political platform. By its radical doctrines on the subject of the land, which it declared 'irrevocably . . . the property of the people' *Komuch* alienated the landlords; its uncompromising insistence on the authority of the dispersed Constituent Assembly antagonized the *Kadety*; while its demands for democracy in the army and its natural incompatibility with the officers soon led to serious conflicts.[15] Its political inexperience was manifested in its failure to subordinate the army commanders from the start to its own civil authority. It enjoyed a measure of popular support, as the results of some local elections in mid-August 1918 showed. But this support was of a negative rather than a positive nature ; the population were glad enough to be rid of the Communists, and had indeed played a large part in their overthrow, but they were not ready to join any army, or to take part in any fighting away from their own homes.[16] There was one notable exception to this general feeling, the case of the industrial towns of Izhevsk and Votkinsk, which lie north of Samara on the river Kama, between Ekaterinburg and Kazan'. Encouraged by the capture of the former by the Czechs from the Communists on 25 July, and of the latter on 6 August, the workers of Izhevsk overthrew their local Soviet government on 8 August. In the course of some three weeks Izhevsk had rallied to its side a peasant and worker 'army' of 25,000, which grew to 30,000 by the adherence of the neighbouring Votkinsk. By September this insurgent army was said to number 50,000 or more, and to control a territory of twelve

---

[15] For a declaration of policy by *Komuch*, dated 24 July 1918, see *Bunyan*, pp. 283–5. A picture of the Samara government can best be obtained by contrasting *Maisky* (an account by the menshevik member, who subsequently became a Communist) and *Klimushkin* (an account by a socialist revolutionary member).

[16] The socialist bloc obtained about half the votes in Samara, and rather more than half in Orenburg—*Maisky*, p. 145. Of the army of 120,000 recruited by 1 September 1918 only 10,000 were volunteers. Its morale was appalling—*Klimushkin*, pp. 82–9.

thousand square *versts*, and a population of 700–800,000. The insurgents were headed by a committee, which declared its adherence to *Komuch*. It is notable that this committee, in contrast to *Komuch*, consisted of right wing socialists and included one *Kadet*. When in November Izhevsk and Votkinsk were recaptured by the Red Army, the entire population, according to the Soviet historian of these events, withdrew with the anti-communist forces across the Kama. This insurgent army continued to fight the Communists under various banners long after *Komuch* had ceased to exist. Remnants of it were fighting to the last until the evacuation of Vladivostok in 1922.[17]

In contrast to the government at Samara, the government at Omsk soon became socialist in little more than name. The socialist revolutionary Commissariat, set up on 30 May, was within a month succeeded by the mainly right wing Provisional Government of Western Siberia, headed by P. Vologodsky. It declared the independence of Siberia, and among other reactionary measures proceeded to restore the expropriated land to its former owners. The new government immediately came into conflict with the Siberian Provincial Duma, which had been elected in November 1917 at Omsk, and was socialist revolutionary in its majority.

The Red Army, by the summer of 1918, was fast gathering strength under Trotsky's command. The only chance of survival for the anti-communist democratic front lay in unity. The divergence of political outlook between the two main governments concerned made this unity unlikely. Further conflict was aroused by the separatist policy of the Omsk government, while relations between all concerned were constantly exacerbated by the inability of the army officers and of the socialists to find any common ground for agreement. With the encouragement of the Czechs, a unification conference met at Chelyabinsk on 15 July 1918 and again on 20 August 1918, but achieved nothing. However, a conference which met at Ufa on 8 September was successful to the extent of reaching agreement on the setting up of an All-Russian Provisional Government.

[17] For an account of these events see N. Sapozhnikov 'Izhevsko-Votkinskoe vosstanie', in *Proletarskaya revolyutsiya*, no. 8–9 (31–2), 1924, pp. 5–42. There is also an account in *Zarya*, nos. 3 and 4, 1923, by a right-wing menshevik participant, I. Upovalov. See also *Varneck and Fisher*, p. 255.

Some hundred and fifty delegates attended the Ufa Conference, of whom nearly half were Socialist Revolutionaries. The various anti-communist governments were represented; a number of national governments which had sprung up, such as the Bashkir, Turkestan, and Estonian governments; and the main political parties, including the *Kadety* and the *Edinstvo* group (Plekhanovites). Maisky and two other Mensheviks, though acting in defiance of the official policy of their party, claimed to represent it.[18] The socialist revolutionary delegates were not agreed among themselves. About half of them, headed by Vol'sky and Rakitnikov, formed an uncompromising left wing of the conference, which insisted that the new government must recognize and be based upon the Constituent Assembly. A large number at the conference, including the *Kadety*, was not prepared to accept this. The *Kadety*, who were supported by other moderate groups, such as the *Edinstvo* representatives, held to their opinion that the first task of the conference was to establish a strong government which would not confuse liberty with licence; they proposed the setting up of a directorate which would not be responsible to any elected body. The right wing of the Socialist Revolutionaries was ready to accept a small, strong government, provided that its powers were exercised within the limits of the legislation which had already been passed by the shortlived Constituent Assembly. This right wing included Avksentiev and Zenzinov, the former of whom acted as chairman of the conference. Their moderation, tact, and endeavour to achieve a workable compromise provided a striking contrast to the behaviour of many members of their party. After a fortnight's debate an All-Russian Provisional Government or Directorate of five was formed. As originally constituted it consisted of Avksentiev, Astrov, a leading *Kadet*, the veteran Chaykovsky, a comparatively moderate general Boldyrev, and Vologodsky, the head of the Siberian Provisional Government. It was to exercise sovereignty until the Constituent Assembly could be convened early in 1919. Its tasks were to build up an army to continue the fight against both Germany and the Communists, to restore

---

[18] Maisky, with the support of some members of the local menshevik organization, had joined *Komuch*. He and his supporters were expelled from the menshevik party—see Chapter XI.

order, to maintain civil liberties, and to promote fair labour legislation. The land was to be left to its *de facto* holders until the Constituent Assembly could ultimately decide what was to be done about it.[19]

The Directorate was a compromise doomed to failure from the start. Neither those of the right nor of the left, whom it purported to unite, were prepared to give it honest support. Within a short time of the formation of the new All-Russian Provisional Government, *Komuch* had lost most of its territory to the Red Army (Samara was captured on 8 October) and the right wing Siberian government began to regret the compromise it had made with the left wing *Komuch*, which now no longer controlled any important territory. While the unification conference was still in session the more reactionary members of this Siberian government had gained the upper hand. With the support of the army they had forcibly dissolved the Siberian Provisional Duma, which had a socialist revolutionary majority and was in sympathy with *Komuch*, and had forced the resignation of the two socialist revolutionary members of the Siberian government. The exasperation of the right wing of this government, who were mostly moderate conservatives, with the intransigence of the Socialist Revolutionaries at a time when unity was essential is easy to understand. But, like *Komuch*, they had never succeeded in subordinating the army commanders to the civil power. Within a short time of the right wing victory in Siberia there were several murders of prominent socialists, all of which could be clearly laid at the door of the officers. Moreover, the behaviour of the army officers—their open contempt for all socialists, however moderate, and the singing of 'God Save the Tsar'—did not make compromise between them and the socialists an easy matter. On the other hand, the left half of the socialist revolutionary party was not far behind the military in its intransigent attitude to the Ufa compromise. Chernov, the leader of the party, who had not been present at the conference, but who belonged to the left wing, soon showed his opinion of the new All-Russian Provisional Govern-

---

[19] The proceedings of the Ufa Conference are reprinted in *Russkiy istoricheskiy arkhiv*. See also an illuminating article by V. L. Utgof, 'Ufimskoe gosudarstvennoe soveshchanie 1918 goda', in *Byloe*, no. 16, 1921, p. 15; and *Bunyan*, pp. 339-56.

ment by remaining seated when the rest of the audience stood at a public meeting convened to celebrate its formation.[20] Within a month the socialist revolutionary Central Committee had repudiated the All-Russian Provisional Government. It complained of the government's weakness in dealing with the Siberian government, and ordered the mobilization and military training of all party forces 'in order to be able to withstand at any moment the attacks of counter-revolutionists who organize civil war in the rear of the anti-bolshevik front'.[21] Some three weeks later, on 18 November 1918, the All-Russian Provisional Government was overthrown, and supreme authority was assumed by Admiral Kolchak.

The rapid collapse of the Directorate resulted in the virtual disintegration of the socialist revolutionary party. Two of its ablest members, Avksentiev and Zenzinov (the latter had acted as a member of the Directorate as the replacement for Chaykovsky) left Russia and established themselves in Paris. Here they formed a group which endeavoured to enlist Allied support for more determined military intervention against the Communists. They failed in their object. According to Avksentiev's account, in some circles they were regarded as reactionary extremists because they contended that the Communists had 'destroyed both democracy and socialism'; while in others they were regarded as half Bolsheviks because they did not 'crawl on their stomachs before Kolchak', and because they 'talked about democracy'.[22] The remainder of the party, under the leadership of Chernov, attempted to pursue what it rather grandiloquently called the fight on two fronts—both against the Communists, and against right wing reaction. On the Volga remnants of the organization continued to resist the advance of the Red Army. In the interior of Siberia

[20] See a letter of 31 October 1919 from Avksentiev to members of his party, intercepted by the Communists, and reprinted in *Proletarskaya revolyutsiya*, no. 1, 1921, pp. 116–17.
[21] The text of the resolution is reprinted in *Bunyan*, pp. 362–5. According to Chernov, his draft of this resolution was toned down by his colleagues—see his *Pered burey*, p. 389. The Socialist Revolutionaries in the Directorate voted against this resolution, and were prepared to order a legal investigation and to take action against the party if the investigation warranted it—see Zenzinov, *Gos. perevorot*, pp. 172, 192–3. It is doubtful if more than half of the members of the party present when the resolution was voted supported the policy expressed in it. *ibid.*, pp. 68–9.
[22] See Avksentiev's letter in *Proletarskaya revolyutsiya*, *loc. cit.*

some attempt was apparently made to organize a force for the overthrow of Kolchak.[23]

But before long the Communists succeeded in dividing the party. Early in 1919 they approached the Socialist Revolutionaries through some Left Socialist Revolutionaries with a proposal for reconciliation. They were successful in persuading a significant number of socialist revolutionary leaders, though not Chernov, that now that Germany was defeated, and hence the main cause of disagreement, the peace of Brest-Litovsk, had been removed, there was every prospect of collaboration with the Communists on the basis of a joint effort to defeat Kolchak. A number of leading Socialist Revolutionaries, including Vol'sky, Rakitnikov, Burevoy, Shmelev, Svyatitsky, and Chernenkov arrived in Moscow on 3 February 1919. The following day the People's Commissar for Foreign Affairs, Chicherin, was already making propaganda capital out of their surrender. A note to the Allied Powers referred to the well-known Socialist Revolutionaries 'who have declared themselves with great emphasis against the Entente intervention in Russia'.[24] On 8 February a conference of the socialist revolutionary organization in Petrograd likewise renounced armed struggle against the Soviet régime. Its resolution called for the rallying of all effort towards 'the overthrow of the reactionary governments and the reunion of their territories with Russia',—terms which incidentally recalled socialist revolutionary resentment over the separatist tendencies of the Siberian government. The conference further 'decisively rejected any attempt at the overthrow of the Soviet government by force of arms' which, in view of the weak and scattered resources of democracy and the growing might of counter-revolution, would only play into the hands of reaction. It also rejected any further attempts at coalition with the bourgeois parties, and called for open political activity, without however indicating how, in Soviet constitutional conditions of 1919, a socialist party was to carry out such activity. The conference appears to have had some doubts on the question itself, since its resolution did not 'consider it possible to put up party

---

[23] V. Chernov, *Mes Tribulations*, p. 18.
[24] *Cumming and Pettit*, p. 301, where the declaration by the group against intervention is also reprinted.

candidates for elections to the soviets until the voices of all workers' parties are given the legal right to be heard'.[25]

As a result of this resolution, on 25 February 1919 the Central Executive Committee revoked its decree of expulsion of 14 June 1918 in favour of those Socialist Revolutionaries who accepted Vol'sky's policy. This legalization made next to no difference in practice. For nine days, from 20 March 1919 to 28 March 1919, the newly-legalized party was allowed to publish *Delo Naroda*, one of the socialist revolutionary organs which had been closed down in January 1918. The short period of free press was brought to an untimely end by the too insistent demands of *Delo Naroda* for free elections. Perhaps the only result of the legalization was that once again isolated Socialist Revolutionaries appeared in the composition of the next few Congresses of Soviets, though they were seldom allowed to speak, and never allowed to vote. They were prevented from marring the unanimity of the by then solidly communist and pro-communist All-Russian Soviet Congresses, by the device of being admitted to the congresses as delegates with a 'consultative voice' only. Vol'sky, for example, was thus allowed to speak at the Seventh Congress in December 1919.[26]

But outright capitulation did not represent the policy of the whole party. Many of the illegal organizations in existence in Russia[27] regarded the action of Vol'sky and his followers with considerable suspicion as a communist attempt to penetrate the party, and it is unlikely that his group had the support of more than a small section of the party. The majority view was expressed in a declaration of the socialist revolutionary Central Committee on 5 April 1919 that armed struggle had only been given up for lack of resources to continue the fight on two fronts, that the 'best champion of counter-revolution is the bolshevik system itself', and that when the people 'inevitably' rose against it, the place of the socialist revolutionary party would be 'as always', at the head of the people's struggle for its rights.[28] The Ninth Conference of the party,

[25] *Obvinitel'noe zaklyuchenie*, pp. 35–6. See also Chernov, *Mes Tribulations*, pp. 21–37.

[26] For his speech, see *Vs. syezd VII*, pp. 68–71. For the popularity of the shortlived *Delo Naroda* among the workers see Chernov, *Pered burey*, p. 406.

[27] There was a wide network of illegal organizations still in existence in June 1919 when the Ninth Party Conference met—see *PSR IX sovet*, pp. 3–4.

[28] *Obvinitel'noe zaklyuchenie*, p. 37.

which took place illegally in Moscow between 18 and 20 June 1919, condemned both the pro-communist Vol'sky group, and the pro-allied group headed by Avksentiev in Paris. Two members of Vol'sky's group, who were also members of the Central Committee, Burevoy and Rakitnikov, then resigned, and the group as a whole issued a proclamation. This called for an armed struggle against 'reaction', but without 'either asking or demanding anything in return from the Bolsheviks'. The Central Committee thereupon voted to disband Vol'sky's group, as a result of which Vol'sky and his supporters left the party on 30 October 1919.[29]

The resolutions adopted at the Ninth Party Conference stressed that the decision to abandon armed struggle against the Communists was a tactical one only, and must on no account be interpreted as acceptance either of the dictatorship, or of the 'absurd and harmful illusion' that the communist régime could in the course of time evolve along more democratic lines. The Socialist Revolutionaries condemned both Allied intervention and any attempt at fomenting local rebellions or riots, which were viewed as a waste of resources. They resolved that the main efforts of the party must be directed to the villages, where 'peasant brotherhoods' should be formed. But the object of these brotherhoods was not to be preparation of a rebellion. Any sabotage of sowing must be discouraged, and the struggle against the 'kulaks' must be regarded as a 'fundamental task'.[30] The brotherhoods must train the peasants 'to wait patiently for the moment when great events of a political character' would be followed by 'corresponding tactical appeals by the party'. These appeals would be 'the signal for a more decisive form of struggle to win back the rights of which the peasants have been deprived'.[31] Such evidence as there is, which is mostly from Soviet sources, does not suggest that the socialist revolutionary party ever exercised any significant influence over the extensive peasant risings which characterized the first few years of the Soviet state. No doubt many individual Socialist Revolutionaries continued

[29] *Obvinitel'noe zaklyuchenie*, pp. 38–9.
[30] This part of the resolution may be contrasted with the usual assertion by Communist and pro-Communist writers, that the Socialist Revolutionaries championed the interest of the 'Kulaks'.
[31] *PSR IX sovet*, pp. 9–23.

to join what anti-communist fighting there was, and disregarded the scruples of their party. But the policy of the party as a whole remained until 1921 one of steadfast refusal to have anything to do with any armed rising unless it could fully approve of its pure *Narodnik* character, and was satisfied that it did not assist counter-revolution. On 13 May 1920 the Central Committee reiterated that the policy of the party was to organize village discontent into a universal protest against the Communists which would take the form of a demand for a referendum. This pacific policy infuriated many sections of the party, and at a party conference in September 1920 the Central Committee was faced with a demand for more resolute leadership, in view of the rising tide of peasant revolt throughout the country. The Conference was, however, only prepared to commit itself to the extent that it foresaw 'the inevitable renewal by the party of armed struggle against the bolshevik power' now that the liquidation of Denikin had removed the fear of counter-revolution.[32] Thereafter the party did apparently give some support to peasant risings, but, as the Central Committee later explained, only where it was satisfied that they 'bore the character of a healthy struggle with communist dictatorship for the affirmation of the rights of the labouring people'; but not to those risings which followed 'the false path of pogroms, violence, and murders'. The peasants did not always find it easy to understand the distinction drawn by the Socialist Revolutionaries between healthy and unhealthy risings, and were somewhat bewildered by what appeared to them the failure of the party to give them a lead. One peasant partisan, when informed that the local Socialist Revolutionaries were not prepared to support a particular rising which had been planned, replied: 'It looks as if we shall have to act on our own. But in that case you had better look out too, when we get to Tambov we'll bump you off with the rest of them!'[33]

The current picture of the Socialist Revolutionaries as opponents of the Soviet régime by force of arms throughout the civil war is at most a half-truth, and a misleading over-

[32] *Obvinitel'noe zaklyuchenie*, pp. 41–3; *Revolyutsionnaya Rossiya*, no. 1, 25 December 1920, pp. 31–2.

[33] *Obvinitel'noe zaklyuchenie*, p. 44. For socialist revolutionary policy, as laid down at the end of 1921, see *Revolyutsionnaya Rossiya*, no. 11, 1921, pp. 2–7.

simplification. Their support of armed struggle was neither resolute, continuous nor unqualified. They remained faithful according to their lights to their *Narodnik* traditions. They continued to believe that the overthrow of communism must come by the act of the people itself, by the 'people's verdict'. Above all, they were throughout restrained in their activity by the fear lest in opposing the Communists they should unwittingly help to put a reactionary dictatorship into power.

When after the end of the civil war, the Soviet government was concerned to justify in the eyes of foreign socialists and communists its treatment of the Russian socialist parties, it endeavoured to portray the Socialist Revolutionaries as ruthless opponents and supporters of counter-revolution whom they had been constrained to destroy. It was with this object that a trial of some leaders of the socialist revolutionary party was held in June 1922. The intention to hold this trial was announced by the Russian government in February 1922, and caused some consternation among foreign socialists. In April 1922, at a meeting in Berlin between Bukharin representing the Third International, and leaders of the Second International, assurances were given by Bukharin that facilities would be afforded to the accused for a fair trial and proper defence, and that no death sentences would be carried out.

The trial was held in Moscow between 8 June and 25 July 1922. The three judges, with G. Pyatakov presiding, were all communist party members of long standing. The defendants were divided into two groups; one group headed by Gots, Gendel'man, and Timofeev, consisted of those leading Socialist Revolutionaries whom the Communists held in captivity, including a number of members of their Central Committee. Their defence was conducted by the socialist Vandervelde and by some members of the Russian Bar, notably Murav'ev. The second group, headed by Ratner, consisted of a number of renegades from the party, or of Socialist Revolutionaries who had long made their peace with the Communists. Their 'defence' was conducted by Bukharin, and by several pro-communists, including Sadoul. The leading members of Vol'sky's group, including Vol'sky himself, were stated to have been amnestied and were exempted from trial.[34] Of the

---

[34] *Obvinitel'noe zaklyuchenie*, p. 107.

two groups, only the first was genuinely on trial. The members of the second group, and their defending counsel, vied throughout the trial with the prosecution to incriminate both themselves, or their clients, and the members of the first group.[35]

Within the limits of a trial in which the elementary principles of natural justice were not observed, the real defendants, aided by their counsel, endeavoured to defend themselves against the charges. Murav'ev, in particular, fought for his clients with spirit and considerable courage. But before long both Vandervelde and Murav'ev, after a series of protests against the denial to their clients of their right to call witnesses or produce documents, and other obstructions, withdrew from the defence. The occasion of their departure was an organized demonstration which took place in the court and demanded the conviction of the accused. When the judges on 23 June rejected the protests of Vandervelde and Murav'ev against their conduct in permitting this demonstration, all the advocates defending the first group of accused left the court. Murav'ev ended his last speech to the judges with the words: 'Woe to that country, and woe to that nation which treats the law with disrespect, and mocks at those who stand up in defence of it.'[36]

The object of the trial was to fasten on the socialist revolutionary Central Committee responsibility for the attempt on Lenin's life in August 1918, and other terroristic acts; and to show that the ostensible abandonment by the party leaders of armed struggle in June 1919 had been merely a blind for a continued policy of acts of terror and conspiracy, underground resistance, and co-operation with Denikin's Russian Volunteer Army. The evidence adduced was that of a number of renegade Socialist Revolutionaries. Quite apart from the unreliable nature of such evidence (and it is significant

[35] The fullest report of the trial which has been published is the incomplete account of the proceedings in *Pravda* of 8 June to 25 July 1922. A summary of the evidence is contained in the long Act of Indictment drawn up at the end of the trial (*Obvinitel'noe zaklyuchenie*). One of the many protests by Vandervelde related to the refusal of the Court to honour a promise made by Bukharin in Berlin that the defence would be allowed to make its own shorthand record of the proceedings —*Pravda*, 15 June 1922, p. 3. The official stenogram was apparently never published.

[36] *Pravda*, 24 June 1922, p. 3.

that the cross-examination of these witnesses was for the most part omitted from the published press reports of the trial), it cannot be said that the prosecution achieved its object. The defendants did not deny that they had engaged in open armed struggle against the communist régime from May 1918 until June 1919. But they maintained that thereafter they had given up forcible resistance, without in any way becoming reconciled to communism, and had done no more than give their support to spontaneous peasant revolts against the injustices of Soviet rule.[37] The picture which emerged from the trial was the one which has been sketched in the preceding pages, and which is itself based mainly on the evidence at the trial—rejection by the party as a whole of armed opposition soon after Kolchak's coup d'état, hesitant support of peasant risings, and conspiratorial activity by isolated individuals unconnected with the party organization and acting without its approval. In particular the prosecution failed to establish the fantastic charge of collaboration with Denikin. The defendants in the first group were eventually convicted. Some were sentenced to terms of imprisonment, and some to death. The death sentences were duly suspended, in accordance with the promise made in Berlin. Since none of the defendants has ever been heard of again, alive or dead,[38] this leniency has proved little more than academic.

The existence of a comparatively large number of Socialist Revolutionaries who were prepared to capitulate to the Communists was not an accident. The two groups of defendants at the trial in 1922, the real and the sham, symbolized in some ways the dualism which often lived within the heart of the average Socialist Revolutionary. One half of him saw the Bolsheviks as usurpers, as betrayers of socialism, and as tyrants. But the other half saw the communist state as something, which, however distorted, was of the Russian people. The 'revolution' was sacred, even if its present form was repulsive. No true *Narodnik* should dare to lift a hand against this revolution. His duty was to wait until the spontaneous wrath of the people should rise to sweep away what was evil, though pre-

[37] See the opening speech of Timofeev in *Pravda*, 11 June 1922, p. 3.
[38] For a report that Gots and Gendel'man were alive in 1939, see *Sots. vestnik*, 1950, no. 10, p. 199.

serving what was good. When the people delivered their 'verdict', but not before, the true *Narodnik* could take his place at their head to help them to execute their will. These conflicting emotions contributed to make the Socialist Revolutionaries after the October Revolution into a party in which there was little unity of purpose. But upon one thing all Socialist Revolutionaries were agreed: the overthrow of the communist dictatorship must not be accomplished at the price of restoring a monarchist dictatorship.

CHAPTER X

THE LEGAL OPPOSITION
THE BACKGROUND

Up to the end of 1920, when the civil war was virtually over, an officially tolerated, but in practice persecuted, political opposition continued to play some part in Soviet political life. 'Our party has for some years been the only legal party in the country,' wrote Zinoviev in *Pravda*, on 7 November 1921. Yet it was not primarily by legal enactments, but mainly by a process of arbitrary violence, increasing in intensity between 1917 and 1921, that the communist party by 1921 achieved its monopoly of power. Lenin's writings leave little doubt that he, at any rate, had no intention of ever sharing power with the Socialist Revolutionaries or Mensheviks as a permanent policy. His alliance with the Left Socialist Revolutionaries had been a temporary tactical move. The political function of the Right Socialist Revolutionaries and of the Mensheviks, from his point of view came to an end with the October Revolution. Hitherto, their co-operation had, whether they intended it or not, been a valuable factor in bringing about the general disintegration which made the bolshevik seizure of power possible. Between March and November 1917 spontaneous assumption of power by local bodies helped to undermine the wavering authority of the Provisional Government. Many local soviets, in which Bolsheviks did not predominate, had anticipated the Bolsheviks by seizing power well before November. Such was the case in Luga, where in March 1917 the Soviet, with a majority of Socialist Revolutionaries, had seized power and had become thenceforward the only governing body recognized by the population. Strongly anti-bolshevik, it withdrew its representatives from the Petrograd Soviet in October after the Bolsheviks had secured a majority there; it supported Kerensky after the October Revolution, and was then dispersed by the Petrograd Military Revolutionary Committee.[1] There were many

[1] *Ryabinsky*, p. 100; *Proletarskaya revolyutsiya*, no. 1, 1921, p. 13. The Luga Soviet, which represented some 200,000, and was the largest after the Petrograd

other similar instances.   But local anarchy, though a valuable ally for the seizure of power, was for some time to come to prove a serious obstacle to the Bolsheviks in consolidating it. Moreover, even when the bolshevik seizure of power had won support, or at any rate, not been opposed in the provinces, this support in many cases turned to hostility as the nature of the new government became apparent with the closing down of the socialist press, the Brest-Litovsk peace, the forcible seizure of food in the countryside, and the excesses of the *Vecheka*.   The peace with Germany is even said to have undermined for a time the loyalty of some communist-dominated soviets, of left views, which repudiated the peace and declared themselves in a state of war with Germany.[2]

For some time the central government struggled against provincial anarchy without any adequate apparatus with which to deal with it.   During this process of consolidation its first aim was the elimination of the influence of the socialist parties to whom the population might look for an alternative government.   The general lawlessness ·and impatience of authority throughout the country, where the rule was 'each for himself', presented a major problem even where the local organs were communist in sympathy.   As late as June 1918 a report of the Military Inspectorate speaks of the need to 'put a most decisive end to the indiscipline of the organs of Soviet power in the provinces, and to the disastrous irresponsibility of the workers'.[3]   The problem could not be solved solely by the elimination from local organs of non-communists, since there was as yet no way of ensuring that even the communist members of these local organs would implicitly obey the directions of the centre.   It was some years before the communist party was built up into the disciplined 'monolith' which it has since become.   Still, the task of the centre could be considerably simplified by ensuring communist majorities in the local organs of power.

The local soviets soon after November displaced from power

Soviet, seems to have done useful work in creating order.   It had a large menshevik and a negligible bolshevik component, in addition to its socialist-revolutionary majority.   For an account of its activities, see the memoirs of its chairman, N. Voronovich, 'Zapiski predsedatelya soveta soldatskikh deputatov' in *Arkhiv grazhdanskoy voyny, vypusk vtoroy*, Berlin, n.d.

[2] *Vyshinsky*, p. 719.   [3] *Po sovetskoy Rossii*, p. 7.

such pre-revolutionary local government machinery as still survived. But they in turn rapidly declined in influence. Government was in fact carried on through a variety of improvised forms of local control: such were the Committees of the Poor, set up on 11 June 1918 primarily to enforce the collection of grain in the villages; the praesidia of the executive committees of the local soviets; and different kinds of local committees. There were also emissaries from the central government. On 30 November 1918, when civil war was already raging in a wide area of the country, the Council of Workers' and Peasants' Defence was formed. This council, while having no concern with military operations, which remained under the direction of the Revolutionary War Council (set up on 13 June 1918), was given as its main tasks the supply of the Red Army and the 'militarization of the most important branches of industry' and of the population, for such tasks as the collection of food. Its orders were obligatory on 'all organs of government, local and central, and on all citizens'.[4] Its chairman was Lenin, and its members included Trotsky, as chairman of the Revolutionary War Council; Nevsky, the Commissar of Communications; Bryukhanov, the deputy Food Commissar; Krasin, who had by now rejoined the Communists and was chairman of the Extraordinary Commission for Supplies; and Stalin, representing the Central Executive Committee of the Soviets. It was thus linked both with the Central Executive Committee, still theoretically the highest legislative organ in the country between Soviet Congresses; and with the Council of People's Commissars, of which Lenin was chairman, and which was rapidly superseding the Central Executive Committee as the chief legislative organ. By the end of 1918, therefore, a great deal of authority was already concentrated at the centre. For the execution of their orders the central authorities relied on the rapidly growing communist party, and on the *Vecheka*.

The survival of opposition parties was no easy matter in a country in which the legal system, roughly thrown together in the first weeks of the revolution, offered little protection against the executive. Besides, it soon became evident that such protection as the law provided could be freely disregarded with complete impunity. But before considering the history

[4] *Sistematicheskiy sbornik*, pp. 62–3.

of the opposition parties something must be said of the main features of the communist state in its early years, so far as they related to freedom of expression, person, and franchise.

A resolution of the Central Executive Committee of 17 November 1917 had promised an allocation of paper to all representative shades of political opinion. But it soon proved of no effect, and after July 1918 few non-communist organs were still in existence.[5] Acute shortage of paper in addition to political considerations may have encouraged the communist zeal for closing down all papers but their own. But from the start purely executive action against the non-communist papers proved too unpopular to be workable, possibly owing to the opposition of the largely menshevik printers' organizations.[6] In December 1917, Steinberg, then People's Commissar for Justice, attempted to regulate the legal position of the press, as a concession to public feeling, in a decree put forward on his own authority. The details of his measure have not been published. But it raised angry opposition from Lenin in the Council of People's Commissars, and a new decree was eventually adopted by the council on 28 January. This set up special press tribunals throughout the country, each consisting of three members appointed by the soviets, which were given jurisdiction in the widest terms over all 'crimes committed against the people by means of the press' such as 'all untrue or distorted statements about public life'. They also had the power, without right of appeal, to close down any paper guilty of this offence and to fine or imprison those responsible for its publication.[7] The members of the tribunals were invariably Communists, who identified any criticism of the party with counter-revolution—a fact which severely restricted the range of subjects on which it was possible for non-communist organs to express themselves without fear of being closed down.

The safeguarding of the rights of the individual depended upon the *Vecheka* and the Revolutionary Tribunals. The Revolutionary Tribunals were set up on 7 December 1917.

[5] See Chapter V for the closing down of newspapers immediately after the bolshevik coup d'état.

[6] See *Dokumenty I*, p. 117, for printers' opposition to the closing down of newspapers by the Military Revolutionary Committee in 1917.

[7] *Kozhevnikov*, p. 48.

The first instruction issued to these tribunals did not confer the right of death sentence, but this was granted by a further instruction issued on 16 June 1918 (i.e. some three months before the so-called 'Red Terror'). On 19 December 1917 the Council of People's Commissars, approved Dzerzhinsky's plan for the setting up of the All-Russian Extraordinary Commission of the Council of People's Commissars for the Struggle with Counter-revolution and Sabotage and Speculation (the *Vecheka*),—in one of the few early decrees which does not appear to have been drafted by Lenin.[8] The *Vecheka* was originally designed for investigation only, and its powers of punishment were limited to confiscation of property and deprivation of ration cards. The trial of all offenders was supposed to take place before the newly-created Revolutionary Tribunals. Although no further decree conferred any increased power upon them, both the *Vecheka* and the provincial *Cheka* almost immediately assumed the right of disposing of cases without trial, frequently carrying out executions.[9] By the end of 1918 some attempts were being made to keep the lawlessness of the *Vecheka* within bounds. On 8 November 1918, the All-Russian Soviet Congress called for strict observance of legality, and specifically restricted extra-legal activity by the executive to cases where the conditions of the civil war and the struggle with counter-revolution required it. In each instance (where extra-legal powers had been resorted to) the Council of People's Commissars was to be informed in writing.[10] On 17 February 1919 the Revolutionary Tribunals were reorganized, and at the same time the *Vecheka*'s power of inflicting direct administrative punishment by imprisonment in corrective labour camps was restricted to cases of open armed rebellion. The tribunals were specifically charged with jurisdiction in all cases of counter-revolution, the *Vecheka* being bound to hand all accused over to them for trial after a pre-

---

[8] *Kozhevnikov*, pp. 59–61. Dzerzhinsky's plan was first discussed in the Military Revolutionary Committee on 4 December—see *Lyubimov*, p. 187.

[9] *Kozhevnikov*, p. 60; although the 'terror' properly so-called did not start until September 1918, after the attempt on Lenin's life, it was common knowledge, not denied by the Bolsheviks either at the time or since, that numerous shootings by the *Vecheka* took place in the first few months of power. See *B. & F.*, p. 574, note 27, for estimates of victims during the first six months of the *Vecheka*'s existence.

[10] *Kozhevnikov*, pp. 46–59; *S.U.R.*, 1918, § 908 of no. 90. *S.U.R.* 1919, § 130 of no. 12; § 138 of no. 14.

liminary investigation. Not long after, on 25 April 1919, an order was issued to free all political prisoners not regarded as dangerous. In practice all these provisions remained to a very great extent a dead letter. Side by side with the legal safeguards there developed a widespread disregard for the law on the part of the *Vecheka*, local *Cheka* and the local soviet executive committees, and by Communists throughout the country, which the central authorities did nothing to discourage. In particular, administrative arrests increased and multiplied, soon to be followed by administrative deportations to the forced labour camps. These were first set up on 15 April 1919 by a decree which established the present pattern of exploitation of forced labour for state economic projects under the control of the Commissariat of the Interior, the N.K.V.D.[11]

That such administrative convictions and deportations were taking place without any constitutional authority is evident from the fact alone that the decrees of amnesty issued during 1920 specifically include the category of those under administrative arrest. Since the power of the *Vecheka* of inflicting imprisonment by administrative action was by the decree of 17 February 1919 restricted to those guilty of open armed rebellion, who were in any case excluded from every amnesty, this was a category which legally did not exist. The illegal practice was finally legalized on 21 March 1921, when administrative organs were first officially empowered to impose sentences of imprisonment and exile, limited to five years. This power of inflicting administrative sentences extended vaguely to 'persons recognized as dangerous to the Soviet structure'.[12] But, at any rate in theory, the distinction between political and other prisoners, which had had so long a history in Russia, was preserved. Political arrest and imprisonment, as the *Vecheka* frequently emphasized in its orders, was preventive, not punitive. To remedy the violations in practice of this theory an order of 30 December 1920 drew attention to reports that members of the various political parties were being detained in 'extremely bad conditions' and that they were being treated 'incorrectly, and often even roughly'. The order goes on to direct that such prisoners

[11] *S.U.R.*, 1919, § 124 of no. 12; § 130 of no. 12.
[12] *S.U.R.*, 1921, § 138 of no. 22.

must be treated as persons detained for reasons of public safety, and not as persons undergoing punishment.[13] There is overwhelming evidence that these political prisoners were treated with savage brutality in very many instances. But it was probably true that this treatment was often due more to local excesses than to any deliberate policy, unless the indifference of the centre to non-observance of the law and to local excesses could be called a policy.

Freedom of the voter or candidate in elections to the soviets was no better protected than freedom of press or person. On 10 July 1918 the Fifth All-Russian Congress of Soviets adopted the constitution of the Russian Socialist Federal Soviet Republic (R.S.F.S.R.). There was nothing in this constitution to deprive socialist parties of their right to existence, except the vague provisions of paragraph 23: 'To safeguard the interests of the working class as a whole, the R.S.F.S.R. denies to individuals and groups rights which they may use to the detriment of the socialist revolution.' Certain categories of persons were denied both the vote and the right to be candidates for election to the soviets, but these persons (such as 'kulaks', priests, or former police officials) would not in any ordinary interpretation of the term have included many members of the socialist parties. But the door to illegal practices was thrown wide open by the provisions relating to elections. The election of any candidate could be annulled by the next higher soviet in the hierarchy (paragraph 76). Elections were to take place both in accordance with local electoral custom and in accordance with central instructions.[14] No central instruction appears to have been published in these early years. But elections were invariably conducted by a show of hands, the secret ballot being despised as degrading to a socialist state.[15] A draft instruction on electoral procedure, prepared by Vladimirsky (the leading authority on the subject up to 1921), no doubt represents practice in Russia in 1920–1. One of the provisions of this draft was that the electoral commission in each district (appointed by the communist dominated executive committee of the local soviet) should 'on the day of the elections . . . take steps to remove from the electoral premises all persons having no right

[13] Quoted in *Latsis*, p. 62.
[14] For the constitution, see *Bunyan*, pp. 507–24.　　　　[15] *Mikhailov*, p. 17.

to participate in the elections. All those who have been known to engage in malicious agitation against the soviet power . . . shall be arrested and handed over to the courts.'[16] There was no provision to help these all-powerful commissioners to decide exactly where legitimate criticism ends, and 'malicious agitation' begins.   It is not difficult to imagine the abuses to which such a system gave rise in practice.   To this should be added the fact that the ratio of representation varied from place to place, with the result that by increasing the representation, for example, in the case of individual pro-communist factories or regiments and at the same time lowering the total composition of a soviet, it was always possible to reduce the relative influence of the anti-communist element in a particular district.   A declaration addressed to the Moscow Soviet by its menshevik 'fraction' on 6 March 1920 gives a picture of the electoral machine at work.

> We say nothing of the innumerable instances of direct acts of violence against the will of the electors, terrorization, pressure and other abuses, which took place in the [recently concluded] electoral campaign.   But it is impossible to be silent about the shocking inequality of electoral rights conceded to different categories of workers.   Unheard of privileges are conferred on the higher organs of such organizations as are in communist hands.   Thus, for example, the Moscow *Guberniya* Council of Trade Unions, consisting of one hundred and thirty delegates, is represented here [in the Moscow Soviet] by nearly one hundred (94) deputies.   Constituency boundaries are manipulated at will. . . .   Twenty-four hour limits for the nomination of candidates play straight into the hands of the party which enjoys the monopoly of means of communication. . . .   With compulsory open voting in the immediate presence of representatives of government authority . . . and . . . the almost open fusion of the electoral organization with the organization of the communist party—who can affirm, in such conditions, that the results of the election can with any degree of accuracy represent the real will and feeling of the workers?[17]

Such provisions and practices made illegal repression of the

---

[16] M. Vladimirsky, *Organizatsiya sovetskoy vlasti na mestakh*, pp. 30–3.
[17] Reprinted in *Guins*, Vol. II, pp. 564–5.   There is ample evidence in Soviet publications of the habitual forcible frustration of elections, without any pretence at legal authority for it—see e.g. V. P. Antonov-Saratovsky, (ed.) *Sovety v epokhu voennogo kommunizma*, Vol. I, pp. 401 *et seq.*

opposition parties an easy matter, and it is a tribute to the courage and persistence of these parties that until 1921 they succeeded, in spite of all efforts directed against them, in retaining substantial representations in soviets. Thus in 1920, for example, menshevik delegates in provincial soviets numbered: in Kharkov 205, in Ekaterinoslav 120, in Kremenchug 78, in Tula 50, and 30 each in Smolensk, Odessa, Poltava, Kiev, and Irkutsk.[18] The size of the anti-communist contingents in the soviets was not measured solely by the Mensheviks, the main, indeed often the only opposition party, so much as by the non-party delegates, who were often menshevik sympathizers in disguise. Thus, in the second half of 1919, according to an official computation, the 'non-party' contingent on the local soviet executive committees averaged nearly one-seventh throughout the country, and from the fact that 'communist sympathizers' were separately listed it is a fair deduction that 'non-party' in this context was equivalent to 'anti-communist'.[19] In practice, however, the importance of this opposition was reduced to nil by the fact that the real power was vested in the praesidia of these executive committees, in which Communists invariably predominated. Moreover, in the absence of proportional representation and fair elections, representation in the local soviets bore no relation to the composition of the annual All-Russian Congresses of Soviets, upon which after 1918 only Communists and pro-communist non-party deputies enjoyed the right of vote, their resolutions being invariably adopted unanimously. Tiny representations were allotted to the legally recognized opposition parties—the Mensheviks, the Vol'sky group of Socialist Revolutionaries, an occasional Anarchist, the Maximalists, and, at any rate after 1920, a few Left Socialist Revolutionaries. Moreover these parties were represented not by elected deputies, but by delegates selected by virtue of a decree of 28 November 1919, which first admitted the tolerated opposition parties to the Seventh Soviet Congress with a 'consultative voice'.[20] This meant that they could not vote. The

[18] See F. I. Dan, in Martov, *Geschichte*, p. 318.
[19] See M. Vladimirsky, *Sovety, ispolkomy i syezdy sovetov, vypusk I*, pp. 7, 9.
[20] *S.U.R.*, 1919, § 557 of no. 59. cf. Dan, *Dva goda skitaniy*, pp. 93–4, for a description of his summons to and appearance at the Eighth Soviet Congress in December 1920.

practice continued in the congresses held in 1920 and 1921. Immediately before the meeting of a congress the leaders of these parties, for example, the Menshevik Dan or Steinberg in 1920, would be suddenly summoned to attend as deputies 'with a consultative voice'. Here, to the accompaniment of jeers, catcalls, and interruptions (faithfully recorded in the stenogram), the opposition delegates were permitted to make their speeches and to put forward their resolutions, which had no possibility of securing a single vote. This curious practice had several advantages from the Communists' point of view. It enabled them to point to the tolerant nature of their régime —and, so far as foreign observers were concerned, apparently to succeed in convincing them, in view of the legend which persists to this day in many accounts of the early years of the R.S.F.S.R., that opposition parties were freely permitted to function until 1921. It exhibited in the glare of publicity the representatives of the parties concerned as discredited remnants without a following and without support. Above all, as Lenin once explained, their speeches served as useful reminders to critics within the communist party that such criticism bore a striking similarity to that of the opposition parties, and was therefore, by implication, playing into the hands of counter-revolution.[21]

The most important legal opposition, the Mensheviks, requires separate treatment.[22] The working of a 'legal opposition' in the early years of communist rule is illustrated by the fates of a number of minor parties which never succeeded in exercising any serious influence.

Three small groups of Socialist Revolutionaries maintained for a few years some degree of independent political existence. One such group was the Union of Socialist Revolutionary Maximalists, which since 1906 had existed as a left extremist group inside the main party. Before the revolution the Maximalists were particularly active in armed expropriations, which had brought them into close contact with the Bolsheviks. They were also insistent in their demand for the socialization of industry, and attempted to a greater extent than the main party to win a following among the proletariat. After the October Revolution they supported the Bolsheviks but endeavoured to

[21] *Vs. syezd VIII*, p. 57.   [22] See Chapter XI.

act as a 'ginger group' to keep them on the true left path. They agitated for a 'labouring republic' and advocated socialization and workers' control in place of the communist policy of nationalization and centralized control. Like the Left Communists, they criticized the replacement of workers' initiative by dictation from above. They opposed the peace treaty, though they recognized its inevitability, fearing much as did Bukharin and Obolensky that it heralded degeneration of the pure revolutionary spirit. They did not in principle object to terror, conceding the necessity for 'inequality of rights and even deprivation of the right to life' in the case of those who refused to work and of 'enemies of the working people'. They also accepted restrictions on the freedom of the press if it became 'harmful to the community'.[23] There was little in all this to divide them from the Communists, though here and there maximalist voices were raised already in 1918 against the atrophy in the one-party soviets, the growing isolation of the Communists from the masses, the misdeeds of local communist commissars, and the like.[24] The Maximalists were allowed to publish a weekly paper, *Maksimalist*, and returned a few delegates to the soviets. But it was not long before they split into a pro-communist majority and an anti-communist minority. In April 1920 the pro-communist majority of the party decided to fuse with the Communists, while the anti-communist minority soon thereafter disappeared into prison and exile.[25]

The other two groups, the Revolutionary Communists and the Populist (*Narodnik*) Communists, came into existence shortly after the left socialist revolutionary rising in July 1918. They neither attempted any serious opposition to the Communists, nor attained any political influence. The Revolutionary Communists were founded by a number of prominent Left Socialist Revolutionaries, including Ustinov, Kolegaev, Cherny, and Bitsenko. Natanson inspired the foundation of this party, but did not himself participate either

---

[23] See *Maksimalist*, no. 4, 7 October 1918, pp. 9–10, for the text of their draft constitution for the 'Labour Republic' adopted in May 1918. See also Soyuz S-R Maksimalistov, *O rabochem kontrole.*

[24] *Maksimalist, loc. cit.*, p. 14.

[25] *Pravda*, 19 December 1919; *Bol'shaya sovetskaya entsiklopediya*, Vol. XXXVII, pp. 771–2.

in its inauguration or in its subsequent activities.   The programme of the Revolutionary Communists differed little from
traditional socialist revolutionary policy—workers' control of
industry through an elected organ of trade union representatives, and common ownership and enjoyment of land.   But
they recognized the temporary need for government compulsion exercised through the soviets, in which 'free election of
deputies from among the toiling masses . . . guarantees a
maximum of democracy in the conditions of the transitional
period'.   The programme, while rejecting the dictatorship of
one party, is silent on all the essential minimum guarantees
of personal freedom.   By thus refraining from any criticism
of communist practices, the Revolutionary Communists pur-
chased a period of free existence.   Nor need their doctrines
have been an embarrassment to the Communists, but rather
the contrary, since both explicitly and implicitly they accepted
the premiss that the communist régime was moving forward
towards a state in which the human personality would ultimately enjoy that freedom which socialist revolutionary doctrine
upheld.   For two years this little party enjoyed the privilege
of publishing a periodical and of sending its representatives
to the soviets without fear of arrest.   But it exercised no
political influence.   In 1919 many of the leaders of the
party, including Bitsenko, Kolegaev, and V. Cherny joined
the Communists, and there were also defections to the right.
In September 1920 the Revolutionary Communists decided to
fuse with the Communists.[26]   The Populist Communists only
survived for a few months.   They decided in November 1918
to cease independent existence and to merge with the Communists, justifying their decision by the argument that the
Narodnik parties (i.e. all Socialist Revolutionaries) had stopped
halfway, and had 'failed in their historic mission of uniting the
poorest peasantry and the town proletariat on the path towards
the common aim—the liberation of labour'.   During their
short period of independent existence they published a paper,

---

[26] See *Lenin*, Vol. XXIII, pp. 582–4; their main periodical was entitled *Trud
i bor'ba*.   See also the broadsheets (undated) issued by the party, 'Zemel'nyy
vopros', and 'Kak dolzhno byt' organizovano narodnoe khozyaystvo pri vlasti
trudyashchikhsya', both brought back by the British Labour Delegation in 1920,
now in the British Museum.   The Revolutionary Communists also published
some provincial newspapers during 1919 and 1920.

Znamya trudovoy kommuny, edited by G. Zaks, A. Oborin, N. Polyansky, and E. Kats.[27]

The much more numerous Anarchists represented a political tendency rather than a political party. The heterogeneous groups which went under this name never attempted to form themselves into a single organization. Between March and November 1917 the Anarchists had been growing in influence and numbers.[28] Their hostility to all state authority made them ready and welcome allies of the Bolsheviks in the making of the revolution, and many of their number played a useful part in the seizure of power. As Lenin's opponents were quick to point out, bolshevik and anarchist slogans were in many instances identical. The position was very different after the Bolsheviks had seized power. Lenin's hostility to the indiscipline of anarchism, his impatient realism, and his belief in the need for the survival of a strong state for a long period after the revolution all placed him worlds apart from anarchism so far as theory was concerned. The imposition of centralized, disciplined control over the country which the Bolsheviks set themselves as their first aim, had no greater enemy than anarchism. Its unpractical idealism and impatient, if understandable, dislike of authority, held powerful attraction for the Russians, and could have proved a disruptive force without itself having either the organization or the unity to offer an alternative to bolshevism. 'The majority of Anarchists think and write about the future, without understanding the present,' Lenin said to Nestor Makhno in June 1918. 'That is what divides us Communists from them.'[29]

The Russian Anarchists between 1917 and 1920 were a varied conglomeration of harmless idealists, active terrorists, groups of anarcho-syndicalists, partisans, theorists, and some criminal elements. They were united in one determination alone—to resist union into any more disciplined organization

---

[27] *Lenin*, Vol. XXIII, pp. 581–2.

[28] See an article by Polonsky in *Novaya zhizn'* of 15 (28) November 1917, on the growth of anarchism from insignificance to a 'power which must be reckoned with' in the course of the few months before November 1917. See also *Sukhanov*, IV, pp. 283–8, for evidence of a not inconsiderable following among the workers enjoyed by the Petrograd Anarchists in June 1917.

[29] N. Makhno, *Russkaya revolyutsiya na Ukraine*, kniga II, *Pod 'udarami kontr-revolyutsii*, Paris, 1936, p. 131. Lenin nevertheless helped Makhno to return to occupied Ukraine to reorganize the anarcho-communists.

than their own loose form of confederation of groups and individuals; for they believed, with the example of the Communists before them, that centralized organization and discipline were the death of political integrity. When Kamenev in 1920 offered the Moscow Anarchists freedom to issue their papers and to run their clubs and bookshops in exchange for their adoption of party discipline and a purge of the criminal and irresponsible elements which had infiltrated into their membership, they indignantly rejected the offer.[30]

Many Anarchists had worked closely with the Bolsheviks in the preparation for and in the seizure of power. The peace treaty and the growing authoritarianism soon alienated the majority of them. Yet there were still many individual Anarchists who believed that 'every revolution is an epoch of progress for humanity',[31] and looked beyond the immediate transitory period of state tyranny to a more libertarian future. Such were Herman Sandomirsky and Alexander Shapiro, who worked with Chicherin in the Commissariat for Foreign Affairs, and there were many others. Kropotkin himself spent his last years aloof from political activity, writing a book on ethics, and confident that anarcho-syndicalism would yet save the revolution. In the last letter he wrote, he still believed that the Russian revolution, although it 'has inevitably taken a centralist and authoritarian turn', nevertheless 'presents the possibility of a transition from capitalist society to socialist society'. To the British Labour Delegation, which visited Russia in the summer of 1920, he sent a message: Though dictatorship of one party was 'doomed to failure', the revolution had nevertheless introduced new social conceptions 'which have come to stay'.[32]

In addition to valuable collaborators in the higher administration, the Communists also found among the less reputable elements of the Anarchists many useful recruits for the *Vecheka*. These two factors, fear of the Anarchists as a disintegrating element in the country, and hope that they could individually be attracted to soviet service, led to a policy alternating between wholesale persecution and minor concessions. The injustice

---

[30] V. Serge, 'The Danger was Within', in *Politics*, March, 1945, p. 76.
[31] P. Kropotkin, *Parizhskaya kommuna*, p. 25, written in 1907.
[32] See his letter to De Rejger of 23 December 1920 in the *Communist Review*, no. 1, May 1921, p. 20. *B.L.D. Report*, pp. 89–92; cf. *Goldman*, Chapter XVII; Emma Goldman visited Kropotkin when she was in Russia in 1920.

of this policy caused men like Volin (V. M. Eichenbaum) to prefer life in prison to the alternative of working for the Communists (he had been offered the post of director of education in the Ukraine). It is plain from the evidence collected by the anarchist groups in Berlin that communist repression of Anarchists was not restricted to criminal elements, as usually asserted by the communist leaders, including Lenin. No less than one hundred and eighty prominent Anarchists were listed by these Berlin groups with circumstantial details of their fate, up to 1921. Of these thirty-eight had been shot, seventy were in prison or in exile, and the remainder driven by persecution to their death or to flight from Russia.[33]

The Anarchists were the first political opponents of the Communists to be the victims of an organized attack. In April 1918 an armed raid was conducted on their premises in Moscow and some six hundred arrested. This was apparently the result of a complaint by Colonel Robins (the unofficial United States representative), whose automobile they had assailed. The alacrity with which the Communists agreed to take action showed that the raid was not carried out solely to please Colonel Robins.[34] It led to a stormy debate in the Central Executive Committee, which at that date still included a small vocal and active opposition. The *Vecheka* claimed that the incident had been of no political significance, and that all except the criminals had been released. Many, if not all of the arrested were eventually released. While it is clear that communist action was aimed at the party quite as much as at any criminal elements, there also seems little doubt, as the Anarchists admitted, that there were quite a few criminals among their number. Moreover the Anarchists, both in Moscow and elsewhere, had of late acquired and maintained a private militia, which had been organized during the weeks of the Brest-Litovsk negotiations, in preparation for resistance to the Germans if they renewed their attack. The Communists were not unnaturally anxious to disband it.[35] The raid in

[33] *Goneniya na anarkhizm v sovetskoy Rossii*, pp. 27–63. For the subsequent fate of some Anarchists see also the *Bulletin*, published, at any rate up to April 1926, in Berlin by the Joint Committee for the Defense of Revolutionists imprisoned in Russia.
[34] See *U.S. Foreign Relations*, Vol. I, p. 497.
[35] See the debate in *Protokoly VTSIK IV*, pp. 153 ff. *Popov*, Vol. II, p. 25 says quite openly with regard to this and similar raids that anarchism was played out

April 1918 disorganized, but certainly did not destroy the anarchist organization. In contrast to the Socialist Revolutionaries and the Mensheviks, the Anarchists were never at any time officially outlawed by decree. For the next few years their organization maintained in spite of frequent arrests a precarious existence, at times underground, at times openly. The Anarchists also succeeded in spite of considerable difficulties in publishing a variety of periodicals. Although individual publications were frequently suppressed, and for long periods no daily papers appeared, it is apparently true to say that until the spring of 1921 there was no time during which at least some of their groups did not enjoy some vehicle of self-expression. Moreover, they were able to keep their clubs going until 1921, and it was to these that they looked as the main instrument for spreading their ideas. The principal anarchist organizations were *Nabat* in the Ukraine, and *Golos Truda* and *Vol'nyy Trud* in Petrograd and Moscow respectively, grouped round newspapers of those titles. The two latter were anarcho-syndicalist groups which advocated emancipation of the trade unions from the hold exercised over them by the state, and urged that they should take over its economic functions.[36] They had some influence in the trade unions—in the Bakers' Union in Moscow for example, and in the Post and Telegraph Workers' Union in Petrograd.

In the Ukraine, *Nabat*, of which the main theorists were Volin and Aaron Baron, preached the coming 'third revolution' on anarchist lines; and it was partly under the influence of its ideas that the leader of the Ukrainian anarcho-communists, a Ukrainian schoolteacher, Nestor Makhno, organized his peasant guerrilla army of many thousands, which fought valiantly against the forces of Denikin and Wrangel, but generally refused to co-operate with the Red Army. Not unlike the Ukrainian partisans of twenty-five years later, Makhno's wild warriors fought the common enemy (the White Armies in this case) when the Red Army was remote, and turned against the Red Army when the latter changed its rôle into that of occupying army. During the lull in the fighting at

as a revolutionary force, and under the conditions of the proletarian dictatorship, it was becoming one of the forces of bourgeois counter-revolution', i.e. it was becoming anti-communist.

[36] *Maximoff*, pp. 368–78.

the end of 1919, an anarchist peasant republic inspired by *Nabat* was set up in the extensive area controlled by Makhno. As in most partisan movements, banditry played its part in this one. To Trotsky, who had an eye to the future problem of the occupation of the territories cleared of the anti-communist forces, Makhno's ill-disciplined bands were anathema, in spite of the military assistance which they provided. A secret order which he had issued to the Ukrainian Front at the end of December 1919 stressed that these bands must in no circumstances be incorporated in the Red Army as units, but that only individual partisans who had been retrained should be recruited; and that no territory should be occupied until the Red Army was strong enough to clear it of 'anarchy and banditry'.[37] In the case of Makhno and the Ukraine, the Communists were successful in liquidating both political and military problems in one blow. In October 1920 they agreed, in return for his co-operation against General Wrangel's forces in the Crimea, to grant an amnesty to Anarchists all over the country (except such as had taken up arms against the state) and to tolerate their organizations. Makhno, in return, in additon to a promise of his military co-operation, agreed that his army should now constitute 'an integral part of the armed forces of the (Russian) Republic', though 'retaining its already established internal régime'. The question of the future organization of his anarchist republic was left open for later discussion. It was a bargain which obviously neither side was likely to keep for long. Immediately on the conclusion of the military operations in November 1920 in which Makhno carried out the first part of his agreement, the Communists accused his forces of a whole series of crimes, organized a raid on them, and shot the principal guerrilla leaders. Makhno himself fought his way out of the raid, and, after some months of fighting against the Red Army, eventually escaped abroad.[38] At the same time mass arrests of Anarchists were carried out in Moscow and elsewhere. It was virtually the

---

[37] *Trotsky, KVR*, Vol. II (i), pp. 308–10.

[38] The most objective account of the Makhno events is *Chamberlin*, II, pp. 232–9. For the pro-Makhno account, see *Arshinov*, pp. 171–89; for the Soviet account see *Grazhdanskaya voyna*, Vol. III, pp. 511–12; *Kubanin*, pp. 153–63; for the Soviet charges against Makhno's forces, which led to the raids, see *Petrogradskaya Pravda*, 5 and 8 December 1920. See also *Voline*, pp. 509–690.

end of freedom for the Anarchists. A few of them were still to enjoy one day of liberty, when they were released from prison in Moscow to attend Kropotkin's funeral on 13 February 1921.[39] Members of organizations which still survived after the arrests of 1920 were forcibly rounded up after the Kronstadt rising in March 1921; these last repressions extended even to harmless idealists like the Universalists, who at the end of 1919 had issued a manifesto: 'We proclaim the whole earth for all the peoples!', and to the followers of Tolstoy. The last surviving anarchist periodicals, such as *Vol'naya Zhizn'* and *Universal* were closed down.

The indiscriminate repression of the Anarchists aroused considerable public feeling, and it is significant that none of them was ever brought up for public trial. Many members of the communist party, who were ready to accept repressions against socialists, were disturbed by repressions against men with many of whom they had fought side by side in the revolution and felt a good deal of kinship. That the Anarchists were often a disrupting element which made communist rule even more difficult in the early years is no doubt true. But it is also probable that the senseless violence practised against them contributed to the rising popular discontent with communist rule. In May 1921 the Central Committee of the communist party, in a circular which showed a certain sensitiveness to the Anarchists' complaint that they were treated worse in Soviet Russia than in any capitalist country, justified the arrests which followed the Kronstadt rising by the familiar charge that the Anarchists had now become 'counter-revolutionary'.[40] The truth was that even if some Anarchists had in the past years resorted to arms against the Soviet power, they had suffered considerable provocation.

There remains the question of Lenin's attitude to arbitrary action by the executive. There is no doubt that, at any rate

---

[39] There are several good descriptions of this funeral, see e.g. V. Serge, *loc. cit.*, p. 78; *Berkman*, pp. 288–90. For the anarchists' appeal to Lenin for permission to attend the funeral see *Anarkhicheskie organizatsii*, no. 1657, 13 February 1921, a broadsheet published by the anarchist organizations who were responsible for making arrangements for Kropotkin's state funeral. See also a special issue, *Anarkhicheskie organizatsii pamyati Petra Alekseevicha Kropotkina*, Moscow 8/13 February 1921. Both these were legally printed, ostensibly 40,000 copies of each.

[40] See the text of this document reprinted in *Maximoff* from *Vestnik agitatsii i propagandy*, at pp. 454–61.

in the early years, he retained some generosity to political opponents which has long disappeared in Soviet politics. Veterans like Vera Zasulich or Vera Figner could live unmolested. Plekhanov, though for long a severe critic of Lenin and of bolshevik policy, was buried with dignity when he died in May 1918, and Lenin never failed to stress the importance of his contribution to marxism. Martov suffered nothing worse than a public rebuke in 1918 for some tactless revelations about Stalin, and an occasional house search. Until the end of 1918, at any rate, Lenin was making personal efforts through the *Vecheka* to curb some of the excesses of its officials.[41] But it is doubtful whether it was much use writing notes to the *Vecheka*, if at the same time he was writing such letters as that to the Elets Communists quoted in an earlier chapter.[42] The lawlessness of communist rule was of his own making. Whether without it he and his party could have survived in sole power is another matter, and of the necessity for such survival at any price he never allowed himself to doubt. He certainly grew impatient with some of the grosser vulgarities of the terror, such as Latsis' outpourings in the short-lived periodicals published by the *Vecheka*. But of the need for terror, for arbitrary executive powers of repression, as a permanent state instrument (at any rate until the remote realization of socialism), he seems in 1922 to have had no more doubt than in 1918. In a letter of 17 May 1922 to the Commissar of Justice, Kursky, he wrote in connection with the new criminal code then in preparation, that for the courts to promise the abolition of terror would be a deception. 'The paragraph on terror', he wrote, 'must be formulated as widely as possible, since only revolutionary consciousness of justice and revolutionary conscience can determine the conditions of its application in practice'. The paragraph of the Soviet criminal code which has become the basis for the current wide and arbitrary exercise of repressive power in Soviet criminal law is in essence Lenin's work. His rough draft of the paragraph reads as follows:

Propaganda, or agitation, or participation in an organization, or co-operation with organizations, having the effect (i.e. the

[41] See his notes to the *Vecheka* collected in *Leninskiy sbornik*, Vol. XXI, pp. 228–38.   [42] See Chapter VII.

propaganda or agitation) of helping in the slightest way that part of the international bourgeoisie which does not recognize the equal rights of the communist system coming to take the place of capitalism, and which is endeavouring to overthrow it by force, whether by intervention, or blockade, or by espionage, or by financing of the press, or other means,—is punishable by death or imprisonment.[43]

This new law was not intended as a temporary measure, but as the foundation of a permanent system of justice to replace the system in use during the civil war. But experience had shown that any criticism whatever could be effectively silenced by describing it as 'agitation having the effect of helping . . . the international bourgeoisie', or what was in communist terminology the same thing, 'counter-revolution'. No one knew better than Lenin that the application of the law, which he was proposing as a permanent basis for soviet criminal justice, would in practice be extended to every criticism of the Soviet system to which the rulers of the country objected. With or without the *Vecheka*—and there is no single line after 1917 in Lenin's writings to suggest that this was to be a short-lived institution[44]—it spelt the end of that free criticism which he had once described as the 'duty of the revolutionary'.[45]

[43] *Lenin*, Vol. XXVII, p. 296.
[44] At the end of 1920 Lenin told the Spanish socialist Fernando de los Ríos that a very long time, 'perhaps forty or fifty years', would be necessary in Russia for the transitional period of dictatorship. See Ríos, F. de Jos, *Mi viaje a la Rusia sovietista*, p. 63.
[45] On 23 November 1917, in the Central Executive Committee, *Lenin*, Vol. XXII, p. 76.

CHAPTER XI

THE LEGAL OPPOSITION
THE MENSHEVIKS

None of the opposition parties which have been discussed was faced with the same problem as the Mensheviks. This party alone, of all those which opposed the Communists, set itself from the first a task which it ceaselessly pursued for four years—that of ousting them from power by strictly constitutional means. The Socialist Revolutionaries looked to a popular rising to put an end to communist rule, and never attached serious importance to the winning of a victory in the Soviets. The Anarchists also did not seek an electoral victory, while of the remaining parties none was ever in a position to command a significant following.

For a time after November 1917 menshevik party counsels were still divided. A minority was in favour of immediate active struggle against bolshevism. Others, like Dan (who had smuggled Lenin's *What is to be Done?* in a false-bottomed suitcase into Russia fifteen years before, and should have known the Bolsheviks better) still believed that the bolshevik party would split, that the majority of them were reasonable, and that a coalition of all socialists would result. By the end of 1917 Martov and his internationalist group were once again working closely with the rest of the party. The internationalists had continued to maintain some contact with the new government after the departure of most of the Mensheviks from the Second Soviet Congress had made Trotsky's task so very much easier. But it was only a fragmentary representation which struggled bravely for a hearing in the Central Executive Committee. Martov was undoubtedly the outstanding menshevik figure. When once the bolshevik seizure of power and the subsequent peace had become established facts, the principal source of conflict within the menshevik ranks disappeared, and it was natural that Martov should have become the undisputed leader of the party. In May 1918 the breach in the menshevik ranks was finally healed when he and his followers decided, against only one dissenting vote, to reunite with the rest of the party.[1]   The majority now led by him and Dan formulated the main lines of menshevik policy as they were to remain as long as the party survived inside Russia,—namely, opposition to bolshevik one-party rule by all legal means, but no armed resistance, and no support of foreign intervention.   A minority, led by Lieber, favoured some understanding with the Allied Powers, but this difference of view did not prevent a greater measure of agreement on policy at a menshevik conference held in May 1918 than probably ever before in the party.   Resolutions were adopted denouncing intervention and demanding the recall of the Constituent Assembly and independent, freely elected soviets.[2]   In the following December a further party conference made one important modification in policy: the demand for recall of the Constituent Assembly was now dropped, on the grounds that it had become a slogan which could be exploited by the forces of counter-revolution.[3]

The influence of the Mensheviks in the country had sunk to insignificance by October 1917, by which time most of their supporters had been won over to the Bolsheviks.   But the unpopularity of government policy after the revolution was beginning to win many of them back.   By the middle of 1918 the Mensheviks could claim with some justification that large numbers of the industrial working class were now behind them, and that but for the systematic dispersal and packing of the soviets, and the mass arrests at workers' meeting and congresses, their party could eventually have won power by its policy of constitutional opposition.   In the elections to the soviets which were taking place in the spring of 1918 throughout Russia, arrests, military dispersal, even shootings followed whenever Mensheviks succeeded in winning majorities or a substantial representation.   Innumerable instances of violence figure at this time in the pages of the menshevik party press.

---

[1] *Ermansky*, pp. 184–5.   The dissenting vote was Ermansky's.

[2] See *Oldenbourg*, pp. 390–5, for the menshevik conference in December 1917; for the May conference, see *Bunyan*, pp. 187–8; *Vardin*, pp. 83–7.   The menshevik Central Committee in June 1918 consisted of the following: Abramovich, Astrov, Akhmatov, E. Broydo, Gorev, Dalin, Dan, Ermansky, Kuchin, Lieber, Maisky, Martov, Martynov, Trifonov, Troyanovsky, Cherevanin, Erlich, Yugov, and Yakhontov.

[3] *Partiynoe soveshchanie R.S.-D.R.P.*, pp. 23–5.

Many of our comrades in the provinces are arrested, then released, then once again arrested. . . . In Saratov, the newspaper *The Proletarian's Word* has been closed down, in case it should be used for counter-revolutionary articles. In Tula the menshevik newspaper is constantly changing its name. . . . In Tambov the Soviet has been declared dispersed for ever . . . In Yaroslavl' the Soviet is dispersed . . . In Tambov the Postal and Telegraph Congress has been dispersed, and the delegates told to leave in forty-eight hours.[4]

In March 1918 even Martov, whose integrity no Communist ever dared to challenge, had found himself on trial before one of the newly set up press tribunals. He had accused Stalin in his paper *Vpered* of raising funds for the Bolsheviks before the revolution by armed hold-ups in Baku, and alleged that he had therefore been expelled from the social democratic party. The trial came to a hurried and inconclusive close when Martov secured an adjournment to enable him to collect evidence, and in the end he was merely reprimanded. The public prosecutor appealed against the mildness of this sentence to the Central Executive Committee, which upheld his appeal in principle, but did nothing further in the matter.[5]

On 14 June 1918 the Mensheviks, along with the Socialist Revolutionaries, were expelled from the Central Executive Committee.[6] Immediately thereafter they were also expelled from soviets throughout the country. The effect of the decree was to render the Mensheviks (or as they now called themselves, the Russian Social-Democratic Labour Party) illegal. But it did not make much difference to their daily political life, in which arrests had become normal. Before long their entire press was closed down, and they never recovered it. The central menshevik organ, *Rabochaya gazeta*, had been closed down on 1 December 1917 by the Military Revolutionary Committee. It reappeared next day as *Novyy luch*, which survived until May 1918. In fact, until the middle of 1918 there was quite an extensive party press in existence, including *Vpered* (closed in May), *Novaya zarya*, *Partiynyya izvestiya*, *Rabochiy internatsional*, *Professional'nyy soyuz*, *Rabochiy mir*,

---

[4] See *Novaya zarya*, no. 1, 22 April 1918, pp. 31–8.
[5] See *Wolfe*, pp. 470–1, for an account of this trial; and see also *Protokoly VTSIK IV*, pp. 194–7, for the sequel.
[6] See Chapter IX.

Prodovol'stvennoe delo, and *Strakhovanie rabochikh*. A few periodicals appeared sporadically up to the spring of 1919, most, if not all of them, in the territories occupied by the White Armies; and the Moscow Printers' Union, which remained menshevik in majority until its forcible dispersal, published a journal until April 1919.[7] Otherwise the Mensheviks had to rely on illegally handprinted news-sheets which they succeeded with considerable skill in distributing widely.

When on 14 June 1918 the Mensheviks in company with the Socialist Revolutionaries were expelled from the Central Executive Committee, the reason alleged was that they, in common with the Socialist Revolutionaries, had been guilty of fomenting risings on the Don and in Siberia. Henceforward this charge of violent opposition would be made again and again, and the Communists, from Lenin downwards, constantly associated the two parties together in an endeavour to show that both were active supporters of intervention and of counter-revolution. The charge was untrue in relation to the Mensheviks, and the Communists, if they ever believed it, never succeeded in establishing it. A few Mensheviks did participate in the Yaroslavl' rising organized by Savinkov in July 1918, but they were expelled from the party, for they had acted without its knowledge.[8] Maisky, a member of the Central Committee who left the Mensheviks in the summer of 1918 on the grounds that they were insufficiently active against the Bolsheviks, and joined the anti-bolshevik government in Samara, was expelled from the party in September 1918. There were a few similar instances involving individuals or groups who rejected the party's official policy of confining opposition to strictly constitutional means. At the menshevik party conference in December 1918, several local party organizations, whose members had advocated either co-operation with the *Kadety* and the Socialist Revolutionaries, or

---

[7] *Gazeta pechatnikov*, from 8 December 1918 until the end of April 1919. Other menshevik publications were: *Mysl'*, a weekly appearing in Kharkov from January to July 1919; *Gryadushchiy den'*, of which two issues, ending April 1919, appeared in Odessa; and *Yuzhnoe delo*, occasionally in Kiev at the end of 1918.

[8] See Savinkov's evidence at the trial in *Boris Savinkov*, pp. 69–70. For Martov's account see *Sotsialisticheskiy vestnik*, 16 April 1922, pp. 6–7; cf. also Martov's 'Liniya sotsial demokrata' in *Oborona revolyutsii i sotsial demokratiya*, pp. 4 ff.; and his speech in reply to Lozovsky at the Halle Congress of the USPD in 1920: Martov, *Bolshevizm v Rossii i v internatsionale*, pp. 25–8.

support of Allied intervention, were condemned. Among these was the Samara local menshevik organization, some of whose members supported Maisky's adherence to the Samara government. The conference also instructed the Central Committee to use its powers to expel individuals and organizations for such deviations from party policy.[9] The expulsion of Maisky, followed by a refusal to reconsider the decision, showed that the Central Committee, though never over-anxious to use disciplinary measures, did make use of its powers.

To the general campaign of anti-menshevik abuse, the Communists added in 1920 the organization of two trials which were designed to demonstrate the complicity of the menshevik party in counter-revolutionary activity, and in fact failed to do so. It should be observed that the Soviet government at this period had not yet learned the art of the staged trial, with rehearsed confessions. The trials of 1920 and 1921 were often unfair, inasmuch as they frequently denied to the accused elementary rights such as that of calling witnesses, but they were to some extent judicial trials. Such was the so-called Tactical Centre Trial in August 1920, a trial of alleged participants in a right-wing anti-bolshevik conspiracy. A British Labour Delegation on a visit to Russia in June 1920 was informed that this trial would establish the counter-revolutionary activities of the Mensheviks—apparently in an effort to justify to that delegation the presence in prison of so many socialists. In fact the trial at most demonstrated that a few individuals on the right wing of their party had participated, as individuals, in an anti-communist organization.[10] Little more convincing was the trial of the members of the Rostov-on-Don (Menshevik Social Democrat) Committee in April 1921, who had been arrested in May 1920. Their arrest had caused a great deal of feeling and excitement among the Rostov workers who were largely menshevik in sympathy, and the Bolsheviks, to pacify them, promised a local trial alleging collaboration with Denikin in the Ukraine. No such local trial was ever held, but, in the manner usual after such mass arrests in 1920, some of those arrested were released and some

---

[9] See *Partiynoe soveshchanie*, pp. 25–8; cf. *Maisky*, pp. 35–41; *Klimushkin*, pp. 58–9. Maisky, the future Soviet Ambassador in London, subsequently joined the Communists.

[10] *B.L.D. Report*, pp. 55, 57; and *Krylenko*, p. 48.

sentenced by the security authorities without trial. It was only in April 1921 that seven members of the Committee were brought to public trial, not in Rostov, but in Moscow, some of them having been re-arrested specially for the purpose. They were denied proper rights of defence, including the right of calling witnesses, and were duly convicted and each sentenced to five years. The circumstances of the trial alone leave little doubt of the fact that the charge was trumped up. The charge and the evidence adduced were never published. The few lines which the press devoted to the matter merely stated that 'the accused had attempted at first to deny the charges', but that the questioning of the prosecutor and the 'course of the trial' had shown up their 'treachery to the working class and their complete solidarity with the bourgeoisie'.[11] If the charge against them was collaboration with Denikin during his occupation of the Ukraine in the second half of 1919 it was untrue. A detailed account of this period published later by a Soviet author discloses no evidence of any such collaboration by the menshevik-controlled trade unions with Denikin's administration. It does show, however, that the Mensheviks did not hesitate to criticize the Communists and their methods in their party press.[12] The Georgian Mensheviks had, it is true, invited the intervention of the Allied Powers in order to resist intervention by the Bolsheviks. But the Georgian organization was entirely separate from the Russian social democrat organization, with which, after the October Revolution, it had no contacts. The menshevik party conference in Moscow in December 1918 resolved that the conduct of the Georgian Mensheviks made the preservation of any organizational link between them and the Russian party 'unthinkable'.[13]

The charge against the Mensheviks, as a party, of supporting armed anti-communist activity was manifestly false, although constantly reiterated. That the Communists knew it to be so is further shown by the fact that at the height of the Polish campaign in 1920, of which the Mensheviks vociferously disapproved as an attempt to spread communism

[11] *Izvestiya*, 24 April 1921; *Sots. vestnik*, 1 February 1921; 4 May 1921; 20 May 1921; 5 June 1921; 3 April 1922.
[12] *Kolesnikov*, pp. 171 *et seq.*
[13] *Partiynoe soveshchanie*, pp. 25–8.

by force of arms, there were no less than twenty Mensheviks working in prominent official positions in the military administration. Had the charge of collaboration with the enemies of Soviet power been true, they could not have been retained in these positions. The Mensheviks in vain challenged the Communists at this date to dismiss these men from their posts, or to withdraw the general accusations of counter-revolutionary activity. But the best proof of all that the menshevik party was not 'counter-revolutionary' is the fact that it was allowed some semblance of political activity throughout the civil war, and was only finally liquidated well after the war had ended. If the accusations of armed assistance to the Allied intervention and to counter-revolution had been even remotely true, one could surely have expected the position to have been reversed.

The officially illegal existence of the Mensheviks did not continue for long after the decree of 14 June 1918, for on 30 November 1918 the Central Executive Committee repealed it. But the practical difference this made was small. The 'revolutionary majority' of the local soviets ignored the decree and the Mensheviks remained as before subject to arrest by the security authorities with little or no reason assigned.[14] One of their newspapers (*Vsegda vpered*) reappeared, only to be suppressed in a month, after fourteen issues. The 'legalization', coupled with the continued arrests and occasional shootings, seems to have somewhat bewildered Lenin's followers, because he took care to explain it to them at the Eighth Communist Party Congress of 1919. The inconsistent policy of the Communists was provoked, he explained, by the inconsistent policies of the socialist parties themselves, who could not make up their minds whether to support the Communists or not.[15] The 'legalization' of the Mensheviks on 30 November 1918 is indeed something of a problem. Ostensibly the reason for it was a resolution adopted by them in October, known as the October Theses. In these Theses they recognized that the October Revolution 'represents an historical necessity' and rejected 'any form of political co-operation with the classes which are hostile to democracy'. At the same time, they demanded abolition of the communist methods of terror; and

[14] *Partiynoe soveshchanie*, pp. 21-2.
[15] *Protokoly VIII*, p. 18.

promised active support for the Red Army in its operations.[16] There was in fact little difference between these theses and the policy pursued by the party since the spring of 1918, and it is unlikely that it was just as a reward for the theses that the Communists decided to 'legalize' it.   To some slight extent the communist concession was probably due to the remnants of faith in the value of free discussion which certain sections of the communist party retained for some years.   But it may also have owed something to the hope that, in the circumstances of civil war, national unity would prevail over party differences, and that the majority of the Mensheviks would be persuaded by this concession to join the communist party.   Nor at the end of 1918 was this a wild hope.   Many enemies of communist methods were to make their peace during the Civil War.   Gorky, for example, whose outspoken criticism of the behaviour of the Communists had led to the closing of his paper *Novaya Zhizn'* in July 1918, was by 3 December 1918 appealing in the pages of *Pravda*: 'Follow us in the struggle against the old order ... to freedom and to a beautiful life.'

The tolerance, at any rate on paper, of the central authorities, exemplified in the repeal of the decree of 14 June 1918, was short-lived.   In the spring of 1919 the communist Central Committee ordered the arrest of all prominent Mensheviks of whom it was not 'individually known' that they were ready 'actively to help us' in the struggle against Kolchak.[17]   This order, which was interpreted as a blank authority to arrest any Mensheviks, was officially justified on the grounds that the existence at liberty of so many of them, openly criticizing the Soviet power, took up the time of security officers who could better be employed at the front.[18]   But the arrests, which were in most instances only temporary, did not destroy the party machine.   There were, however, many defections to the

---

[16] *Lenin*, Vol. XXIV, p. 760.   But see also Martov, 'Liniya sotsial demokrata', in *Voprosy sotsial-demokraticheskoy politiki, vypusk I*, pp. 5–7.

[17] *Izvestiya Ts. K.*, no. 1, 28 May 1919, quoted in *Protokoly VIII*, pp. 473–5. cf. an order by the *Vecheka*, printed in *Izvestiya* for 1 March 1919, that in view of the fact that the Mensheviks and Left Socialist Revolutionaries were disorganizing the army, industry and transport by their activities, they would be arrested and held as hostages 'whose fate would depend on the conduct of both these parties'.

[18] See *Otchety*, pp. 4–5.   (Ironically enough, as the Communists themselves admitted, it was the Mensheviks and Socialist Revolutionaries who were jointly responsible for the overthrow of Kolchak's government—see Varneck and Fisher, *Testimony of Kolchak*, p. 3.)

Communists by Mensheviks to whom the prospect of further resistance seemed hopeless, or to whom unity in face of the common enemy during the civil war appeared more important than any political differences.[19]   It was such considerations which eventually decided a majority of the Jewish Social Democratic *Bund* to fuse with the Communists in April 1920.[20] But the menshevik organization as a whole survived the repressions of 1919 and 1920, and struggled on as a constitutional opposition.

The popularity of the Mensheviks among the workers, which waxed as discontent with communist rule grew, became an increasing source of concern to the communist authorities. The Mensheviks advocated freely elected soviets, free trade unions, and freedom of speech and press for all workers' parties.   Their obviously justified criticism of the repeated failure of any attempt to observe the provisions of the constitution was a constant embarrassment to the Communists.   'When we hear such declarations, coming from people allegedly in sympathy with us, we say, "Yes, terror by the *Cheka* is absolutely necessary",'[21] said Lenin, in answer to Martov's criticism at the Seventh Soviet Congress.

In the summer of 1919 the Mensheviks elaborated their programme in a manifesto, bearing the somewhat incongruous title (in view of its association with Lenin) of 'What Is to be Done?'.   In the political sphere the manifesto demanded a franchise in the elections to the soviets which would include all workers, free and secret ballot, and unhampered electoral agitation; the subordination of all officials to the Central Executive Committee, restored to its constitutional position of a supreme legislature, with control over all legislative acts; freedom of speech and freedom of press for all workers' political parties; abolition of terror, free election of all members of revolutionary tribunals, and full jurisdiction of the latter over all complaints regarding the actions of officials; abolition of

[19] By Lenin's special instructions those Mensheviks who did join the Communists were the first to suffer during the great purge of the communist party in the autumn of 1921.   See *Lenin*, Vol. XXVII, pp. 12–13.

[20] The fusion did not in fact take place until March 1921.   The *Bund* made a last effort to preserve its autonomous organization, resolutely resisted by the Communists.   Ultimately the *Bund* yielded to an 'arbitral award' by the Communist International, which decided on its dissolution.

[21] *Vs. syezd VII*, p. 75; and pp. 56–73 for Martov's formidable indictment.

the death penalty and of all organs of investigation and administrative punishment, such as the *Cheka*.[22] The extension of the rights of free speech, indeed of any rights, to persons who did not fall within the category of workers, was not part of menshevik policy, at any rate for the immediate future. According to their view, 'the new labour democracy is the democracy of those who take part in public productive labour. Therefore, the complete or partial forfeiture of civil rights by social groups outside this labour democracy (i.e. outside public productive labour) does not violate the democratic principle of class dictatorship.'[23] In economic policy the Mensheviks advocated a series of measures almost indistinguishable from the New Economic Policy to which Lenin turned in the spring of 1921 in a sudden effort to avert the collapse of communist rule. The manifesto demanded the 'retention in the hands of the government of the basic branches of industry and transport, while at the same time permitting participation in them of private capital under state control; the denationalization of internal trade and of medium and small industrial undertakings; the securing to the peasants of their lands; the building up of a system of food supply on the basis of agreement between consumers and producers, with the active participation of free co-operatives; and the retention under state control of the monopoly of foreign trade'.

The Mensheviks had early in 1919 published a protest against Allied intervention, and had appealed 'to all socialist classes and to all trade unions to work for an agreement between the Entente and Lenin's Government'.[24] In the autumn of 1919 they launched a campaign of mass meetings for recruitment to the Red Army and active participation in the civil war, and endeavoured to enlist communist support for their activities on these lines. The Communists were considerably embarrassed by this offer of help. At the centre, the authorities were reluctant to encourage a campaign which

[22] Summary by Martov in 'Nasha Platforma', *Sots. vestnik*, 4 October 1922, pp. 3–8. See also Vardin, in *Za pyat' let*, pp. 46 ff. For the menshevik criticism of the atrophy of the Central Executive Committee, which played little part after 1918, as well as the atrophy of the provincial soviets, and of the development of an irresponsible bureaucracy into a state within the state, see their proposed resolutions and speeches at the Seventh and Eighth Soviet Congresses, *passim*.
[23] Theses adopted on 10 April 1920, reprinted in *B.L.D. Report*, pp. 73–9.
[24] *Humanité*, 5 March 1919, quoted in *Cumming and Pettit*, p. 302 note.

might prove more awkward politically than helpful militarily. In the provinces the Soviet authorities, for lack of a firm central directive, varied in their reaction from the usual arrests to tolerant indifference.[25]

In the course of 1920 the Mensheviks extended their criticism to communist foreign policy, and denounced the subordination of the Third International to the interests of the survival of communist rule in Russia, and its neglect of the revolutionary aims for which it stood. Martov, in particular, was loud in such criticism, both in the Moscow Soviet of which he was a member and elsewhere. He drew attention to the danger inherent in the fact that the Russian communist party had acquired an 'exceptional position' for itself in the Third International, that of 'standing outside the control of international socialism' in its foreign policy. In the autumn of 1920, by which time he was a very sick man, he was readily given permission to leave Russia to attend the Halle congress of the German Independent Socialist Party—the congress at which this party split, the majority deciding to join the Third International. In his speech Martov endeavoured to dissuade the pro-communist majority of the German Independent Socialist Party from accepting the Third International's conditions for membership and he dwelt not only on the repressions to which socialists in Russia were subjected, but also on Russian foreign policy. He attacked Russian policy towards the Eastern peoples, alleging that in the interests of consolidating Soviet power, and in particular of improving Soviet relations with Britain, the Communists had betrayed their mission to help these peoples towards their liberation from the imperialist yoke. He also criticized the fact that in the government of the Far Eastern Republic, formed after the overthrow of Admiral Kolchak, Communists were sitting in a coalition side by side with right wing socialists and liberals.[26] It was a telling attack, likely to find ready response among the growing radical opposition inside the ranks of the Communists outside and inside Russia. But Martov did not return, and there were few, if any, among the remaining menshevik leaders

---

[25] Martov, *Voprosy sotsial-demokraticheskoy politiki, vypusk I, passim.*
[26] For Martov's speech at the Halle Congress see his *Bol'shevizm v Rossii,* which is a reprint of it. For his criticism of Soviet policy in Poland in May 1920 in the Moscow Soviet, see *Sten. mosk. soveta,* no. 4, p. 73.

inside the country who had his qualities. Years of ridicule had not been successful in discrediting his personal reputation for integrity. The loss of his leadership was a very serious one, especially as Dan, his successor, was scarcely able to replace him. But in Berlin, in February 1921, he founded the *Sotsialisticheskiy vestnik* as the central organ of the Russian Social Democratic Party. Its numerous contacts all over Russia enabled it to give a full picture of the fate of menshevism inside the country. The issues of the paper, freely introduced, in spite of occasional confiscation, were widely circulated inside Russia and helped to take the place of the party press which no longer existed.[27]

Throughout 1919 and 1920 menshevik influence grew steadily in the trade unions. The six million or more members of the trade unions represented in 1920 the great bulk of the Russian industrial class. By 1920 there was little love left for the communist party in the largely non-communist rank and file union membership. The Mensheviks, who demanded freedom of the trade unions from communist control, but at the same time advocated radical socialist measures, gained at the expense of the Communists. It is not possible for lack of data to estimate with any accuracy the menshevik following among the industrial proletariat at the end of the civil war. All that can be said with certainty is that Mensheviks, pro-Mensheviks, and other anti-communists together far outweighed the Communists and their sympathizers. Zinoviev, who was prone to exaggerate, estimated in 1921 the total anti-communist following among the industrial workers at 90 or even 99 per cent. Even Trotsky, who ridiculed this as a 'monstrous exaggeration', conceded that the anti-communists were 'very numerous', and was constrained to justify the party dictatorship on the grounds that it 'was more important than some formalistic principle of workers' democracy' in that it defended the fundamental interests of the working class 'even during a period of a temporary wavering in its mood'.[28] In spite of all the Communists' efforts to counteract their influence, the Mensheviks still managed to return quite a considerable

---

[27] As Lenin said of Martov, who was then his neighbour in exile, in a letter of 8 March 1898, 'Fortunately the lad is not one to lose heart.'
[28] *Protokoly X*, p. 353.

delegation to the Second All Russian Trade Union Congress in January 1919. At this congress, together with the kindred party of Internationalists headed by the still impenitent Lozovsky, they gathered 67 votes as against 430 for their opposition resolutions demanding trade union independence from communist control. Lozovsky's outspoken criticism of the activities of the communist cells throughout the country in stifling free union activity was shouted down.[29] At the Third All Russian Trade Union Congress in April 1920, the Mensheviks and their supporters now only numbered 70, out of a total of over a thousand delegates. It is certain that their influence in the unions was much greater than this figure suggests; they had an enormous majority in the powerful printers' union, and according to one of the delegates, Ber, in three of the other principal national unions—the metalworkers', the chemical workers' and the textile workers'.[30] This was the last trade union congress at which the Mensheviks enjoyed any significant representation—in the following year, 1921, the number of their delegates at the Fourth Congress was negligible—nine in all.[31]

But this decline in the number of their delegates to the trade union congresses did not correspond to a decline of menshevik influence inside the unions. On the contrary, by the beginning of 1921 it was obvious that their influence within them was still growing. The danger of this from the communist point of view lay in the fact that there already existed by this date an important group within the communist party whose opposition to centralized party control of the trade unions was becoming a serious problem. This group demanded, in terms not unlike those of the Mensheviks, more active participation by the working classes in the organization and direction of industry, through freely elected trade union representatives.[32] The communist campaign against the Mensheviks had to proceed side by side with a campaign to eliminate opposition within their own party. One after another during 1921 congresses of trade unions upon which Mensheviks and their

[29] *Vs. syezd prof. II*, pp. 97, 65, 32–3.   [30] *Vs. syezd prof. III*, pp. 43, 110.
[31] See *Vs. Syezd prof. IV*, p. 59, for Shtul'man's account of the numbers of menshevik trade unionists in prison at that time.
[32] For the opposition within the communist party see Chapters XII to XVII. For the menshevik policy on trade unions see their Theses adopted on 31 March 1920, reprinted in an English translation in *B.L.D. Report*, pp. 80–2.

supporters secured majorities were forcibly closed down, and union organizations were disbanded and replaced by others upon which Communists predominated. One instance out of many will illustrate the methods adopted. On 26 March 1921 the Moscow Union of Chemical Workers elected Martov as their honorary chairman, instead of Lenin, the rival candidate. On 27 April 1921 the All Russian Central Committee of this union which was entirely communist in composition resolved to take the 'most decisive measures' to 'reorganize' the Moscow Union. But it was some time before they were successful in achieving this. In the autumn of 1921 a congress of the Union of Chemical Workers in Moscow, adopted by a small majority a resolution which, though not ostensibly menshevik in character, contained a demand for the independence of trade unions, which was a doctrine invariably associated with menshevik policy. The communist minority left the congress and forcibly seized the union premises. Another carefully chosen congress was then summoned, which condemned the policy of the old congress and obediently passed a resolution in the approved terms.[33] Repressions against union organizations were followed during 1921 by mass arrests of the workers, who protested with strikes and demonstrations.

During these years, 1919–21, the Mensheviks fought against similar tactics in elections to the soviets. One of the difficulties with which they were often faced was the arrest of their entire organization immediately before an election. Sometimes charges were brought, sometimes administrative sentences were passed, usually the arrested members were released after the election had been concluded. Candidates arriving for an election would often be arrested and detained until it was over, and then released with an apology that they had been mistaken for someone of a similar name. Successful candidates would frequently be declared illegally elected by the electoral commissions, or would be arrested and sentenced on some trumped-up charge—usually for speculation. Since election was by show of hands, it was easy for those workers who were known to sympathize with the Mensheviks to be singled out for

[33] For repressions against unions, see *Sots. vestnik*, 20 April 1921, 20 May 1921, 5 June 1921, 1 September 1921, 15 December 1921. For the action against the chemical workers in the autumn of 1921 see also *Pravda* of 7 and 9 October 1921. And see below for the suppression of the Printers' Union in Moscow.

reprisals, and this made them reluctant to vote for the menshevik lists. Yet, in spite of these difficulties, the Mensheviks
were still succeeding in 1921 in getting a small number of their
delegates into the soviets. The Communists viewed with
uneasiness the fact that, as was the case in the trade unions,
the Mensheviks' reiterated demands for freedom from arbitrary
executive action were beginning to find an echo in some
sections of the communist party. In the Moscow Soviet,
elected in the spring of 1921, the tiny menshevik 'fraction'
succeeded, with the support of communist deputies, and in
defiance of the chairman, Kamenev, in putting through a
resolution that no deputy to the Soviet should be arrested
until the Praesidium of the Soviet had been informed and in
any case not without the consent of the full meeting of the
Soviet.[34] The spectacle of Communists joining with Mensheviks in defence of personal freedom could hardly have been
a welcome one to the communist leaders. The position had
changed from 1918 or 1919 when the very reference by an
opposition speaker to the word 'freedom' was certain to raise
in any communist audience a chorus of jeers, whistles, and
shouts of 'shame!'

The adoption of the New Economic Policy was the signal
for intensified action against the Mensheviks. Lenin gave it
his full approval. 'The place for the Mensheviks, and the
S.R.'s', he wrote in the middle of April 1921, 'both the open
ones and those disguised as "non-party", is in prison, (or on
foreign newspapers, by the side of the White Guards—we
willingly allowed Martov to go abroad)'.[35] The Mensheviks
had for long advocated some such economic policy as that
adopted by Lenin in March 1921. To have left them at
liberty even with such restricted political freedom as they had
enjoyed in 1919 and 1920 would have invited the obvious
question why the party, whose policy had hitherto failed, should
not yield power to the party whose policy was now being
adopted. Economic concessions were inevitable in 1921 if the
communist monopoly of power was to survive. Without the
accompanying rigid political dictatorship this monopoly would

---

[34] *Sots. vestnik*, 8 July 1921. See *ibid.*, I September 1921, for a menshevik
success in the same soviet in getting a debate going on the treatment of political
prisoners in the Moscow prison.

[35] *Lenin*, Vol. XXVI, p. 348; cf. Dan, in Martov, *Geschichte*, p. 319.

have been doomed, since the communist leaders had lost much support not only among the workers but even within the ranks of their own party members.   It was not therefore an accident that the final elimination from political life of the Mensheviks coincided with the first, and most important effort to put an end to freedom of discussion within the ranks of the communist party as well.

The final assault on the Mensheviks began during February 1921 on the eve of the Kronstadt rising, and continued in the weeks following it, during which the New Economic Policy was launched.   Some two thousand were arrested during the first three months of the year, including the whole of their Central Committee.   This wave of arrests coincided with the measures taken to put an end to opposition within the communist party at the Tenth Party Congress in March 1921. This time the arrested were, for the most part, not released, and the menshevik organization suffered a blow from which it never recovered.   There was little menshevik following either among the peasants or among the sailors, and menshevik influence on the Kronstadt rising in March 1921 was negligible. But their political activity was an important factor in the industrial unrest which, in Petrograd and elsewhere, had preceded the Baltic sailors' revolt.   For over a year their leading members remained in prison; yet their organization, although largely broken, continued for a time as best it could its political activity in elections to the soviets.   It was not, however, very successful.   In the Moscow Soviet elected in January 1922 for example there was one Menshevik out of two thousand deputies. The arrested members of the Central Committee conducted from their prison in Moscow a campaign of agitation against the *Vecheka* as represented by Unschlicht, then one of Dzerzhinsky's deputies.   Threatened early in 1922 with the prospect of administrative mass exile to distant provinces, they went on hunger strike, which was successful to the extent that some dozen of them were permitted to leave the country as an alternative to exile.   About ten, including Dan and Nikolaevsky, availed themselves of this choice and reached Berlin in February.[36]   Some thirty-five others from Moscow and many

---

[36] Dan, *Dva goda skitaniy*, Chapter X.   According to what Dan was told by Unschlicht, the decision to permit this alternative of emigration was taken by the

more from the provinces went into exile in distant parts of Russia. By the middle of the year the menshevik organization had ceased to exist inside Russia. No decree or other legal enactment had been passed outlawing the party, since its official 'legalization' in the autumn of 1918. It was destroyed by force and by fraud. In the summer of 1922 the menshevik Central Committee in Berlin decided no longer to permit party members to participate in elections to soviets, since to do so would have exposed their supporters among the workers to increasingly severe reprisals.[37]

In June 1920 a delegation of the British Labour Party visited Russia. Its members had full opportunity of meeting representatives of the opposition parties, and were witnesses of an example of communist methods of suppressing democracy in the unions. In June 1920 there still survived in Moscow a separate menshevik organization of the Printers' Union, with its own central committee, despite the fact that in August 1919 an official new communist central committee had been set up at an all-communist congress—which incidentally represented less than half of the union membership. For some time the Moscow Central Committee, almost entirely menshevik in composition, existed side by side with the new, official, communist Central Committee. This Moscow Central Committee now organized for the benefit of the British visitors a mass meeting of workers, (the last free meeting of its kind, as claimed by the Mensheviks). The proceedings were enlivened by a surprise appearance of Victor Chernov, the socialist revolutionary leader then in hiding, and by his success in evading the efforts of the *Vecheka* to capture him. While the British visitors were still in Moscow this last surviving free trade union paid the penalty. Its leaders (some forty) were arrested, and the offending organization dissolved. The British delegation published full details of this incident.[38] The British

Politbureau by a vote of 3 to 2, with Trotsky voting against it—pp. 249–50. Apparently, according to Radek's account in 1922, Zinoviev wished to have all the menshevik leaders in Petrograd shot when they were first arrested, but the Central Committee of the Communists overruled him—pp. 135–8.

[37] *Sots. vestnik*, 3 February and 23 February 1922. *Sots. vestnik*, 21 September 1922, p. 12; resolution of 12 August 1922.

[38] For the August 1919 congress see *Milonov*, pp. 221–22; for the dissolution of the Moscow Printers Union, see *B.L.D. Report*, pp. 63–72; see also *Revolyutsionnaya Rossiya*, no. 5 (1921), pp. 23–4, where a protest is reprinted signed by a number of the leading printers from prison and giving details of the fates of many of

delegates could have left the country with no illusions as to what was happening in it at the time.   Speaking a few months later in Geneva, one of them, Shaw, stated that 'le prolétariat n'a aucun droit en Russie, et n'a ni la liberté de réunion, ni la liberté de la presse.   Il n'a pas le droit de choisir ses représentants.   L'oppression du peuple russe est aussi grande que sous le tsarisme'.[39]—Yet the report published by the delegation on its return merely refers to personal freedom and freedom of speech as being 'severely repressed in the case of all those whose activities are supposed to threaten the Soviet régime', without explaining that this applied to all socialists.[40] Among the many documents brought back by this delegation was an illegally printed appeal of 40 Right Socialist Revolutionaries, 80 Left Socialist Revolutionaries, 28 Maximalists, 5 Mensheviks, and 55 Anarchists imprisoned in the Moscow prison, addressed to anarchists and socialists of all countries, and asking for their support.   Yet the delegation did not think it necessary to publish this document, two copies of which have remained deposited in the British Museum.   The main purpose of its report was to urge an end to Allied intervention in Russia.   The delegates appear to have accepted the explanation Lenin had given them at an interview, that 'the real authors of the terror are the English imperialists and their allies.   Our terror is the defence of the working class against the exploiters'.[41]   That the real reason for the suppression of political freedom was neither intervention nor the civil war is evident from the fact alone that it was extended and consolidated only well after the end of both.

The *Kadet* leader and historian, Milyukov, suggests that for a brief period in 1921 the communist leaders considered the idea of sharing political power with the Mensheviks, but that the ensuing conversations came to nothing owing to Dan's demands for guarantees of political freedom.   There is nothing

them.   The protest was presumably smuggled out of prison and printed by the Socialist Revolutionaries in their organ; see also Dan, *Dva goda skitaniy*, pp. 7–15; and Chernov, *Pered burey*, pp. 409–12.

[39] *Dixième Congrès*, etc., p. 41.
[40] *B.L.D. Report*, p. 9.
[41] *Lenin*, Vol. XXV, p. 264.   Bertrand Russell, who travelled with the delegation but was not a member of it, produced in his *The Practice and Theory of Bolshevism* an analysis of the reasons underlying communist repression of freedom which has stood the test of over thirty years.

in Dan's memoirs covering the period to corroborate this rather unlikely story. More probable is the account by the Menshevik Liberman, who was working at that time in an important post in the state timber administration, that attempts were made in 1921 to attract individual leaders into the communist party, without in any way relaxing the restrictions on the party as a whole. He confirms that there was a feeling among some of the communist leaders, including Kamenev and Bukharin, 'that it was time to bring other socialist parties into the picture'. Lenin was however opposed to anything more than the admission of individuals into governing bodies.[42] It is more possible that some idea of safeguarding the (ostensibly) legal status of the menshevik party was for a short time in Lenin's mind early in 1922 before the Eleventh Party Congress. There are some grounds for supposing that by this date Lenin, who had given up all active work, no longer saw eye to eye on a number of important questions of policy with the rising party leaders, Zinoviev and Stalin.[43] In a manuscript note for an article which he prepared at the time of this congress there are several brief unexplained references to 'legalization' of the Mensheviks. It is possible, therefore, that for a short time he was considering the idea that repression had gone too far. But nothing of the kind was in fact referred to in his speech, so whatever scheme he may have had in mind must have been abandoned by the time of the congress. In Lenin's notes for his speech at the congress there are no references to 'legalization'. One short entry summarizes the policy to the socialist parties which he outlined: 'Mensheviks and S-Rs: to be shot if they show their noses.'[44]

Indeed, so long as they did not 'show their noses' the Communists remained ready to welcome the services of individual Mensheviks in state organizations. The Mensheviks, in turn, were ready to serve on those conditions, believing it to be their duty to help in the rebuilding of the country.[45] Even

[42] See *Milyukov*, Vol. II, pp. 258–9; *Liberman*, pp. 69–70. According to Milyukov, based on private information, the approach was made by Stalin to Troyanovsky, a member of the menshevik Central Committee, who later became a Communist. [43] See Chapter XVII.
[44] *Lenin*, Vol. XXVII, pp. 525–6; and cf. *Protokoly XI*, p. 27.
[45] Many of the defendants in the trial of the Mensheviks in 1931 had worked in Soviet institutions for years. This outlook was not confined to the

in exile, the Mensheviks, headed by Martov, continued to stress their rejection of any form of violent overthrow of the Communists, characterizing their relation to the Communists as that of a party 'not of revolution, but of opposition',[46] and hoping that the economic concessions of the N.E.P. would in due course be followed by political concessions. It was a vain hope. The Twelfth Conference of the communist party, which met in August 1922, devoted considerable attention to the question of the Mensheviks and other 'anti-soviet' parties and tendencies. The conference was alarmed by a new 'dangerous phenomenon'; the anti-soviet parties had 'changed their tactics', and were endeavouring to 'exploit the legal opportunities of the soviet structure', such as public conferences and 'so called social organizations'. These parties were systematically endeavouring to 'transform rural co-operatives into an instrument of kulak counter-revolution, university chairs into a platform for undisguised bourgeois propaganda, and the legal publishing firms into a means of agitating against the workers' and peasants' power'. The party was enjoined to deal with the new danger by the combined means of 'repressions' directed against opposition parties and intensified propaganda designed to offset their influence.[47]

Thus the Mensheviks perished without firing a shot. By the irony of history, their faith in democratic freedom had contributed not a little to their undoing. By refusing to take power themselves and by failing to support the coalition of anti-bolshevik parties between March and November they helped Lenin to power. After the October Revolution, with large numbers of the working class behind them, an advantage which no other opposition party ever enjoyed, they refused to resort to anything but strictly constitutional means to overthrow him.

Mensheviks. In mid 1921 a group of mainly socialist revolutionary and *Kadet* intellectuals, which became known as the *Smena vekh* ('Change of Landmarks') group, in Prague and in Paris, resolved that the Russian revolution was a national revolution, and that their duty lay not in supporting intervention from without or revolt from within, but in helping Russia to heal her scars (see *Smena vekh*, passim.).

[46] According to Dan, in 1922. A number of right wing Mensheviks broke with Martov on this issue in Berlin in 1922 and formed the *Zarya* group—see *Zarya*, no. 8, 1922, p. 239.

[47] *VKP(b) v rez.*, pp. 553–8.

PART III

TOWARDS THE MONOLITHIC PARTY

CHAPTER XII

EARLY DISSENSIONS
IN THE COMMUNIST PARTY

The disputes within the communist party between 1919 and 1921 differed in character from those of 1918. The patent anarchy which had resulted from the over-hasty putting into practice of extreme socialist doctrines, especially workers' control, had cured the utopian left wing of its illusions. Its intellectual leader, Bukharin veered gradually to the right. By 1920 he fully accepted the need for disciplined management of industry and state compulsion as the inevitable accompaniments of the long transitional phase to communism, when all compulsion would at last cease to be necessary.[1] The acrimonious wrangles of the years of 'war communism' (as the years of extremist socialism which preceded the introduction of Lenin's New Economic Policy in 1921 came to be known) sprang from causes quite different from those which had engendered Lenin's disputes with the left communist intellectuals in 1918. The party struggles of this period can be divided into two phases: the first phase, up to the spring of 1920, during which a fairly united party leadership struggled against a wave of disappointment and dissatisfaction in the lower ranks of the party; and the second phase, culminating in the Tenth Party Congress, in March 1921, during which a struggle for power among different groups within the party leadership was going on at the same time as a struggle by the centre for control over a more organized and clearly-defined opposition from below. These party conflicts took place against the background of the civil war and of a rapidly declining national economy, which by 1920 was verging on complete collapse. They cannot

[1] See his *Ekonomika perekhodnogo perioda*, pp. 114–22.

therefore be analysed without some reference to the main reasons for this collapse.

Three main causes underlay the economic crisis: the disorganization inherited at the October Revolution; the peace treaty with its inevitable consequence, the civil war; and 'war communism', an attempt, as Lenin later described it, at 'an immediate transition to socialism without a preliminary period of adapting the old economic system to a socialist economy'.[2] But serious as the economic situation was by 1920, the core of the problem which confronted the Communists was the fact that the October Revolution, and the consequent dictatorship of the proletariat, had failed to win over the support of the great majority of the population, as theory required. The peasants, whose anarchical seizures of land had helped Lenin to power in 1917, were not prepared to support him in 1919 and 1920. Having got the land which they wanted, their interests as small-holders were little served by socialist measures. The industrial workers, on the other hand, who had been attracted by the promises of workers' control and by the happy anarchy of 1917, fell back when they realized that the socialist utopia was a good deal further off than they had been led to believe. Many of them, as the popularity of menshevism showed, were also repelled by communist methods of government. Engels had foretold the situation which would result from the premature seizure of power by an extremist class party when, at the time of the European revolutions of 1848, he had analysed the peasant rising of the early sixteenth century in Germany.

The worst thing that can happen to the leader of an extremist party [he wrote], is to be forced to take power at an epoch when the movement is not ripe for the leadership by the class which he represents, nor yet for the putting into effect of the measures which leadership by this class demands. What he can do in such a case does not depend on his will. It depends on the level to which the conflict between the various classes is forced, and on the degree of development of the material conditions of existence together with the state of production, commerce, and other circumstances upon which the degree of development attained by the class conflict at the time depends. . . . He thus neces-

[2] In October 1921. See *Lenin* (1), Vol. XVIII, Part I, p. 391.

sarily finds himself in an insoluble dilemma: that which he finds it possible to do is in contradiction with all his utterances hitherto, his principles, and the immediate interests of his party. At the same time, what he ought to do, cannot be done. In a word, he is forced to act in the interests not of his own party and class, but in the interests of that class for the rule of which the movement happens to be ripe. He is thus forced to promote, in the interests of the movement, the interests of a class which is alien to him. At the same time, he is forced to placate his own class with phrases and promises that the interests of that alien class are really its own interests. He who once lands in this crooked position is lost beyond redemption.[3]

In Russia the 'crooked position' had a twofold effect on the communist party. On the one hand it made for unity in face of the common danger of being overthrown. But on the other, it caused grave heart-searchings in those members who, while not prepared to give up the monopoly of power which their party was building up, were disturbed by the difference between the revolution in fact and the revolution of their dreams.

The peace treaty with Germany and the isolation consequent upon the civil war had struck a crippling blow at Russia's economy. But although the Communists had lost more than half the wheat production, all the petrol, and the greater part of the coal, it should have remained possible for the area controlled by them to feed itself, since it still retained a slight potential excess of grain production over its needs.[4] The failure of war communism was therefore primarily a failure of mechanism—a failure of the attempt to base the exchange of village food for town products not on trade, but upon quite separately organized and uncoordinated food collection on the one hand, and distribution of manufactured goods on the other. The forcible collection of food from the peasants was centralized at the end of 1918 under the Commissariat of Food and Supply, acting through commissars in the *gubernii*. The commissars, in turn, organized the armed detachments of industrial workers and of poor‚peasants in the villages who

---

[3] *Der Deutsche Bauernkrieg*, pp. 105–6. Although this work was published in 1850, Engels had been working on the question of the peasant revolt in Germany for some years before.

[4] The potential excess was reduced from the pre-revolution figure of 775 million puds to 87 million puds, as the result of the loss of the most valuable areas. —*Kritsman*, p. 52.

enforced the collection of produce from the more prosperous peasants. At the Sixth Soviet Congress in November 1918, the somewhat anarchical Committees of the Poor were embodied in the village soviets, and thereby brought under more effective control by the central government system. Industrial production was centralized under the elaborate machinery set up in 1918 by the Supreme Council of National Economy. This body, the chairman of which was a member of the Council of People's Commissars, operated in 1920 entirely through its small praesidium, controlling some forty central directorates of the main branches of industry and a number of other central organs of management. In theory, the industrial products of the towns were to go to the villages and thus provide a return for the food collected. The failure of the theory in practice is most graphically illustrated by the fact that, in spite of severe repression, right up to 1920 the illegal market accounted for more food supplied to the towns than the legal system of distribution, which was independent of any market. The illegal market was not limited to food. Side by side with the nationalized organization of industry there developed a semi-legal 'underground' organization of capitalists upon whom the state machine was at times entirely dependent for the raw materials which it was unable itself to supply.[5] The two main causes which prevented the legal system from working were the resistance of the peasants to the forcible collection of the compulsory quotas of food; and the failure of the government's centralized control of industrial production. Although a central planning institution (*Gosplan*) was set up in February 1920, it did not begin to function for some years. The individual directorates of industry worked without either plan or co-ordination, with consequent maldistribution of available raw materials, resulting in the simultaneous accumulation of surpluses in one area, and suspension of production for lack of materials in another. Moreover, although the process of nationalization of industry was completed on paper by the end of 1920, the centralized machine was incapable in practice of managing the vast network of

[5] See an article of 26 June 1920 by Sokol'nikov in *Ekonomicheskaya zhizn'*, quoted in *Zagorsky*, p. 317; and cf. Zagorsky in *Sovremennyya zapiski*, no. 1 (1920), pp. 136 ff.

enterprises, large and small, which it had taken over. Hence a considerable part of nominally nationalized industry in fact succeeded in escaping all central control,[6] with each undertaking working as best it could for its own ends, and swelling the illegal market.

By the end of the civil war the consequences of the failure of this system were becoming disastrous. Lack of industrial goods to induce the peasant to part with his produce caused food supplies to decline severely, and it is estimated that the villages sent to the towns and the army only two-fifths to one-third of the pre-war delivery. This fall was caused not only by the fact that the recalcitrant peasants were sowing a smaller area, but also by the breaking up of the larger estates among the peasants. The agricultural population had by this time largely become a community of smallholders, and was now producing not for sale, but for its own consumption. However, starvation fell very unequally on different parts of the country. The town population was the worst off, especially in those parts of the country which were food consuming and not food producing. Here food consumption was estimated at 41 per cent of the pre-war level. Even among the peasantry of the food-consuming areas, always better fed than the townsfolk, the consumption of food was slightly lower than that enjoyed by the state-assisted starving peasantry during periods of famine before the war. In contrast, the peasantry in the food-producing areas remained almost at their pre-war level of consumption right up to the bad harvest of 1920.[7] This condition of affairs naturally exacerbated relations between town and country, since to large sections of the town workers (and to many within the communist party) it appeared that the only class to have benefited by the revolution were the peasants. The results of starvation told on industry. Production per worker fell drastically. The drain of industrial workers to the villages in search of food had halved the industrial proletariat by 1920 as compared with 1917. Moscow lost half its population, Petrograd rather more. Production in heavy industry fell to nearly a fifth of the pre-war

---

[6] Over 30,000 nationalized undertakings in 1920 were, according to *Kritsman*, pp. 131–2, not even on the lists of the central authorities.

[7] *Kritsman*, pp. 184–5.

figures. In light industry, less dependent on mechanical power, and more able to supply itself with raw materials from unofficial local sources and hence to short-circuit the central bureaucratic apparatus, the fall in production was only between a third and a half. Over seven million are estimated to have died from malnutrition and epidemics between January 1918 and July 1920, and the general death rate more than doubled.[8] Moreover the civilian population had to suffer from the fact that the bulk of production, such as it was, went to the army, though some of the army supplies found their way back to the civilians through the illegal market.

The abundant evidence of the failure of 'war communism' still did not appear to shake the confidence of the majority of the communist leaders in the efficacy of the system. At the end of 1918, at the Second Congress of Councils of National Economy, Larin, in a very bold and critical speech, painted a picture of the growing chaos (which Lozovsky described as 'only a hundredth part of what each one of us knows') and advocated a transition to a modified form of free trading with the villages. His views found little support.[9] The final argument, in which the great majority of the communist leaders supported Lenin, was that any system not based on a forcible campaign against the peasants would enable the latter to hold up the régime to ransom, and starve it into submission. By the beginning of 1920, however, free trade had found an advocate in Trotsky. His proposals, which apparently differed little from the New Economic Policy adopted the following year, were rejected in February 1920 by the Central Committee by eleven votes to four.[10] With unimpaired confidence in its policy the communist party, in a resolution of its Ninth Party Congress in the following month, noted 'with satisfaction the indisputable signs of a rise in productivity among the foremost sections of the workers'.[11] Even at the end of 1920 confidence in yet further centralization and compulsion as the solution for all ills seems to have remained unshaken. On 29 November

---

[8] *Kritsman*, p. 187   [9] See *Trudy II*, pp. 140–1.

[10] See *Ma Vie*, Vol. III, pp. 179–80; *Protokoly X*, p. 352. Trotsky's own account is largely confirmed by a note of the Marx-Engels-Lenin Institute in its annotated edition of the Proceedings of the Tenth Party Congress, published in 1933.—See *ibid.*, p. 848.

[11] *VKP(b) v rez.*, pp. 386–98. This resolution on economic policy, though critical in detail, did not in any sense depart from the basic principles of war communism.

1920 the Supreme Council of National Economy, although incapable of controlling the enterprises already nationalized, proceeded to nationalize the smallest undertakings which still remained in private ownership. At tne end of the year, Obolensky's proposal for a system of centrally controlled and planned sowing in the villages was adopted in its essentials; if it had not been overtaken by the New Economic Policy, which was introduced just in time for the spring sowing, this plan would have entailed centralized management of no less than eighteen million farmsteads.[12] The over-loading of an already inefficient bureaucratic machine, which, in comparison with 1913, contained double the number of employees in relation to workers engaged in productive tasks,[13] was one of the causes of the decline in production. But the majority of the communist leaders seemed to have retained sufficient confidence that this machine could, in spite of all the evidence to the contrary, be made to work. At the same time, the policy of 'war communism' cannot be explained solely in terms of over-confidence in socialist doctrine. To the Communists the main object during these years was at least as much to smash the existing machinery of the state and of the national economy —the co-operatives, the owners of industry, and the civil service—as to build the new economy. Though 'war communism' failed as a system of organizing national economy, it helped to lay the foundations for the dictatorship of the communist bureaucracy which was designed to replace the old machinery of the state.

In view of the widespread discontent caused by economic hardship, the vital problem from the point of view of the communist leaders in 1920 was to ensure sufficient support in the country to survive in power. In the army, centralized political compulsion exercised through the communist party had, at any rate, been successful in neutralizing opposition.[14]

[12] *Kritsman*, p. 134. For Obolensky's scheme, which was adopted with modifications, see his *Gosudarstvennoe regulirovanie krestyanskogo khozyaystva*. Obolensky, one of the leading Left Communists in 1918 and by this date one of the principal advocates of 'democratic centralism', rejected out of hand the proposal of some 'to replace the monopoly of food supplies by a tax in kind' (i.e. the basis of Lenin's New Economic Policy) as leading to free trade and signifying a 'pro-kulak policy' (p. 16); and see on this question generally *Farbman*, Chapter XVI.

[13] The exact calculation is not easy in view of many factors involved which make comparison difficult, but this conclusion seems to be well founded on the figures analysed by *Kritsman*, pp. 197–8. [14] See Chapter XIII.

The problem was more complicated in the country as a whole. While the civil war lasted, the peasants for all their hostility to a government which took (or tried to take) all and gave virtually nothing in return, in the last resort preferred the Bolsheviks, who did not threaten their newly acquired land, to the White generals who did. But this slender support disappeared when at the end of 1920 victory in the civil war removed the threat of the White Armies. The discontent of the peasants had no normal legal method of voicing itself. Even the local soviets, in which they were nominally represented, were long atrophied by 1920. They were in any case carefully packed and all critics of the régime were eliminated. Within the communist party, members officially classified as of peasant origin formed a quarter in 1920.[15] But the reports of the debates in the party congresses during the years of the civil war nowhere voice the peasant point of view. It seems therefore that the figure of one quarter of party members of peasant origin was inaccurate or it included peasants so-called, who had long lost all contact with the land. No influential opposition group within the communist party sponsored any policy for improving the lot of the peasantry and the advocacy of their interests was left mainly to the stifled voices of the Mensheviks and the Left Socialist Revolutionaries.[16] Hence peasant discontent expressed itself in other forms—sabotage of the food requisitioning, desertion from the Red Army, extensive murders of commissars and of other government functionaries, and a wave of armed risings throughout the country, mounting at times to guerrilla war. Some ten thousand partisans were engaged in the Tambov peasant rising, which began in the summer of 1920. In the Ukraine, during the first three months of 1921, twenty-eight partisan detachments,

---

[15] *Bubnov*, p. 615. The proportion of peasants in the party was beginning to rise at the end of 1920. The official percentage for 1921 is 28·12 per cent, but at the Tenth Party Congress in March Sosnovsky claimed that in some districts, e.g. in industrial Ekaterinburg, the party organization was two thirds peasant in composition—*Protokoly X*, p. 84. As will be seen in Chapter XV, by 1922 the influx of peasant elements into the party was seriously disturbing Lenin.

[16] An exception should be made perhaps for the Communist G. I. Myasnikov, in 1920 and 1921 linked with the Workers' Opposition, but always highly individualistic in his views. Myasnikov advocated the formation of peasant unions in order to heal the growing breach between the peasantry and the proletariat —see e.g. his article 'Nereshennyy vopros' in *Petrogradskaya Pravda* of 19 November 1920.

some of them a thousand and more strong, were operating in eight *gubernii*. Though individual Socialist Revolutionaries played some part in these risings, there was little political ideology behind them, beyond the simple slogan: 'Down with the Communists!' The peasants' hostilities were directed primarily against the commissars and the armed requisitioning units, from whom they extracted a heavy toll of victims.[17]

The industrial workers, however, could voice their discontent. Outside the communist party it was reflected in the increasing influence of the Mensheviks, in spite of the efforts of the authorities to repress them. Within the party a serious crisis was developing by the autumn of 1920, which threatened the Central Committee with isolation. General weariness, and discontent with rigid party dictatorship, were rallying supporters to several opposition groups which were emerging inside the party. The Central Committee was thus confronted with the additional problem of retaining sufficient support within its own party to maintain itself in power. Its task was further complicated by the fact that it was itself rapidly becoming disunited, torn asunder by rival factions. Nor did there as yet exist, in 1920, either a fully centralized party machine, such as Lenin had envisaged many years before, to ensure the implicit support of party members and to direct all their activities; or effective control by the party over the trade unions. The party statute, adopted in December 1919, had, it is true, provided for a large measure of control by the communist party over all organizations in which it was in a majority. It provided for the setting up in every non-party organization, such as a soviet or a trade union, of a cell, or 'fraction', which was to be 'completely subordinate to the party'. Every question on the agenda of the trade union or other organization concerned must be debated in preliminary discussion by the 'fraction', which was obliged to follow the ruling of the local party committee. Above all, the statute provided that 'candidates for all the more important posts in the organization or body concerned in which the fraction works are appointed by the fraction jointly with the appropriate party

---

[17] See *Revolyutsionnaya Rossiya*, no. 6, April 1921, pp. 23–8 (Tambov); no. 11, August 1921, pp. 22–5 (Ukraine); cf. no. 14/15, Nov./Dec. 1921, pp. 33–6 (Tobol'sk). cf. the speech of Skvortsov-Stepanov at the Tenth Party Congress, *Protokoly X*, pp. 69–72.

organization. Transfer from one post to another takes place in the same manner'. The appropriate party committee was also given the power to appoint or recall any party member to or from any 'fraction'. Thus, in a trade union, for example, a 'fraction' member need not necessarily have anything to do with the trade concerned. The authority of the Central Committee was ensured by the provisions enjoining implicit obedience of local party committees to its directives.[18] But in 1919 this extensive central power on paper did not yet correspond to practice. It was in the struggles of 1920 and 1921 that this salient feature of the Soviet state became a reality.

The communist party had grown steadily in size in the three years since the revolution. It numbered over 600,000 in March 1920 as compared with 200,000 in August 1917. The main increase had taken place after 1919.[19] Thus, the party consisted of adherents of whom at most one member in three had joined when the issue was still doubtful, and could be reckoned among the 'old guard'. Many of the new influx joined for what they could get in the way of privilege and power. The revolution had encouraged a system of unbridled licence for Communists in authority and this inevitably attracted the careerist type of party candidates in whom a sense of duty took second place. The percentage of workers was rapidly sinking. Official figures show a decline to just over 40 per cent in 1920 as compared with 60 per cent in 1917. In fact, the decline was a good deal more rapid, and there was much truth in the allegation frequently made by Shlyapnikov, and others, that many workers were leaving the party in 1920 and 1921. It is likely that the official figures give a misleading picture by including as 'workers' many who had long ceased to be anything but professional politicians or administrators. For example, in 1922 the percentage of workers is given as 44·4 in a party then numbering 514,800, i.e. about 225,000. Yet in the same year the official total figure for *all* Communists in *all* workers' groups and cells in *all* factories and workshops was only 90,000.[20] Thus, of all party members

[18] *VKP(b) v rez.*, pp. 370–7.   [19] Figures in *Bubnov*, p. 612.
[20] *ibid.*, p. 615; *The Communist International between the Fifth and Sixth World Congresses*, p. 500.

classified as 'workers' fewer than half were in fact working in factories or workshops,—since otherwise they must have been included in the total figure for membership of factory groups and cells. Similarly, in the Petrograd communist party in 1920, 60·4 per cent of the whole party were classified as 'workers', although only 20·2 per cent were in fact workers in the sense that they were employed at factory benches.[21] Besides in 1920, 30 per cent of the communist party were classified as 'employees, etc.'. In view of this social composition, it is easy to understand the growing rift in 1919 and 1920 between the minority of bench workers and the career politicians who were beginning to form the majority of the party. The Central Committee in its report to the Tenth Party Congress in March 1921 analysed the various forms which disunity assumed in the summer of 1920: in some cases it took the form of the struggle of rival groups for influence, in others of a struggle by local organizations against the discipline and authority of the *guberniya* committees, or of discord between workers and intellectuals, or between peasant and town Communists. The Central Committee attributed this disappearance of 'the former unifying party solidarity' to exhaustion from war conditions, hunger, the over-rapid expansion of the party, and to the 'rift in the case of a significant number of the party leaders in the centre and in the provinces . . . between them and the broad working masses'. The leaders, says this report, were gradually ceasing to attend party meetings and were losing the confidence of the rank and file. Inequality of living conditions and privileges of the higher party officials, which at first had been the exception, 'were beginning to become widespread' and increased discontent.[22]

Two opposition groups were already discernible within the communist party in 1920—the groups which were to become known as the Workers' Opposition and the Democratic Centralists. The Workers' Opposition, which was entirely

---

[21] See A. S. Pukhov, 'V Petrograde nakanune kronshtadtskogo vosstania v 1921 g.', in *Krasnaya letopis'* No. 4 (37), 1930, at pp. 95–6.
[22] *Izvestiya Ts. K.*, no. 29, 7 March 1921. It is a melancholy reflection on the standards of research into Soviet history in this country that this publication, essential for the study of the history of the party, was found by the present writer in the British Museum in 1950 with its pages still largely uncut.

proletarian in its following, grew up among the communist trade unionists in the course of 1919. It developed out of the discontent of the workers with the official policy of employing bourgeois specialists in responsible positions in industrial undertakings. The leaders of this group of critics within the party—for it was nothing more in 1919—were all prominent trade unionists, notably Shlyapnikov and Lutovinov. In addition to attacking the specialists in industry, the Workers' Opposition in course of time began to complain of the diminishing part played by the workers in the control of industry, and deplored what they regarded as the tendency of the leading Communists to become more bureaucratic and less proletarian in their outlook, and to lose their contact with the working masses. An observant visitor to Russia, who attended a meeting of the Central Executive Committee on 26 February 1919, at which Glebov, also a trade unionist, spoke on the subject of the hated specialists, noted the 'clear indication of the political undercurrent towards the Left which may shake the Bolshevik position'.[23] But there was no desire among this group of critics to shake the position of the party dictatorship. Not long after, at a meeting of the communist fraction of the Central Trade Union Council, in the spring of 1919, Shlyapnikov proposed a resolution that the unions should assume the leadership of the growing mass dissatisfaction, and by directing it and endeavouring to remove the causes of it, 'fight with all our power against the tendency towards the outbreak of strikes by explaining the disastrous nature of this policy'.[24]

In the course of 1920 the Workers' Opposition, or, more accurately, those individuals who were later to become its leaders, extended their criticism. At the Ninth Communist Party Congress in March Kiselev was complaining that there existed 'a great tendency at the centre to kill, diminish, and weaken all party thought in the provinces'.[25]

[23] *Ransome*, p. 107.
[24] See *Protokoly X*, pp. 869–70 for the text. cf. also Shlyapnikov's article in *Pravda* of 27 March 1919, which complains that the recourse to the specialists is a desperate attempt to cure the rift between the workers and industrial management. Soviet historians (e.g. *Yaroslavsky*, Vol. IV, p. 440) normally omit the sentence quoted, in an endeavour to display Shlyapnikov as already embarked on a policy of 'counter-revolution'.
[25] *Protokoly IX*, p. 67.

In contrast to the Workers' Opposition, the Democratic Centralists were largely a group of intellectuals. Their leaders, such as Obolensky, Sapronov, and Maksimovsky had all in their time played a prominent part in the left communist opposition of 1918. Sapronov, however, was a working man, one of the bolshevik 'old guard'. Whereas the Workers' Opposition saw their aim as the defence of the rights of the workers against the state apparatus, the Democratic Centralists were concerned to restore the democratic provisions embodied in the soviet and party constitutions, but which had disappeared in practice almost from the first. They claimed to voice the opinion, not of the army, nor of the trade unions, but of 'civilian soviet culture'.[26] At a communist party conference in December 1919, which dealt with state structure, Sapronov was successful against the official party spokesman, Vladimirsky, in securing the adoption of his draft resolution. This provided for alterations in the composition of the Central Executive Committee which aimed at making that body more representative; and for reforms designed to restore real power to the executive committees of the local soviets. The drafts of both Vladimirsky and Sapronov were debated at length in a commission of the Seventh Congress of Soviets, which followed immediately after this party conference, and the final resolution adopted was based on Sapronov's draft, and embodied most of his proposals.[27] This resolution which, it may be added, was the product of one of the very few instances of constructive public debate in Soviet history, remained a dead letter. The Democratic Centralists in the course of 1919 and 1920 also urged the need for greater freedom within the party. They demanded that the Central Committee should not manage the party, but guide it, giving it a general direction, but not interfering in details. They insisted that every important question should be widely discussed among the party rank and file before a decision was taken on it. Central Committee meetings, other than secret meetings, should be open to all party members. In party elections representation

---

[26] According to Obolensky at the Ninth Party Congress in March 1920—see *Protokoly IX*, pp. 123–4.

[27] For the December conference, see *Pravda*, 4 December 1919; for the debates in the Congress see *Vs. syezd VII*, pp. 209–50; for the resolution adopted see *Postanovleniya 7-go vserossiyskogo syezda sovetov*, pp. 15–19.

of minority views should be assured, and such minorities should be given facilities for publishing their views.[28] 'Comrade Lenin says,' Obolensky said at the Ninth Party Congress in March 1920, 'that the essence of democratic centralism is contained in the fact that the [party] Congress elects the Central Committee, while the Central Committee manages [the party]. We cannot agree with this somewhat fanciful view. . . . We believe that democratic centralism . . . consists in the putting into effect of the directives of the Central Committee by the local organizations, in the responsible autonomy of the latter, and in their responsibility for their spheres of work.'[29]

Neither of these groups was an opposition in any real sense of the term. They had no separate organization, no fixed membership, no press or publications of their own, and no platform or policy as an alternative to the official communist programme. The very name of Workers' Opposition was apparently a nickname invented much later by Lenin, at the end of 1920 or early in 1921. The members of these groups were little more than the spokesmen for a somewhat utopian idealism. At the same time they were conscientious adherents to what many believed were the true principles of their party within an organization which seemed to them to be rapidly degenerating. They accepted the policy laid down by the party and voted, after discussion, for party resolutions, even when they did not entirely agree with them. The two groups, the Workers' Opposition and the Democratic Centralist, only became distinct opposition groups in 1921 and then only because this was forced upon them by the Central Committee.[30]

The position by 1920 was also becoming critical in the trade unions. The unions could not be regarded as representative of proletarian opinion as a whole. Their communist mem-

[28] From Obolensky's speech at a Crimea conference of party leaders (in 1919 or early 1920), which is summarized by Smilga in *Na povorote*, pp. 21–2.

[29] *Protokoly IX*, p. 130. It is not clear to what precise statement by Lenin he was referring, but his summary was not far off Lenin's view. Thus, cf. the 21 conditions for communist parties adopted by the Second Congress of the International, of which the original draft of Point no. 13 by Lenin, published in July 1920, defines 'democratic centralism' as 'iron discipline' in each party, with the 'party centre as a mighty authoritative organ with full powers and widest rights of action, enjoying the universal confidence of members of the party'— see *Lenin*, Vol. XXV, pp. 279–84.

[30] See Chapter XV.

bership formed a very small proportion of the total—some 500,000 out of seven million, by official reckoning in 1921.[31] Nevertheless they acted exclusively through communist officials and councils. At all conferences Communists composed the overwhelming majority: if, as frequently happened, even the managed elections did not produce a sufficiently large communist majority, force was used to produce the required result. Non-communist trade union Central Committees, such as that of the Moscow printers, were disbanded by force. By the end of the civil war even the government did not disguise the fact that the Russian proletariat was in its majority anti-communist. Early in 1921 Vyshinsky, a recent recruit from the Mensheviks, who was exercising his talents in the organization of 'non-party' discussion meetings of workers, could regard it as a welcome sign of progress that a communist resolution had secured 760 votes as against 900 at one such meeting.[32] As Lenin admitted to the Tenth Party Congress: 'We have failed to convince the broad masses.'[33]

It is, however, the ruling communist 'fractions' within the trade unions which must be examined, because it is here that opposition to official party policy was fast gathering strength in 1920. The trade union Communists had put up little resistance in the early months after the revolution to the official aim of making the unions executants of state policy rather than defenders of workers' rights. Logically, with the victory of the working class, it seemed to them that there could be no more room for antagonism between the workers' state and the workers' organizations, and at their first All-Russian Congress in January 1918, the trade union Communists, who formed 66 per cent of the delegates, had approved this proposition in principle. They also recognized that the factory committees should become incorporated into the central machinery as branches of the trade unions.[34] There was little, if any,

[31] Virtually the entire communist party membership was enrolled in the trade unions. It follows that of these 500,000 only a small proportion were workers in the ordinary sense of the term. For example, at a vital meeting of the communist 'fraction' of the Metal-workers' Union Congress in March 1922 there were present such distinguished metal-workers as Lenin, Zinoviev, Stalin, Molotov, Kamenev, Cachin, Kolarov, and Clara Zetkin.
[32] See his article in *Pravda* of 12 April 1921.
[33] *Protokoly X*, p. 382.
[34] See the resolutions of the First All-Russian Congress of Trade Unions, 23 January 1918, reprinted in *B. & F.*, pp. 639–41 and 642. The menshevik

sympathy at that date among the union Communists for the opposition on union questions which existed outside the communist party. Opposition to the communist policy of destroying all union independence was voiced in 1918 mainly by Mensheviks, and by the ex-Communist Lozovsky.[35] Even the programme laid down by the Supreme Council of National Economy at the end of 1918, which was designed to put an end to the anarchical interference by the factory committees of workers in the running of industry, did not arouse any immediate opposition from the union Communists. They fully accepted the principle that workers' control must now be transferred to the state, which would henceforward exercise it in co-operation with the unions at the top, through the Supreme Council of National Economy, with the union management acting in turn through partly appointed and partly elected local committees—all strictly subordinate to the centre. At the Second Congress of Trade Unions early in 1919 the menshevik voices of warning were drowned in derision. The communist resolution, adopted unanimously with only two abstentions, (the Mensheviks had no vote), roundly condemned the slogan of trade union independence as a screen for what was asserted to be in reality a struggle against Soviet power; and recognised that the trade unions had now 'passed from the control over production to its organization, actively participating both in management of individual enterprises and in the economic life of the whole country'.[36] This congress also approved the concentration and centralization

resolution will also be found there. And see *ibid.*, pp. 644–5, for the resolution of the Fifth Conference of Trade Union Leaders of 12–17 March 1918. Shlyapnikov, the future Workers' Opposition leader, was fully behind this policy—see his speech of 19 May 1918 quoted in *Bunyan*, p. 384.

[35] Lozovsky, it will be recalled, the leading communist trade unionist in 1917, had been expelled from the party early in 1918 for his advocacy of trade union independence. He had gathered a number of other dissident trade union leaders around him, who resisted not only the communist policy of turning the unions into state instruments, but also their methods of subjugating those unions which showed any signs of opposition. For Lozovsky's expulsion from the party before the First Trade Union Congress, see *B. & F.*, pp. 639–41. His group published for a short time a paper, *Proletariy*. It will also be recalled that Lozovsky had been one of the most forthright critics of the bolshevik refusal to form a coalition with the socialists and of repressions against freedom of speech and press in November 1917. See *ante* Chapter V.

[36] See *Vs. syezd prof. II*, pp. 400–2; see also *ibid.*, p. 82, for Martov's speech and pp. 32–3 for Lozovsky's criticism of the communist trade union cells as organs of the *Vecheka*.

on functional lines of the trade union organization, which at that date still presented a very variegated picture. (This centralization was virtually achieved by 1921.)[37] If some uneasiness was beginning to appear among the communist rank and file workers over their decreasing say in the management of industry (and Martov in his speech at the Congress certainly hinted at the existence of dissensions on this question), it did not appear on the surface. The policy of centralization was however tempered by an official promise. It was contained in the party programme, adopted in March 1919: 'Being already . . . participants in local and central organs of industrial management, the unions must achieve the actual concentration in their hands of all management of the entire national economy as a single economic unit.'[38]

As time went on, this promise became a source of acrimonious debate. The critics of the government among the trade union Communists repeatedly argued that all that they were demanding was that it should be honoured. It is true that the trade unions were, in a sense, integrated into the central system of control through the directorates set up by the Supreme Council of National Economy. Trade union representatives sat on the praesidium of the Supreme Council at the centre, and on the praesidia of the subordinate councils in the *gubernii*. The unions were also given a voice in the composition of the directorates of the branches of industry formed by the Supreme Council of National Economy, and in the sub-directorates. The percentage of members of factory managements in 1920 classified as 'workers' was 63, and in the management boards (or *collegia*) of the main industrial directorates it was 26.[39] But the same process was taking place among the union Communists as in the party as a whole—a rift between the rank and file and the trade-union officials. Participation in the centralized machine satisfied the professional Communists, who acquired with it the privileges and status of government officials. It did not appease the ordinary worker Communists, who felt that they were being edged out of any

[37] By the end of 1921 there were only 22 unions, embracing 9,451 union organizations. *Kritsman*, p. 85.
[38] *VKP(b) v rez.*, p. 336.
[39] *Kritsman*, pp. 93–7, quoting figures from a report of the Supreme Council of National Economy of December 1920.

participation in management, and subjected to orders from the party bosses. They not unnaturally longed for the early days of the revolution, when the workers' committee had been a law unto itself in each factory. Many of the union Communists had been drawn from these factory committees, which the Bolsheviks had won over to their side by the promise of workers' control, and to them communism meant the power which workers' control had once seemed to offer. Now they were beginning to learn in the words of J. S. Mill that 'The "people" who exercise the power are not the same people with those over whom it is exercised'. To quote an official Soviet historian of the trade unions, 'the transfer of the centre of gravity of activity to the summits of the unions created a whole row of abnormal and unhealthy results: estrangement of the masses, insufficient sensitiveness to what was happening among the union members, and a formalistic attitude towards members'.[40]

The communist workers were also dissatisfied over the leading positions in industry held by bourgeois experts, the 'specialists'. Early in 1919 this discontent had found a staunch champion in Shlyapnikov, at that date chairman of the Metal-workers' Union, and a member of the Central Council of Trade Unions. His outspoken criticism, to which reference has already been made, was, no doubt, a considerable source of embarrassment to the communist leaders, and it was not unnatural that his dispatch on a long mission to Norway later in the year, and his replacement by Gol'tsman as chairman of the Metal-workers' Union should have given rise to suspicion that he had been removed for his oppositional activities. The accusation was indignantly denied by Lenin, and was probably ill-founded.[41] Repressions against critics within the communist party were still the exception rather than the rule in 1919. But, like Trotsky in the army, Lenin was fighting a battle for the 'specialists'. The problem was not only to force the specialists on to the reluctant communist workers in the

[40] *Lozovsky*, p. 197. (This was written in 1922, after Lozovsky had rejoined the communist party.)
[41] Seè on this incident *Protokoly IX*, pp. 62, 86, 93. According to Lutovinov, another trade unionist and a close collaborator of Shlyapnikov, he had not been exiled. But, in general, Lutovinov maintained that the method of exile was already being applied 'on the widest scale'.

factories. It was also necessary to moderate the overzealous attentions of their communist colleagues or of the *Vecheka*, for fear that persecution might make their very existence intolerable, and their services accordingly of little productive value.[42] The Communists were on the whole successful in combining the persecution of the class or party to which their specialists belonged (many of them were Mensheviks) with the retention of their services until such time as they could replace them with indoctrinated communist specialists.

It was mainly over the question of one-man management in industry that the trade union opposition first came to a head. A compromise system had been originally devised for the management of branches of industry, and of industrial undertakings, to conciliate the opposition to the specialists. This was the board, or collegiate, system, in which responsibility was vested in a number of joint managers, one of whom would in most cases be a non-communist specialist, and the others party members. This system pacified the critics, but did not lead to efficient management. By 1919 Lenin had become impatiently disciplinarian in outlook. No more was heard from him of the assurances so frequent before, and for a short time after, the revolution, that the talent of the masses for organization could by itself achieve socialism, when once they were freed from capitalist oppression. The failure of the rash experiments of war communism had shattered this illusion. The resolution of the Ninth Party Congress in 1920, calling for a struggle against 'the ill-bred self-conceit of those ... demagogic elements ... who think that the working class can solve its problems without utilizing the bourgeois specialists in the most responsible posts',[43] if not drafted by Lenin, accurately reflects what he had been urging for over a year. His ceaseless campaign for one-man management in the

---

[42] For a picture of the life of a specialist in communist society see a letter to Lenin by one of them, quoted by Lenin in *Pravda* on 28 March 1919. 'A specialist who only joins you to save his skin' wrote this unknown correspondent, 'will not be of very great use to the country.' See *Lenin*, Vol. XXIV, pp. 184–7, where Lenin's not very convincing reply will also be found. There seems little reason to doubt the figures of a 'gallup-poll' among specialists, quoted by *Kritsman*, pp. 148–9, which show that of engineers in Soviet employment, who had held responsible posts before the revolution, fewer than a tenth were in sympathy with the Soviet régime.

[43] *VKP(b) v rez.*, p. 394.

interests of efficiency was bound to create opposition from many quarters, since it was obvious that the manager would have to be, in most cases, a non-communist specialist who knew the work. This aroused the resentment of many of the senior trade union officials, and of the members of the local councils of national economy, who saw in the proposal a threat to their vested interest; of the ordinary worker Communists; and of the intellectual Democratic Centralists, who opposed one-man management as a system which facilitated centralized control and thereby destroyed local initiative.

Lenin's efforts to persuade his party to adopt his policy met with immediate serious resistance. On 12 January 1920 he was outvoted in the All-Russian Central Council of Trade Unions party 'fraction'. At the end of January the Third All-Russian Congress of Councils of National Economy adopted a resolution in favour of board management. One-man management was rejected at party conferences in Kharkov and in Moscow *guberniya*. Theses in opposition to Lenin were put forward by Tomsky, the most prominent trade union leader, and a member of the Central Committee; and by the Democratic Centralists.[44] On 15 March 1920, a fortnight before the Ninth Party Congress, Lenin was opposed at the Third All-Russian Congress of Water Transport Workers, and on the same day, Bukharin, defending one-man management, met with heated opposition in the party 'fraction' of the All-Russian Central Council of Trade Unions.

The greatest potential obstacle to Lenin's policy lay in the hostility shown towards it by the majority of the senior trade union communist officials. As the succeeding eighteen months were to show, the discontent of the party rank and file could be neutralized as a political factor by an adequate overhaul of the central party organization. But the upper ranks of the trade union hierarchy were an important force to be reckoned with, since on their co-operation and organizational talent depended the only hope of winning control over the recalcitrant trade unions. However, in spite of their opposition to Lenin on this issue, leaders like Tomsky, Andreev, Schmidt, and Rudzutak had already shown themselves quite accommodating to party policy on other matters, even when it conflicted with

[44] *Lenin*, Vol. XXV, pp. 543–8, 593–4.

trade union interests.[45] Lozovsky, once a bitter opponent of communist policy towards the trade unions, had capitulated in December 1919, when he, at the head of his small Socialist Labour Party of Internationalists, had fused with the communist party. If they were tactfully handled there was every reason to hope that the trade union leaders, or the majority of them, would throw in their weight with the official policy rather than with the discontented masses.

It was only at the Ninth Party Congress in March 1920 that Lenin finally succeeded in overcoming all opposition and in putting into effect one-man management from the top downwards, from the directorates which managed the branches of industry down to the individual factories.[46] The communist party accepted the unpopular policy after debate, without a split or even a threat of a split. The opposition at the congress came mainly from the Democratic Centralists, who voiced the views of the restive local party and soviet organizations, and from Lutovinov, as spokesman for a minority group of trade union leaders. Lutovinov demanded a policy which was completely irreconcilable with that of Lenin: a form of syndicalism in which the responsibility for, and control of, each branch of industry should ultimately pass to the appropriate trade union. This novel view, which developed out of opposition to management by specialists, had first been circulated by Shlyapnikov in a series of Theses in mid 1919. These Theses have not been preserved (nor was their author present at the congress), but their general purport emerges from the speech of Shlyapnikov's close supporter, Lutovinov. But all opposition finally melted away. At the end of the congress Lutovinov declared that he, and those of a like opinion, though still convinced that their view was right and that of the Central Committee wrong, would henceforward work loyally to put through one-man management in accordance with the decisions of the congress—and that 'not out of fear, but as a matter of conscience'.[47] Most suprising of all,

---

[45] They had not resisted, for instance, the forcible dispersal of properly elected unions already during 1918—see the criticism levelled at Tomsky and Schmidt at the Second Trade Union Congress, *Vs. syezd prof. II*, pp. 28–30.

[46] According to *Kritsman*, p. 206, of 2,000 large undertakings investigated at the end of 1920, 1,720 were already under the management of a single individual.

[47] *Protokoly IX*, p. 257.

there was no serious opposition from Tomsky, and the trade union leaders of like opinion. Tomsky contented himself with a speech in defence of his own opposition theses, and with a proposal for a compromise amendment to the official resolution, both so mild in tone as to give rise to the suspicion that they were little more than face-savers and that he had already been won over before the congress. Skilful compromise had apparently played its part in Lenin's victory. The resolution finally adopted made a number of concessions which showed that the vested interest of the senior trade unionists would not be too seriously affected by the change over to one-man management. Thus, in the various forms of one-man management proposed, trade unionists could still participate as assistants to the specialist manager, or as commissars attached to him; or again the manager could be a trade unionist with a specialist assistant attached to him. The right of the central trade union organs to be consulted on appointments was retained. Boards of management which had proved themselves capable of working in harmony could be preserved.[48] Those senior trade unionists who were not in sympathy with the discontented workers, nor finally edged out of any position of control over industry, had reason to be satisfied with Lenin's handling of the acute problem of management.[49]

The putting through of this policy after so much initial resistance was one of Lenin's last major personal triumphs in control of his party. But such party solidarity, the last of its kind, owed its existence partly to the fact that the civil war was not yet won. Nor had the personal rivalries, which a few months later began to rend the Central Committee, come into play. Above all, Lenin's success in March 1920 was due to the fact that he had once again, as so often in the past, correctly assessed the forces arrayed against him at the time. He also seized the chance to tighten up party control over the unions. In contrast to the policy which the party programme had proclaimed in 1919, the unions, it was now laid down, 'in

---

[48] For the resolutions adopted at the Ninth Congress, see *VKP(b) vrez.*, pp. 391–92 (one-man management), pp. 393–4 (specialists), and particularly pp. 400–2 (on the current tasks of trade unions).

[49] According to *Kritsman*, p. 206, a high percentage of managers were 'workers'. This may well have been true in the sense that they were ex-workers who had graduated from the bench to the more tempting positions offered by the trade union party machinery.

no way managing the economy of the Soviet Republic either as a whole or to the exclusion of others', participate in the organization of production, but no union organization 'interferes directly in the management of undertakings': the factory committee was to concern itself with labour discipline, with propaganda, and with educational work. The party 'fractions', obligatory in each union, were to be strictly subordinate to the Central Committee of the party. The tasks of the unions were primarily educative, and they could best carry them out as one of the 'components of the apparatus of the Soviet state'. All talk of the unions as something separate from the economic organization of the working class was denounced as a deviation from marxism. Finally the party resolved that the 'personal composition' of the unions must be strengthened by the 'pouring into them' of the 'most reliable and hardiest Communists' chosen as far as possible from those with civilian experience.[50] Trotsky's method, applied, as will be seen, with such success in the army, was to be tried out in the unions.

For a time after the Ninth Congress it seemed that Lenin's assessment had been right. No dissensions of any kind appeared in the debates on the relation of the trade unions to the state at the Third Trade Union Congress which followed shortly after the Ninth Party Congress, and Lozovsky was able to record with satisfaction that the hopes of those anti-communists who expected that the discussions over one-man management would lead to a split between the trade unions and the party had been disappointed.[51] On the communist Central Committee elected by the Ninth Congress, Andreev and Rudzutak, both leading trade unionists, now served in addition to Tomsky, who had been a member since the previous year. The fact that men like Tomsky and Andreev, after some hesitant opposition in 1921, and a number of other trade unionists prominent in 1920, were to serve for years in posts of great importance in the party machine (Andreev remained

[50] VKP(b) v rez., pp. 398–402.
[51] Vs. syezd prof. III, p. 2. Tomsky was the main speaker. From the fact that only Bukharin and two Mensheviks took part in the debate which followed, and from the general applause which apparently greeted the menshevik speakers' demand for trade union independence, it seems not unreasonable to suppose that the debates at this congress were carefully stage-managed, and that there was still much dissatisfaction among the rank and file unionists.

a member of the Politbureau until 1952) is evidence of the skill with which Lenin had won over to his side the all-important senior trade union officials.

Thus, in March 1920, Lenin succeeded in preserving unity in his party in spite of the opposition with which he was confronted at the outset. Little remained of this unity by the end of the year. Although the Ninth Party Congress accepted in principle centralized and disciplined control of industry, the carrying out of this policy proved no easy matter. Meanwhile communist policy had been meeting with comparable difficulties in the Red Army.

CHAPTER XIII

THE MILITARY OPPOSITION

Before the seizure of power, the aim of the Bolsheviks had been the destruction of the imperial army from within. The Petrograd Soviet had already started the process, with its famous Order No. 1. The network of army committees which it set up in all military units enabled bolshevik influence to grow. It was not, apparently, the aim of the Bolsheviks ever to use the existing army as the basis for a new army. The 'armed people' of the future socialist state was identified with the Red Guards, while the disintegrating army was looked upon as a mere reservoir of manpower on which the Red Guards could draw.[1] But the destruction of the army and the attempt to replace it by the Red Guard were not merely tactical moves. The existence of a standing army was inconsistent with socialist principles, which demanded an armed people's militia in its place. At a military conference of delegates from the front held in June 1917 the speakers demanded the 'immediate destruction of standing armies everywhere and their replacement by a national militia and the universal arming of the people'. Lenin had repeatedly asserted that the replacement of the army by a militia was bolshevik policy.[2] In June 1917 a bolshevik military conference demanded that election of officers, self-government, and initiative from below should replace appointment, discipline, and obedience, as the basis for the new militia. The election of all officers by the troops and the abolition of all saluting and marks of rank were duly decreed at the end of December, and put the finishing touches to the disorganized army. However, election of officers was abolished within three months, as soon as Trotsky, in March 1918, set about rebuilding a new, Red Army from the ruins of the old. As Trotsky

[1] *Fedotoff White*, p. 28; cf. *Antonov-Ovseenko*, p. 147. In fact it was only in a few instances, notably the Lettish Rifle Regiment, one cavalry division, and some armoured car detachments, that the Bolsheviks reorganized units of the old army into formations of the new army.

[2] *Lenin*, Vol. XX, pp. 121, 139; cf. Engels, *Anti-Dühring*, p. 192.

frankly explained to the Central Executive Committee, election had never been intended as 'a method of appointing commanders, but as a method of class struggle'. His realistic and determined policy to build up with little regard for socialist theories an army which could fight aroused violent opposition within the party from the start.[3] There were many Communists who were not yet ready to jettison their utopian vision of the army of the socialist future, in which no discipline was required, because comradeship and loyalty to the revolution took its place. Such idealists took some time to be persuaded.

An attempt had been made in January 1918 to create the new army on a volunteer basis. But, except for a short period between the time when the Germans resumed their hostilities in February, and the signing of the treaty of peace in the following month, the attempt did not prove a success. The Germans, in disregard of the treaty, were streaming across the new frontier. On 22 April compulsory military training was introduced. There was no opposition from the communist members to this measure when the Central Executive Committee debated it.[4] But the building up of even some measure of centralization inside the new army took many months. The civil war was in full progress by the middle of 1918, but until 1919, at least, the main brunt of the fighting was borne by improvised partisan or guerrilla detachments of the Red Guards operating each on its own, with no discipline, and with supreme contempt for the military science of the old order.

Trotsky rightly perceived that without a fully centralized army the civil war could not be won. But he made many enemies in breaking the opposition of the guerrilla leaders to his attempt to mould their disjointed units of Red Guards and workers' volunteers into a united army. The self-made communist partisan leaders resented absorption into a centralized machine. Nor was their resentment likely to be allayed by the open contempt with which Trotsky treated

[3] For Trotsky's speech and the debates in the Central Executive Committee on this question, see *Protokoly VTSIK IV*, pp. 169–93.
[4] The main opposition came from the Mensheviks, whose spokesman, Martov, rejected as a danger to the revolution any form of armed force which was distinct from the people—see *Protokoly VTSIK IV*, pp. 180, 192.

them. His speech at the Fifth Soviet Congress on 10 July 1918 reveals his attitude: 'Naturally, you have heard it asserted here that what we need, if you please, is not an army constructed on a military basis, but partisan detachments . . . It is essential for us to introduce the strictest centralization. We are meeting with opposition all over the country, and I am afraid that we shall meet with it even from some of the comrades who are present here today. Still, this is understandable. The rule of the [old] centralized, bureaucratic régime created a state of mind which makes them feel that now that they are rid of this régime it is necessary for each to act independently on the principle "we can manage by ourselves, don't you know, we can do it all by ourselves without any threats or interference from the centre".' Trotsky went on to describe as 'utter childishness' the local patriotism which led each district to try to amass as much military material as it could for itself.[5] It was plain that Stalin and Voroshilov (though not present) were among the comrades whom Trotsky had in mind. His collisions with Stalin and Voroshilov, who were at that date at Tsaritsyn in charge of a food collecting expedition which had grown into a military operation, are sufficiently familiar from Trotsky's writings.[6] By the end of 1918, Trotsky had succeeded in acquiring some of the powers necessary for centralized military command. I. I. Vatsetis, an ex-colonel of the imperial army, had been appointed Commander-in-Chief on 8 July, while on 2 September 1918 the Revolutionary War Council was set up, of which Trotsky became chairman, and in which the supreme command was incorporated, to co-ordinate all operations of the Red Army throughout the country.[7] It was proof of Trotsky's

---

[5] *Vs. syezd V*, pp. 169, 175.

[6] The best documented account is in his *Stalin*, Chapters IX and X. (These chapters were completed posthumously by the editor of this work from Trotsky's rough outline.)

[7] Its powers at first extended to questions of military supply as well as to operations. But Trotsky's authority was curtailed to some extent by the setting up on 30 November 1918 of the Council of Workers' and Peasants' Defence with full powers in all matters relating to the organization of the resources of the country in the interests of defence. Lenin was its first chairman and the council consisted of Trotsky, Nevsky, Bryukhanov, Krasin, and Stalin. (Except for a period of a few weeks, Stalin was never a member of the Revolutionary War Council.) For the text of the two decrees see *Bunyan*, p. 276. An Operation Department had already been formed by Trotsky in May, but it made little headway against the anarchy of the 'local patriots'—see *Fedotoff White*, pp. 36–8.

growing authority that on 4 October 1918 he finally demanded and obtained the recall of Stalin from Tsaritsyn.

The first problem in building a centralized and disciplined army was to ensure a supply of experienced officers. From the start it was Trotsky's policy to utilize the ex-officers of the imperial army to help to build the Red Army. To soften the blow of bringing back the unpopular ex-officers they were invariably now called 'military specialists'. A number of these officers (including the future Commander-in-Chief, S. S. Kamenev)[8] had already joined the infant Red Army before the civil war began in order to help with the defence of their country against the renewed German advance. This may have prepared them for co-operation with the Red Army for the defence of communist Russia in the ensuing civil war. Many officers were persuaded to join as an alternative to prison or death. It is not surprising that during the three years of fighting there should have been many instances of desertion by the officers to the anti-communist forces. But it is beyond doubt that without them the civil war could not have been won, since it was only towards the end of it that the newly-trained Red commanders were able to play even a slight part in the control of military operations.[9] It was inevitable that the throwing together of ex-officers and Communists, should have caused friction, and resentment.[10] There had been opposition from the start in the communist party to Trotsky's policy of bringing the old officers in to the new army and even Lenin had at first had some misgivings. But he did not interfere with Trotsky's handling of the problem. In March 1918 the Left Communists had

[8] Sergey Sergeevich Kamenev: not to be confused with Lev Borisovich Kamenev, the communist leader.
[9] In 1918 ex-officers and ex-non-commissioned officers numbered 7/8ths of all commanders, and in 1919, 4/5ths. Even then the new Red commanders were necessarily in junior posts. The increase of commanders under training, from 1,172 in 1918 to 11,000 in 1919 could not in essentials affect the balance before the end of the civil war—see *VKP(b) i voennoe delo*, pp. 235–6. On 15 August 1920 the Red Army contained a total of 314,180 'military specialists', including 214,717 'ensigns' (junior lieutenants and non-commissioned officers), 48,409 officers of the rank of lieutenant and up, and the remainder doctors, etc.—*Wollenberg*, p. 73.
[10] See *Fedotoff White*, p. 59 *et seq.*, for a discussion of this question. The general impression to be gleaned from descriptions of the relations between these ill-assorted colleagues is that the comradeship of joint military service often overcame the friction—see e.g. an interesting account in *Barmine*, Chapters VIII to XIII of the relations between the young communist commanders and the ex-officers.

opposed this policy as part of their general charge that the pure stream of socialist doctrine was being defiled. But it was not socialist doctrine which caused most opposition to the officers. Much of it came from the partisan detachment leaders of the early days of the revolution and the civil war, who viewed with suspicion and contempt any return to the despised military science of the old capitalist days.

> We are always being told [wrote one spokesman of the partisans' point of view] that conduct of a war is so delicate a matter that we cannot hope to manage without the military specialists. Well, maybe military matters are a delicate affair, but they are no more than a component part of a much more delicate business—the running of the whole state machine. We had the audacity at the time of the October Revolution to take the running of this machine into our hands,—and somehow or other we managed it! [11]

The introduction into the Red Army of an increasing number of officers whose loyalty to the new régime could not be implicitly relied upon, accentuated an acute political problem which already existed in the army. It was inevitable that any conscript army in Russia should be overwhelmingly, peasant in composition, and the loyalty of the peasants to the new communist rulers was questionable. They showed a natural reluctance to be once again uprooted from the land and forced into uniform; their loyalty was to the land, and not to any party or government. When faced with the choice between the rule of the Communists and that of the White Army generals, whose forces successively overran their farmsteads, the peasants, for fear of losing their newly-acquired land, on the whole preferred the Communists. Trotsky attributed victory in the civil war primarily to this factor.[12]

[11] A. Kamensky, 'Davno pora', in *Pravda*, 25 December 1918. This article was part of a whole series of articles on this and other questions, which appeared in the months before the Eighth Party Congress—see N. I. Podvoysky in *Pravda* of 31 October 1918; V. Sorin, 'Kommandiry i kommissary v deystvuyushchey armii', *Pravda*, 29 November 1918; G. Sokol'nikov, 'Pis'ma s fronta', *Pravda*, 31 January 1919; a directive of the Central Committee of the party 'O politike voennogo vedomstva', *Pravda*, 26 December 1918. For Trotsky's views see 'Voennye spetsialisty i krasnaya armiya', *Izvestiya*, 10 January 1919; cf. *Trotsky*, *KVR*, Vol. II, pp. 135, 142–5, 154–61. His Theses for the Eighth Congress which also dealt with the question were published in *Pravda* on 25 February 1919.

[12] *Trotsky, KVR*, Vol. I, pp. 14–21. cf. *ibid.*, Vol. III (2), p. 7.

But peasant support was nevertheless precarious, and liable, after a communist victory, to turn into hostility.[13] It was from the peasants that the astronomic total of deserters during the civil war was drawn, and the numerous partisan bands operating on their own, many of them against the Soviet régime, were replenished.[14] It was inevitable that a coherent and disciplined army could only be formed out of such material if the peasant mass were leavened by a proportion of the more politically malleable proletariat. As Lenin told a secret session on military questions of the Eighth Communist Party Congress in March 1919 'without iron discipline wielded by the proletariat over the middle peasantry, nothing can be achieved'.[15] So far as general economic policy was concerned, this congress decided on concessions to the 'middle' peasantry, that is to say the small-holders. But it was quite clear that these concessions were not intended to apply inside the army. The policy of subordinating peasant to worker in the army was justified by results, which showed that the fighting value of military units was directly related to the proportion of proletarian elements in those units.[16] The presence of a potentially antagonistic officer class together with the need for stiffening the morale of the unreliable peasants in the Red Army thus raised very special problems of political organization. Trotsky solved them with a ruthless disregard for the susceptibilities of the party members, to the benefit of the Red

[13] Their hostility to the Communists was not to be explained away by the familiar communist argument that it was inspired by the well-to-do 'kulaks'. This class had by the end of 1918 virtually disappeared. The percentage of peasants employing hired labour was on the average only 2 before the revolution, and was 'negligible' in December 1918—see Larin's speech at the Second Congress of Councils of National Economy, *Trudy VSNKh II*, p. 99.

[14] The total number of deserters *recaptured* during 1919 and 1920 was 2,846,000, of whom about half surrendered voluntarily. The total strength of the Red Army was 3,000,000 by the end of 1919 and 5,500,000 by the end of 1920. See *Grazhdanskaya voyna*, Vol. II, p. 83. Soviet writers claim that the large number of voluntarily returning deserters was due to the mild penal measures applied to them as well as to the intensive propaganda in the villages. In the last eight months of 1919 out of 1,500,000 deserters only 10,000 were imprisoned, and 600 shot. See A. Geronimus, *Partiya i krasnaya armiya*, p. 73.

[15] Quoted from the archives of the congress in *Yaroslavsky*, Vol. IV, p. 414. cf. Trotsky in secret session at the Tenth Party Congress in 1921: 'Do not forget that our army consists in its overwhelming majority of young peasants. It represents a bloc of the directing worker minority and the peasant majority directed by it.'—Quoted in *Antonov-Ovseenko*, pp. 185–6.

[16] The percentage of workers in crack divisions varied from 19·6 to 26·4, while in divisions of low combat value it was 10·5—figures quoted from *Voennyy vestnik* in *Fedotoff-White*, p. 105.

Army as a fighting machine, and to the detriment of his own political future.

The main features of the system of political control envisaged by Trotsky were: complete centralization; freedom from control by the civilian party machine; the resolute putting down of the initiative of the local military party cells; and, above all, the organized shifting around of party members from one part of the country to another, to meet emergencies as they arose at different parts of the widely scattered front. To make the employment of former officers less hazardous, he devised the system of political commissars. 'Every specialist must have a commissar on his right and on his left, each with a revolver in his hand,' Trotsky told the Central Executive Committee in July 1918.[17] The system of dual command, with the political commissar counter-signing every operation order, so as to guarantee the absence of any counter-revolutionary intention behind it, was obviously unsatisfactory from the military point of view and it was never regarded as permanent. The aim from the beginning was to develop as soon as possible a system of unified command. 'The more the commissar begins to penetrate into combatant work, and the commander to assimilate the political work, the nearer we are getting to unified command, where the person placed at the head of a unit will be both commander and commissar,' Trotsky said at the end of 1918.[18] To some extent this process of fusion did in time take place. Many political commissars found that their appetite for the purely military duties grew, and were in time transferred to positions of military command. During 1920 some of the Red commanders had acquired the necessary experience to be promoted to greater authority. Wherever the unification of command was achieved, efficiency was increased and friction avoided.[19] But Trotsky was determined that the fusion of commissars and commanders should not take place any faster than efficiency warranted, and his pace was too slow for some of the communist leaders.

[17] *Protokoly VTSIK V*, pp. 78–80.　　[18] *Trotsky, KVR*, Vol. I, p. 184.
[19] See for example *Putna*, p. 15, for a description of the effect of the introduction of unified command in his division at the Polish front, in March 1920. According to him it both increased the authority of the commanders and improved political life in the division, since the former commissars became deputy commanders in charge of political matters, and were able to devote their full time to political activity.

Trotsky initiated his centralized system of control during 1918 by setting up a number of political departments. These were attached to the revolutionary war councils of fronts and armies,—that is to say, to the subordinate military *cum* political authorities framed on the model of the Revolutionary War Council of the R.S.F.S.R., of which Trotsky was chairman. In May 1918 the Political Administration of the R.S.F.S.R. (known in its abbreviated form as P.U.R.) was formed at the head of these political departments. By the spring of 1919 political departments were also formed in the divisions. Their function, the co-ordination of all political activity in the army along the lines laid down by the central party authorities,[20] accorded ill with the spirit of independence which was manifesting itself in the political life of the army. During 1918 there had been an extensive and apparently quite spontaneous growth of communist party cells throughout the army. Unconnected from the beginning with any central party authority, they had by 1919 grown very considerably in power, interfering in army affairs and attempting to exercise direct control over commanders. They were even building up a party hierarchy of their own by electing divisional and army bureaux. This local political enthusiasm was viewed with great distrust by Trotsky since it cut right across his plan for a centrally controlled party machine.

> The partisan spirit [observes the leading historian of political structure in the Red army] which the communist party was burning out with a red hot iron in the army, was reappearing in the peculiar guise of 'army syndicalism' within the [army] party organization, thus thwarting the general policy of the party of strengthening the centralization which was beginning to take shape in the direction of military affairs.[21]

In January 1919 an 'Instruction on Party Cells' in the army issued by the Central Committee put a stop to the creation of any kind of elected committees or bureaux in the army, and provided for the absorption of existing communist party committees into the centralized system of appointed political departments. With the development of the centralized

---

[20] But P.U.R. was not subordinated to the Central Committee of the party until 1925.

[21] See *Geronimus*. pp. 39, 86–8.

political administration (P.U.R.) and of the political departments, the commissars became an integral part of the new machinery. The Eighth Party Congress in March 1919 empowered the political departments, i.e. the branches of P.U.R. in the field, to appoint the commissars, at the same time 'removing from their number all unreliable and careerist elements'. The political departments were to act under the 'immediate direction of the Central Committee'.[22] In this way there grew up a fully centralized machine for all political activity in the army, namely, P.U.R., itself directed by, though not subordinate to, the Central Committee, and in turn controlling through the subordinate political departments of divisions both the commissars and all political activity within units.

The 'Instruction on Party Cells' of January 1919 made clear what the function of army party cells in the new political system was to be—not interference in the conduct of military affairs, but the creation within units of a nucleus of shock troops who by their example of self-sacrifice would strengthen the morale of the rest of the unit.[23] Trotsky, intolerant from the first of the tendency of party members to acquire privileges for themselves on the strength of their political position, had made this function of Communists as a 'ginger group' his main aim, with more regard for military efficiency than for his own popularity. To him belongs the credit of first defining and developing in practice the nature and function of a communist party member—that of an obedient spy and faithful agent of the party hierarchy, with no mind of his own, yet at the same time fired by selfless and disinterested devotion to duty. 'Send me Communists who know how to obey,' he had wired Lenin when he first arrived to take charge of military operations at Sviyazhsk, near Kazan', in August, 1918. A year later, in an order of the day, he warned all Communists that their rights were no greater than those of others, but that their penalties for delinquency would be doubly severe.[24] In an order of the day in May 1920, issued to the Western Front, he defined in clear terms his views of the function of the Communist in each

---

[22] *VKP(b) v rez.*, p. 347. The All-Russian Bureau of Political Commissars was disbanded on 18 April 1919.

[23] *Grazhdanskaya voyna*, Vol. II, pp. 119–22; *Fedotoff-White*, pp. 94.

[24] *Trotsky, Ma Vie*, Vol. III, pp. 145–6.

unit. His duties were 'to watch over the morale of his fellow-soldiers', to exhort them hour by hour, to 'keep careful check on their work' and to inspire them by his example. Political departments in turn must keep a close watch over the behaviour of all Communists, and ruthlessly eliminate or punish those lacking in obedience, decision, or courage.[25]

A big drive for party members in the autumn of 1919 produced a further 35,000–40,000 Communists for the army,[26] a mass which no doubt had the effect of swamping any intractable elements among members of the old anarchical cells and committees, thus making the task of P.U.R. and its departments easier. But the most powerful and effective weapon in the hands of P.U.R. was the section which dealt with the transfer of Communists from one part of the front to another. This section enabled P.U.R. to keep complete control over the party machine, to strengthen the front at any point as required, to eliminate obstreperous Communists from places where their influence was likely to do most harm, and to break up undesirable cliques or groups. Thousands of Communists were thus drafted by this organ—over 24,000, for example, between April and November 1920.[27] A further important stage in the growth of centralized political control, was the decree of 21 February 1919, which removed the so called special branches of the army, responsible for security inside the armed forces, from the control of the *Vecheka* and placed them under the Revolutionary War Council.[28]

It was inevitable that this policy should arouse fierce opposition. Not only did it put down local political initiative and transform party cells into obedient tools of the central disciplinary machine, but it also struck a blow at the privileged position to which many party members aspired. The opposition asserted itself at the Eighth Party Congress in March 1919. The main spokesmen for the opposition were the former Left Communists, V. M. Smirnov, Sapronov, and Yaroslavsky, as well as Voroshilov, who, with Stalin at

[25] *Trotsky, KVR*, Vol. II, (2), p. 126.
[26] *Grazhdanskaya voyna*, Vol. II, p. 123.
[27] *Izvestiya Ts. K.* no. 29, 7 March 1921, p. 3. By the end of the civil war the number of cells at.the front and in the rear was 7,000, with a total of 280,000 party members—*Grazhdanskaya voyna*, Vol. II, p. 126, note.
[28] *Sistematicheskiy sbornik*, p. 55.

Tsaritsyn, had presented a solid front of obstruction to Trotsky. The deliberations of the congress were held mainly in secret and the minutes were never published, but the salient lines of the 'military opposition' (as it became known) are clear enough from the speech of V. M. Smirnov in open session. The opposition complained of the growing power of the 'specialists', and demanded increased influence in military affairs for the commissars. It also complained of excessive discipline and of the bureaucratic methods of the new centralized political machine, and urged greater participation in army affairs by the local party organizations 'on the basis of the comradely welding together of Communists by combining appointment from above with spontaneous initiative'.[29] Trotsky was at the time of this congress engaged at the front, though he had prepared a series of Theses for it embodying the Central Committee's views in defence of centralization. This official view was supported by Lenin, Pozern, Zinoviev, Sokol'nikov, and Stalin.

Stalin's position at the congress is of interest. There is little doubt that he was the main inspiration behind Voroshilov's opposition, and he had certainly fomented insubordination to Trotsky. He supported the official Theses, but as he himself later explained, 'I did not attack the military opposition with quite so much hostility as perhaps Comrade Trotsky might have wished, because I considered that among the military oppositionists there were many splendid workers without whom we could not manage at the front.' At the same time he appears to have urged the need for a strictly disciplined army.[30] The military question was discussed in a commission of the congress, in which the opposition secured a majority against the official policy. A conciliation commission was thereupon appointed in an endeavour to reach agreement. Stalin, with Pozern and Zinoviev, was a member of this conciliation commission. Thus he was already showing the political skill which enabled him, without coming out openly against the Central Committee, to retain the support of the friends in the Red Army whom he was gathering up on the

---

[29] *Protokoly VIII*, pp. 159–60.
[30] Stalin, *Ob oppozitsii*, pp. 668–9, where a paragraph from his speech (not apparently published elsewhere) is reprinted. cf. *Istoriya VKP(b)*, pp. 224–5.

wave of discontent caused by Trotsky's unpopular measures. In the end Trotsky's Theses were adopted in the form of a resolution, with no more than editorial changes, as Yaroslavsky said in his report. The resolution approved the principles of political organization in force in the Red Army, and made a number of recommendations as a result of which the centralized political machine was further strengthened in the course of 1919.[31] The military opposition did not recover from its defeat in March 1919. Moreover, the critical eighteen months of fighting which followed helped to relegate inner party disputes to the background. With the end of the civil war in sight the old discontent flared up again in a somewhat new form.

In the spring of 1920, at the Ninth Party Congress, a number of local civilian party organizations demanded that control over political activity in the army should be handed over to them. In view of the scattered nature of operations in the civil war during which many sections of the widely extended front were quiescent for long periods, this was a natural enough demand. But it was just such interference that the army system of political control was designed to avoid. The Central Committee did not succeed before 1921 in gaining complete control over the local civilian party organizations, and in 1920 these still retained a measure of autonomy. Any form of subordination of army political work to local organizations in 1920 would have destroyed the centralized system of control regarded as essential for discipline, and for Trotsky's policy. The demands of the local civilian organizations made little headway at the congress.[32] But the rivalry between them and the centre grew to more formidable proportions later in the year, particularly after the extension of the military model of party organization to spheres other than the army. By the time of the Tenth Party Congress in March 1921, when all-round opposition to the Central Committee's dictatorship had reached fever heat, there was a considerable movement for a revision of the whole system of political control in the army. Podvoysky, the most radical of the leading Communists on military questions, included in the Theses he submitted to the congress a demand for the reform of political activity in the

[31] For the full text of the resolution see *VKP(b) v rez.*, pp. 344–51.
[32] *Geronimus*, p. 115.

army by linking military political work as closely as possible with civilian party organizations—a suggestion obviously aimed at some form of decentralization. Delegates from the political departments of the Ukraine, of the South-West Front and of Kharkov Province, presented Theses which contained a demand not only for closer links between military and civilian party organizations, but also for reforms designed to make the party cell of each military unit the basis of all political work, and for a system of elected commissars.[33] However, the congress, which was in session during the Kronstadt revolt, reaffirmed the existing political system of control in the army and navy. Its resolution on military questions branded as 'politically dangerous and capable of evoking and strengthening the disintegration of the Red Army and therefore completely inadmissible' the demand of certain groups and individuals that the political organization of the Red Army should be changed by introducing elected commissars subordinated to the party cells. The resolution proposed that the Central Committee should take 'definite steps to ensure the complete elimination of such disorganizing agitation'.[34] Experience had proved in 1917 and 1918 with what rapidity the system of elected officers led to disintegration of army discipline.

Thus, the military opposition had made little headway by 1921, so far as influencing party congress decisions was concerned. Its importance lay in the fact that it united a powerful group of antagonists inside the Red Army against Trotsky. This in turn enabled Trotsky's enemies in the Central Committee, Zinoviev and Stalin, to build up support for themselves inside the army. Stalin's skill at the Eighth Party Congress has already been referred to. Zinoviev's campaign in the Baltic Fleet, in 1920 and early 1921, against the political directorate of the fleet is described later.[35] By his conduct in the direction of the army, Trotsky had to some extent given his enemies the opportunity which they sought. Intolerant and often tactless and domineering, he had no time for the theorists, the careerists, or the second rate. A latecomer to

[33] *Protokoly X*, pp. 674–6, 682–4. These Theses were apparently also supported by the Workers' Opposition.
[34] *Protokoly X*, p. 620. This resolution was kept secret and not published until 1933—*ibid.*, p. 617, *note.*
[35] See Chapter XIV.

the party, lacking the bond of the early days of struggle to link him with the old Bolsheviks, he always tended to maintain the distance of authority between himself and them. At all times, and above all throughout the civil war, he regarded the building up of the army and the winning of the war as a job to be done. It absorbed all his energies, and left no time for the consolidation of his own political position. The result was that, at the end of the civil war, it was among the younger party members within the army and the Red commanders, the newcomers who perhaps instinctively recognized that the building of the Red Army had been accomplished by him almost single-handed, that his supporters were mostly numbered.[36] But by the time Trotsky's position in the army came to be seriously threatened by his rivals for political power, personal popularity with the party rank and file was of little importance. The political machine within the army, which he had himself created, ensured that those who now controlled it at the top could easily neutralize any mass support on which he might have relied. When once the control of the army party machinery had slipped from his grasp, his position in the army was doomed.

There were also during the years of the civil war discussions on military doctrine between Trotsky and the communist military theorists which were of importance in that they alienated from Trotsky the men who were later, under Stalin, to oust him and to become the main leaders of the Red Army —men like Gusev, Frunze, and Voroshilov.[37] In the war-time debates on military doctrine Trotsky brushed aside the new theories with contempt and impatience. Again and again in his speeches of those years the refrain was the same: this was no time for theories, the practical problem was to train an army of largely illiterate peasants to handle a rifle, to grease their boots, and to keep themselves free from vermin. But in defending this practical point of view he placed himself on the side of the conservatives and reactionaries—the side, incidentally, of the ex-officers—and became an opponent of the more revolutionary elements of the party who wanted

[36] *Geronimus*, p. 167.

[37] Frunze was appointed Commissar for War in January 1925, but in fact became the effective head of the army when he was appointed deputy to Trotsky in February 1924.

military doctrine to be linked with what they considered to be marxist principles, and with the task of promoting world revolution. The main exponents of this 'Unitary Military Doctrine', as it became known, were Gusev and Frunze. The doctrine had already appeared in 1919 as an aspect of the opposition to the military specialists. In the new class army, so ran the argument of the opposition, there was no room for specialists of the old enemy class, since both tactics and strategy should be subordinated to 'marxist principles'. In the absence of any authoritative definition of what marxist principles of military art were, the doctrine of the opposition amounted in practice to advocacy of a war of manœuvre conducted by small, highly mobile detachments, as against positional warfare. To this end, they argued, the Red Army should be constructed for the specific needs of the civil war and not built up on the old military principles with the aid of former officers.[38] However, this idealization of the partisan warfare of the early days of the Red Army (which is what it amounted to) contained a number of valuable practical suggestions, such as the increased employment of cavalry and of highly mobile detachments, all later embodied with success in Red Army military practice. It was easy for Trotsky to dismiss this early advocacy of marxist military doctrine as ridiculous, since it appeared to be part and parcel of the campaign against the ex-officers, whom the great majority of the party leadership (including even Stalin) supported. By the end of the civil war, however, the doctrine was revived by several of the victorious communist commanders. The 'Unitary Military Doctrine' as elaborated by Frunze in 1921, was put forward in a series of Theses in collaboration with Gusev for the Tenth Party Congress in March of that year.

In its essentials this elaboration of the doctrine differed little from the early form. It demanded a unitary system of training in the army to prepare it for its coming task of promoting world revolution. The army should be trained throughout in a spirit of offensive action, with defence regarded only as

[38] The early exponent of these views was Tarasov-Rodionov. See *Trotsky, KVR,* Vol. II (1), pp. 59, 452; *Fedotoff-White,* pp. 159-60. Neither Gusev nor Frunze was, however, a supporter of the campaign against the officers, or of guerrilla methods generally in 1918 or 1919—see e.g. Gusev's articles collected in his *Grazhdanskaya voyna.*

an aspect of attack. It must be united from top to bottom by its political ideology and by its determination to carry out the tasks with which the proletariat would shortly be faced. Moreover, 'the task of working out a unitary proletarian military doctrine in the conditions of the developing world revolution and in the circumstances of the forms of civil war most probable in the immediate future cannot be entrusted to the narrow specialists of the military type'. The general staff must immediately be enlarged by the inclusion of the more important political workers in the military sphere.[39] Yet, although backed by Frunze, who had a victorious campaign against Wrangel to his credit, the new doctrine made little apparent headway at the congress. The 'ridiculous theses', as Trotsky described them, were in the end withdrawn,[40] and Trotsky's views officially prevailed. 'It is not verbiage and noisy chatter about innovations that we need,' Trotsky said in the course of the debate, 'not this gibberish, this enunciation of new military doctrines, but systematization of experience, improvement of organization, and attention to details.' Trotsky was no less determined on the question of what the tasks of the army should be in bringing about world revolution. Army policy, argued Trotsky, must keep in step with the policy of the Communist International, where the order of the day is 'lengthy preparatory work of a defensive character'. It would not be possible to start a war which would lead to world revolution by mere propaganda to the effect that the 'interests of the workers are the same all over the world'. Nor would world revolution necessarily be achieved through military intervention which is like 'the obstetrician's forceps, applied in time they can relieve the birth pangs, but applied prematurely they can only produce a miscarriage'.[41]

---

[39] See Frunze, *Sochineniya*, Vol. I, pp. 207–27; *Protokoly X*, pp. 676–82. Frunze's article 'Edinaya voennaya doktrina i krasnaya armiya', which became the foundation of the new ideas, was published in *Armiya i revolyutsiya* in July 1921, after the Tenth Congress. As in the case of Tarasov-Rodionov, there can be no doubt that from the military point of view there was much that was excellent in his ideas, particularly his advocacy of war of manœuvre against positional warfare. There was also much that was calculated to appeal to the army Communists, such as the view that military discipline should be based on 'that comradely fusion and mutual understanding between the upper and lower ranks, which is the main guarantee of the physical and spiritual might of the Red Army'.

[40] *Trotsky, KVR*, Vol. III (2), p. 242; *Protokoly X*, p. 682, *note*.

[41] *ibid.*, pp. 210–239; *Antonov-Ovseenko*, pp. 182–98.

For the time being Trotsky could be sure of his majority. The disastrous failure of the Polish campaign not long before had been in part due to a mistaken confidence, which Lenin shared, that the advance of the Red Army would start a revolution in Poland. Lenin, who had profited by this experience and who regarded the Frunze doctrine as right from the long-term point of view, but wrong at the moment,[42] was still there to lend his weight to Trotsky's authority.

At the same time Trotsky's defence of caution and conservatism and his spirited attacks on a doctrine dear to all full-blooded revolutionaries within the party and to many of the communist Red Army commanders, inevitably lost him support. The election at the Tenth Congress of Frunze, Voroshilov, and Gusev (the latter as a candidate) to the Central Committee indicated their growing authority within the party. Frunze's views grew in popularity. Although his doctrine did not officially prevail the following year at the Eleventh Party Congress, yet he won a considerable measure of support shortly before at a conference of Ukrainian army commanders, which adopted a resolution on training in the Red Army based on his principles of the revolutionary offensive.[43] The time was not yet ripe at the Eleventh Congress for the adoption of any resolution in open opposition to Trotsky, but the ground was already well prepared for the attack on his position in the army. It was not, however, by doctrines of world revolution nor by 'marxist principles' that the Red Army was built up into the outstandingly efficient machine it eventually became, but by the more orthodox methods of intensive training and stern discipline. When most of the old commanding caste of ex-officers was eventually eliminated, it was not in accordance with any revolutionary doctrine, but in pursuance of a general policy of eliminating potentially hostile elements. But the debates on military doctrine in 1920 and 1921 were much more than mere academic discussions. They concealed a struggle which was going on within the communist leadership for the control of the army. The men who were hoping to displace Trotsky used the debates to rally supporters under the

[42] According to Frunze himself,—see quotation by A. S. Bubnov, the editor, in his *Sochineniya*, Vol. I, p. xxvi.
[43] Trotsky, *KVR*, Vol. III (2) pp. 242 *et seq.*

banner of an attractive revolutionary military doctrine. Trotsky's failure to realize this, or his inability to counter the move against him, helped to bring about his eventual downfall.

The relevance of these disputes on military questions to the political history of 1920 and 1921 is threefold. In the first place, the model of centralized political control in the army was at the end of the civil war adapted to civilian life, with momentous results. This, in turn, enabled Zinoviev and Stalin, by attacking an unpopular policy associated with Trotsky, both to discredit him and to win support inside the party for themselves. Most important of all, the disturbance caused in the party by the adaptation of the military pattern of political direction to civilian conditions, gave Zinoviev and Stalin their opportunity to undermine and then capture the party apparatus.

CHAPTER XIV

THE BEGINNING OF THE CRISIS

Lenin had succeeded in March 1920 in reconciling the many trends of opposition inside the trade unions, at any rate to the extent of persuading the unions to approve his policy. But the precarious balance of forces which he had achieved was disturbed by the intervention of Trotsky. In 1920, though still retaining command of the army, Trotsky had turned his indefatigable energies to the critical situation on the domestic front. With the rejection in February of his proposals for the abolition of war communism, he seems to have drawn on his army experience and to have turned his thoughts not only to increased discipline and improved methods of central control of industry, but also to the construction of some system by which the hegemony of the proletariat over the peasants might be made to work as successfully in civil matters as it had worked in the army. According to a scheme for a gradual transition to a militia system which he put forward to the Ninth Party Congress in March 1920, the territorial army was to be co-ordinated with industrial centres in such a way 'as to ensure that the industrial nuclei, with their agricultural peripheries drawn into their orbits, should become the basis for military units', consisting of proletarian cadres whose military tasks would be closely co-ordinated with the industrial life of their district. This system, though fully approved by the congress, was not, however, put into operation. By the following year, the majority of the party, including Trotsky, had come to the conclusion that transition to a militia would be both 'incorrect and dangerous in practice'.[1] But Trotsky succeeded in 1920 in putting through an idea to which he attached great importance, the conversion of certain of the military formations into labour armies for industrial tasks. This involved more than merely putting the soldiers to civilian tasks, since his scheme in fact amounted to the total militarization of whole areas, with wide administrative authority vested in each labour

[1] *VKP(b) v rez.*, pp. 407–9; 465–7.

army command. The First Revolutionary Labour Army, formed in the Urals by a decree of 15 January 1920, was given limited authority over local administrative organs.[2] Moreover, as in the Red Army, the entire political direction was to be concentrated at the top, cutting right across the existing party organizations within the area controlled by the labour army. It was an ambitious, though not a very successful plan. Although the scheme never got so far, it was apparently envisaged by Trotsky as a part of the militarization of entire civilian life, with strict centralization of both political and practical work within a series of large areas, each controlled by the revolutionary council of the appropriate labour army.[3] That such a project should have aroused opposition is not surprising, nor did the First Labour Army with its headquarters in Ekaterinburg in fact ever succeed in capturing political control from the existing party organizations.[4] Stalin was put in charge of the labour army formed for industrial reconstruction in the Ukraine in February 1920. He followed exactly the same pattern of subordination of all political activity to his central political department as did Trotsky in the Urals.[5] This fact did not prevent him later from pouring contempt on the whole plan, in retrospect.

The labour armies were not a successful economic experiment. From a vast apparatus there emerged a very small return. Trotsky, however, did not lose his conviction that the methods which had proved their value in the army could be successfully translated into economic life. His speeches and writings during 1920 urge incessantly the need for strict military discipline in industry, for one-man management, for planned control from the centre, and at the same time for development of initiative, not in the form of interference by the ignorant worker in management, but by easier promotion of the ablest workers from the ranks into the administrative hierarchy.

No social organization [he wrote] except the Army has ever considered itself justified in subordinating citizens to itself in

---

[2] For the text of this decree see *Sist. sbornik*, pp. 97–9.
[3] See, e.g., some theses of the Central Committee on militarization of the national economy, reprinted from *Pravda* of 22 January 1920 in *Protokoly IX*, pp. 525 *et seq.*, in which it is not difficult to detect Trotsky's inspiration, if not his hand.
[4] See Dan, *Dva goda skitaniy*, pp. 45–6 (Dan was in Ekaterinburg at the time).
[5] See *Proletarskaya revolyutsiya*, no. 3 (1940), pp. 169–70.

such a measure and to control them by its will on all sides to such a degree as the state of the proletarian dictatorship considers itself justified in doing and does. . . . The young Socialist state requires trade unions, not for a struggle for better conditions of labour—that is the task of the social and state organizations as a whole—but to organize the working class for the task of production, to educate, discipline, distribute, groups . . . in a word, hand in hand with the state to exercise their authority in order to lead the workers into the framework of a single economic plan.[6]

He was closely supported in his ideas by Gol'tsman, a prominent trade union leader, who developed his proposals for the emergence of a 'workers' aristocracy', the creation in industry of an officer class composed of managers trained up from the ranks. Gol'tsman's idea was for a time also supported by Lenin, as an alternative much to be preferred to board management. It was indeed a system which would have enabled workers to have a stake in industrial management, without endangering efficiency by dividing responsibility for management between an expert and untrained workers sitting together on a management board. The main opposition to the idea of the 'workers' aristocracy' came from the senior trade union officials, who possibly saw in it a threat to their own positions; and also, to a certain extent, from the communist workers, because it did not go far enough to satisfy their aspirations for an immediate large measure of control over industry. Zinoviev attacked the idea in the columns of the organ of the International.[7]

During part of 1920 Trotsky also occupied the position of People's Commissar for Transport, and it was in the organization of transport that a policy of militarization was most thoroughly applied in practice, and aroused most opposition, the main odium for which fell on Trotsky. The critical condition of this service by 1920 certainly called for stern measures.

---

[6] See his *Terrorism and Communism* (published in May 1920), where these ideas are fully developed, especially at pp. 130–2, 152.

[7] See his *Sochineniya*, Vol. VI, p. 344. 'The task of communist workers in the trade union movement', he wrote, 'cannot consist in the separating out and grouping apart of the qualified workers, who represent a minority in the working class.' For Gol'tsman's views see *Pravda*, 26 March 1920; on the 'bloc' between Gol'tsman and Trotsky at the Ninth Party Congress and for Lenin's views on the question, see *Protokoly IX*, pp. 164 (Lenin), 247 (Ryazanov), 210–12 (Trotsky). An extract from Gol'tsman's *Pravda* article is at p. 171 *ibid.*

The inability of the railway shops to keep up with current repairs had drastically reduced the replacement of stock upon which continued service depended. Over half the engines were out of commission, compared with 17 per cent in 1913.[8] The railways had already since 1919 been organized quite distinctly from the rest of industry, and on a military pattern: —the various departments under the People's Commissar of Transport were headed by single managers, with political commissars attached to them, though in many instances the commissar and the manager were, as in the army, fused in one person. As in the army, all political activity was organized centrally, under a directorate (known as *Glavpolitput'*), which cut across both the local and the trade union party organizations. Early in 1920 water transport was removed from the control of the Supreme Council of National Economy, and also placed under the People's Commissar of Transport and under *Glavpolitput'*. Thousands of Communists were drafted into the party structure subordinate to *Glavpolitput'*.[9] This system of wholesale appointments from the centre, with disregard in most cases for the views of local and trade union party organizations, gave rise to considerable resentment inside the party, which the assurance of the Ninth Party Congress that *Glavpolitput'* was a temporary emergency organ, and would in time fuse with the normal union communist organizations and disappear,[10] did little to allay. To many members of the party the military pattern of political control adopted in the railways may have appeared as the thin end of the wedge, the forerunner of the end of all independence of local party organizations. Indeed Obolensky expressly charged Trotsky (who did not refute the charge) with harbouring a secretly prepared plan to extend this system of centralized political control to all the main branches of industry.[11] The antagonism of both the union and the local communist party organizations was further aroused by the setting up in August 1920 (in spite of the protests of Tomsky in the Central Committee of the party) of a Joint Central Transport Committee (known as *Tsektran*) consisting 'princi-

[8] *Kritsman*, pp. 183–4.
[9] 3,000 already by the middle of May 1920—*Otchety*, p. 29. This tendency increased as the demand of the army for political manpower decreased.
[10] *VKP(b) v rez.*, pp. 394–5.   [11] *Protokoly IX*, pp. 132–3.

pally' of the members of the Central Committee of the Railway and Water Transport Workers' Unions. The proposal to create *Tsektran* was adopted by a majority of the Central Committee including Lenin, Zinoviev, and Stalin. The latter was charged, jointly with Bukharin and Krestinsky, with putting the scheme through the communist 'fraction' of the All-Russian Central Council of Trade Unions—no easy task.[12] *Tsektran* consisted of twenty members, including Gol'tsman, and Trotsky became its chairman.

It is not difficult to understand the union opposition to this new committee: it cut across the authority of the All-Russian Central Council of Trade Unions and substituted a centralized government control over the unions, in practice exercised by Trotsky, for that hitherto exercised by the central authorities of the unions concerned. There is little doubt that *Tsektran* was rough in its methods and intolerant of opposition. Above all, Trotsky made no attempt in his administration of transport to win over the trade union leaders. He made no secret of the fact that he intended as chairman of *Tsektran* to use his full powers of redistributing officials within the unions, even to the extent of threatening the recalcitrant with imprisonment.[13] On the other hand, the policy of dictatorial control of transport was the policy of the Central Committee, and had been first put into effect before Trotsky became People's Commissar of Transport. The political commissars appointed by *Tsektran* held office with the authority of the government as a whole, and were therefore entitled to the support of the government in their actions. For one member of the Central Committee to exploit the unpopularity of *Tsektran* in order to discredit another member of the Central Committee, primarily associated with it in the popular view, was nothing but political chicanery. Yet this was the policy openly pursued by Zinoviev towards the end of 1920 and in the beginning of 1921. In the pages of the Petrograd *Pravda* (which he edited) vitriolic articles attacked the system of compulsion over the workers practised by *Tsektran*, such as its 'police methods of dragooning the workers from above with the help of specialists'. The same line of attack was used in speeches up and down the

[12] *Protokoly X*, p. 872. [13] *ibid.*, pp. 372–3.

country. Trotsky was not far wrong when later at the Tenth Party Congress he characterized Zinoviev's campaign as 'hypocrisy': 'It is not to be tolerated that one man should preach democracy among the workers and when it leads to complications, say to another on the telephone "now, the stick if you please, that is your speciality".' The commissars working under *Tsektran*, Trotsky argued, were only carrying out the will of the Central Committee, and Lenin himself had insisted on placing none but 'tsektranists' in the Railways Commissariat. Trotsky's speech was punctuated by applause.[14] Among the 'complications' to which he referred was the wave of industrial strikes at the end of February 1921 in Petrograd, which immediately preceded the Kronstadt sailors' revolt.

Another aspect of Zinoviev's campaign against Trotsky was his attack on the political direction of the Baltic Fleet. As head of the Petrograd communist organization, he exploited the dislike of the sailor Communists for the centralized political structure in the fleet, which left no initiative to their local political cells. A revealing account of this campaign was later published by A. S. Pukhov, based on archival records of the party organizations. It developed in the form of a conflict between the Petrograd Communist Party Committee, of which Zinoviev was the head, and the political department of the Baltic Fleet, *Pubalt* (which was subordinate to P.U.R., the overall military political administration which Trotsky controlled). Zinoviev was eventually successful in persuading the sailors of the Baltic Fleet that they would gain by exchanging one master for another or, at any rate, that the master they did not know could hardly be worse, and might be better, than the one they did—*Pubalt* and its commissars. The conflict appears to have started at least as early as March 1920, at which date the Petrograd committee was openly urging the party organizations controlled by *Pubalt* to disregard the latter's authority. In November 1920 a formal demand that political direction over the Baltic Fleet should be transferred to the Petrograd party was adopted in the Petrograd committee. The 'abnormal relations' between the 'Trotskyist direction of the fleet' and the Petrograd com-

[14] *Protokoly X*, p. 395.

mittee, observes Pukhov, led to 'loss of authority by *Pubalt*' and encouraged the growth of 'unhealthy tendencies among the communist masses'. On 15 February 1921 at a stormy meeting of party organizations of the Baltic Fleet, a resolution was passed condemning *Pubalt* and accepting the Petrograd committee's demand. A number of delegates also 'demanded abolition of all political departments in the fleet'. A fortnight later the Kronstadt sailors revolted against the communist party. Their revolt was not, of course, against *Pubalt* in favour of the Petrograd committee, but against the entire communist party. But the spectacle of open conflict in the party leadership for twelve months before had beyond doubt played its part in encouraging the revolt. As in the case of *Tsektran*, centralized political control in the fleet, independent of the civilian party organization, had been introduced with the full authority of the Central Committee of the party and approved at successive party congresses. This campaign, and other similar campaigns dealt with below, can only be understood as part of an attempt to break Trotsky's authority, a fact which Pukhov (writing in 1930) no longer bothers to conceal.[15] Lenin did not in any way publicly dissociate himself from Zinoviev's campaigns against either *Tsektran* or *Pubalt*. He may, however, have been instrumental in procuring the passing of a resolution by the Central Committee on 12 January 1921 condemning the campaign against *Tsektran*.[16] But the resolution does not in any case appear to have had much effect.

The charge against Trotsky that he wanted to 'militarize' industry in 1920, and that his policy in this respect differed radically from Lenin's, has been reiterated so often, not only by Soviet authors but by many who have written on the disputes of 1920 and 1921, that it is necessary to examine it with some care. The individual proposals and even methods that he advocated or put through during his administration of transport undoubtedly represented the official policy of the party. The unpopular *Tsektran* had been officially set up by the Central Committee. If it was true that Trotsky wanted to

---

[15] See A. S. Pukhov, 'Kronshtadt i baltiyskiy flot pered myatezhem 1921 goda' in *Krasnaya letopis'*, no. 6 (39), 1930, pp. 174–97.
[16] See Trotsky's article 'Tsektran' in *Pravda*, 14 January 1921.

incorporate the unions in the state machine, that was no more than a resolution of the Ninth Party Congress in March 1920 had declared: 'the trade unions . . . must gradually transform themselves into auxiliary organs of the proletarian state'.[17] Again, while it was the case that Trotsky was ready to nullify the machinery of electing union officials by the wholesale infusion of reliable Communists, this too had consistently been the policy of the Central Committee, reaffirmed at the Ninth Party Congress. His introduction of military methods into the political organization of transport was also carried out with the full approval of the Central Committee, and was a continuation of the policy initiated in 1919. Nor is there anything to show that Lenin was not fully behind these decisions. On the other hand, as he had already shown in his administration of the army, Trotsky was intolerant, devoid of political tact, and careless of the repercussions of a policy on his own political position or upon the stability of the party dictatorship. Lenin early in 1920 had triumphantly steered the unpopular one-man management through the party congress, and had yet at the same time retained the support of the administrative talent of the trade unions. Trotsky in a short time undid most of Lenin's work. But the fault for this lay not only with him, but with the faction within the Central Committee, including Zinoviev and Stalin, who set out in the course of 1920 to bring about his downfall. They succeeded in 1920 to the extent that by the end of the year he was replaced as Commissar for Transport by Emshanov. For this some of the responsibility must attach to Lenin who at the critical moment was either unable or unwilling to rescue him. Perhaps in his heart Lenin in 1920 felt a closer kinship with the political cunning of the supporters of his policy like Stalin and Zinoviev, than with the more brilliant, but tactless, outspoken and politically inept Trotsky, and he may have been right, from his own point of view. It was a critical time, and a false step might have meant the end of communist power in Russia. 'Trotsky', Lenin wrote later in his Testament, with express reference to 1920 and 1921, 'is distinguished not only by his exceptional abilities . . . but also by his too far-reaching self-confidence, and a disposition to be too much attracted by

[17] *VKP(b) v rez.*, pp. 398–9.

the purely administrative side of affairs.'[18]   Trotsky himself
admitted that the criticism was fair.[19]

But the attack on Trotsky for his policy towards the trade
unions was only one part of the struggle for power which was
taking place inside the Central Committee during 1920 and
1921.   This struggle was waged primarily around the whole
question of the centralization of authority within the party,
and those who professed to oppose centralization emerged
victorious, only to introduce a greater degree of centralization than had existed before.

By the end of 1919 virtually all authority in the Soviet state
was concentrated at the centre.   Not only had the local soviets
ceased to have any importance, but the local executive committees had become little more than officials under the orders
of the centre.   Even at the centre, the representative Central
Executive Committee, originally intended to be the main
legislative body to which the Council of People's Commissars
should be responsible for its policy, had lost most, if not all,
of its importance.   At the Seventh All-Russian Congress of
Soviets in December 1919, the Mensheviks alleged, with
justification, that the Soviet constitution had completely
degenerated: the All-Russian Soviet Congress had not met
for over a year, instead of meeting once every six months; the
Central Executive Committee had scarcely met at all and had
barely debated or voted a single decree; all legislation was
conducted either by the Praesidium of the Central Executive
Committee, or by the Council of People's Commissars (the
two bodies were largely identical in composition) while in the
provinces there was the same atrophy in the local soviets.[20]

As the party extended its influence over the entire life of
the country and the central party authorities tended increasingly to subordinate all local party activities to their control,
real power became concentrated in the Central Committee
of the party.   The Central Committee was elected at the party

[18] Trotsky, *The Real Situation in Russia*, p. 321.
[19] See Trotsky, *Stalinskaya shkola*, pp. 40–1; 'I think that these words correctly
characterize the very root of the dispute at that period.'
[20] See *Vs. syezd. VII*, pp. 23–4, 60–2.   Certain recommendations were made
at this congress with the object of improving the working of the machinery, but
they were not in fact carried out and the position remained very similar at the
next Congress of Soviets, in December 1920—see *Vs. syezd VIII*, pp. 55–6, for
Dan's proposed resolution in very much the same terms as the year before.

congresses, which during the early years were held annually. Until 1922, at any rate, the Central Committee was forced, to a varying extent, to moderate its policy to the temper of the congress. The Central Committee elected at the Ninth Congress in March 1920 consisted of the following: A. Andreev, A. Sergeev (Artem), N. Bukharin, F. Dzerzhinsky, M. Kalinin, L. Kamenev, N. Krestinsky, V. Lenin, E. Preobrazhensky, K. Radek, Kh. Rakovsky, Ya. Rudzutak, A. Rykov, L. Serebryakov, I. N. Smirnov, I. Stalin, M. Tomsky, L. Trotsky, and G. Zinoviev, nineteen in all. In addition there were twelve candidate members:—G. Petrovsky, E. Yaroslavsky, M. Muranov, V. Milyutin, P. Stuchka, V. Nogin, S. Gusev, I. Pyatnitsky, A. Beloborodov, P. Zalutsky, V. Molotov, and I. Smilga.

The Political Bureau ('Politbureau'), destined before long to become the main organ of party control, was not in 1919 or 1920 independent of the Central Committee. Originally set up in 1917, it had played no part as a formal organ of the party, and was reconstituted by the Eighth Party Congress, in March 1919, as a sub-committee of the Central Committee consisting of five members with the responsibility of taking urgent decisions which could not wait for the full committee to meet. The members elected in 1919 were: Lenin, Trotsky, Stalin, Kamenev, and Bukharin. Its resuscitation was greeted with some suspicion in the party, especially by Obolensky. But during 1919, 1920 and the first half of 1921, the Central Committee still remained the main organ of party direction, notwithstanding the fact that the influence of the Politbureau necessarily increased during the absence on war duties of many members of the Central Committee, which thus made the frequent summoning of the full committee impossible.[21] The omission of Zinoviev from the Politbureau in 1919 was

[21] Thus, during the period March to September 1920, the Politbureau dealt with 629 matters, as against only 99 dealt with by the Plenum; but between September and December 1920 (i.e. when the civil war was almost over) the Plenum was meeting four times a month and dealt with more than twice as many matters as the Politbureau. After the Tenth Party Congress in March 1921 meetings of the Plenum became gradually less frequent. In June–August the Plenum met five times for 27 questions, the Politbureau 24 times for 264 questions. The figures for later months are similar—see *Izvestiya Ts.K.*, no. 22, 18 September 1920; no. 26, 20 December 1921. During 1922 the Politbureau became the governing body, with the Central Committee meetings becoming more infrequent and dealing mainly with ratification of policy—see *Lenin*, Vol. XXVII, p. 402.

not an indication that he lacked important influence. His authority as virtual dictator of Petrograd was considerable. Moreover, during 1919 and 1920 he was the main agent of the Central Committee for questions of party organization, and all important changes in this sphere were steered through by him.

The concentration of political force at the top created fresh difficulties for the Central Committee. Its wide responsibilities and growing appetite for power tended more and more to make it interfere directly in the spheres of the local party organizations. At the same time, in the absence of an adequate apparatus, it lacked the means to quell the impatience and opposition which its interference evoked. Until 1919 the Central Committee had worked without a secretariat, and without any personnel department to deal with party appointments. The death of Sverdlov, shortly before the Eighth Party Congress in March 1919, upon whose memory and organizational talent the Central Committee had been able to rely, made a reconstruction imperative. The congress accordingly set up a Secretariat, with a single secretary, and an Organizational Bureau of five (Orgbureau) to deal with party appointments, both to be responsible to the Central Committee. The congress further declared the need for a determined struggle inside the party against bureaucratic methods, so as to heal the rift between the communist masses and the party leaders, of which the first signs had appeared early in 1919.[22] The implementation of the recommendations of this congress and of succeeding party congresses and conferences for remedying these ills became the responsibility of the Secretariat. But since the causes of these unhealthy signs in the party were deep rooted in a whole series of factors quite beyond the control of any secretariat, its task of restoring harmony in the party was far from easy. The Orgbureau, on the other hand, as the department responsible for the moving around of party members on an ever increasing scale, was bound to be unpopular.

Krestinsky was the first secretary appointed in March 1919. In the following year the number of secretaries was increased to three by the addition of Preobrazhensky and Serebryakov.

[22] *VKP(b) v rez.*, p. 352.

There was as yet no first or General Secretary, but owing to the illness of both Krestinsky and Serebryakov during 1920, much of the work fell on Preobrazhensky. The Orgbureau, as originally set up in March 1919, consisted of Stalin, Krestinsky, Serebryakov, Beloborodov and Stasova. However, the composition of this body was variable and included at different times Trotsky, Kamenev, Dzerzhinsky, and Rakovsky, until on 15 April 1920 its membership was fixed as follows: Stalin, Rykov, Krestinsky, Serebryakov, and Preobrazhensky, with Dzershinsky and Tomsky as candidates.[23] All three secretaries thus became members of the Orgbureau early in 1920. The interdependence of Orgbureau and Secretariat, the absence of Stalin on war duties in the second half of 1920, the weakness and insignificance of Rykov—alike contributed to make the three, Krestinsky, Serebryakov, and Preobrazhensky, the real masters of the new apparatus. All were members of the Central Committee.

In its power of making appointments within the party the Orgbureau possessed what could be a most effective weapon for dealing with discontent and unrest. By means of a systematic redistribution of party members throughout the country, it could break up potential cliques before they had time to gather strength, and exploit to the maximum, and on the widest scale, the restorative influence of the more reliable party members. It thus played in the civilian party organization the part which corresponded to that of P.U.R. in the army. The need for systematic redistribution of party strength had already been laid down at the Eighth Party Congress in March 1919.[24] It was not, however, until the spring of 1920 that the Orgbureau had worked out a plan for such a redistribution involving 52 *gubernii* in all. Hitherto it had been carried out 'as occasion demanded'. Moreover, it was only in March 1920, at the Ninth Party Congress, that the Orgbureau had been given the power to make all transfers and appointments in the party without reference to the Politbureau, except for appointments within the central apparatus.[25] But a planned redistribution of party strength depended upon an efficient

[23] *Otchety*, pp. 27–8.   [24] *VKP(b) v rez.*, p. 354.
[25] *Protokoly IX*, p. 330; *Otchety*, pp. 30, 31. The increased activity of the Orgbureau at this period is shown by the fact that it was now meeting twice daily on an average.

card index of all available members, the responsibility for which rested with a special section of the Secretariat. Some reorganization had taken place in this section during 1920, in preparation for the major operation. But it had far from completed its vital work of card-indexing. Only in September 1920 had a card index of party members been instituted grading members as: (1) most active and reliable; (2) promising; (3) the rank and file,[26] and even this remained incomplete. According to Molotov (not an impartial witness on this question since it was he who replaced Preobrazhensky in 1921), the indexing up to 1 July 1921 was only planned to cover 30,000–32,000 party members,[27] nor was it until the autumn of 1920 that the first attempt had been made, at a conference of *guberniya* party secretaries, to introduce a uniform system of records in local party organizations. Indexes of members in the provincial party organizations, on which the central index must necessarily have depended, were only instituted in January 1921.[28]

By September 1920 the Orgbureau had dealt with transfers of over 25,000 party members. It was an unpopular operation, in spite of the Central Committee's assurances that transfers of party members were 'as a general rule' devoid of any punitive character, and intended merely to implement the party congress resolutions.[29] This major redistribution aroused much antagonism in the provinces. The comparatively mild and conciliatory Krestinsky attempted to meet this opposition by carrying out his transfers in consultation with, and on the recommendation of, the local organizations.[30] He claimed that his policy had been successful. But the Orgbureau, by 1921, had probably hardly scratched the surface of a task which the more energetic successors of Krestinsky and Preobrazhensky were eventually to complete.

During the same period the Secretariat, under Krestinsky and Preobrazhensky (Serebryakov was absent through illness) was vainly endeavouring to deal with discontent in the party. In 1921 the problem would be tackled with more ruthlessness and thoroughness than these men, both of a comparatively

---

[26] *Izvestiya Ts.K.*, no. 22, 18 September 1920. [27] *Pravda*, 21 July 1921.
[28] *Spravochnik I*, p. 54. [29] *Otchety*, p. 43.
[30] *Otchety*, p. 66; and see *Spravochnik*, I, p. 79, for the instructions signed by Krestinsky to local organizations, dated 20 December 1920.

tolerant and compromising temperament, were either able or willing to bring to it. They saw the solution in terms of discussion, persuasion, exhortation, compromise, and conciliation. Preobrazhensky made no secret of the fact that he regarded freedom of discussion as one of the prizes of victory in the civil war. 'This possibility of greater freedom of criticism represents one of the conquests of the revolution,' he wrote in *Pravda* on 22 January 1921, in an article in which he reprimanded some organizations, and especially the Petrograd organization, for their 'exaggerated' tone of criticism. Nor was he alone in his view, since until the end of 1920, at any rate, many members of the Central Committee saw the solution of the crisis in the party in terms of increased freedom of discussion.

The Secretariat grew rapidly in 1920. Its staff increased from 30 in 1919, to 602 by February 1921. In the autumn of 1920 a secret cipher department was set up, to enable it to maintain direct contact with the local party organizations.[31] The Ninth Party Congress in March 1920, when it increased the number of secretaries to three, laid down a policy of closer contact between the centre and the local organizations, of increased propaganda, and encouragement of independent local party activity.[32] Judging by its reports for 1920, there is little doubt that the Secretariat fully shared the opinion that more discussion, more guidance, more contacts with local workers would cure the discontent of the rank and file. But the directives of the party congress were easier to lay down than to implement: for one thing, communist practice, whatever its theory, did not conduce to free discussion in the party, and there were constant complaints in the provinces during 1920 of victimization of those who were inclined to criticize official policy.[33] Moreover, there is an unreality about the reports prepared periodically by the Secretariat which suggests that it had failed to grasp the magnitude of the problem with which it was confronted. On the very eve of the trade union discussion which at the end of 1920 and early in 1921 split the party into many hostile groups, it reports in the name of the Central Committee: 'Thus none of those ideological

[31] *Izvestiya Ts. K.*, no. 22, 18 September 1920.   [32] *VKP(b) v rez.*, pp. 404–7.
[33] *Izvestiya Ts. K.*, no. 29, 7 March 1921.

rifts between party and trade unions now exist, the dissensions on the management of industry have disappeared as well as the dissensions in the sphere of central and local administration.'[34] It was in fact already apparent by July 1920 that the problem of discontent inside the party was far from solved. The situation was not made any easier by the antagonism which had grown up between Zinoviev and Preobrazhensky.

The whole question of healing party discontent was discussed at a special party conference in September 1920, at which both the Democratic Centralists and the Workers' Opposition were strongly represented. In addition to the official report presented by Zinoviev on behalf of the Central Committee, Sapronov, on behalf of the Democratic Centralists presented a minority report. He demanded freedom of discussion within party organs as the only means of uniting the sundered ranks. On behalf of the Worker's Opposition Lutovinov called for the immediate putting into practice of the widest possible workers' democracy, complete abolition of the system of making appointments (to posts supposed to be filled by election), the strictest purge of the party and, above all, the emancipation of the highest Soviet and trade union organs from excessive interference by the Central Committee of the party. Zinoviev did not apparently oppose these suggestions.[35] The party conference in the end worked out a new charter for party democracy which, on the face of it, completely accepted the demands of the opposition. It represented a continuation of the policy of conciliation and compromise which Krestinsky and Preobrazhensky had been pursuing. Its resolution called for equality for all within the party and an end to the system under which privileged bureaucrats ruled over the rank and file by edict. Inner party discussion was to be developed to a much wider extent than hitherto, both locally and centrally. Though recognizing the necessity in 'exceptional cases' for appointments by the centre to be made to posts required to be filled by election, the resolution enjoined the Central Committee to use the method of recommendation, rather than appointment. In no circumstances should transfers of party

[34] *Otchety*, p. 45 a report for the period up to 15 September 1920.
[35] See *Lenin*, Vol. XXVII, p. 494. cf. *Aleksandrov*, pp. 29–30, for an account based on the official record of the proceedings of this Conference. This record, which is very rare, has not been available.

workers take place as a punitive measure 'against comrades on the grounds that they hold different opinions on one question or another.'[36]

The report of the Central Committee prepared by the Secretariat for the Tenth Party Congress the following March claimed considerable success in the carrying out of the directives of the September conference. The practice of appointments to posts supposed to be filled by election, declared the report, had been reduced, repressions against oppositionists inside the party had ceased, party officials had been 'compulsorily returned to work among the masses'. There had been a 'sharp change' after September, in that complaints of victimization against oppositionists had become 'comparatively rare'. Above all, success was claimed for the policy of permitting free inner party discussion and criticism, which it stated had been put into practice on a very wide scale. These discussions had led to a reduction of the strength of the opposition, said the Secretariat in the name of the Central Committee. Moscow was characteristic in this respect. The Moscow *Guberniya* Party Conference in November 1920 had included a very significant and 'extremely hostile' opposition group consisting of three-fifths of the delegates. Three months later this same organization was 'healthy and united', with an opposition forming no more than one-sixth of its members.[37]

It is not easy to assess the weight to be attached to this report as evidence of the value of free discussion, since the policy towards party opposition was radically changed after the Tenth Party Congress, and the system of free discussion was therefore never given a fair trial. It is true that the secretaries responsible for this report had in the past shown a tendency to view the state of the party in a more favourable light than the facts warranted. On the other hand, experience had hitherto shown that the most bitter opposition within the party could in the end be ironed out by full and free discussion of the issues concerned—the case of the Left Communists in 1918 was one instance, and, more recently, Lenin's tactical

---

[36] See *VKP(b) v rez.*, pp. 411–16, for the published resolution. In an account of this conference Preobrazhensky stresses that, in spite of criticism, it was characterized by its complete unity and solidarity—see *Izvestiya Ts. K.*, no. 24, 12 October 1920.

[37] *Izvestiya Ts. K.*, no. 29, 7 March 1921.

triumph on the issue of one-man management. More recently still, at the Moscow *Guberniya* Party Conference, at the end of November 1920, Lenin had succeeded in smoothing over an actual split, when the Workers' Opposition group broke away and held its meeting separately from the rest of the conference. The committee newly elected at this Moscow conference included members of the opposition group, yet it ultimately passed a resolution condemning separate groups and cliques.[38]

At the party conference in September, Zinoviev, as spokesman of the Central Committee, had not opposed the suggestions of Sapronov. He was, however, successful in accomplishing the main task with which he had been charged, the setting up of Control Commissions, which were eventually to prove an effective remedy against opposition within the party after the policy of permitting free discussion had been abandoned. The central and local Control Commissions, composed of the 'most impartial comrades enjoying universal confidence' were instructed to examine all complaints and to deal with them, however trivial. Nothing was laid down about their legal powers. Dzerzhinsky was appointed to the Central Control Commission, but left it after a very short time. Preobrazhensky also became a member, though he was replaced within a few months by Sol'ts. The third member was Muranov. A separate Control Commission was set up for Moscow. Owing to the shortage of living accommodation, the privileges which leading party members had acquired for themselves had created special circumstances in the capital. An instruction on the Control Commissions issued by the Central Committee emphasized that they had been set up for the sole purpose of dealing with questions of breaches of party ethics, and to help to heal the unhealthy state of the party.[39]

Throughout 1920 Zinoviev constantly strove to exhibit himself as the champion of party democracy against every form of tyranny. His campaign in Petrograd against the political direction of the Baltic Fleet, and his attacks on *Tsektran* were a part of this activity. At a Petrograd Party Conference on 4 October 1920 he welcomed 'healthy criticism' in the party, which could only help to keep it 'absolutely pure'. At the

[38] *Lenin*, Vol. XXV, p. 642.
[39] *VKP(b) v rez.*, pp. 415–16; *Izvestiya Ts. K.*, no. 26, 20 December 1920.

same time he blamed the military authorities, 'especially certain ones at the top' (i.e. Trotsky) for the discontent in the party. By the end of the year Zinoviev was holding out promises of a new era of freedom in the All-Russian Congress of Soviets.

> We will set up a more intimate contact with the working masses, we will organize meetings in barracks and camps and factories, and the working masses will then . . . immediately understand that it is not just a joke when we say that a new era is about to dawn, that at the first opportunity of drawing breath freely we will transfer our political meetings to the factories. . . . We are asked, what do we understand by worker-peasant democracy, and I reply: nothing more nor less than what was understood by it in 1917. We must restore the principle of election to worker and peasant democracy. It must be understood that new times call for new songs. It must be made clear that if hitherto we have been repressing our organizations, if we have all been denying ourselves what should be the most elementary democratic rights of the workers and the peasants, the time for this has come to an end.[40]

It would have been understandable had the conciliatory policy of the three secretaries, in the face of growing unrest within the party, exasperated the more determined members of the Central Committee, such as Tomsky, Stalin, or Zinoviev, whose views on opposition within the party were perhaps of a less tolerant nature, whatever Zinoviev may have said. But it was not for its inefficiency, or tolerance, or inaction that the Secretariat, or rather the Orgbureau, was eventually attacked. It was attacked for what were said to be its dictatorial methods and its self-seeking lust for power. Moreover, the division in the Central Committee on the question of the Orgbureau was now openly advertised to the entire party—with Tomsky, Zinoviev, and Stalin shown to be on the side of those who opposed the secretaries' tyrannical methods. In December 1920, Zinoviev had said in the communist fraction meeting of the Eighth Congress of Soviets, 'There are a few individuals among our comrades who sometimes imagine that all our

---

[40] For the Petrograd Conference see *Petrogradskaya Pravda*, 5 October 1920; for Zinoviev's speech at the Soviet Congress in December, see *Vs. syezd VIII*, p. 324. For a forceful attack on this speech see Smilga, *Na povorote*, a pamphlet written for the Tenth Party Congress.

institutions might, if you please, be replaced by the Orgbureau. Then, don't you know, all would go smoothly and quickly, everybody would just have to obey their masters' orders . . . and government work would be very simply distributed: the Orgbureau decides and all other institutions just carry out its orders.   We will not stand for this!'[41]   The Central Committee at the instance of the three secretaries discussed this attack on 30 December.   The result of the voting, which was published in the party organ, disclosed a clear alignment within the Central Committee which had, beyond doubt, been forming for some time past.   For one resolution, fully supporting the Orgbureau, and 'accepting full responsibility for it' there voted: Andreev, Bukharin, Preobrazhensky, I. N. Smirnov, Trotsky, Rykov, Serebryakov, Krestinsky, Rakovsky, and Dzerzhinsky.   For the second resolution, in more frigid terms of approval yet 'seeing no need to reconstitute the Orgbureau' there voted: Tomsky, Zinoviev, Stalin, Petrovsky, Kalinin, and Rudzutak.[42]   Lenin was apparently not present at the meeting.

A campaign for democracy, emanating from Zinoviev, was not likely to carry conviction with the shrewder party members who saw through it without difficulty—the wittier speakers could always raise a laugh by quoting some of Zinoviev's choicer utterances in the defence of freedom.   But the campaign served its purposes.   First, it discredited Trotsky and his dictatorial methods.   Next, it helped to win support for the faction within the Central Committee which had ranged itself against the alleged dictatorship of the Orgbureau—Stalin, Zinoviev, Kalinin, and the trade unionists Tomsky and Rudzutak.   Above all, by undermining the authority of the three men who controlled the unpopular party apparatus—Preobrazhensky, Krestinsky, and Serebryakov—it paved the way for the capture of this apparatus by new men at the next Party Congress.   But while Zinoviev thus held out these promises of party freedom, Lenin dropped a strong hint of the course which the future was to take.   In one of his speeches at the Moscow *Guberniya* Party Conference in November 1920 he formulated his views on opposition, and sounded a note of

[41] Zinoviev, *Partiya i soyuzy*, pp. 106–7.
[42] *Izvestiya Ts. K.*, no. 27, of 27 January 1921.

warning. There was much that is justified and healthy in the opposition, he told the conference. At the same time,

> when opposition becomes opposition for opposition's sake the time has come to put an end to it. . . . It is not only freedom of criticism that must be considered, but also its content. It is time to say that, having regard to our experience, we must make a whole list of concessions, but we must also tell ourselves that in future we will not tolerate the slightest deviation in the direction of cliques.[43]

But when does opposition become 'opposition for opposition's sake' or a 'clique'? The new party leaders, who with Lenin's help were to rise to power a few months after these words were spoken, had no difficulty in answering that question. The men whom they displaced were none of them of the calibre or temperament to carry out the ruthless measures which were now considered necessary to put an end to opposition. Their downfall in March 1921, and the rise of the men who replaced them, heralded a new era in the political history of Russia. But before these changes took place a revolt at a plenary meeting of *Tsektran* at the end of 1920 led to an open split in the Central Committee of the communist party.

[43] *Lenin*, Vol. XXV, pp. 493–6.

CHAPTER XV

OPEN DISSENSION
IN THE CENTRAL COMMITTEE

The trade union Communists had never accepted the decision to organize transport on military lines. The unpopularity of *Tsektran* was only equalled by that of *Glavpolitput'*, with its rough and ready methods of moving around any Communist it chose as occasion demanded. However, the new system did bring about some slight improvement in the catastrophic transport situation which had been reached by spring 1920.[1] Aware of the unpopularity of its policy among the union Communists, the Central Committee of the party at first attempted to placate them with resolutions. One such resolution, passed in September 1920, stressed that the Central Committee rejected any 'petty interference' in the internal life of the unions, and that *Tsektran* and *Glavpolitput'* were to be regarded as temporary organs, destined to fuse with the normal union machinery and to disappear.[2] It is unlikely that the union Communists found this very convincing, though it was true that in some instances this fusion of the *Glavpolitput'*, *Tsektran*, and normal trade-union officials was beginning to take place both at the centre and in the provinces.[3] But it was not an easy task to put through a policy of the most determined dictatorship, while at the same time keeping up the appearance of avoiding undue interference in union affairs. It was a diplomatic game quite beyond the impatient directness of Trotsky, who was mainly responsible for the relations between the Central Committee and the railway-workers' and water transport unions. Zinoviev's campaign for party democracy and the knowledge in party circles that he could be

---

[1] The percentage of locomotives out of repair fell from 60 per cent in the spring to 58 per cent in the early autumn and the repair programme was carried out in the early autumn in excess of the number planned. See E. Preobrazhensky, *Trekhletie oktyabr'skoy revolyutsii*, pp. 10–11.

[2] *Spravochnik*, I, p. 120; cf. a circular letter on the same lines issued by the Secretariat, quoted in Zinoviev, *Sochineniya*, Vol. VI, p. 601.

[3] Report of the Central Committee for period ending 15 September 1920, *Otchety*, pp. 40–1.

relied on to champion an attack on Trotsky in general, and on *Tsektran* in particular, could not have rendered Trotsky's problems much easier. By November the situation in the trade unions had become explosive.

Matters came to a head at an All-Russian Trade Union Conference, which opened on 2 November 1920. Trotsky bluntly disclosed his intentions. His speech emphasized the need for a wholesale reorganization of the unions by appointment, and not by election. 'We have built and rebuilt Soviet state economic organs,' he said, 'smashed them, and then rebuilt them once again, carefully selecting and checking the various workers, and their various posts. It is quite obvious that it is necessary now to set about the reorganization of the unions, that is to say, first of all, to pick the directing personnel of the unions.'[4]

Trotsky's speech evoked immediate protest from Tomsky, then chairman of the All-Russian Central Council of Trade Unions and a member of the Central Committee of the party. Tomsky was no doubt aware that in an attempt to overthrow *Tsektran* he could count on support from at any rate some members of the Central Committee. He was also sure of backing from the spokesmen of the rank and file, who were discontented with the 'bureaucratic bosses'. Though little interested in the personal conflict between Trotsky and Zinoviev, they were only too ready to join in condemning 'bureaucracy in the guise of *Tsektranism*'.[5] As a result, a collision between *Tsektran* and the union Communists became inevitable. On 8 November Tomsky decided to raise the question of the relations between the two at a meeting of the Central Committee, and attacked *Tsektran*. He was supported by Lenin, who blamed *Tsektran* for having alienated the trade union Communists. Lenin's speech in the Central Committee is not preserved, but his views appear from what he wrote a short time later: 'if the party quarrels with the trade unions, then it is the party's fault, and this is certainly the end of Soviet power'.[6] He at

---

[4] For this extract from Trotsky's speech see Tomsky's speech at the Tenth Party Congress, *Protokoly X*, p. 372; for Lenin's views, see *Lenin* (1), Vol. XVIII (1), pp. 22–5.

[5] See e.g. an article by Lutovinov on this Trade Union Conference in *Vestnik truda*, no. 2, December 1920, pp. 11–14.

[6] *Lenin*, Vol. XXVI, p. 100.

once drafted a report in strong terms for adoption by the communist 'fraction' of the All-Russian Trade Union Conference, which was still in session. This report, as Lenin later admitted, was too violent in the terms in which it attacked *Tsektran*, and it caused a sharp difference of opinion in the Central Committee. In an attempt to overcome this disagreement, in which Trotsky and Lenin were ranged on opposite sides, a group consisting of Kamenev, Tomsky, Bukharin, Serebryakov, Sergeev, Dzerzhinsky, Radek, Krestinsky, Rykov, and Zinoviev met together to work out a compromise. They prepared by a majority a draft resolution which proposed that Zinoviev should replace Lenin as the Central Committee speaker at the Trade Union Conference; that he should present a 'businesslike and not a polemical report'; and that the disagreement within the Central Committee should not be openly discussed in the party. Trotsky inquired whether the members of the Central Committee who held a minority view could express their opinion in the 'fraction' meeting of the Trade Union Conference. He was told by the Central Committee that this would be 'undesirable'. The proposal of the Zinoviev group was then adopted by the Central Committee against the votes of Trotsky, Andreev, Rykov, and Krestinsky; Preobrazhensky abstained.[7] Zinoviev was thus put in charge of the difficult situation which had arisen at the Trade Union Conference, and he alone was to be permitted to speak at this conference in the name of the Central Committee. If the solution adopted was intended to heal the breach which had arisen between Trotsky and Lenin in the Central Committee, it is difficult to think of a less suitable candidate than Zinoviev for the handling of the thorny question of *Tsektran*.

On the following day the Central Committee met again. It now had before it rival theses on the whole trade union question, prepared by Lenin and Trotsky. The Central Committee was fairly evenly divided on these: eight voted for Lenin's, and four against. Seven voted for Trotsky's, and eight against. Sixteen members of the Central Committee were present.[8] A draft resolution intended for adoption by the communist 'fraction' at the All-Russian Trade Union Conference was then passed, by eight votes to six.

[7] *Lenin* (1), Vol. XVIII (i), p. 28. [8] *Lenin*, Vol. XXVI, p. 624.

Since it was designed to placate the union Communists, its terms contained a concession to their point of view.

It is necessary to wage a most energetic and systematic struggle in order to eradicate the degeneration of centralization and of militarized forms of work into bureaucracy, self-conceit, and petty officialdom and interference with the trade unions. Healthy forms of militarization of labour will be crowned with success only if the party, the soviets, and the trade unions succeed in explaining the necessity of these methods, if the country is to be saved, to the widest masses of the workers. . . .

The draft resolution went on to recommend that *Tsektran* should 'increase and strengthen the normal methods of proletarian democracy within the unions'.[9] A commission was also set up by the Central Committee, under the chairmanship of Zinoviev, charged with the duty of working out means for the wider application of democratic practice in the unions; for the encouragement of their participation in the control of production; and for a re-examination of the whole question of the employment of specialists. No member of the Central Committee, except Zinoviev as the chairman of this commission, was to be allowed to publish or to speak at any party meetings on the question of the trade unions.[10] Apart from Zinoviev, the commission as appointed included Tomsky, Rudzutak, Rykov, and Trotsky. Trotsky refused to serve on it. He justified his refusal on the grounds that the question of trade unions was one of long-term importance and could only be solved by way of 'ideological work on a mass scale', and also because he would not serve unless he was given equal opportunity with others, i.e. Zinoviev, to voice his views in the press.[11] It is understandable that Trotsky should have declined to leave his reputation in the trade unions in the hands of a commission of which the chairman had not hesitated to attack him publicly in the past. Moreover, he could neither control what the chairman might say outside the commission, nor would he be allowed to contradict him. But Trotsky's refusal to co-operate on the commission did help to precipitate an open split in the Central Committee.

[9] *Otchety*, pp. 47–8.
[10] Zinoviev, *Sochineniya*, Vol. VI, p. 606; *Lenin* (1), Vol. XVIII (1), p. 419.
[11] Trotsky, *O zadachakh profsoyuzov*, pp. 15–21.

The Central Committee had thus on 9 November expressed no decided preference between the views of Lenin and Trotsky on the function of the trade unions. Indeed, although these views as formulated in their respective theses subsequently gave rise to much controversy, there was not in reality very much difference between them on basic principles. Neither for a moment contemplated control of industry by the trade unions, independently of the party, or any relaxation of party control over the unions. Both emphasized the need for the strictest discipline and for the application of methods of compulsion. But where Lenin's theses are a masterpiece of diplomatic understatement, Trotsky's are a defiant challenge: this is what proletarian goverment means, he seems to be saying; it is not particularly pleasant, but it is the only way to win through. Lenin's theses are an appeal to the trade union masses, by a half-promise of freedom: Trotsky's appeal is to robuster instincts, by telling the union Communists the worst. A few contrasting passages may serve to illustrate this difference.

> In the workers' state . . . [says Trotsky] the parallel existence of economic organs and of trade union organizations can only be tolerated as a temporary phenomenon. . . . The thoughts and energies of the communist party, of the unions, and of the government organs must be directed towards fusing in the more or less near future economic organs and trade unions. . . .

In Lenin's formulation the idea was expressed as follows: 'The rapid fusion of the trade unions in the state would be a great political mistake. . . . The trade unions are already at present carrying out certain state functions', and 'these state functions will gradually increase'. But he rejected 'any artificial speeding up of the tempo of fusion of state and unions'. The difference between the two men is particularly apparent in their respective treatment of the question of compulsory methods. As he had often done in the past, Trotsky quite openly urged militarization and compulsion as the normal methods of the proletarian state. Even to differentiate between so-called military methods, and so-called trade union methods such as propaganda or the teaching of self-reliance, was nothing but 'a Kautskyite-Menshevik-S-R prejudice'. In Trotsky's view, in a workers' state there could be no better method for inculcating self-reliance in industry than militarization. The same vexed question is treated much more cautiously by Lenin: 'The principal method of the trade-unions is not compulsion, but persuasion—though this in no way prevents the unions, where necessary, from successfully applying the method of proletarian compulsion. . . .' Finally Trotsky had openly urged the need for central party control over union appointments, but Lenin now seemed to promise some freedom to the union Communists in this matter.

> It is necessary to put into practice in the unions, before all else, election on a wide scale of the members of all organs of the trade union movement, and to eliminate the method of appoint-ment . . . The selection of the directing personnel of the trade union movement must, of course, take place under the overall control of the party.[12]

The theses did not define 'control of the party'. To Lenin this undoubtedly meant the Central Committee; the union Communists may have been led to hope that it meant their own party cells inside the unions.

Trotsky both in his theses and in his speeches and articles at this time made much use of the phrase 'productive democracy'. This had little to do with democracy in the sense of self-government, but meant at most ampler discussion by the communist workers without any interference in actual manage-ment; and, as in the army, an opportunity for all to rise by their merits in a strictly disciplined organization. His lavish use of this term, 'democracy', has however given rise to the completely unfounded view that he was at this period advocating some form of freedom for the workers from the dictatorship of the party.[13] What he did advocate was something more on the

---

[12] Lenin's original theses have not been preserved, but they were the founda-tion for the 'Platform of the Ten', as it became known, the official programme at the Tenth Party Congress, from which the quotations are drawn. This is re-printed in Zinoviev, *Partiya i soyuzy*, pp. 9–32. Trotsky's original theses are to be found *ibid.*, pp. 354–60.

[13] Thus, e.g., *Rosenberg* at p. 153: 'Although Trotsky showed great caution in formulating his proposals in detail, his purpose was clear: the restoration in Russia of working-class democracy by means of the trade unions. If a million trade unionists seized control of production and economic life in general (the idea of productive democracy here makes its appearance) there would be an end to the dictatorship of the communist party.' But Trotsky advocated nothing of

lines of the 'Workers' Aristocracy' of his friend and colleague Gol'tsman during 1919, in an attempt to outbid the senior trade union officials. Thus, in a further set of theses prepared some time after, Trotsky urged the 'flow of fresh creative power from below . . . the flowering of the most gifted sons' of the proletariat. The obstacle to this he saw not in the masses, 'but in the more conservative sections of the trade union bureaucracy'.[14] In the army Trotsky had once, by the recruitment of Communists on a mass scale from among the more promising soldiers, swamped the opposition of the army party bureaucracy. He no doubt hoped now, by encouraging a flow of new Communists from the ranks of the workers, to replace the recalcitrant trade union leaders by more malleable men. His principal anxiety was summed up in his conclusion that discontent would continue so long as industrial production was not increased, and to this end steps must be taken to ensure that 'comrades Tomsky and Lutovinov and the comrades who are used to working by military methods should find a common language'.[15] Past experience had, however, shown that what Trotsky meant by this 'common language' was that the trade union leaders should learn to submit to military methods.

The Zinoviev Commission on the trade unions, without Trotsky, but enlarged by the addition of four trade unionists, Andreev, Lozovsky, Shlyapnikov, and Lutovinov, immediately set to work. At the meeting of the communist 'fraction' of the All-Russian Trade Union Conference on 9 November, the Central Committee's conciliatory resolution was adopted, after heated discussion, by a majority of two hundred, with twelve abstentions.[16] It was Zinoviev's first, and last, success at conciliation. Hatred of *Tsektran* was too strong for any freely negotiated compromise with it to last. In the first week of December at a meeting of the enlarged plenum of *Tsektran*, the communist representatives of the water transport workers together with a large number of communist railwaymen left the conference room as a protest. On 7 December in the

the sort. It was the Workers' Opposition which advocated control of production by the trade unions, and there is certainly no evidence of any sympathy with their views on Trotsky's part at any time.

[14] From Trotsky's theses for the Tenth Party Congress; see Zinoviev *Partiya i soyuzy*, pp. 249–50.

[15] Trotsky, *O zadachakh profsoyuzov*, pp. 21–2.

[16] Zinoviev, *Sochineniya*, Vol. VI, p. 606.

Central Committee Zinoviev now demanded that *Tsektran* should be abolished, that the political directorate of transport (*Glavpolitput'*) should be disbanded, and that the organization of transport should be assimilated to normal trade union organization. Faced squarely with the question of the immediate dissolution of *Tsektran*, it was inevitable that the Central Committee should split into the two factions which had been forming within it for some time past. Lenin, backed by Stalin and Tomsky, supported Zinoviev, and together they urged the immediate abolition of *Tsektran*. By a vote of eight to seven the Central Committee refused to adopt this drastic course, and accepted instead a compromise resolution proposed by Bukharin. This advocated the immediate abolition of the unpopular political directorates, but proposed to leave *Tsektran* in power until February, when a new *Tsektran* would be elected at a congress of railway and water transport workers. Bukharin's proposal also included an important concession to the union rank and file. It insisted that all candidates for union positions should be selected 'not only for their political reliability, but also for their industrial talents, their administrative experience, organizational ability, and practical proof of their interest in the material and spiritual welfare of the masses'.[17] The hand of Trotsky, who supported this resolution, is clearly to be seen in this sentence. Lenin's characterization of the compromise as a 'scrap of paper' was not far wrong, since it was immediately rejected by the dissident water transport Communists, who now defied the communist party by resigning from *Tsektran* on 9 December.[18]

Lenin laid the blame for the deadlock between the trade union Communists and the Central Committee, and for the consequent split in the Central Committee, squarely on Trotsky. He maintained that Trotsky's refusal to serve on the trade union commission headed by Zinoviev had made the split inevitable.[19] He also repeatedly reproached Trotsky for having unnecessarily antagonized the trade union leaders, such as Tomsky and Lozovsky, by his attitude on the trade union question.[20] Lenin still believed that not all the ground gained by him at the

[17] *Otchety*, pp. 47–9; *Lenin* (1), Vol. XVIII (1), p. 29.
[18] *ibid.*, p. 28.   [19] *ibid.*
[20] See e.g. a speech at the end of January 1921, *Lenin*, Vol. XXVI, pp. 97–108.

Ninth Party Congress in March 1920 had been lost, and that the trade unionists, if properly handled, would still be prepared to co-operate with the Central Committee. He was never tired of emphasizing that the party had not paid enough attention to some theses which Rudzutak, a leading trade unionist, had proposed to, and which were in the end accepted by, the All-Russian Trade Union Conference in November. These theses had emphasized the need for the strictest work discipline, and for the closest co-operation by the unions with the central organs. They had also dwelt on the educational mission of the unions, both in the improvement of work discipline and in the struggle against bureaucratic methods—all matters near to Lenin's heart.[21] But in his praise for Rudzutak's theses, Lenin omitted to mention that at the very same conference the same Rudzutak was also demanding that the unions should take 'at any rate a part of the control of industry directly into their own hands'.[22] This was suspiciously close to the demand of the Workers' Opposition, which Lenin was always the first to condemn in the most stringent terms as 'anarcho-syndicalism'. Evidently, the trade union leaders were not all quite so ready to accept the surrender of trade union independence as Lenin hoped.

Trotsky in turn blamed the deadlock between the unions and the Central Committee on Zinoviev's immoderate attacks on *Tsektran*.[23] That Trotsky's lack of tact in handling the unions had contributed to the crisis is clear. On the other hand, had the Central Committee, and in particular Lenin, given their own creature, *Tsektran*, honest backing, the crisis could perhaps have been overcome. What made any compromise solution impossible was the knowledge inside the trade unions that the Central Committee was not united on the question of *Tsektran*. Zinoviev's well-known hostility against this body and his general championship of democratic methods had made it clear that some members of the Central Committee would back the unions against Trotsky in a demand for the immediate abolition of *Tsektran*.

Bukharin's compromise move to save *Tsektran* had thus failed, and the Central Committee was therefore divided on

[21] Rudzutak's theses are printed in Lenin (1), Vol. XVIII (1), pp. 23–4.
[22] Quoted by Larin in *Diskussionnyy listok*, no. 2, p. 3.
[23] See Zinoviev's speech on the subject, *Partiya i soyuzy*, p. 88.

the question of the immediate abolition of *Tsektran*. On Trotsky's side were ranged the three secretaries, as well as Andreev, Bukharin, and Dzerzhinsky—exactly as they were to be three weeks later in the vote on 30 December on the subject of the Orgbureau, to which reference has been made in the last chapter. That Trotsky and the three secretaries were thus aligned together was probably due less to ideological affinity, than to the fact that they were the objects of two aspects of the same campaign. (Even the prosecution at the trials of Trotsky's former supporters in 1937 and 1938 did not allege any bloc between Trotsky and the three secretaries at this early date.)[24] Zinoviev's attack on *Tsektran* and his championship of democratic methods against Trotsky had proceeded side by side with his intrigues against the masters of the party apparatus, Krestinsky, Preobrazhensky, and Serebryakov.

The split in the Central Committee made an open discussion in the party of the issues involved inevitable, in the absence of any other method for determining which faction was to have the upper hand in the Central Committee to be elected at the forthcoming Tenth Party Congress, in March 1921. The debate lasted in full vigour for two months. During this time the question of the policy to be pursued towards the trade unions filled the press and formed the main subject at innumerable party rallies, conferences, and meetings. As shown above, the dissensions which led to the great debate arose partly as a result of a difference of opinion between Trotsky and Lenin on the best tactics to be adopted in putting through a policy of strict control of industry, on which in principle they were both agreed; and partly as the result of personal conflicts within the Central Committee. It soon became apparent that there were wide sections of the party to whom the trade union question was one of subordinate interest only. They welcomed the opportunity for free debate, and used it to ventilate deeper grievances: the dictatorship of the Central Committee and the stifling of local initiative.

[24] The accusation of forming such a bloc in October 1921 for treasonable activities, which was also said to include Radek, was only made against Krestinsky in 1938, but not against either Serebryakov or Radek at their trial in 1937. Nor was Preobrazhensky who in 1938 (if still alive) had been in prison for years, either brought to trial or called as a witness to support the accusation.

Faced with this menace to their authority, the members of the Central Committee became more united, more ready to sink their differences and to join to eliminate the common danger; while their opponents, aware of the solid front against them in spite of personal disagreement in the Central Committee, developed their criticism with increasing bitterness.

The ground for free party discussion had to some extent already been prepared by the Secretariat's policy of allowing debate on the vexed question of the relations between the rank and file and the party leaders. Lenin was, however, reluctant to allow an open ventilation of the question of *Tsektran* and the trade unions. Nevertheless, in spite of the fact that the Central Committee only resolved to permit free discussion on the trade union issue on 24 December, it had already been widely debated in party circles since 9 December, when the breach which had arisen inside *Tsektran* was revealed by the resignation of the water transport workers. According to his own account, which was corroborated by Zinoviev, Trotsky succeeded in persuading Lenin that an officially sponsored discussion might have the effect of drawing away support inside the trade unions from the Workers' Opposition. He maintained that by laying stress on the vital rôle of the trade unions in production, the best elements in the party could be attracted away from the temptation to use the trade unions as the fulcrum of a political opposition. The demand of the Workers' Opposition for the control of all industry by the unions was a powerful magnet to the dissatisfied union Communists. Lenin rightly appreciated that the possible loss of some of his supporters in the party to Trotsky was a far less serious threat to the authority of the Central Committee than that presented by the Workers' Opposition. Trotsky's theses were accordingly published in pamphlet form and the party discussion officially opened.[25] Trotsky is apparently right in his assertion that he did not, before this decision of the Central Committee, openly voice his views.

The great debate began with a meeting in Moscow on 30 December in the Bolshoy Theatre. The trade union Communists were represented in strength, and the entire communist

---

[25] *Protokoly X*, p. 396; *ibid.*, p. 872; for Trotsky's theses see Zinoviev, *Partiya i soyuzy*, pp. 354–60.

'fraction' of the Eighth All-Russian Congress of Soviets, then in session, was also present. The main feature of the meeting was the debate between Zinoviev and Lenin on the one hand, and Trotsky on the other. But other trends of opinion were also revealed at this meeting. Bukharin and Shlyapnikov produced theses of their own on the question of the trade unions, and Nogin and Ryazanov also presented joint minority reports, expressing their views on the question.[26] All these theses and 'platforms' and some others were soon afterwards printed in the pages of *Pravda*. After opening in Moscow, the discussion passed to Petrograd and to the provinces.

In all eight 'platforms' appeared in the course of the debate. In addition to Trotsky's theses and those of Lenin and Zinoviev, which became known as the Platform of the Ten (the other signatories were Tomsky, Rudzutak, Kalinin, Kamenev, Lozovsky, Petrovsky, Artem (Sergeev), and Stalin),[27] no less than six other 'platforms' were made public in the first weeks of January 1921: those of Bukharin, of the Workers' Opposition, of the Democratic Centralists, and of small groups formed around Nogin, Ryazanov, and Ignatov.[28] Only three survived to be discussed at the Tenth Party Congress in March 1921: the Platform of the Ten, the theses of Trotsky, and the theses of the Workers' Opposition. The views of Nogin, Ignatov, and Ryazanov were little more than personal opinions. The Democratic Centralists also did not represent any wide sections of opinion, and they were anxious at all costs to prevent a split in the party. Their leading spokesmen in this debate were Obolensky, Sapronov, and Bubnov—all former Left Communists. (Bubnov was a candidate member of the Central

[26] A verbatim account of this debate was printed early in 1921 in a pamphlet entitled 'O roli professional'nykh soyuzov v proizvodstve—doklady tt. Zinovieva i Trotskogo, rech' tov. Lenina, sodoklady tt. Bukharina, Nogina, Shlyapnikova, i zaklyuchitel'nye slova tt. Trotskogo i Zinovieva na soyedinennom zasedanii delegatov VIII Syezda Sovetov, V.Ts. S.P.S. i M.G.S.P.S.—chlenov RKP, 30 dekabrya 1920 g.' A selection of articles, theses, speeches etc. on the subject of the trade unions also appeared early in 1921, edited by Zinoviev (*Partiya i soyuzy*).

[27] See Zinoviev *Partiya i soyuzy*, pp. 9–32, for the text.

[28] For Bukharin's theses, which were also signed by Larin, Preobrazhensky, Serebryakov, Sokol'nikov, and Yakovleva, see *Partiya i soyuzy*, pp. 371–7; for those of the Workers' Opposition see *ibid.*, pp. 361–70; for the theses of the Democratic Centralists, see *Lenin*, Vol. XXVI, pp. 573–6; for those of Ignatov see *ibid.*, pp. 576–8. Nogin's views will be found in an article 'Dolzhny li professional'nye soyuzy byt' neytral'nymi po otnosheniyu k sovetam?' reprinted in *Partiya i soyuzy*, pp. 304–16.

Committee). The Democratic Centralists regarded the trade union crisis as only an aspect of the general crisis within the party caused by over-centralization. In their opinion there was little difference between the views of Trotsky and Lenin, which they regarded as merely 'two tendencies of one and the same group of militarizers of the national economy'. They considered that party discontent could be obviated by compromise and by more respect for the principle of party democracy. But at the Tenth Congress in March they refused to be separately represented on the praesidium, and withdrew their platform, leaving their supporters (who were only a handful) to vote as they thought fit.[29] The Democratic Centralists had no sympathy with the Workers' Opposition. In spite of some identity of views on over-centralization in the party between the two groups, the Democratic Centralists were essentially intellectuals, whereas the Workers' Opposition was entirely proletarian. The Democratic Centralists were therefore perhaps more ready to be appeased by promises contained in party resolutions. The Workers' Opposition was more interested in practical results.

The theses of the Workers' Opposition carried the signatures of leading Communists in the Metal-workers' Union, headed by Shlyapnikov; of the Miners' Union, headed by Kiselev; of some other trade unionists and industrial officials; and of Chelyshev, a member of the Central Control Commission. They recalled that the programme of the party enjoined that the trade unions 'must achieve actual concentration in their hands of all management of the entire national economy'. They accordingly now demanded that control over industry should pass to the trade unions, and that it should be exercised by a central organ specially elected by the unions, grouped according to branches of production. Within individual undertakings, control should be vested in an elected workers' committee, subordinated only to the trade union organization next in the hierarchy. Inside the unions, the principle of the election of officers must in all cases prevail. Clearly, therefore, this policy was aimed at breaking the power of the Central Committee of the party and even of the local party organizations over the unions. If once it lost its power

[29] *Protokoly X*, pp. 7, 370.

of appointing union officials and the members of union committees the central apparatus would not be able to put its policies into practice through the agency of suitably selected obedient party members, irrespective of the views of the union 'fractions'. There was, however, nothing in the theses of the Workers' Opposition to suggest that, within the all-powerful unions envisaged by them (in which the Communists in 1921 formed a small and unpopular minority), anyone other than members of the communist party was to have any influence. They did not propose that the workers should be given an opportunity by free elections to choose their representatives from other parties if they so desired.

Bukharin's theses, which were published in *Pravda* on 16 January 1921, justly earned Lenin's taunt that they had been written without any thought. Somewhat inaccurately known as the 'buffer' or 'compromise' theses, the views of Bukharin and his co-signatories went a long way towards advocating a system which would ultimately have left little room for the central party organs in the control of the trade unions. They rejected any form of party appointments to the trade unions, and demanded that all union nominations to posts on the economic directorates of the Supreme Council of National Economy should be binding on the party. It is plain that this did not represent the real convictions of the signatories. For within a few weeks of the publication of their theses they were won over by Trotsky, whose ideas on the question of party control were of a different order. Trotsky's theses, prepared for the Tenth Congress, which were fundamentally the same as his earlier theses, were now also signed by Bukharin, Andreev, Dzerzhinksy, Krestinsky, Preobrazhensky, Rakovsky, and Serebryakov—all members of the Central Committee; by Pyatakov and Kon, both prominent members of the Ukrainian Communist Central Committee; by a number of leading trade unionists, including Kossior and Gol'tsman; and by a few well-known Moscow Communists, such as Larin, Sokol'nikov, and Yakovleva. Bukharin now threw union independence overboard. He and his co-signatories fully endorsed Trotsky's views that the solution to the trade union question lay in the combination of two methods: fusing the unions as soon as possible in the state apparatus on the one hand; and developing what Trotsky called 'productive democracy' on the other, i.e., encouraging the emergence in the militarized industry of an aristocracy of the most talented workers to replace the existing party bureaucracy of officials. Thus, as had happened in the army, both central control by the party and work discipline would be strengthened, but prospects would be opened up to the more talented rank and file to rise in the hierarchy.[30] The proposals were designed to steal some of the thunder from the Workers' Opposition, against which Bukharin and Trotsky were now firmly united. Indeed, in view of the zeal with which Bukharin attacked the Workers' Opposition in debate at the Tenth Party Congress it would seem that he was anxious to disclaim any sympathy with their policy, which his original theses may perhaps have suggested.

Thus, at the beginning of 1921, the Central Committee was united against the Workers' Opposition (which no single member supported) but at the same time divided into two factions, the formation of which had already begun in 1920. Lenin and Zinoviev headed the supporters of the Platform of the Ten. The Platform of the Ten started with the overwhelming advantage of carrying Lenin's approval. In the many public meetings organized at the end of December 1920 and early in January 1921 it soon became evident that Lenin's views were quite sure of a majority in the party in any representative vote taken on the subject. In some instances meetings, after voting by a large majority in favour of Lenin's policy, nonetheless also passed a vote of confidence in Trotsky.[31] But though Trotsky could still command a good deal of personal support, the prestige of Lenin made a majority vote against him at any party meeting virtually unthinkable.

But the dispute on the trade unions was of secondary importance compared with the personal struggle, aimed at the control of the party apparatus, which was in progress at the same time. Zinoviev now made an important move in this struggle, which was fully endorsed by Lenin,[32] and was crowned with success.

[30] Text in *VKP(b) v rez.*, pp. 800–10.
[31] See e.g. *Pravda*, 4 February 1921.
[32] *Protokoly X*, p. 546.

On 3 January 1921 the Petrograd party organization which he headed, took it upon itself to issue an appeal to all party organizations. This appeal called for elections to the forth-coming Tenth Congress to be conducted on the basis of the various platforms on the trade union question. It drew sharp public protests both from Trotsky and from the Moscow party organization, which resented this attempt by Zinoviev to take upon himself the leadership in what was supposed to be a free debate. An even sharper rejoinder followed from the Petro-grad Communists. There was, however, more behind this move than appeared at first sight. By forcing the election of delegates committed in advance to the support of this or that programme, the signatories of the Platform of the Ten compelled their adversaries to crystallize into open opposition groups, and also, incidentally, in the absence of secret voting at party meetings and conferences, forced all party members to reveal their affiliations. On 12 January 1921, the Central Com-mittee by eight votes to seven approved the election of delegates to the congress by platforms. Trotsky, Bukharin, Krestinsky, Dzerzhinsky, Serebryakov, Preobrazhensky, and Andreev voted against. The resolution adopted also stressed the importance of the fullest freedom of discussion.

The first fortnight of open discussion had revealed the cleavage in the Central Committee, and the personal anta-gonisms behind it which extended beyond the issue of the trade unions. The Central Control Commission, appalled by the relations between members of the Central Committee disclosed by the incident, decided to intervene. This Com-mission (first set up in September 1920) retained, during the early period of its existence, a certain degree of independence and could not, in January 1921, be manipulated by rival factions of party intrigue. In an appeal to the Central Com-mittee, the Control Commission deplored the fact that the discussion had been taking the form of personal conflict and attacks, and of 'irresponsible criticism'; it went on to say that 'the impression was being created that even within the Central Committee itself there was no unanimous opinion on such exhibitions'. The Control Commission accordingly proposed that the Central Committee should take the discussion in hand, rather than leave it to the Petrograd party organization, and try to lead it along more dignified lines.[33] Lenin's public participation in the discussion had hitherto been confined to one speech, on 30 December, at the meeting in the Bolshoy Theatre. Although it was generally known that he had not wanted a public discussion, and viewed its progress with alarm and distaste, he does not appear to have attempted to restrain the form which his supporter Zinoviev had chosen to give to it, any more than he attempted to restrain the attacks on *Tsektran* and the Orgbureau. Now, probably as the result of the Control Commission's intervention, and its rebuke to Zinoviev, he once more entered the discussion. In an article and a pamphlet he called for more conciliation and more tact. With more regard for precept than for practice, he once again rated Trotsky soundly for antagonizing the union leaders, and blamed him for starting the discussion by refusing to serve on the Zinoviev conciliation commission.[34]

But although Lenin had not wanted the discussion, and took comparatively little part in it, he was, at any rate, determined to utilize it to the utmost to create a unified party at the end of it. To Zinoviev the discussion was a welcome opportunity to continue the campaign against *Tsektran* and Trotsky which he had been waging for some time. As Trotsky said later: 'Every village now knows what *Tsektran* is. It is a kind of animal which takes away the grain, it has a stick in its hand, and does not allow the workers to breathe freely. And then, when the worker is tired out, *Tsektran* offers him vinegar in place of the milk which comrade Zinoviev has at his disposal.'[35] The part played by Zinoviev during these months was not an attractive one. But he was a weak man, and a demagogue liable to be carried away by his own oratory. It may be that much of the responsibility for his conduct must fall on shrewder men, who did not hesitate to use him as a cat's-paw. Stalin, on the winning side from the first, took little public part in the

---

[33] Texts of the Petrograd resolution with replies and rejoinders and the account of the Control Commission's intervention are reprinted in *Protokoly X*, pp. 777–83, 847–8.

[34] See 'Krizis partii' published in *Pravda* on 21 January 1921; and 'Eshche raz o profsoyuzakh, o tekushchem momente, i ob oshibkakh tovarishchey Trotskogo i Bukharina' on 25 January—*Lenin*, Vol. XXVI, pp. 113–45. For Trotsky's reply 'Est' raznoglasiya, no k chemu putanitsa?' see *Pravda* of 29 January 1921.

[35] *Protokoly X*, p. 358.

campaign beyond one modest article.[36] But he was active behind the scenes. 'Not only in Petersburg under comrade Zinoviev,' said Rafail, a Democratic Centralist, at the Tenth Party Congress, 'but also here, in Moscow, instead of military communiqués . . . we have communiqués of the party front under the supervision of that military strategist and arch-democrat, comrade Stalin.'[37] Trotsky campaigned with the vigour which always characterized him in debate. To Zinoviev he showed no mercy. But a personal loyalty, in which he had not wavered since 1917, restrained him from any attacks on Lenin. Besides, he fully identified himself with the hostility of the entire Central Committee to the Workers' Opposition and other critics of centralization in the party. Indeed, at the first opportunity, he readily joined with Lenin in attacking them in public.[38] To the members of the Workers' Opposition in turn, the policies of Lenin and Trotsky with regard to the trade unions had always appeared as a distinction without a difference.[39] But, though far from united among themselves, the leaders of the communist party were induced by the threat to their own position, to accept in the spring of 1921 the new policy of the party—the creation of unanimity by the forcible elimination of critics.

Indeed early in 1921 the need for unity in the Central Committee, if it was to survive in power, was grave. Its precarious position was further shaken by a rather dramatic development in the Workers' Opposition, which had been until now a somewhat colourless trade union movement. None of the signatories of the theses in January had either the personality or the ability for national leadership, or any particular talent in debate. They were an easy prey to the combined skill of Lenin, Trotsky, and Bukharin. But in the course of the debates in January and February 1921 a forceful and colourful personality, Alexandra Kollontay, joined the Workers' Opposition and the movement became transformed. Kollontay, who since her excursion into left communism in 1918 had

[36] 'Nashi raznoglasiya', *Stalin*, Vol. V, pp. 4–14.
[37] *Protokoly X*, p. 101.
[38] At the Second Miners' Congress on 22–24 January 1921—see *Protokoly X*, pp. 125, 854. Over a quarter of the communist delegates to this congress voted in favour of Shlyapnikov's resolution—61 out of 229; 137 voted for Lenin, 8 for Trotsky. See *Lenin*, Vol. XXVI, p. 636.
[39] A. Kollontay, *The Workers' Opposition*, pp. 37, 48.

been devoting her energies to the harmless subjects of free love and communist family life, now threw herself whole-heartedly into the discussion. Although hardly cast for the rôle of a national leader, she was a brilliant speaker and a debater of considerable force, and her personal charm added to her powers of persuasion. Her close friendship with Shlyap-nikov gave extra zest to her advocacy of his views. In her hands the somewhat dry doctrine contained in the Workers' Opposition theses (of which she had not been a signatory) was transmuted into a general criticism of the communist régime, with a potentially much wider appeal than the theses, which were addressed mainly to communist trade unionists. Hatred of the privileged commissar, anger at the suppression of initiative by the party hierarchy, and dislike of the bureau-cracy, were all issues which were troubling much wider sections of the party. In January and February many Communists were leaving the party in disgust, according to the Control Commission.[40] Kollontay's views were expressed in innumer-able speeches up and down the country, and in a vigorous pamphlet which she was allowed to publish early in March 1921 just before the Tenth Congress.[41] That her agitation was effective is evident from the tone of the attacks on her writings and speeches delivered at the Tenth Congress by Lenin and Bukharin, when compared with their milder and more academic strictures on the doctrine propounded in the original theses. Proletarian in outlook and origin and Bol-sheviks of old standing, the Workers' Opposition leaders now heard with genuine dismay and astonishment the accusation made against them by Lenin and other members of the Central Committee, both shortly before and at the Tenth Party Con-gress, that their criticisms of the party's shortcomings were a compound of menshevism and of petty bourgeois ideas.

[40] See two articles by Sol'ts in *Pravda* of 6 and 21 February 1921.

[41] Entitled *Rabochaya oppozitsiya*. According to Kollontay it was officially published, ostensibly in an edition of one and a half million copies, according to a statement printed on the cover. But only 1500 copies were in fact published 'and that with difficulty'—*Protokoly X*, p. 103. The rarity of this work in the Russian version rather supports Kollontay's statement. The pamphlet is freely available in the English and German versions published abroad in 1922, after the condemnation of the Workers' Opposition at the Eleventh Party Congress in March. (Kollontay maintained that these foreign translations and publica-tions took place against her will.)

Bukharin even discovered in Kollontay traces of 'disgusting, sentimental Catholic beastliness'.[42]

Nothing could have been less 'petty bourgeois' than the views of Kollontay, as expressed in her pamphlet. The kinship of her views with menshevism (she had been a Menshevik until 1916) was limited to the fact that the Mensheviks, until their voices were stifled, likewise criticized the dictatorship of the communist party. But the Mensheviks, unlike the Workers' Opposition, supported the participation in the government and in industrial management of all workers, and not merely of the minority who were members of the communist party. Kollontay emphasized that the trade union dispute was only one aspect of a much graver problem, the loss of faith by the communist party in the mission of the working class. Bourgeois principles were beginning to soil party policy as set out in the programme, and she saw the beginning of this process in the rejection of collective industrial management in favour of one-man management by specialists. Organization of industry by the workers was the 'essence of Communism'. The party, she asserted, was dominated by middle-class elements and by the peasants. The percentage of workers in vital posts scarcely exceeded seventeen.[43] No one had gained from the revolution except the peasants, and the party leaders were becoming estranged from the masses. 'The workers ask—who are we? Are we really the prop of the class dictatorship, or are we just an obedient flock that serves as a support for those who, having severed all ties with the masses, carry out their own policy and build up industry without any regard to our opinions and creative abilities under the reliable cover of the party label?'[44] Kollontay demanded, as did the Workers' Opposition theses, control of industry by the unions and local administration by the workers. But she added an important new point. She attributed the origin of the stranglehold of the bureaucracy on the life of the country

[42] *Protokoly X*, p. 327.

[43] This figure was based on an analysis by Tsyurupa. cf. Shlyapnikov's detailed analysis of figures for 1922 which gives a very similar result, in an article published on 18 January 1924, reprinted in M. Zorky, (ed.) *Rabochaya oppozitsiya*, at p. 149.

[44] Kollontay, *The Workers' Opposition*, p. 23. The quotations in the text are taken from the rather inadequate English translation. The Russian original has not been available.

to the party's fear of criticism, its 'heresy hunting', its stifling of initiative and of discussion. 'There can be no self-activity without freedom of thought and opinion, for self-activity manifests itself not only in initiative, action, and work, but in independent thought as well.'[45] The only way of curing bureaucracy was by reverting 'to that state of things, where all cardinal questions of party activity and soviet policy are submitted to the consideration of the rank and file and only after that are supervised by the leaders. . . . There is nothing more frightful and harmful than sterility of thought and standards of routine.'[46]

The charge was to be made later that Kollontay, and the Workers' Opposition generally, were at this date openly aiming at a split in the party, i.e., the setting-up of a new party in opposition to the Communists. There is not a word in her pamphlet, or for that matter in any of the Workers' Opposition speeches at the Tenth Party Congress or elsewhere, to support this view. The emphasis throughout is that the party as a whole will ultimately see the justice of the criticism of the Workers' Opposition, and that through such criticism it will in the end be saved from degeneration. 'The Workers' Opposition alone', Kollontay wrote, 'will not and must not compromise. This does not, however, mean that it drives to a split. Even in the event of defeat at the Congress, it must remain in the party and step by step stubbornly defend its point of view, save the party, and clarify its class lines.'[47] And again, 'only those will fall out who attempt to evolve into principles our temporary deviation from the spirit of the Communist Programme, which was forced upon the party by the prolonged Civil War. . . . All that part of the party which has been accustomed to reflect the class point of view of the evergrowing giant proletariat will absorb and digest everything that is wholesome, practical, and sound in the Workers' Opposition.'[48]

In preparation for the forthcoming congress the Workers' Opposition now put forward, in addition to their theses on the trade unions, a draft resolution embodying its somewhat drastic recommendations for restoring the party to health. This called

---

[45] *ibid.*, pp. 54–5.
[47] *ibid.*, p. 48.

[46] *ibid.*, pp. 59, 61.
[48] *ibid.*, pp. 62–3.

for a radical purge in order to eliminate all the careerists and those who, without being either proletarians or poor peasants, had joined the party after the October Revolution for what they could get out of it. The resolution demanded that manual work should be made compulsory for all party members, irrespective of their offices. Unless medically exempt, every party member should spend three months in each year at such work. Finally, it called on the party to recognize the right of party members to complete freedom of criticism and discussion 'upon the compulsory condition that the directives of all higher party authorities are carried into effect'.[49]

The arguments of Kollontay were thus strictly limited in their appeal to the communist party. For instance, they made no demands for any relief to the peasants; on the contrary they voiced the hostility of the town proletariat towards the comparatively more prosperous peasantry. Nor did they in any form criticize the domination by the communist minority over the majority of the proletariat. The fundamental weakness of the case of the Workers' Opposition was that, while demanding more freedom of initiative for the workers, it was quite content to leave untouched the state of affairs in which a few hundred thousand imposed their will on many millions. 'And since when have we [the Workers' Opposition] been enemies of *komitetchina* [manipulation and control by communist party committees], I should like to know?' Shlyapnikov asked at the Tenth Party Congress. He went on to explain that the trade union congress in which, as he and his followers proposed, all control of industry should be vested would 'of course' be composed of delegates nominated and elected 'through the party cells, as we always do it.' But he argued that the local trade union cells would ensure the election of men qualified by experience and ability in place of those who are 'imposed on us at present' by the centre.[50] Kollontay and her supporters had no wish to disturb the communist party's monopoly of political power. But they did not admit the necessity of adopting the Central Committee's methods of preserving it. In spite of the popular appeal of many of their points, there was never a time when the Workers' Opposition was anywhere near winning a majority in the party. With more susceptible audiences,

[49] Text in *Zorky*, pp. 244–50.   [50] *Protokoly X*, p. 391.

such as the young officer cadets at the army schools, Alexandra Kollontay could occasionally gather a large following.[51] But in the numerous party meetings the votes for the Workers' Opposition platform were almost invariably a long way behind the votes secured by the Platform of the Ten.[52] Lenin's prestige was still too high to be shaken by criticism of the Central Committee, however telling.

There was nothing in the aim which the Workers' Opposition set itself which was inconsistent with what had been party policy hitherto. In the past, ventilation of differences inside the party had helped to preserve unity. No one early in 1921 denied that the party was far from healthy. Bureaucracy, abuse of power and privilege, and the indifference of some leaders to the masses were only too obvious. There was therefore nothing in any way improper or inconsistent with the party rules in the fact that the Workers' Opposition sought to play the part of a critical group within the communist party. But before the Tenth Party Congress concluded its deliberations on 16 March, two events happened which sealed the fate of free opposition and criticism within the Russian communist party: the revolt of the Kronstadt sailors against party dictatorship, and the launching of the New Economic Policy. Both these developments decided Lenin to pursue the course which he had already hinted at in November 1920:— concessions, but no 'opposition for opposition's sake', or 'cliques'. The carrying out of this policy involved the reshaping of the central political machinery and the removal of those members of the Central Committee, such as Preobrazhensky and Krestinsky, who stood for a policy of freedom of party criticism and conciliation of opposition.

[51] See *Barmine*, p. 92.
[52] e.g. in the Moscow *Guberniya* Party Conference on 19–21 February the voting was: Platform of the Ten 217; Shlyapnikov and Ignatov 45; Trotsky-Bukharin 52; Democratic-Centralists 13, see Zinoviev, *Sochineniya*, Vol. VI, p. 623. In the Sverdlov University at the end of January out of 1200, 115 voted for Trotsky, 91 for the Workers' Opposition, the rest for Lenin—*Pravda*, 29 January 1921.

CHAPTER XVI

THE KRONSTADT REVOLT AND THE NEW ECONOMIC POLICY

The wave of strikes and workers' demonstrations in Petrograd at the end of February 1921 and the revolt of the population and sailors of the naval base of Kronstadt against the dictatorship of the communist party have been much distorted in the telling by many Soviet, and some other historians. Most of them labour to demonstrate, with scant regard for the facts, that these events were inspired and directed from outside Russia by enemies of the Soviet state. The allegation is unsupported by evidence, and has been rejected by every serious historian of the period. The opponents of Trotsky—and their number naturally increased after his fall in 1927—strive to show that in Petrograd, where Zinoviev was in control of the party organization, order was much more easily restored and the threat much less serious than in Kronstadt, where, so far as the fleet was concerned, the party organization was subordinated to the military machine, and therefore to Trotsky. Trotsky and his supporters, on the other hand, are concerned to establish that the sailors' revolt was only possible in 1921 because of the change in their social origins as compared with 1917. Although there appears to be some truth in each of these contentions, neither of them gives by any means the whole explanation of events which were due to much more complex causes.

The strikes and industrial unrest which began in Petrograd in the last week of February and extended to practically the entire city, were only in part a political manifestation. There was enough to explain them in the hardships caused by the collapse of the industrial life of the city, without looking for a political motive. The situation was aggravated in February by a fuel crisis which led to the closing of many factories. Moreover, in Petrograd, the heaviest category of workers, the transport workers, were receiving only 700 to 1,000 calories of food a day. The Petrograd workers attempted to organize food collecting expeditions in the neighbouring countryside, in defiance of the prohibition of free trading. The government's action in suppressing these expeditions raised discontent to fever heat. That this question of food collection was uppermost in the minds of the demonstrators and strikers is evident from the fact that all the resolutions passed at the numerous strikers' meetings demanded the right to trade freely with the villages, and the abolition of the punitive detachments which existed to suppress such trading as was carried on illegally. Nevertheless, a political undercurrent was also reflected in some of the resolutions passed, in which menshevik and socialist revolutionary influence was apparent.[1]

The Mensheviks were certainly active at the time of the Petrograd strikes. They had a large following among the workers of the city, and they endeavoured, in accordance with their policy of open opposition by all legal means, to urge the demand, not merely for piecemeal concessions, but for a radical reform of the whole government structure— freely elected soviets, freedom of expression for all workers, release of socialists under arrest, and an end to the terror. The Mensheviks mostly conducted their propaganda in small groups inside the factories, so as to avoid arrest for as long as possible, and they also distributed leaflets. Individual right wing Mensheviks went so far as to urge open revolt against the government, but this did not represent either the views or the policy of the Menshevik Central Committee.[2] The Socialist Revolutionaries mainly urged the convocation of the Constituent Assembly.

The strikes and demonstrations, which were assuming the character of a general strike, were quickly and effectively suppressed by the Petrograd Committee of the communist party, by the combined methods of force and concessions. There is no evidence that any section of the communist party organization in Petrograd supported the strikers. On 24 February the Petrograd *Guberniya* Communist Committee declared a state of emergency, mobilized the whole party for dealing with the situation, and among other measures of

[1] See A. S. Pukhov, 'V Petrograde nakanune kronshtadtskogo vosstaniya v 1921 g.' in *Krasnaya letopis'*, no. 4 (37), 1930, pp. 107 ff., for these resolutions, quoted from the archives of the Petrograd communist party.

[2] Dan, *Dva goda skitaniy*, pp. 105–14.

wholesale repression, arrested all the members of menshevik and social revolutionary organizations still at liberty.[3] But at the same time an important concession was made to public feeling: food-finding expeditions by the workers were sanctioned, and a large quantity of food was hastily rushed to Petrograd. Thus in Petrograd the incipient revolt soon collapsed, partly owing to the discipline of the communist party, and partly because hunger outweighed political discontent as a motive force.

The circumstances were very different in the isolated naval base of Kronstadt, which is situated on an island in the Finnish Gulf, about seventeen miles west of Petrograd.[4] The sailor Communists of Kronstadt, the 'pride of the revolution', had been from the earliest days the most unruly element in the party. In the disturbances of July 1917 it was only with the greatest difficulty that they had been dissuaded from attempting an immediate seizure of power in defiance of the Central Committee. When in January 1918 two sick ministers of the Provisional Government, Shingarev and Kokoshkin, were murdered in a Petrograd hospital, an inquiry ordered by Lenin clearly fixed the guilt on certain sailors of the Baltic Fleet. When the fleet refused to hand them over, Lenin preferred to drop the inquiry rather than to defy the sailors.[5] There were other later instances which showed that the sailors with whom Lenin was wont to threaten his recalcitrant Central Committee were well beyond his own control. The Mensheviks had no influence whatever in the Baltic Fleet, and no evidence

[3] Pukhov, loc. cit., pp. 105–6; Dan, op. cit., pp. 114 ff.
[4] The Kronstadt Revolt has been closely studied in a number of well documented anarchist publications, notably Ida Mett, La Commune de Cronstadt; Voline, pp. 409–506; E. Yarchuk, Kronshchad v ruskata revolyutsiya, Sofia, 1923. The most important source of information is the file of the daily paper (Izvestiya) published by the Provisional Revolutionary Committee of the Sailors, Soldiers, and Workers of the City of Kronstadt, reprinted in 1921 in Prague by the Socialist Revolutionaries, in a publication called Pravda o Kronshtadte. Fourteen issues in all appeared, between 3 and 16 March 1921. There is also much valuable material quoted in a series of articles published in the historical journal of the Leningrad party Krasnaya letopis', of which use has been made in the account of the events given here. The best Soviet account is A. S. Pukhov, Kronshtadtskiy myatezh v 1921 g. See also a recent article, Robert V. Daniels, 'The Kronstadt Revolt of 1921: A Study in the Tyrannies of Revolution' in American Slavic and East European Review, 1951, p. 241. The best account published in English and the most detailed, is Fedotoff-White, Chapter V. I have also had the advantage of seeing in manuscript Dr. G. Katkov's forthcoming study of the Kronstadt Revolt.
[5] Steinberg, Als ich Volkskommissar war, pp. 139–63.

of any participation by them in the revolt has ever been adduced by Soviet writers, though assertions to this effect are frequent. There is even some evidence to show that the Petrograd Mensheviks, so far from supporting the revolt, refused to have anything to do with it.[6] On the other hand, the anarchist influence in the fleet was fairly strong, and the Left Socialist Revolutionaries also had some following. Moreover, whereas in Petrograd the relations between townsfolk and peasantry had been exacerbated through the extortionate barter prices which the peasant exacted on the black market for his food, in Kronstadt many, if not the majority, of the sailors were of peasant origin and consequently felt more sympathy than townsfolk with the hardships which the forcible state food collection inflicted on the peasantry. The political picture in the two towns was therefore entirely different. Again, the communist party organization in the fleet differed not only from the political organization in Petrograd, but also from the army political organization. Whereas in the army the authority of the commissars had grown with the progressive fusion of commissars and commanders, there were no Red commanders in the fleet, and the commissars normally sided with the ratings against the imperial ex-officers.[7] The authority of the commissars and the authority over them of the higher command had also suffered considerably as the result of Zinoviev's campaign against the political direction of the fleet. The opportunities presented by the debate on the trade unions had also been exploited by Zinoviev to undermine Trotsky's position. Raskol'nikov, the Political Commissar of the Baltic Fleet, and Batis, the director of *Pubalt* (the Political Directorate of the Fleet) accused Zinoviev, in a complaint addressed to the Central Committee, of conducting a campaign in which Trotsky was being portrayed as the main advocate of compulsion, in contrast with Zinoviev who was portrayed as the champion of the revival of full democracy.[8] It is not difficult to imagine the effect of this campaign on discipline, not only among the political commissars, who were subordinate to Trotsky, but among the ratings as well.

[6] See P. Bogomil, 'Pis'mo iz Rossii', in *Zarya*, no. 1, 1922, pp. 21–5.

[7] *Fedotoff-White*, p. 154.

[8] A. S. Pukhov, 'Kronshtadt i baltiyskiy flot pered myatezhem', *Krasnaya letopis'*, no. 6 (39), 1930, at pp. 188–9. (And see Chapter XIV.)

The contrast between the atmosphere in the communist parties in Petrograd and in Kronstadt was immediately apparent. When a state of emergency was declared by the communist party in Petrograd, the political commissar in Kronstadt refused to take similar steps, though advised to do so from Petrograd.[9] Yet discontent in the naval base had for many months past been assuming proportions as menacing as in the capital. Dissatisfaction with material conditions as well as political unrest had been giving rise to serious apprehension in the party.[10] No less than 22·7 per cent of the Communists in the fleet had been purged in September 1920, and an equal number had at the same time resigned. There have been many attempts to prove the assertion, primarily originating from Trotsky, that the communist party both in Kronstadt and in the Baltic Fleet contained a much higher proportion of peasants than elsewhere. They are not, however, convincing. Thus, peasants formed 66·7 per cent of the Communists in the Baltic Fleet in 1921. But this was not a higher percentage of peasants than in the communist cells in the Red Army, where in 1921 peasants formed the majority.[11] Similarly, in the civilian party in the town of Kronstadt, peasants formed 30·9 per cent in 1921. Again, this scarcely differs from the percentage in the civilian party throughout Russia in 1921, which was 28·2 according to official figures, and probably in fact higher.[12] It was, however, true that a large number of the older Bolsheviks had been drafted out of the fleet, largely no doubt because they were required for service in other fields, particularly in transport,[13] but also in some instances with the additional

---

[9] A. S. Pukhov, 'V Petrograde nakanune kronshtadtskogo myatezha', *ibid.*, no. 4 (37), 1930, at pp. 117–18.

[10] Pukhov, 'Kronshtadt i baltiyskiy flot', etc. pp. 149 ff.

[11] In 1925 the percentage of peasants in army communist cells was still 58·2, and it would have been higher in 1921—see *Ivanovich*, p. 174.

[12] See Pukhov, 'Kronshtadt i baltiyskiy flot', etc., pp. 176–7, for figures on the Kronstadt party. The percentage of peasant Communists may have been high as compared, for example, with the Petrograd party.

[13] A special commission was set up after the revolt to carry out the drafting back into the fleet of old Bolsheviks who had been drafted away, principally on duties in transport—see *Izvestiya Ts. K.*, no. 31, 20 July 1921; cf. a resolution of the Tenth Party Congress, *VKP(b) v rez.*, p. 468. This resolution was, of course, a reflection on Trotsky who would have been mainly responsible for the unwise drafting away of reliable sailor Communists for transport duties in 1920.

object of breaking up any growing centres of discontent among the sailors by removing the ringleaders.

The unrest in Petrograd at the end of February was the spark which set off the explosion in Kronstadt. The sailors had made some contact with the Petrograd strikers, and confidently expected that their own demands would be supported by the discontented workers in Petrograd. On 28 February the crew of the battleship *Petropavlovsk* voted the resolution which became the charter of the revolt. The main demands of this resolution were: The immediate re-election of the soviets by secret ballot and upon the basis of free political agitation, 'in view of the fact that the existing soviets do not express the will of the workers and peasants'; freedom of speech and press for 'workers, peasants, and for the Anarchists and the left socialist parties'; freedom of meeting, and free trade unions and the formation of peasants' unions; liberation of all socialist political prisoners and of all workers, peasants, soldiers, and sailors imprisoned in 'connection with workers' and peasants' movements'; the setting up of a commission to review the cases of all who were detained in prisons and concentration camps; abolition of all special political departments (in the army, navy, and transport) 'since no one party can enjoy privileges for the propaganda of its ideas and receive money from the state for this purpose'; equal rations for all, except those engaged in work detrimental to health; abolition of all special communist detachments; full rights for the peasants to 'do as they please with all the land' and to keep their own cattle, 'provided that they use no hired labour'; and the right of individual small scale manufacture, again without the employment of hired labour.[14]   It was a popular resolution.   Not even the ingenuity of communist historians can easily bring it within the frame of any of the non-communist opposition parties.   The omission of any reference to the Constituent Assembly, for example, which the Kronstadt rebels rejected, proves that socialist revolutionary influence

[14] *Pravda o Kronshtadte*, pp. 46–7.   The main points of the Kronstadt programme were little different from the demands which were being voiced in the country by both workers and peasants who were desperate or courageous enough to open their mouths.   See for example a resolution passed at a protest meeting of Moscow workers on 23 February 1921 demanding a coalition government; freedom of meeting and of the press; and the release of all political prisoners, printed in *Revolyutsionnaya Rossiya*, no. 5, April 1921, pp. 23–4.

did not predominate in it, since the recall of the Assembly was fundamental to socialist revolutionary policy. The stress on the rights of the peasants is sufficient to dispose of any suggestion that the resolution was menshevik inspired. But the sailors' political programme may well have derived some of its home-made qualities from anarchist contacts of the sailor leaders. It is no doubt because of its obviously popular character that this resolution, which is very rarely reprinted or even quoted in Soviet sources,[15] is often described by communist writers as a 'disguised' demand for the restoration of capitalism.[16]

The news of this openly anti-communist resolution sent Kalinin, the chairman of the Central Executive Committee of the All-Russian Congress of Soviets, hurrying to Kronstadt the following day, 1 March 1921. He was accompanied by Kuz'min, one of the two political commissars attached to the Revolutionary War Council of the Baltic Fleet. A mass meeting was held in the Anchor Square, long famous as a revolutionary forum. The two officials were received with military honours. It was a turbulent meeting. When Kalinin began to speak, the crowd at first calmed down, but soon angry voices were to be heard from all sides. 'Drop it, Kalinin, you manage to keep warm enough! Look at all the jobs you've got, and I expect you draw a ration for each of them!' shouted a bearded sailor. Kuz'min, who endeavoured to remind the sailors that they were the 'pride of the revolution' was met with a sharp retort from the crowd: 'Have you forgotten how you had every tenth man shot on the Northern Front? Kick him out!'[17] The most serious aspect of this meeting from the communist point of view was that the Kronstadt and Baltic Fleet Communists either supported or did not openly oppose the critical crowd. When the *Petropavlovsk* resolution was put to the vote of the meeting it was adopted against the sole dissenting votes of Kalinin and Vasiliev, the chairman of the local Soviet Executive Committee. The

[15] It is, however, reprinted in full in A. S. Pukhov's detailed history of the revolt.
[16] The most recent example of this type of assertion is to be found in A. Rothstein, *A History of the U.S.S.R.*, London, 1950, p. 145. 'The leaders of the rebellion did not come out openly for capitalist restoration. . . . But the true significance of the rising was well understood abroad.'
[17] *Kuznetsov*, pp. 62–86

Communists, present in strength in the vast crowd (about twelve thousand people in all were present at this meeting) either voted for the resolution or abstained. This feature distinguished the Kronstadt revolt from all disturbances which had hitherto taken place in Soviet Russia. The number of Communists who actively supported the insurgents was at the lowest estimate 30 per cent of the local party; 40 per cent were 'neutral'.[18] During the short period in which the Kronstadt garrison remained in the hands of the insurgents, of the total communist strength of two thousand, civilian and naval, about a quarter resigned.

The communist Central Committee, in the persons of Zinoviev and Trotsky, immediately branded the sailors' revolt as a counter-revolutionary attempt organized from abroad by the White Guards and led by imperial ex-officers. Lenin, in an incautious moment, admitted that in Kronstadt 'they do not want the White Guards, and they do not want our power either'.[19] But in general he fully associated himself with the party line—to the bitter disappointment of the sailors, who 'had never believed a word that Zinoviev or Trotsky uttered', but did not expect Lenin to associate himself with the general 'hypocrisy' in the party.[20] On 2 March 1921 a Provisional Revolutionary Committee was set up by the insurgents. It consisted entirely of peasant and proletarian ratings, headed by Petrichenko, a naval clerk on the battleship *Petropavlovsk*.[21] Far from leading the revolt, the few imperial ex-officers who supported it and were involved in it were at loggerheads with the Provisional Committee. The officers wanted to seize a bridgehead on the mainland immediately with the object of giving the revolt every chance of spreading to the capital. The committee, naïvely confident that the justice of their cause would prevail, rejected their advice and refused to resort to arms, except in self-defence in the event of an attack on the fortress.[22] The Soviet government immediately demanded

[18] According to Trotsky's view, as quoted by Smilga, 30 per cent actively anti-communist, 40 per cent neutral, 30 per cent pro-communist—see *Protokoly X*, p. 225; and see A. S. Pukhov, in 'Kronshtadt vo vlasti vragov revolyutsii', *Krasnaya letopis'*, no. 1 (40), 1931, pp. 5–80, and *Kornatovsky*, pp. 13–15, on communist support for the revolt.
[19] At the Tenth Party Congress—see *Lenin*, Vol. XXVI, p. 248.
[20] Quoted from the insurgents' *Izvestiya* in *Pravda o Kronshtadte*, pp. 150-1.
[21] List in *Pravda o Kronshtadte*, p. 131; *Mett*, p. 36.
[22] See A. S. Pukhov, 'Kronshtadt vo vlasti vragov revolyutsii', *loc. cit.*, pp. 36–9.

the surrender of the Kronstadt Provisional Committee, a demand which the insurgents rejected on 2 March. Military operations led by Tukhachevsky were started on 7 March and the fortress was finally stormed across the ice on the Finnish Gulf on 18 March. It was not an easy task to drive the Red Army, stiffened by young communist cadets from the army schools, against the sailors.[23] Two hundred delegates to the Tenth Party Congress (which met during the rising, on 8 March) were mobilized to the Kronstadt front. The victims of the reprisals after the fall of Kronstadt numbered hundreds, if not thousands. From these many victims the Soviet government selected for publication a list of thirteen alleged ringleaders, among whom were five ex-officers, one former priest, and seven peasants.[24] No public trial was ever held in connexion with the Kronstadt revolt.

The revolt of the Baltic sailors was welcomed by non-communists both inside and outside Russia, from the Anarchists to the *Kadety*. The Socialist Revolutionaries, whose headquarters were then at Reval, offered military aid to the insurgents, but this offer was rejected by an overwhelming majority of the insurgents at a meeting held to discuss it.[25] Milyukov, in an article in *Posledniya Novosti* in Paris, of 11 March 1921, invented for the benefit of the insurgents the slogan 'Soviets without the Communists' which has been foisted on them ever since, but which they in fact never used.[26] Outside Kronstadt, the communist party leadership was unanimously behind the Central Committee and approved the forcible suppression of the revolt. Some foreign anarchists then in Moscow endeavoured to mediate between the Communists and the Kronstadt sailors so as to stop bloodshed, but could find no one in the communist party prepared to raise

[23] *Kuznetsov*, pp. 75–6, admits that the soldiers were driven into battle at the point of the revolver, but says this was due to their fear of going onto the ice. There is no doubt that there was a certain amount of unrest among the armed forces on the mainland inspired by the sailors' revolt. The seamen of the Naval Aviation Detachment at Oranienbaum voted in support of the *Petropavlovsk* resolution on 3 March. Although they did not take up arms against the government, forty-five were executed—see P. E. Dybenko, *Iz nedr tsarskogo flota k velikomu oktyabryu*, Moscow, 1928, pp. 199–200, quoted in *Fedotoff-White*, p. 156. For other instances of army unrest see *Fedotoff-White*, pp. 153–4.

[24] *Pravda o Kronshtadte*, pp. 38–9.

[25] See an article by Vardin in *Pravda* of 7 April 1921, based on the interrogation of captured Kronstadt insurgents; and see *Pravda* of 13 July 1922, p. 2.

[26] A quotation from Milyukov's article is printed in *Lenin*, Vol. XXVII, p. 496.

the question in the party leadership. The delegates from the Tenth Party Congress to the Kronstadt front included both Democratic Centralists and members of the Workers' Opposition. The very same army cadets who had voted so enthusiastically not many weeks before for Kollontay's fiery resolutions were the most reliable fighters against the insurgents.[27] During the rising Lutovinov, then in Berlin, publicly associated himself with the military action in progress. He explained that the liquidation of the revolt was taking some time because the Soviet government was anxious to 'spare the population of Kronstadt'.[28] Trotsky was not only fully behind the suppression of the Kronstadt revolt at the time, but caused somewhat of a stir in anti-Stalinist left wing circles many years later by reiterating that the forcible suppression had been fully justified, and that the rising was in essence bourgeois in character and therefore counter-revolutionary. Although he accepted full responsibility for the military action, as Commissar for War, he did not himself participate in the operations, in view, so he says, of the personal conflict between him and Zinoviev. The sailors of the Baltic Fleet had voted in favour of political direction by the Petrograd Party Committee, headed by Zinoviev, and against the political directorate of the Fleet, *Pubalt*, controlled by Trotsky.[29] He therefore feared as he says, that his presence might have been interpreted as a political manœuvre to discredit Zinoviev. However, in 1938 Trotsky no longer attempted to maintain the view immediately broadcast by him in 1921 that the Kronstadt rising was organized by the White Guards.[30]

On the face of it, therefore, Lenin and the Central Committee had little reason to fear that any of the oppositionists, and in particular the leaders of the Workers' Opposition, were likely to harbour secret sympathies for the Kronstadt rebels in March 1921. The hostility which the supporters of the Workers' Opposition felt for the peasantry in general made it

---

[27] *Barmine*, p. 95.

[28] *Humanité* of 18 March 1921, quoted in *Mett*, p. 78. There is no authority for the statement in *Deutscher*, p. 220, that 'some of the leaders' of the Kronstadt revolt were 'Left Communists', and it is extremely improbable.

[29] See Chapter XIV.

[30] See two articles by him in *Byulleten' oppozitsii*, 'Shumikha vokrug Kronshtadta', nos. 66–7 (1938), pp. 22–6; and 'Eshche ob usmirenii Kronshtadta', no. 70 (1938), pp. 10 ff.

even less likely that this group would approve of a programme which was markedly peasant in character. Why then should it have been necessary to silence the Workers' Opposition at the Tenth Party Congress, and to justify this step in part, at any rate, by the allegation that the Kronstadt revolt had been facilitated by the existence of opposition within the party?[31] One obvious answer is that criticism within the party had proved embarrassing in the past and was likely to prove even more embarrassing in the future; and that the revolt provided a convenient pretext to silence it. There were other reasons too. Around the outer fringe of the Workers' Opposition there were some elements who were prepared to espouse the cause of the peasantry—dangerous elements from the point of view of the Central Committee, as Kronstadt had revealed. Such was G. I. Myasnikov,[32] a stormy individual opposi-tionist who, though not a signatory of the Workers' Opposition platform, was at times prepared to support this group. Myasnikov had been urging since 1920 the need for the creation of peasant unions to heal the breach between the proletariat and the peasantry.[33] Similarly, the history of the small group headed by Panyushkin, although it belongs to the period after the Tenth Party Congress, nevertheless shows that the Com-munists may have had reason to suspect at the time of the congress that there were elements in the communist party outside Kronstadt whose sympathies with the peasantry were strong. Panyushkin, a sailor Bolshevik, who had distinguished himself in the early days of the revolution by particularly atrocious murders, formed soon after the Tenth Party Congress a group which called itself the 'Workers' and Peasants' Socialist Party'. This group presented a petition to the Moscow Soviet in the summer of 1921 calling for 'All power to the Soviets, and not to parties', and was promptly arrested. Before arrest Panyushkin and his supporters did succeed in organizing

[31] *VKP(b) v rez.*, p. 430. And see the next chapter.
[32] Not to be confused with A. Myasnikov, who was not associated with any opposition activity.
[33] See his article 'Nereshennyy vopros' in *Petrogradskaya Pravda*, of 19 November 1920. And cf. for a fuller exposition of his views on this question *VIII Syezd sovetov, ezhednevnyy byulleten' syezda*, no. 6, 26 December 1920, p. 10, which embodies the proposals prepared by him for the Eighth Congress of Soviets. Shlyapnikov was quite right in his denial in 1924 that Myasnikov had ever been representative of the opinion of the Workers' Opposition—see *Zorky*, p. 154.

one public meeting.[34] The Panyushkinites made some tentative overtures to the Workers' Opposition in the early summer
of 1921, but were treated by them with considerable suspicion,
and there is no evidence of any formal link between them.[35]
But apart from these minor danger signals, there was good
reason for silencing the Workers' Opposition, when once
Lenin had decided on the reversal of war communism in
favour of a new policy of concession to private enterprise.
In its full form, this New Economic Policy (N.E.P.), as it
became known, consisted of three elements: the substitution
of a tax in kind for the exaction from the peasants of arbitrary
quotas of food, so as to increase their incentive to produce;
the legalization of a wide measure of freedom of internal trade;
and the granting of concessions to private capitalists for the
running of industrial enterprises. Lenin's original decision to
make this fundamental change in policy could not, it would
seem, have been directly connected with the Kronstadt revolt.
In the first place this reversal of policy, if it was to have immediate effect in encouraging greater food production by the
peasants, had in any case to be introduced in time to precede
the spring sowing. On 14 February, Lenin had had a discussion with a delegation of peasants from Tambov *guberniya*,
where at the time peasant disturbances amounting to a guerrilla war were raging. It is at the least likely that his conversations with emissaries from the principal centre of peasant
discontent were in some way connected with the decision on a
question of policy of such vital importance to the peasantry.
Moreover, the question of a change in economic policy was
first raised in the Political Bureau as early as 8 February 1921,
and Lenin's draft of a resolution on the subject was completed
before 18 February.[36] All this took place some weeks before
the sailors' revolt. In accordance with a decision of the
Political Bureau, two articles appeared modestly in *Pravda*, on

[34] See Sosnovsky in *Pravda* of 17 December 1921. cf. Molotov's account at
the Eleventh Party Congress, *Protokoly XI*, p. 49; cf. *ibid.*, p. 652. See also Dan,
Dva goda skitaniy, pp. 209–10. Panyushkin recanted his errors at the end of 1921
and was re-admitted to the party.

[35] See *Zorky*, p. 52, where an intercepted letter from a member of the Workers'
Opposition with a contemptuous reference to Panyushkin is reprinted. For a
rather lame attempt to prove a link between Panyushkin and the Workers'
Opposition on the basis of Panyushkin's evidence after his recantation, see
Protokoly XI, p. 698.

[36] *Lenin*, Vol. XXVI, pp. 651–2, 728.

17 February and on 26 February, and attracted little attention. They discussed the question of increasing the peasants' incentive to sow more by introducing a tax in kind in place of forcible requisitions. They did not, however, deal with the second and equally important element of the proposed policy—the legalization of free trading in the surplus produce which would remain to the peasant after he had met his new obligations. On the contrary, the articles assumed that these surpluses would be exchanged by the peasants for manufactured goods with the state alone.

When the question of the New Economic Policy was raised by Lenin at the Tenth Party Congress in March 1921 it had not therefore as yet been discussed in the party. Even at the congress the vital proposal was not introduced by Lenin until the very end of the session when many delegates had already left, and it was hardly debated—the discussion of Lenin's resolution on this momentous reversal of policy occupies some twenty pages in the three hundred and thirty pages of the original edition of the stenogram of the congress proceedings. The debate was speedily cut short after four ten-minute speeches had followed the official proposals made by Lenin and Tsyurupa. One comparatively obscure delegate did succeed in drawing attention to the fact that to leave what is not taken away from the peasants to be sold on the free market was in effect a return to capitalism, and thirty delegates voted against the resolution.[37] Moreover, the resolution passed at this congress was confined to replacement of confiscation of food quotas by a tax in kind, and to the exchange 'on a local scale' of the surplus products which would remain in the peasants' hands. No mention was made of the intended state concession to private capital, which formed an equally important element in the new policy, and which, if not already decided on in the Politbureau, was certainly in contemplation. However, if the decision on the New Economic Policy was not dictated by the Kronstadt revolt, the timing of its introduction probably was. When the delegates from the Tenth Party Congress were sent to the Kronstadt front, it was not for their military experience alone. The significance of their journey was that 'they brought to the hesitant soldier-

[37] *Protokoly X*, pp. 406–49.

peasants [of the Red Army] the news of the new turn in party policy in relation to the peasantry, of the replacement of the forcible grain collection by a tax in kind, and of the increase of free market exchange of goods'.[38]

The reason for Lenin's caution in introducing the new policy to his party is not far to seek. It was obvious that a change which involved the reversal of the basic socialist principles on which the Russian state was ostensibly founded would be opposed from the start. The party, committed to the plan of exacting produce from the peasantry by compulsion, was slow to accept any modification which in any degree recognized the individual peasant producer as a free participant in Soviet economy. In December 1920, at the Eighth Congress of Soviets, when Obolensky's plan for increasing the spring sowing during 1921 by a method of universal compulsion was adopted, Lenin had suggested a modification, providing for the award of premiums to efficient farmers. Reluctant at that date to accept even so moderate a concession to the free enterprise of the peasants, the party 'fraction' rejected this proposal and was only with difficulty persuaded to reverse its decision.[39] Yet what was now contemplated was a far more radical change in the social structure of the country. For many years after 1921 the interpretation of the New Economic Policy and its relation to the ultimate aims of the communist party was to be the kernel of the party controversies and conflicts. But the study of these disputes belongs to a later period of Soviet political history. For the moment it is only necessary to consider the effect on Lenin's tactics of the intention to put through a policy which he anticipated would meet with opposition.

The immediate result of the decision to launch the New Economic Policy was the final elimination of the Mensheviks from the political scene. This was dictated not by the danger of their opposition to this policy, but by the fact that they were likely to support it and welcome it, and had indeed for some time past been advocating it. To them it was a proof of their

[38] S. E. Rabinovich, 'Delegaty 10-go syezda RKP(b) pod Kronshtadtom v 1921 godu' in *Krasnaya letopis'*, no. 2 (41), 1931, p. 32. According to this author, who was well informed on army questions, it was 'solely' this information which brought a 'radical change in the mood of the Red Army men'.

[39] *Popov*, II, pp. 113–14.

contention that the October Revolution, in spite of appearances to the contrary, had in reality been a bourgeois, middle-class revolution, destined to continue as such for some time. The existence at liberty of a non-communist party which had been proved right by events was too dangerous a menace to communist prestige, and even power, to be tolerated. The Mensheviks were therefore now crushed for ever for having committed the offence of being right, when the Communists had been proved wrong. But within the communist party the Workers' Opposition, already severely critical of what it regarded as bourgeois deviations in communist policy, was likely to become even more critical after the introduction of the New Economic Policy. Moreover, the obvious concession to private capitalism implicit in the New Economic Policy was likely to add considerable weight to their arguments. If this group was not to gather strength in the party, it had to be finally discredited before the New Economic Policy was embarked on. Lenin explained his decision to silence opposition inside as well as outside the party by contending that the argument of the communist critics to the effect that the New Economic Policy was a 'radical break in policy' fully coincided with the menshevik and socialist revolutionary points of view. In spite of the fact that the reactions of the socialist parties and of the Workers' Opposition to the New Economic Policy were diametrically opposed, their assessment of it in Marxist terms was the same. Hence Lenin now argued that since the main enemy which the revolution faced was the forces of reaction grouped around the (ostensibly) socialist parties, the silencing of communist critics inside the party who subscribed to the socialists' analysis was equally justified.[40] In other words, since both the Mensheviks and the Workers' Opposition argued that N.E.P. was a bourgeois and not a socialist policy; and since the Mensheviks were 'counter-revolutionaries' it therefore followed that the Workers' Opposition were 'counter-revolutionaries'. Thus there came into being in communist logic the form of syllogism which has so frequently been pressed into service ever since. If A opposes

---

[40] See his speech of 26 May 1921 at a party conference, in *Lenin*, Vol. XXVI, at p. 387. cf. his speech to the Third Congress of the Third International, *ibid.*, pp. 463-4.

C, and B opposes C, it follows that A supports B, and that the aims of A and B are in every way identical. For example, since both the Kronstadt sailors and the 'counter-revolutionaries' were opposed to the communist dictatorship, it followed that the Kronstadt sailors were counter-revolutionaries. To the mind trained in the crude antitheses of the marxist dialectic the obvious fallacy of these arguments is not readily apparent. So now the Communists were for the most part easily persuaded that the critics from the Workers' Opposition were on the side of counter-revolution, whether they knew it or not, because, though they disapproved of NEP, they agreed with the Mensheviks that it was a 'radical break in policy'.

Lenin did not view the New Economic Policy entirely as a short-term measure. As he explained to the Tenth Party Congress, it was not surprising that experiments in collectivization had failed, 'since the task of reconstructing small scale agriculture, transforming all its psychology and habits, is a task demanding generations'. Only large scale industrialization, electrification, and the use of tractors and other technical developments on a mass scale could achieve this. 'When I say that generations are necessary, I do not mean that centuries will be needed'. But the task of industrialization envisaged would in any case require a period of time 'which cannot be calculated in less than decades'.[41] Two months later he expanded his explanation. 'The proletariat directs the peasantry, but this class cannot be driven out of existence as the landlords and capitalists were driven out of existence. It must be re-fashioned over a long period, with great effort and great privations.'[42]

Three and a half years of revolution, with its attendant misery and catastrophe, had thus brought Lenin at long last very close to the view which nearly every marxist had held in opposition to him in 1917: that socialism should only be attempted after a long preparatory stage of evolution. This stage of evolution, according to marxism, must necessarily be both economic and political. Since the political form of the state is an expression of the economic realities, or its 'superstructure', it followed that, so long as any economic power was

[41] *Lenin*, Vol. XXVI, p. 239.   [42] *ibid.*, p. 400.

retained by private capitalists, the form of the state must be at least in some respects middle-class and democratic. In this state the conflicting interests between different classes would be represented by political parties, expressing these interests. During the stage of evolution the proletariat would, moreover, acquire the political experience to administer the state when the time was ripe for it to seize all economic power. Lenin, in 1917, had discarded this stage of evolution. Economic realities now compelled him to admit the need for 'generations' of economic evolution. Logically, therefore, if marxist theory was right, there arose at the same time the necessity for a period of political evolution, involving the co-existence of contending political parties. For over three years a small but resolute communist party had dictated its will to both the workers and the peasants. It had succeeded in this formidable task by forcibly silencing its political rivals. To re-admit them now might conform to logic and marxism, but it would mean the end of communist monopoly of power.

But it was not only political rivals, the Mensheviks and the Socialist Revolutionaries, who constituted the danger. The New Economic Policy created a challenge to Lenin and the Central Committee from within the communist party. Hitherto, in spite of disagreements and dissensions, the party had preserved unity in face of the common peril. The belief that it was building socialism had been strong enough to hold it together. The New Economic Policy would now shatter that belief not only in the minds of the Workers' Opposition, but in the minds of many more, who might think that the criticism by the Workers' Opposition of bourgeois deviations in party policy, and of pampering of the peasants had not been exaggerated. Lenin had to envisage the possibility that a dissident movement might arise within his own party which could in time grow powerful enough to dislodge him from power. Engels had foreseen that the leader of an extremist party who seized power prematurely would find himself in a 'crooked position', and something of the kind had now happened to Lenin. In order to retain power the forcible methods applied to the socialist parties were now to be applied within the communist party. Thus, compulsion must take the place of discussion, and the unity which hitherto had sprung from faith in a common purpose must now be created by force. As Lenin explained some months after the Tenth Party Congress, 'it is necessary to ram home again and again that, after all, the character of meetings, congresses, conferences, and consultations in the communist party and in Soviet Russia cannot be such as it was in the old days, and such as it still is with us, when speeches are exchanged in the spirit of a parliamentary opposition, and then after that a resolution is written down. We must spend our time on business, and not on resolutions'.[43] But if resolutions are not to be prepared after discussions, then an obedient and uncritical party must be created, which will accept implicitly whatever its Central Committee orders. For the creation of such a party a new central apparatus was required, ruthless enough to reshape the organization of the party by force. Zinoviev's attack on the men who controlled the party apparatus had started well before the Tenth Party Congress. The danger signal from Kronstadt, one week before the congress opened, gave Lenin the opportunity to ensure, if for different reasons, that this attack should be crowned with success.

[43] At the Tenth Party Conference, on 26 May 1921, *Lenin*, Vol. XXVI, p. 408.

CHAPTER XVII

'PUTTING THE LID ON OPPOSITION'

The congress which laid the foundations of the Russian communist party organization as it still remains in essentials today was the Tenth Party Congress, which met in Moscow on 8 March 1921. As the result of Zinoviev's successful manœuvre, its membership reflected the election by 'platforms' put forward in the trade union discussions. Out of a total of six hundred and ninety-four delegates with a right to vote, the Workers' Opposition was represented by some forty-five or at most fifty delegates.[1] The congress was the culminating moment of the dispute on the trade unions. Yet by the time it met this problem had been eclipsed by more important questions. The victory of the Platform of the Ten was a foregone conclusion.[2] There was not very much difference in substance between the two platforms put forward by members of the Central Committee, so far as future freedom of activity for the trade unions was concerned. But Trotsky's name was, in the eyes of the rank and file, associated with militarization, Lenin's was not. Many may have believed that the adoption of the Platform of Ten would assure some independence to the trade union Communists. The resolution adopted certainly seemed calculated to give this impression. 'The reconstruction of the trade unions from the top', it ran, 'is quite inadmissible. . . . It is above all necessary to put into practice in

[1] Thirty-seven supporters of the Workers' Opposition attended a private meeting summoned by Lenin towards the end of the Congress, but by that time many of the delegates had left, including some two hundred for Kronstadt. Among those who had left were the Samara and Saratov delegations, which had been hurriedly spirited away by Dzerzhinsky on the ground that their presence was required at home owing to local disturbances (*Protokoly X*, pp. 337–8). Samara was a stronghold of the Workers' Opposition. Thus the total of their supporters must have been higher at the start of the Congress.

[2] The voting figures as published are puzzling. The total of votes cast was 336 for the Platform of the Ten, 50 for the Trotsky-Bukharin Platform, and 18 for the Workers' Opposition. Even allowing for about 200 delegates at the Kronstadt front, there must have been a good few abstentions among those of the 694 delegates still present at the Congress. The figure of 18 for the Workers' Opposition supporters is also odd since there were still 37 of them left at the time of Lenin's meeting.

the trade unions on a wide scale the principle of election to all organs of the trade union movement, and to do away with the method of appointment from the top.'[3] The promise of greater democracy was equally prominent in another long resolution on party structure which was adopted.[4] Proposed by Bukharin, it seemed to meet many of the criticisms of the Workers' Opposition. It stressed that the military form of centralization in the party, dictated by civil war conditions, was no longer applicable.

> Inner party workers' democracy [ran the resolution] means such a form of organization as ensures to all members of the party, including the most backward, an active part in the life of the party, in the discussion of all questions arising in the party, and in their solution. . . . The nature of workers' democracy excludes every form of appointment in place of election as a system, and finds expression in a widespread practice of election in all organizations from top to bottom. . . .

Among the most important methods of party work were listed 'extended discussion of all the most important questions, and public debates on them, with complete freedom of criticism inside the party . . . until such time as a decision binding' on all the party has been reached on any such question'. The resolution also reiterated the familiar recommendations for restoring the party to health,—the drafting of party officials back to factory benches, the struggle against those party members who abused their positions for their own selfish ends, and so forth.

In spite of these resolutions, a very different plan was afoot for dealing with criticism within the party, and in particular with criticism by the Workers' Opposition. The panic created by the alarming news from Kronstadt (the revolt was still in progress when the congress met on 8 March) as well as the personal form which the public discussion of the trade union question had taken, had both created a strong desire at the congress for party unity. The supporters of the Workers' Opposition were in a difficult position. By the Central Committee ruling on election of delegates they had been forced, for the first time, to appear at the congress as a separate group.

---

[3] *VKP(b) v rez.*, p. 439.   [4] *ibid.*, pp. 419-29.

Both the Central Committee factions, that of Lenin and Zinoviev on the one hand, and of Trotsky and Bukharin on the other, were openly ranged against them. Although no resolution condemning their policy had been tabled at the beginning of the congress, it was evident right from the start that something of the kind was in the air, and that before the congress ended something was going to happen to put a stop to their embarrassing criticism. Lenin had said so on the second day: 'We do not need any opposition now, comrades, it's not the time for it. Either here, or over there, with a rifle, but not with the opposition. It is no good reproaching me, it follows from the state of affairs. No more opposition now, comrades. And, in my view, the congress will have to draw the conclusion that the time has come to put an end to opposition, to put the lid on it, we have had enough opposition.'[5] Shlyapnikov in his reply offered full co-operation in any measures designed to restore the party to health. 'But do not', he said, addressing himself to Lenin, 'pick up the stick for a struggle against us. Here you will perhaps crush and break us, but in the result you will only lose.'[6] In spite of Lenin's threat to 'put the lid' on opposition, no resolution condemning it had been tabled by him up to the last day scheduled for the congress, 15 March. Bukharin, however, on 11 March announced his intention of proposing some form of resolution on party unity. Shlyapnikov and Medvedev thereupon immediately filed a declaration that until the intention to put forward such a resolution had been abandoned, the delegates supporting the Workers' Opposition would refuse to nominate any candidates for the Central Committee.[7] The tone of Bukharin's speeches had already made it clear enough that any resolution proposed by him on party unity would be aimed at silencing the Workers' Opposition. Lenin was, however, determined that Shlyapnikov, at any rate, should be elected to the Central Committee, and Shlyapnikov was no match for his tactics. At a private meeting of supporters of the Workers' Opposition (which Lenin convened before the end of the congress) he was successful in conciliating the Workers' Opposition to the extent of persuading them to add

---

[5] *Lenin*, Vol. XXVI, pp. 227-8. [6] *Protokoly X*, p. 78.
[7] *ibid.*, pp. 337, 805.

several of their representatives to the official list of candidates for election to the Central Committee.[8] Shlyapnikov and Kutuzov were duly elected members, while Kiselev was elected a candidate member. In view of the declaration which Shlyapnikov and Medvedev had filed in response to Bukharin's threat, Lenin must either have been successful at this meeting in allaying their fears, or have won them over by some promise or reassurance. On 15 March the chairman of the congress, Rakovsky, announced that it was essential to close it by midnight, but the congress later voted to meet again the following day to discuss the fuel situation.[9] The day came to an end without a mention of any resolution on opposition. At least two hundred delegates had already left. The elections to the Central Committee had been held. The main business of the congress had to all appearances been concluded.

On 16 March the congress met again. Lenin meanwhile had produced a bombshell, in the form of two resolutions, directed against the Workers' Opposition: the first on 'Party Unity' and the second on 'The Syndicalist and Anarchist Deviation in our Party'.[10] The first resolution drew attention to the fact that there were signs in the party of the formation of 'groups with separate platforms and with the determination, to a certain extent, to become self-contained and to create their own group discipline'. It went on to hint that the existence of the opposition had given encouragement to the enemies of the revolution, as the Kronstadt revolt had shown, and laid down the limits of criticism within the party: 'Everyone who criticizes in public must bear in mind the situation of the party in the midst of the enemies by which it is surrounded, and is also bound by his direct participation in soviet and party work to strive for the improvement in practice of the party's mistakes.' The resolution finally called for the immediate dissolution of all groups with separate platforms, on pain of immediate expulsion from the party. An unpublished article of the resolution, which remained secret until October 1923, conferred on the Central Committee the power of expulsion from the party. In the case of members of the Central Committee (a provision of particular interest to

---

[8] For this meeting see a note of the Marx-Engels-Lenin Institute, *ibid.*, p. 891–2.
[9] *ibid.*, pp. 453, 496.   [10] *VKP(b) v rez.*, pp. 429–34.

Shlyapnikov) a two-thirds vote of all members and candidates of the full Central Committee was required.

It may be observed that the emergence of the Workers' Opposition as a group on its own was solely the result of the Central Committee's decisions to allow public discussion of the trade union question and to elect delegates to the congress by 'platforms'. The Workers' Opposition had no press of its own, and there is no evidence of any kind that it had any separate organization or discipline. Nothing in the speeches of its representatives at the party congress could be construed either as proof of an intention to create such a separate organization, or as anything more than the wish to stimulate by their criticism within the party the reforms which they considered necessary. The charge contained in this resolution and aimed at the Workers' Opposition was manifestly false, and everyone present at the congress must have been aware of this. The resolution moreover imposed a very serious limitation on the principle laid down in the party statute, adopted in 1919, that all party questions were open to 'completely free' discussion until such time as a decision had been reached.[11] Nor does the congress seem to have been disturbed by the fact that it was quite inconsistent with Bukharin's resolution on 'Workers' Democracy' which had been adopted only a few days before. Subsequent months were to prove to what abuse the appeal to alleged dangers from external enemies was open as a method of stopping any criticism unwelcome to the party leadership.

The second resolution condemned the views of the 'so-called Workers' Opposition'.

> Marxism teaches us [it ran] that only the political party of the working class, i.e. the communist party, is capable of uniting, educating, and organizing such a vanguard of the proletariat and of the working masses as is capable of resisting the inevitable petty bourgeois waverings of these masses . . . [and] their trade-union prejudices. . . .

Thus the novel views on the rôle of the communist party which Lenin had first developed in 1902 were now established in Russian communist doctrine as a part of marxism. The

[11] The Statute had been adopted in December 1919. See *VKP(b) v rez.*, pp. 370-7, Article 50.

resolution went on to condemn the propagation of the views of the Workers' Opposition on the rôle of the trade unions in the control of industry as 'inconsistent with membership' of the Russian communist party, since they offended against marxism. It should be noted that, whether or not they offended against marxism, the views of the Workers' Opposition on this question do not seem to have been very different from the programme adopted in 1919 by the Russian communist party which declared that the 'unions must achieve the concentration in their hands of all management of the entire national economy'.[12]   Shlyapnikov, outmanœuvred by these surprise resolutions and outwitted by Lenin, announced his resignation from the Central Committee.   This resignation was rejected by the congress, on Lenin's proposal.[13]   The momentous resolutions were duly passed, with twenty-five and thirty dissenting votes respectively.   Lenin gave no explanation of his last-minute move.   His speech introducing the first of the two resolutions occupies eighteen lines in the stenogram.   'I do not think it will be necessary for me to say much on this subject', was his characteristic introduction to a decision which was a turning point in communist party history.[14]   Apart from the Workers' Opposition speakers, no one, not even the Democratic Centralists, opposed the resolutions.   The attitude of the Workers' Opposition was that they had no wish to exist as a separate group, but did demand the right freely to criticize party policy.   Medvedev, in a resolution which claimed the right of free criticism, expressly proposed to condemn all separate groups with their own group discipline.[15]   But neither his speech, nor that of Shlyapnikov, suggests that either of them fully realized that the two resolutions now before the congress would be used to silence them for ever.   To judge by the voting figures, the effect of surprise was such that the supporters of the Workers' Opposition did not vote up to their full strength against both the resolutions.[16]

---

[12] *VKP(b) v rez.*, p. 336.   [13] *Protokoly X*, pp. 538, 545.
[14] *ibid.*, pp. 523–4.   [15] *Protokoly X*, pp. 535–6.
[16] Twenty-five voted against the party unity resolution; 30 against the anarchosyndicalist deviation resolution.   Yet 37 oppositionists had attended Lenin's meeting a few days before, and on 9 March Medvedev collected 45 votes for a resolution condemning the Central Committee for failing to carry out the resolutions of the Ninth Congress—*Protokoly X*, p. 141.   Even allowing for departures, these figures are low.

The rest of the members of the congress, in spite of the misgivings of some speakers, were solidly behind Lenin. Perhaps the attitude of the party was best summed up in the prophetic words of Radek: 'In voting for this resolution, I feel that it can well be turned against us, and nevertheless I support it . . . Let the Central Committee in a moment of danger take the severest measures against the best party comrades, if it finds this necessary . . . Let the Central Committee even be mistaken! That is less dangerous than the wavering which is now observable.'[17] Many of those present at this congress, like Radek himself, would one day become victims of the new system of communist party organization which Lenin that day inaugurated. Their loyalty and their fear of the consequences of disunity led them to support Lenin, possibly in some cases against their better judgment. When, as Radek foresaw, the principle of these resolutions was turned against them, they discovered that by supporting it in the past they had cut the ground from under their feet.

The new Central Committee elected by the congress reflected the change of policy, as well as the ascendancy of many who were to prove themselves loyally on Stalin's side for many years to come. Of the old members of the Central Committee the three secretaries, Krestinsky, Preobrazhensky, and Serebryakov were not re-elected. Neither was Andreev, who had backed the wrong side in the trade union dispute, nor I. N. Smirnov. Among the newly-elected members were a number whose names were already closely associated with Stalin,—Komarov, Molotov, Mikhaylov, Yaroslavsky, Ordzhonikidze, Petrovsky, Frunze, Voroshilov, and Tuntul. Among the new candidate members were Chubar', Kirov, Kuybyshev, and Gusev,—all known supporters of Stalin. Kutuzov and Shlyapnikov were retained on the Central Committee against their will. The control of the party apparatus now also passed to the new men. The full Central Committee met on 22 March to elect its officials. It decided that:

> the only official of the Central Committee is its secretary, there being no chairman. To the Politbureau are elected: comrades Lenin, Trotsky, Zinoviev, Stalin, and Kamenev. The first

[17] *Protokoly X*, p. 540.

replacement member is Molotov, the second Kalinin, the third Bukharin. The secretary has a consultative voice at all meetings of the Political Bureau. Molotov to be appointed the responsible secretary of the Central Committee. Yaroslavsky and Mikhaylov to be appointed to the Secretariat. The Orgbureau to be composed of Molotov, Yaroslavsky, Mikhaylov, Komarov, Stalin, Rykov, and Tomsky. Comrades Dzerzhinsky, Rudzutak, and Kalinin to be appointed replacement members.[18]

Thus not only was the importance of the Secretariat augmented, but Stalin's influence on it through Molotov, who stood close to him, was well assured. The three former secretaries were removed from all positions of influence in the party. Zinoviev was rewarded by elevation to the Politbureau in place of Bukharin. There is nothing to indicate that these changes in leading party personalities took place without Lenin's full approval and support. The official list for the elections to the Central Committee, which was approved by the delegates to the Tenth Party Congress, was prepared by him at a private meeting during the congress.[19]

The Control Commission was also reorganized by the Tenth Party Congress. Neither Preobrazhensky nor Dzerzhinsky had stayed long on the Control Commission after their appointment in September 1920. By November they had both left[20] and Sol'ts (who like Molotov had worked with Stalin on *Pravda* before the revolution) had replaced Preobrazhensky. By the time of the congress it was apparent, if only from the fact that he presented the report on its activities, that he was now its leading personality. Although originally set up solely to safeguard the standards of behaviour of party members, the Control Commission discovered before long that 'it was impossible for it not to take an interest in party unity'.[21] Its intervention in January 1921 in the affairs of the Central Committee has already been noted, and thereafter it demanded and

[18] This minute, of considerable importance in Russian communist party history, is reprinted by Zinoviev, in his *Sochineniya*, Vol. VI, p. 626.
[19] *Protokoly X*, p. 891 (note of the Marx-Engels-Lenin Institute). cf. *Zorky*, p. 157.
[20] As Sol'ts said at the Tenth Congress: 'Comrades Preobrazhensky and Dzerzhinsky have now completely left. This is the result of the fact that the elections to the Control Commission at the September conference were rather hurried', *Protokoly X*, p. 67. It was in fact the case that the elections at this September conference were expressly stated to be temporary—*VKP(b) v rez.*, p. 416.
[21] From Sol'ts's report to the Tenth Congress, *Protokoly X*, p. 62.

obtained the right to be represented at all meetings of the Central Committee.[22] This increase in influence was further marked by changes made at the Tenth Congress. The purpose of the Control Commission was now openly recognized as 'the consolidation of unity and authority in the party'. Both the central and local commissions were given the power to participate in all meetings of both party and soviet committees, to make use of the apparatus of the appropriate party committee, and 'to give instructions to all party comrades and party organizations'.[23] Nevertheless, the members of the Central Control Commission appointed at the congress included Chelyshev, one of the signatories of the Workers' Opposition theses on the trade unions.

Thus the Tenth Party Congress marked the end of an important phase in the history of the Russian communist party. The personal struggle within the Central Committee had ended with a complete victory for Lenin, Zinoviev, and Stalin. In the case of the trade unions, Trotsky's blunt policy of militarization had been defeated by an apparently more liberal policy, which rejected both the immediate incorporation of the unions in the state and the reconstruction of trade union organs by wholesale appointments from the centre. A policy of extensive 'workers' democracy' had been laid down for party life, ostensibly permitting wide discussion and freedom. But at the same time there were indications that the resolutions on party democracy were not likely to get much further than the paper on which they were printed. In the first place, the control of the all-important party apparatus had passed to new men. The men whose policy had been compromise, conciliation, and the encouragement of democratic methods in the party, Krestinsky, Preobrazhensky and Serebryakov, had not only been removed from the Secretariat and from the Orgbureau, but had even been ousted from the Central Committee. Secondly, the resolution directed against the Workers' Opposition did not augur well for the future of democracy in the party. The demand of the Workers' Opposition that the trade unions should control all industry had been condemned as an anarcho-syndicalist deviation from marxism; and the existence within the party of groups with

---

[22] *Protokoly X*, pp. 65–6.   [23] *ibid.*, pp. 621–2.

separate discipline and organization of their own had been forbidden. But, most important of all, a new and very serious limitation had been laid down on the freedom of criticism within the party which alone cast considerable doubt on the value of the other resolutions of the congress. Two diametrically opposed policies thus emerged. Events very soon showed which of the two was going to be put into effect.

Lenin, Zinoviev, and Stalin had, in December 1920, urged the immediate abolition of *Tsektran* against a bare majority of the Central Committee, and the deadlock in the Central Committee over this issue had led to the trade union discussion. It would be natural to suppose that with the victory of Lenin's view at the Tenth Party Congress, the policy, on which ostensibly he and his supporters had broken with the majority of the Central Committee, would be implemented. Yet, immediately after this party congress, *Tsektran* was fully restored at a Congress of Transport Workers. It was a carefully packed congress. No word of opposition to *Tsektran* was heard except from an 'insignificant handful' of Mensheviks and Socialist Revolutionaries who were alleged to have gate-crashed disguised as 'non-party members'.[24] The unpopular transport political directorates, which had been fused with the union party organizations in December 1920, were restored in October 1921 in the form of a special section of the Central Committee for the 'direction and control of party work in transport', with a network of subordinate sections.[25] The iron hand of the Central Committee was soon in evidence in its relations with the trade unions. 'The reconstruction of trade-union organization from the top is completely inadmissible', ran the resolution adopted by the Tenth Congress in March 1921. In May 1921, with the ink on it scarcely dry, a conflict arose with the Metal-workers' Union. This union (the oldest bolshevik trade union) was largely in sympathy with the Workers' Opposition. When the communist 'fraction' of the union rejected the Central Committee's list of candidates for the controlling committee of the union by 120 votes to 40, the Central Committee ignored this vote, and appointed a

[24] *Pravda*, 24 and 31 March 1921.
[25] *Spravochnik*, I, p. 122; II, pp. 68–9.

metal-workers' committee consisting entirely of its own nominees. Shlyapnikov attempted to resign from the Central Committee in protest. His resignation was not accepted.[26]

The Central Committee's policy was also revealed at the Fourth All-Russian Trade Union Congress, which met between 17 and 25 May 1921. The main business of this congress was to consider the tasks of the trade unions in relation to the revival of private capitalist enterprises which was shortly to be put into effect.[27] It was soon made plain that no relaxation of the strictly centralized party control was to be allowed. Tomsky, as chairman of the All-Russian Central Trade Union Council was, together with Tsyperovich, made responsible for the preparation of theses on the new trade union functions, and charged by the Central Committee to ensure their acceptance by the communist 'fraction' in the congress and subsequently by the full congress. The theses were duly adopted by the 'fraction'. However, on 17 May this 'fraction' also accepted by a vote of 1500 to 30 a resolution proposed by Ryazanov. The essence of this resolution was contained in the following: 'The selection of directing personnel for the trade union movement must take place under the over-all control of the party, but the party must make a special effort to put into practice the normal methods of proletarian democracy, and this particularly in the trade unions, where, above all, the selection of leaders should be made by the organized party masses themselves.'[28] This proposal was even milder in its terms than Bukharin's resolution on the same question accepted at the Tenth Party Congress two months before. But the passing of Ryazanov's resolution infuriated the Central Committee. On the following day Tomsky, who had not himself supported it, was replaced as the Central Committee's representative at the congress by Bukharin, Lenin, and Stalin, who were charged by the Central Committee to ensure its reversal in the unruly 'fraction' of the congress. Ryazanov was banned from all further work

---

[26] *Izvestiya Ts. K.*, no. 32, 1921, pp. 3–4. This union, which had led the strike wave in 1905 and had won a majority from the Mensheviks as early as 1913, represented the foremost elements of the bolshevik trade union movement—see *Milonov*, pp. 109–19. See also *Popov*, II, pp. 155, 164.
[27] For details of these new tasks, see *Vs. syezd prof. IV.*, pp. 66–8.
[28] Quoted by Ryazanov at the Eleventh Party Congress, *Protokoly XI*, pp. 277–8.

in the trade union movement. A special commission, headed by Stalin, was set up to investigate the conduct of Tomsky. This commission found that, although Tomsky had not supported the offending resolution, he had not shown sufficient zeal in ensuring its rejection. It severely reprimanded him for his 'criminal indifference' and relieved him of all work in the Central Council of Trade Unions. The 'fraction' was duly persuaded to revoke its resolution of the day before, though it did demand, without success, that the decision with regard to Tomsky should be reversed.[29]

It proved only a temporary eclipse so far as Tomsky was concerned. Ryazanov, who had not endeared himself by his bitter and witty attacks on Zinoviev's tactics, both before and at the Tenth Party Congress, was never allowed to return to political work in the trade unions. As the result of this rebellion, on 30 July 1921 new instructions on party 'fractions' in the trade unions were issued by Molotov, the responsible secretary of the party, and Andreev. (The latter had by now been restored to favour after his short period of very moderate opposition, and had become secretary of the Central Council of Trade Unions.) The new instructions enjoined complete obedience of 'fractions' to directives of the party on pain of expulsion, and prohibited any member of a 'fraction' from speaking at any meeting without leave of the 'fraction'.[30] During 1921 and 1922 control of the Central Committee over all trade union appointments became firmly established. In December 1921 a party conference laid down that only 'old experienced party members' who had not been members of any other party should be drafted to the trade unions, but that this 'renovation' of the directing organs of the unions should take place gradually. A special commission for this purpose (which included Tomsky, restored to favour by this date) was set up in January 1922. Its work had not yet been completed by March 1922 when the Eleventh Party Congress met.[31]

Victimization of supporters of the Workers' Opposition began immediately after the Tenth Party Congress. 'The

[29] *Izvestiya Ts. K.*, no. 32, of 6 August 1921, pp. 2–3.
[30] See *Pravda*, 30 July 1921.
[31] *VKP(b) v rez.*, p. 488; and see Andreev's speech at the Eleventh Party Congress, *Protokoly XI*, pp. 260 *et seq.*

struggle', as Shlyapnikov later recounted, 'took place not along ideological lines but by means . . . of edging out from appointments, of systematic transfers from one district to another, and even of expulsion from the party.' The party would have been within its rights in suppressing the propagation of the demand that the unions should control industry, since this had been declared an anarcho-syndicalist deviation from marxism. But the attack was levelled not for heretical opinions, but for criticism of any kind of the party shortcomings. 'Every member of the party who spoke in defence of the resolution on workers' democracy passed at the Tenth Congress was declared a supporter of the Workers' Opposition and guilty of disintegrating the party', and was accordingly victimized.[32] The resolution on workers' democracy to which Shlyapnikov was referring, was not, be it noted, an opposition resolution, but the official resolution adopted at the congress, on the proposal of Bukharin. Comparison of the lists of delegates to the Tenth and Eleventh Congresses shows that of the thirty-seven oppositionists who attended the private meeting convened by Lenin during the Tenth Congress, with the object of persuading Shlyapnikov to serve on the Central Committee, only four reappeared as delegates with a vote at the Eleventh Congress the following year.

An incident in August 1921 illustrates what Zinoviev and Lenin meant by the professions of party democracy which had ensured their victory at the Tenth Party Congress. At a private meeting of a party cell Shlyapnikov criticized in biting terms a decree of the Praesidium of the Supreme Council of National Economy. On 9 August in the Central Committee, Lenin demanded his expulsion from the Central Committee. He was, however, unable to secure the necessary two-thirds majority required for this step, as laid down by the Tenth Party Congress. But the Central Committee decided (in a resolution which was only made known in higher party circles) that Shlyapnikov's criticism was 'quite inadmissible', and that further utterances might lead to his expulsion. He was also relieved of his duties in connection with the party purge, then in progress. The text of an official report of the party cell meeting, possibly compiled by someone acting as

[32] *Zorky*, pp. 146–7.

an informer for the central apparatus, was quoted some years later by Rykov.[33] No ingenuity can turn Shlyapnikov's words either into advocacy of anarcho-syndicalism, or into an attempt to set up a separate group or 'clique' in the party. At the Tenth Congress Lenin had persuaded him to serve on the Central Committee. Now, five months later, Lenin was demanding his expulsion for a few sharp words of criticism of the bureaucracy, uttered at a private meeting of a local party cell. If he was looking for a pretext, he could scarcely have picked a weaker one.

That there was still at this date some reluctance to take disciplinary action against known Bolsheviks of long standing in the party is illustrated by the case of that rare individualist, G. Myasnikov, perhaps the only Russian Communist after 1917 to advocate freedom of speech for parties other than his own. An old worker-Bolshevik, and a party member since 1906, he had been responsible for the killing of the Grand Duke Michael in 1917. He had been transferred in 1920 from his native Urals to Petrograd where, at the end of 1920, he made full use of the opportunities for free criticism still existing at that period for members of the communist party, to lash the bureaucracy and the shortcomings of the leading party officials in vigorous, if somewhat illiterate, articles and speeches. He went much further than the Workers' Opposition, not only by his advocacy of peasant unions to which reference

---

[33] The report, as quoted by Rykov, is given in full in this note, in order to illustrate the kind of criticism which in Lenin's view justified the expulsion of an old Bolshevik, his principal lieutenant between 1915 and 1917, from the Central Committee: 'In the party cell the former People's Commissar presented a report, —or rather did not so much present a report, as launch into criticism of government decrees. As the basis of his criticism he took the resolution of the Praesidium of the Supreme Council of National Economy on the granting of concessions of industrial enterprises to private capitalists. He began with the paragraph which says "It must be admitted, that national economy has been managed without any organization". Comrade Shlyapnikov, burst out laughing over this sentence. "What *does* this mean? Four years' management, and no organization—it doesn't make sense!!" The second point of his criticism was the part of the resolution which reads: "In spite of the fact that the workers were supplied with clothes and provisions, production dropped to a minimum." This sentence was much criticized by comrade Shlyapnikov, who said that the workers were given pretty well damn all, whereas production at some factories was even higher than before the war. The third point which he criticized was the passage about pilfering at work. Comrade Shlyapnikov said that it was not the fault of the workers, but of the economic departments: they have reduced the workers to thieving. At the end of his criticism he announced that the whole resolution stank of prejudice against the workers, and that the workers should be on their guard.' See *Zorky*, pp. 48–9. cf. *Izvestiya Ts. K.*, no. 33, October 1921.

has already been made,[34] but also in his demands for freedom of speech for all parties without exception, as the only method of ensuring efficiency and probity in the communist party. 'The Soviet power', he wrote, 'must maintain at its own expense a body of detractors as did once the Roman Emperors.'[35] Writing years later, in exile, he attributed the decline in the party to the decisions of the Tenth Party Congress which made free criticism impossible.[36] He did not hesitate to express his views forcibly, not only in Petrograd, but in a report to the Central Committee. Lenin, in a private letter, endeavoured to convince him that greater freedom of speech and press meant in effect freedom for the forces of counter-revolution.[37] In his reply to Lenin, Myasnikov reminded him that the only reason why he, Myasnikov, was not in jail was because he was an old Bolshevik, and that thousands of ordinary workmen were in jail for saying exactly the same things as he did. Even after the Orgbureau had condemned his views, through a special commission appointed for the purpose, Myasnikov succeeded in winning over to his side, against the Orgbureau, the whole of the local party organization of Motovilikhin (in his native Urals). The Orgbureau commission (which included Bukharin and Sol'ts) thereupon voted to expel him from the party and this decision was referred for confirmation to the Politbureau on 20 February 1922. The Politbureau confirmed it, subject to a proviso that he should be readmitted within a year if he mended his ways.[38]

The tolerance shown to Myasnikov was however exceptional. For the great majority of the party, the 'workers' democracy'

---

[34] See Chapter XVI.

[35] Quoted in *Proletarskaya revolyutsiya*, no. 6 (113), 1931, at p. 93.

[36] See his *Ocherednoy obman*, Paris, 1931, p. 40.

[37] See *Lenin*, Vol. XXVI, pp. 683, 473. A selection of Myasnikov's speeches and articles and Lenin's letter and Myasnikov's reply were reprinted 'for party members only' in a very rare pamphlet entitled *Diskussionnyy material* (*Tezisy tov. Myasnikova, pis'mo tov. Lenina, otvet emu, postanovlenie byuro Ts. K. i rezolyutsiya motovilikhintsev) tol'ko dlya chlenov partii*. Moscow, 1921. It was printed in 500 copies only. It has not been obtainable (a copy in Paris was accidentally destroyed by fire) but a summary of its contents will be found in *Sotsialisticheskiy vestnik*, 23 February 1922, pp. 2–4. cf. *Izvestiya Ts. K.* no. 34, of 15 November 1921.

[38] Myasnikov's name recurred for some years as an active oppositionist. Banished and imprisoned after 1928, he eventually escaped to Paris, where he remained until after the war. In 1945, apparently in the belief that the Russian victory would herald an era of political tolerance in which he could once again play a part, he returned to the U.S.S.R.; he has not been heard of since.

which the Tenth Party Coñgress had decided on in theory soon proved of little value in practice, in the light of the new limitation on criticism introduced at the last minute.   Although some discussion was at first encouraged, partly perhaps as a convenient method of forcing opposition into the open, it soon led to the silencing of any outspoken criticism.   In the summer of 1921 a discussion club was set up in Samara, a stronghold of opposition, to debate the policy of granting concessions to private capitalists[39] and, in the second half of 1921, such clubs sprang up all over the country.   But they did not survive many months.   In the case of the Moscow club, for example, the Control Commission, having noticed that its discussions had been 'taking on a demagogic non-party character which had a demoralizing effect on its members', decided to 'liquidate' it after six months' existence.[40]   The resolutions of the Tenth Congress disapproving of central appointments to elective posts in the party were likewise disregarded.   In the case of the Samara party organization, for instance, the Central Committee was 'forced' to remove a number of workers from responsible positions and transfer them to other regions, and to send to Samara a strong group of 'new workers'.   There were expulsions and transfers from the party organs in Simbirsk and Archangel.   In Vologda, after a conflict lasting for two months, the difficulty was solved by the 'drafting of several new workers, unconnected with local groupings'.   Of nine party *oblast'* (provincial) organizations, each controlling a number of *gubernii*, six in 1921 consisted of persons appointed by the Central Committee, and only three, including the Central Committee of the Ukraine, were elected by the local party organizations.[41]

When it became evident that they were being victimized, supporters of the Workers' Opposition appealed to the Central Committee.   Their complaints were investigated and

---

[39] For a report of this see *Pravda*, 14 January 1922, which ascribes the setting up of the Samara club to the desire to 'liquidate' opposition tendencies, but does not state whether this meant liquidation of the critics, or the resolving of doubts in free discussion.

[40] *Lenin*, Vol. XXVII, pp. 536–7.   The closing down of this club was fully endorsed by Lenin—*ibid.*, p. 267.

[41] See the Central Committee's report for the period between the Tenth and Eleventh Party Congresses, reprinted in *Protokoly XI*, pp. 637–64, from *Izvestiya Ts. K.*, no. 4, of 1922.

rejected as untrue.[42] Instructions were however issued that the extensive purge, then in progress in the party under the direction of the Control Commission, should not be used as cover for expelling sympathisers with the opposition. Indeed, it does not appear that the purge was much abused in this manner, possibly in view of the presence on the Control Commission during 1921 of an oppositionist, Chelyshev. In practice repressions against the opposition were more often carried out directly by the central party apparatus, by removing an elected organization, as in the case of Samara, or by the transfer of too outspoken critics to the most remote regions of the country, as well as by dismissals from official appointments.

Thwarted inside Russia, some of the leaders of the Workers' Opposition eventually endeavoured to make their criticism heard in the arena of international communism and to warn foreign Communists of the decline of proletarian influence in the Russian party and of what they regarded as a dangerous tendency towards bourgeois degeneration. They were assured of some sympathy from the left wings of a number of the foreign communist parties. These left wings had been growing in strength in the course of 1920, mainly under the influence of the Dutch Communists, Gorter and Pannekoek. The left wings criticized the Russians for attaching too much importance to the party, and too little to the function of the working masses. The result was, argued the 'left' Communists, that the International tended to see its tasks in terms of the interests of the Russian communist party, and not in terms of the interests of the working masses. 'For the International the masses of Western Europe are merely a means to an end. For the left, they are in themselves the end,' wrote Gorter in the summer of 1920, in reply to Lenin's *Left Communism—an Infantile Disease.*[43] The most important left wing was the German *Kommunistische Arbeiter Partei* (K.A.P.D.), which in the spring of 1920 split off from the German communist party and soon captured the majority of the party in many important centres, including Berlin and Hamburg. In April 1922 the K.A.P.D. formed, together with the Dutch and Bulgarian opposition groups, the so-called Communist Labour International, as a co-ordinating body for all left-wing communist parties in sympathy with the K.A.P.D.[44] It is this body which was at times, somewhat ambitiously, referred to as the Fourth International.

There was clearly something in common between these left wings and the Workers' Opposition, in particular the stress which they all laid on greater confidence in the masses and on their spontaneous participation in the business of socialism. They all shared, moreover, a hostility to the New Economic Policy, if for different reasons: the Workers' Opposition because they regarded it as a betrayal of proletarian interests, the K.A.P.D. because they saw in it a brake on revolution in Western Europe. When Lutovinov, and later Shlyapnikov, visited Berlin after the Tenth Party Congress,[45] they naturally enough established contact with the left wing of the German communist party, including its leader Maslow. Rumours of Maslow's meetings with Lutovinov or Shlyapnikov presumably reached Lenin. In the conditions of open party opposition still prevailing in 1921 it is hardly surprising that these contacts should not have been kept secret from the Russian Central Committee.[46] 'The indiscretion, to use a mild term, in the conduct of this Maslow has had its repercussions even here in Moscow,'[47] Lenin wrote in the summer of 1921. But it is probable that the enthusiasm for the identification of the two groups of dissidents came more from the side of the Western left Communists than from the Workers' Opposition. To the Western European opposition the existence of a group of old Bolsheviks inside Russia who shared their view was valuable support. But for the Workers' Opposition, which had through-out shown no inclination to split off from the Russian com-munist party, to be identified with dissident groups no longer represented in the Third International was a very doubtful political advantage. To the Russian Central Committee the identification of the Workers' Opposition with groups which they were seeking to discredit in the International was no doubt welcome. Shlyapnikov later accused the Central Com-mittee of having attempted by the use of *agents provocateurs* to

---

[44] *Reichenbach*, p. 139.
[45] Shlyapnikov apparently also visited England in 1920—see Vs. *syezd prof. III*, p. 139.
[46] See Ruth Fischer, *Stalin and German Communism*, pp. 181-2.
[47] *Lenin*, Vol. XXVI, p. 490.

provoke the Workers' Opposition into forming a group of the 'Fourth International'.[48]

So far from abandoning the communist Third International, the Workers' Opposition made a rather naïve attempt in 1921 to enlist the support of this body against the Central Committee, when the latter rejected their protest against victimization of oppositionists. At the Third Congress of the International, in June 1921, Kollontay, speaking 'not in the name of the Russian delegation', but for 'a small minority' of the Russian party offered some mild criticism of the decline in Russia of confidence in the masses, and of the loss of initiative by the proletariat. She was attacked with venom by Trotsky and Bukharin, and found no support in the congress, except from the delegates of the K.A.P.D. In spite of her criticism, she did not vote against the resolution approving the policy of the Russian communist party.[49] The disagreements inside the Russian party were at that date scarcely known outside Russia, except in left wing groups, and there was clearly no desire on Kollontay's part to disclose their seriousness at this congress. But in February of the following year, twenty-two prominent supporters of the Workers' Opposition decided to appeal to the International against the Russian Central Committee. In a declaration addressed to the Executive Committee of the Communist International they complained of the decline in the Russian party of proletarian initiative, and of the methods now being adopted to stifle criticism and to suppress democracy in the trade unions and in the party. The signatories of this declaration, of which a copy was sent to the Central Committee, included Shlyapnikov, Medvedev, and Kuznetsov, as well as Chelyshev, the member of the Central Control Commission. Kollontay, not an original signatory, appended her signature later. The Declaration of the Twenty-Two, as it became known, was also signed by Myasnikov, who had been expelled from the party a few days before the declaration reached the Executive Committee of the International. One notable omission from the list of signatories was Kiselev. He had, since the Tenth Party Congress, become chairman of the 'Lesser Sovnarkom', a co-ordinating office within the Council of People's Commissars,

[48] *Protokoly XI*, p. 697.   [49] *Comintern III*, pp. 367–83.

and had broken with the opposition, of which he had been a leading member.

The decision of the Executive Committee of the International was a foregone conclusion. It was hardly conceivable that in 1922 the Communist International should side with an opposition of the serious nature of which it was probably unaware, and which was making accusations against the first socialist state which ran directly counter to everything which all had been led to believe. A commission was appointed under the chairmanship of Kolarov to examine the complaints of the Twenty-Two; it included Clara Zetkin, Cachin, Kreibich, and MacManus. The inclusion of Cachin on the commission was interpreted by the oppositionists as a special insult.[50] The commission heard the statements of Shlyapnikov, Kollontay, and Pravdin at one session; and of Zinoviev, Trotsky, and Rudzutak at another. The complaints presented by Shlyapnikov have been summarized in Soviet sources, presumably from the archives of the International. The summary does not appear particularly exaggerated or inaccurate, though Shlyapnikov later asserted that what he had said had been distorted. He told the commission about the complete party domination over trade unions and over the workers generally, about the flouting of the party congress resolutions on workers' democracy, and criticized the growing petty-bourgeois and non-proletarian composition of the Russian party. As an example, he alleged that of thirty-five *guberniya* party secretaries only three were workers. The Central Committee's methods were driving workers to leave the party. Shlyapnikov also complained of house searches, interception of correspondence, the employment of *agents provocateurs* against oppositionists in the party, and the constant stifling of all criticism. The Kolarov commission duly reported to the Executive Committee of the International condemning the opposition: the Russian party, it found, was fully aware of some of the defects complained of by the opposition, and was taking energetic steps to combat them, while the conduct of the opposition merely provided valuable support to

[50] As Shlyapnikov observed to Alfred Rosmer, then a member of ECCI: 'Vous n'avez pas pu trouver mieux que cette chiffe pour nous condamner.' See A. Rosmer, *Moscou sous Lénine. Les origines du communisme*, Paris, 1953, p. 209.

Mensheviks and 'counter-revolutionaries' generally. Its report was unanimously accepted by the Executive Committee; but four members, two Swiss and two Czech, abstained.[51]

No one could deny the right of the opposition to appeal to the highest instance of the communist hierarchy, the International. But the reaction of the Russian Central Committee, and particularly of Lenin, to this incident is not difficult to imagine. The blow to the prestige of the Russian communist party caused by this action of the Twenty-Two was considerable. Their step was understandable as a last desperate attempt to obtain a hearing. But, as Communists of long experience, they must have known that they had committed an unpardonable sin against the party. The Central Committee proceeded to exploit its victory in the International in order finally to discredit the opposition inside Russia. The measures adopted to silence opposition after the Tenth Party Congress had apparently not yet been successful by 1922. In the first week of March an Extraordinary Congress of the Metal-workers' Union was summoned. In spite of the care with which this very union had been packed by the Central Committee the previous year, and in spite of the participation in the meeting of the communist 'fraction' of this congress of Lenin, Zinoviev, Stalin, Molotov, Kamenev, Clara Zetkin, Cachin, Kolarov, Tomsky, Rudzutak, and Andreev, there were five abstentions in the voting in the 'fraction' on a resolution condemning the Declaration of the Twenty-Two.[52]

A much more serious state of affairs was disclosed at the Eleventh Communist Party Congress which opened on 27 March 1922. In the country as a whole, as Zinoviev's guarded report on the state of the party indicated, critical opposition (now invariably described as 'cliques' and 'group struggles') was widespread.[53] What was more alarming to the Central Committee, the unrest in party life in the country was reflected in the congress proceedings. Lenin's health was already failing. He had ceased regular work in December. He attended only the opening of the Eleventh Congress, to present the

[51] Not all the documents relating to this incident have been published, but such as have been published will be found in *Zorky*, pp. 59–63, and *Protokoly XI*, pp. 693–700, 735–39. See also an article by Kreibich in *Kommunisticheskiy Internatsional*, no. 21, 1922, pp. 5589–5602.

[52] *Lenin*, Vol. XXVII, p. 518; *Zorky*, pp. 62–3.   [53] *Protokoly XI*, pp. 423–4.

report of the Central Committee and to take part in the subsequent debate, and the closing session. The effect of his absence was evident. It proved to be the first congress since the revolution at which the Central Committee was unable, through the praesidium, to control the proceedings. The constant efforts of the chair to silence speakers met with resistance from the floor of the congress, and the stenographic report of the proceedings bristles with interruptions by anonymous voices. A proposal to abolish all local control commissions—which if adopted would have struck a severe blow at the machinery of the Control Commission throughout the country—was greeted with hearty applause, and secured no less than 89 against 223 votes.[54] But the most serious matter of all was the defeat of the Central Committee's endeavour to expel Shlyapnikov, Medvedev, and Kollontay from the party. The Central Committee reported to the congress on the complaint of the Twenty-Two to the International, and proposed to set up a commission, (which included Dzerzhinsky, Stalin, Zinoviev, and Sol'ts among its members) to investigate 'all the circumstances connected with the activities of the former Workers' Opposition group'. The chairman of the congress vainly attempted to silence debate on this proposal. He refused to accept the first vote of the congress on the question whether the proposal to set up the commission should be debated, on the pretext that the 'results of the voting were unclear'. A second vote was then taken, which presumably left no doubt of the feeling of the meeting, and the proposal was thereupon debated. The congress next rejected a proposal from the chair to cut short the debate, before Shlyapnikov and Kollontay had spoken; and it refused to reduce the time allowed to speakers in the debate.[55] The appointment of the commission was agreed to, but the debate revealed considerable uneasiness in the congress. A number of responsible and important delegates were clearly disturbed by the methods which had been adopted in the past year to silence criticism.

At the end of the congress, the commission produced a long report. Its burden was that the Workers' Opposition had defied the resolution of the Tenth Party Congress and had maintained, under the leadership of Shlyapnikov, Medvedev,

[54] *ibid.*, p. 220.   [55] *ibid.*, pp. 188, 196.

and Kollontay, a secret organization of its own. The evidence adduced in support of this charge consisted of one intercepted letter from a certain Mitin which, if genuine, at most established that Mitin, in conjunction with Shlyapnikov and Medvedev, was endeavouring to secure the election of workers in sympathy with their point of view to factory committees in the Donets Basin.[56] The report of the commission leaves no doubt that police methods of search, censorship, and interrogation were at that date being used against the opposition. The commission recommended the expulsion of Kuznetsov and Mitin (the latter it was now alleged was really a Menshevik, who had only joined the Communists in 1920, though he himself in signing the declaration of the Twenty-Two had given his party seniority as 1902), and also of Shlyapnikov, Medvedev, and Kollontay. In the case of these three reinstatement within a year was offered if they mended their ways.[57] In deliberations which are described as secret and of which no account has been published,[58] the congress now defied the Central Committee. It refused to expel Shlyapnikov, Medvedev, or Kollontay from the party. This appears from a comparison of the terms of the resolution as passed by the congress with the recommendations of the commission. But the main proposals of the commission were accepted. The opposition was condemned not for its appeal to the International, but for its continued existence as a separate group allegedly threatening the party with a split. To bolster this charge it was now asserted, without a shadow of truth, that Kollontay had stated in her pamphlet in March 1921 that the splitting off of the Workers' Opposition from the party was inevitable and that it was 'only necessary to pick on the most opportune moment' for such a move.

No mention was made in the resolution adopted by the congress of the main reason for the condemnation of the opposition—its relentless and forceful criticism of the shortcomings in party policy and practice which must have been evident to all.[59] 'They say,' said Ryazanov, in the course of debate on the Declaration of the Twenty-Two, 'that the

---

[56] An extract from this letter is reprinted in *Zorky*, pp. 51–3.
[57] The report is reprinted in *Protokoly XI*, pp. 693–700.
[58] *ibid.*, p. 547, footnote.   [59] *VKP(b) v rez.*, pp. 535–8.

English Parliament can do everything except change a man into a woman. Our Central Committee is far more powerful than that. It has already changed more than one not very revolutionary man into an old woman, and the number of these old women is increasing daily.'[60] He argued that so long as government took the form of the issuing of orders without previous discussion, chaos, bureaucracy, and corruption would be the inevitable results. Yet, like the Tenth Congress before it, this congress too surrendered, in spite of misgivings, to the policy of the Central Committee. The opposition was unorganized, and lacked influential leaders. No single member of the Central Committee (other than Shlyapnikov and Kutuzov, retained there against their wills) had lifted a finger during 1921 in an endeavour to stop or modify the new policy of building unanimity by force. Trotsky, for example, was stoutly against the opposition, in spite of the fact that according to one of his former supporters, Kossior, there had been some victimization of supporters of the Trotsky-Bukharin platform.[61] His temporary rift with Lenin had been completely healed. Zinoviev's campaign against Trotsky had lost its force, and Trotsky was not anxious to jeopardize his own position by defending his past supporters. For the Workers' Opposition it was the end, though it was to take some years before their spokesmen had all either capitulated, or been effectively silenced.

But although the Central Committee once again emerged victorious, the Eleventh Congress revealed that the party apparatus, under the management of Molotov, was as yet far from equal to its tasks of exposing and silencing opposition, and of ensuring implicit obedience to its orders. The fact alone that the Central Committee had been defeated in a vote showed serious mismanagement of the election of the delegates to the congress. The Secretariat, in particular, had been lagging behind. It was only as late as September 1921 that a full system of returns was initiated on the basis of which the centre could inform itself in detail on party activity in local organizations.[62] The indexing of all party officials had not yet been completed by the Eleventh Party Congress.[63]

[60] *Protokoly XI*, p. 83.   [61] *ibid.*, pp. 133–4.
[62] *Pravda*, 10 September 1921.   [63] *Protokoly XI*, p. 52.

Although in the summer of 1921 the Secretariat was already despatching an average of a hundred telegrams a day through its secret cipher department,[64] it does not appear to have made anything like sufficient progress in the basic card indexing of all party members—the foundation for all effective manipulation.[65]

The new Central Committee elected by the Eleventh Congress on 2 April 1922 once again showed the ascendancy of Stalin. Andreev and Kuybyshev were now added to the Central Committee as members, while, among the candidates, Stalin's future supporters were increased by the addition of Manuilsky and Mikoyan. The Central Committee proceeded to make some changes in the party apparatus. It elected Stalin as General Secretary, in place of Molotov, whose designation had been that of 'Responsible Secretary'; Molotov and Kuybyshev were elected as his assistants.[66] According to Trotsky, Lenin expressed some misgivings about Stalin's fitness to prepare anything but 'peppery dishes'.[67] But some doubt is cast on Trotsky's recollection by the fact that he places this story around the Tenth Congress, in 1921. Moreover if Lenin, or for that matter Trotsky, had opposed Stalin's election as Secretary in the Central Committee, one would expect Trotsky to have recorded this fact. Stalin was clearly the best man for the new functions which in the past year had become the peculiar province of the party apparatus. There is nothing to indicate that Lenin, in April 1922, thought otherwise. The congress also reorganized and strengthened the Control Commissions. Of the seven members elected to the central Control Commission the year before, only one, Sol'ts, was reappointed. Both the local and the central commissions were equipped with 'a small apparatus for investigations'.

Thus, the 'workers' democracy' proclaimed at the Tenth Party Congress had proved a sham, no less than the trade

---

[64] *Izvestiya Ts. K.*, no. 34, 15 November 1921, p. 6.
[65] See a report on this aspect of the organization of the Secretariat by the Central Revision Committee appointed at the Tenth Congress, reprinted in *Protokoly XI*, pp. 75–6.
[66] According to *Pravda* of 4 April 1922. According to a note of the Marx-Engels-Lenin Institute the election only took place in May—*Protokoly XI*, p. 758. If the latter date is correct, the election may have taken place in Lenin's absence, since by that date he was already incapacitated by illness.
[67] *Trotsky, Ma Vie*, Vol. III, p. 183.

union programme. No attempt was ever made to implement either. The real policy of the Central Committee was contained in the resolutions directed against the Workers' Opposition. For this an effective apparatus at the centre was vital. The apparatus developed by Stalin after 1922 was no more than the perfection of the apparatus which Molotov had tried, and failed, to create during 1921. It was a necessary consequence of Lenin's policy of eliminating criticism from the party, and of ruling it by decree. There is nothing to show that the routing of the Workers' Opposition at the Eleventh Congress did not correspond to Lenin's views, although it took place in his absence. It was, after all, Lenin who had proposed the expulsion of Shlyapnikov from the Central Committee for a few hard words about the bureaucracy. Yet, before a stroke in May 1922 virtually eliminated Lenin from political life, there were already signs of discord between him and the new masters of Russia. Lenin apparently retained his faith that, side by side with his system of rigid, centralized party dictatorship, the standards of the party could be raised, bureaucracy and careerism checked, and the efficiency and self-reliance of the proletariat developed. During the first few months of 1922 he was bombarding the communist leaders with advice on improvement of the state machine, advice which was consistently disregarded by his successors. On 21 February he wrote to Tsyurupa, the Commissar for Supply:

> There is still, I think a fundamental disagreement between us. The main thing in my view, is to transfer the centre of gravity from the writing of decrees and orders (and we are guilty of stupidity in this matter to the point of idiocy) to the selection of men and to the checking of the carrying out of orders. . . . All of us have been drowned in a putrid bureaucratic swamp of 'departments'.[68]

Lenin also had misgivings about the increasing influence of the Workers' and Peasants' Inspection (*Rabkrin*), though they did not go so far on this subject as Trotsky's.[69] *Rabkrin* was a vast, bureaucratic engine for control over the administration of economic life, which Stalin had headed since 1919. A

[68] *Lenin*, Vol. XXVII, p. 163.
[69] For Lenin's plan for, and difference of view with Trotsky over, *Rabkrin* see *Lenin*, Vol. XXVIII, pp. 285–9, and 542–3, where Trotsky's private letter on the subject is quoted.

letter from Lenin to Stalin of 29 September 1921, at a time when Stalin was still head of this institution, perhaps illustrates more than anything the contrast between the two men. 'The task of *Rabkrin*', wrote Lenin 'is not only, indeed not as much as at present, to "catch" and "expose" people . . . as *to know how to improve them.*'[70] 'Catching' and 'exposing' were however fast becoming the keynote of Soviet government, and proving an effective alternative to 'improvement'. But it was over the vital question of the social composition of the party that the decline of Lenin's influence was most evident by the time of the Eleventh Party Congress. In the second half of 1921 an extensive purge of the party had been carried out. More than a fifth were expelled, two and a half per cent left voluntarily. Nearly half of the members expelled were said to have been peasants.[71] In spite of this drastic measure the party did not become more proletarian in character, and the percentage of actual workers in the party remained very low. Very many of the best worker Communists continued to leave in disillusionment. Lenin, still unable or unwilling to admit that it was in the nature of the machine he had created to attract the worst and repel the best, was early in 1922 seriously concerned at the decline in the proletarian element in the party. The New Economic Policy made it more likely that the party would now be assailed by applicants from among the wealthier peasants anxious to secure the privileges which party membership offered. In a series of letters to the Central Committee early in 1922 Lenin severely criticized Zinoviev's proposal that new members should be accepted into the party after only six months' probation for workers, and twelve months' probation for others. Lenin's view was that the probation periods should be six months for those workers who had had ten years' actual experience in heavy industry, and eighteen months for other workers. For peasants, and for Red Armymen he proposed a probation period of two years, and for all others of three years. The Central Committee refused to accept this suggestion, but finally agreed to increase the probation period in the case of peasants to eighteen months.[72]

[70] *Lenin*, Vol. XXVII, p. 14.
[71] Details given at the Eleventh Congress by Shkiryatov, of the Central Control Commission, *Protokoly XI*, pp. 392–400.
[72] See *Lenin*, Vol. XXVII, pp. 209–12, and 528–9.

At the Eleventh Party Congress it became evident that the views of the new party rulers, Stalin and Zinoviev, did not coincide with Lenin's.   Lenin himself was not present when this question was debated and the resolution on the admission of new members to the party adopted.   Zinoviev's speech on the question of party composition mainly stressed the importance of increasing the representation of the peasantry in the party.   No reference was made by anyone in the course of debate to Lenin's strong views on this question.   The agreement which the Central Committee had reached with Lenin was disregarded.   The probation period for peasants was now fixed at only twelve months, while the period for 'workers and Red Armymen of worker and peasant origin' was fixed at six months.[73]   The new leaders were apparently determined to facilitate the influx of peasants into the party and did not share Lenin's views on the need to increase its proletarian composition.   Such disregard of Lenin's view on so vital a question of policy would have been unthinkable while Lenin was still at work.   There are also some pointers which suggest that in 1922 the method of compulsion and dictatorship, of 'catching' and 'exposing', was in Lenin's view going too far. A comparison, for example, of Lenin's draft resolution on trade unions prepared by him for the Eleventh Congress, with the resolution which was adopted at the congress in Lenin's absence discloses a vital addition: 'The immediate practical task of the *guberniya* committees and of the central committee of the party is the renovation of the composition of the governing organs of the trade unions at the centre and in the *gubernii*.'[74]   There was, of course, nothing inconsistent in this proposal with Lenin's policy in the past year.   'Renovation' of trade union organs had taken place often enough in 1921, and there is nothing to suggest that it took place without his approval.   Still, the omission from his draft of all reference to this policy in 1922 and its addition at the congress by the men who were beginning to replace him, Zinoviev and Stalin, raises the question whether at this date Lenin may have begun already to fear that the policy which he had laboured for the

[73] *VKP(b) v rez.*, p. 513.   These periods were reaffirmed in August 1922—*ibid.*, p. 542.
[74] *ibid.*, p. 502.   For Lenin's draft, see *Lenin*, Vol. XXVII, pp. 147–56.   See also *ibid.*, p. 515.

past year to put into effect was leading to results which he had not anticipated. Certainly, as his 'Testament' showed, by the end of 1922 he had decided that Stalin was too 'crude' to occupy the post of Secretary, and should be replaced. It is no more than a speculation, but if in 1922 Lenin was beginning to have misgivings, it was already too late. He had conjured up a monster which he no longer had the strength to control.

PART IV

CONCLUSIONS

CHAPTER XVIII

LENINISM TRIUMPHANT

Lenin had first formulated his doctrine on the organization of the social democratic party in 1902. This is what he wrote in September of that year to a party worker in a letter which was reproduced and widely circulated:

> While in the matter of ideology and of practical *control* of the movement and of the revolutionary struggle we need the *maximum possible centralization* for the proletariat, so far as concerns *information* on the movement the centre needs the *maximum possible decentralization*. . . . We must centralize control over the movement. We must likewise . . . *decentralize* as much as possible the *responsibility before the party* of each individual member. ., . . We must particularly bear in mind . . . the *centre will be powerless* if we do not at the same time put into effect the *maximum decentralization* both as regards responsibility to the centre, and as regards information at the centre on all the wheels and little cogs of the party machine. . . . In order that the centre should be able not only to advise, to persuade, and to argue (as we have been doing up till now) but really to direct the orchestra, it is essential for it to know in detail who plays what fiddle and where, what instrument he has studied and is studying, and where, who is playing out of tune, and where, and why (when the music begins to grate on the ear), and who should be transferred, and how and whither he should be transferred in order to get rid of the discord, and so forth.[1]

This plan, though designed for the purposes of revolution, was not substantially altered after the revolution had been accomplished. It was not, however, until 1921, with the

[1] *Lenin*, Vol. V, pp. 179–92. cf. his 'Chto delat?,' *Lenin*, Vol. IV, pp. 359–508. The first edition of this work carried as its epigraph a quotation from Lassalle: 'The party strengthens itself by purging itself.'

development of the party Secretariat and Orgbureau, that it began to be put into practice. Nor was it until 1921 that Lenin was able to achieve the other fundamental principle of his scheme of party organization, the monopoly of control over proletariat and peasantry. The latter was only accomplished with the elimination from the political scene of socialist opponents, and especially of the Mensheviks, whose influence in the trade unions presented the most serious competition to the Communists.

Before the revolution the conflict between the two wings of Russian social democracy had centred much more on questions of organization and method than on questions of theory. With the coming of the February Revolution, Bolsheviks and Mensheviks alike did not scruple to jettison theoretical principles to which each had previously adhered. The same process can be observed after the October Revolution, during the years of the civil war. Once again, it was much less dispute over the theory of marxism which divided Bolsheviks and Mensheviks than questions of organization and method. The Mensheviks, in particular, had in practice abandoned, within a year of the revolution, the most cherished tenet of orthodox Russian marxists, that a socialist revolution should only take place after a long period of 'bourgeois' democracy, by conceding the 'historical necessity' of the October Revolution. In introducing his New Economic Policy Lenin did little more than take over and put into practice a doctrine evolved by the Mensheviks—after first removing the Mensheviks from the political scene. Even in the case of relations between the Bolsheviks and the Socialist Revolutionaries, it was to some extent true that what divided the two parties was more often disagreement over methods of government than widely divergent theoretical beliefs. The left wing of the Socialist Revolutionaries immediately accepted the Bolshevik revolution, and only broke with the Bolsheviks on the question of the tactics to be adopted in preserving the revolutionary government in power. But even the rest of the party, who at first repudiated the Bolshevik revolution, accepted it in the end when they found that their struggle against the revolutionary government was helping a counter-revolutionary government to power. The capitulation of many of their number to the Communists, and the hesitations of those who did not capitulate, proved this beyond doubt. Lenin had in turn accepted, at any rate temporarily, the socialist revolutionary theory of land distribution to the peasantry, and had abandoned the bolshevik programme of immediate nationalization. Once again, as before the revolution, the main source of conflict between Lenin and Russian socialism proved to be questions of organization and method—such as the *Vecheka*, the uncontrolled bureaucracy, or the subordination of the trade unions to centralized party control. Above all, the great majority of socialists were not prepared to tolerate the suppression of democratic liberties. The victory of the Bolsheviks over the socialists can of course in large measure be explained by the constant use of force. But there were other causes at work which were also of importance in helping to assure this victory.

The first reason was the war with Germany. The efforts of the Second International had not yet by the summer of 1914 produced unity in the ranks of the great majority of Russian social democrats who rejected Lenin's authoritarian tactics. But on the eve of the war it seemed as if Lenin's tactics were at last going to bring about in Russian social democracy the cohesion which it had hitherto lacked. The war put an end to this movement, which, had it succeeded, might well have left Lenin and his followers by the wayside as an offshoot of the main trend of Russian politics, of little more historical importance than Tkachev before him. For the division caused by the war brought the internationalist wings of both Mensheviks and Socialist Revolutionaries much nearer to Lenin's group of extremists in the Second International than to their own 'defensist' colleagues, who appeared to them to be betrayers of socialist principles. In Russia, during the critical and chaotic months between March and November 1917, large sections of both the Socialist Revolutionaries and of the Mensheviks, namely, the Left Socialist Revolutionaries and Martov's Internationalists, occupied positions much closer to the Bolsheviks than to the 'defensists' in their respective parties. When they realized that Lenin's policy had led not to the promised revolutionary war, but to Brest-Litovsk, they broke with the Bolsheviks, but it was by then too late. Moreover, even among the 'defensist' socialists, if one excepts a few realists like Plekhanov, or romantic patriots like Savinkov, there were many whose outward support of national defence was nevertheless qualified by demands for such action as made effective defence impossible. Their attitude only served to strengthen the hands of the Bolsheviks.

Equally important for the victory of bolshevism was the advantage which the Bolsheviks derived from the moral scruples of their socialist opponents. It is now a commonplace to argue that the Provisional Government, headed by the socialist Kerensky, could easily have prevented the bolshevik revolution by taking effective and timely action against a mere handful of men and their skeleton organization. But, to argue thus is to look at the Bolsheviks through the eyes of 1921, or 1951, and not of 1917. In August or September 1917 the Provisional Government, largely composed of socialists and headed by a socialist prime minister, was understandably reluctant to use the methods of the overthrown autocracy against ostensibly socialist opponents, however extremist their views or actions. When it was goaded into taking some steps against the Bolsheviks after the abortive rising of July 1917, its measures were half-hearted and quite ineffective. It was not for nothing that the bolshevik leaders subsequently maintained that their coup d'état in November 1917 had proved easy beyond expectation.

The hesitation of their political opponents to take up arms against the Bolsheviks played as great a part in their retention of power after 1917. The Mensheviks rejected armed opposition from the first, though a minority of the party was for a short time in favour of it, and a few individuals broke with their party and joined one or other of the anti-bolshevik forces or conspiracies. As regards the party as a whole, such a course was foreign to their tradition, their temperament, and be it said their capabilities. The case of the Socialist Revolutionaries was different. They were neither a marxist not a proletarian party and the peasants whom they represented had given them an ostensible mandate in the elections to the Constituent Assembly against the bolshevik usurpation of power. Unlike the Mensheviks, many of their number were in November 1917 anxious to fight to victory against Germany and the Central Powers, and the bolshevik surrender outraged their patriotic sentiments. Even the internationalist Left Socialist Revolutionaries were not devoid of such sentiment. Their indignation at the treaty of Brest-Litovsk, though primarily due to what they regarded as the betrayal of the cause of world revolution, was not untinged with the romantic notions harboured by their intelligentsia of the enraged Slav masses rising against the invading West. Moreover, violence had always been an influential factor in socialist revolutionary tradition. Yet, the story of the Socialist Revolutionaries' struggle against the Bolsheviks is one of indecision, hesitation, disunity, and divided loyalty. The refusal of the Central Committee of the main party to take up arms in defence of the Constituent Assembly, at a time when there were still armed forces available to support the attempt, lost them an opportunity which never recurred, and dealt a great blow to their prestige. The treaty of Brest-Litovsk goaded them at last into co-operation with the forces of the Western Allies and into an armed struggle against the Bolsheviks. But the weak governments which the Socialist Revolutionaries set up fell, and were replaced by military dictatorships. By November 1918 the ill-assorted partnership of inexperienced and doctrinaire socialists on the one hand, and politically illiterate and reactionary army officers on the other, had come to an end. The Socialist Revolutionaries' insistence on the adoption of a full socialist policy in the midst of a civil war had contributed not a little to the debâcle. Moreover, in November 1918 the defeat of Germany removed the circumstance which in the eyes of many Socialist Revolutionaries had alone justified armed struggle against the Bolsheviks. The fight against Lenin's government could now no longer be viewed as a means of restoring the Eastern front against Germany, but became open civil war. A number of the party capitulated to the Bolsheviks, preferring political extinction to a struggle which, though it might defeat the Bolsheviks, would do so at the cost of putting reactionary monarchists into power. Within Russia the remnants of the party organization renounced recourse to arms for the duration of the civil war. From the end of 1918

onwards the armed activity against the Communists by Socialist
Revolutionaries inside Russia was limited to the participation
of individuals in the fighting in the civil war and in a few
conspiratorial organizations, while abroad groups of émigrés
endeavoured to enlist the support of the Western Allies for
more effective intervention. The party organization waited
to lead a popular rising on a national scale, which never came.
Thus, of the opponents of the Bolsheviks during the years of
the civil war, those who had moral authority to justify their
resistance, the socialists, hesitated to use the method of the
coup d'état. The reactionary White Armies, which remained
in the field against the Bolsheviks, had no such scruples. But
they, in turn, lacked the moral authority which could have won
them popular support, and might have ensured their success.

These were the negative reasons for the Bolsheviks' success.
There were positive reasons as well. In contrast to their
socialist opponents, the Bolsheviks were resolute, and bold in
decision. Under Lenin's leadership, and because of it, they
were not afraid to jettison their doctrine where the all-important question of power was involved—not afraid, in fact,
of that 'opportunism' for which Lenin so frequently reviled his
socialist opponents. Besides this, the personality of Lenin,
his political skill as well as his clarity of thought and incisiveness
in the analysis of a situation, were without rival anywhere on
the Russian political scene. Among social democrats, certainly Plekhanov, perhaps Martov, were his equals as theorists.
Neither of them even approximated to Lenin as a political
leader. Among the Socialist Revolutionaries there is no single
name that even invites comparison with Lenin, whether as a
theorist or as a political leader. But perhaps Lenin's greatest
achievement for bolshevism was his success in harnessing to
marxism the smouldering passions of the Russian people,
which centuries of autocracy had engendered. It is true that
in the last few years before the war it was marxism in its
moderate, Western form of trade unionism and parliamentary
democracy that seemed at long last to be taking some root in
Russia. But this was only the beginning of a new process in a
country in which habits of constitutionalism and legality still
remained to be formed. The more traditional instinctive form
of Russian socialism was not menshevik marxism, but the

Narodnik mystique of the Socialist Revolutionaries, with its belief that it was Russia's destiny to follow a path quite distinct from that of capitalist Europe, and its faith in the natural socialism of the Russian peasant; and with its sense of the dark forces of anarchy which could so easily be conjured up.

> In Russia [wrote Bakunin] the robber is the only true revolutionary. . . . The robbers in the woods, in the cities and in the villages, robbers all over Russia, and robbers imprisoned in the innumerable jails throughout the country make up one, indivisible, closely linked world,—the world of the Russian revolution. . . . He who wishes to plot revolution in earnest in Russia, he who desires a popular revolution, must enter this world.

There was not a Russian socialist, Bolshevik, Menshevik, or *Narodnik*, who did know the significance of this world. But whereas all Mensheviks and the majority of Socialist Revolutionaries recoiled from it in horror, hoping to exorcise it in the end from Russian society, Lenin was not afraid of alliance with it.

The victory of the Bolsheviks in November 1917 did not, however, mean the victory of a united party. The struggles which reached their culmination at the Tenth Party Congress in March 1921 need have caused no surprise. Lenin's rapid and sudden switches of doctrine in response to the exigencies of policy placed considerable strain on the loyalty of his bewildered followers. One need only recall as instances the sudden abandonment in April 1917 of the two orthodox phases of revolution; the repeated promise of revolutionary war jettisoned in favour of an immediate peace on any terms in March 1918; the rapid ending of workers' control; and the sudden and unheralded switch from war communism to the New Economic Policy. To anyone who based his conduct on a political theory it was no easy matter to follow Lenin through the many mutations of his policy. Yet for all this, it was not solely or primarily from the failure of Lenin's followers to realize as rapidly as Lenin the practical reasons for his switches of theory, that the most serious opposition arose inside the Russian communist party.

There was nothing peculiar to Russia in the fact that a

revolutionary theory should have undergone a change when once the attempt had been made to put it into practice. Nor is the difference between political programmes before and after the coming into office of the party which sponsors them confined to revolutionary parties. Lenin's departures from his promises, or from marxist doctrine, could not by themselves have engendered the feverish excitement which characterized the Russian communist party during 1921. Indeed, some of the most fundamental departures both from orthodox theory and from party promises took place without arousing any serious opposition within the communist party at all. Perhaps this ready acceptance by the Russian Communists of the need to subordinate theory to keeping in power is best illustrated by their attitude to that all important question, the state in a socialist society. It will be recalled that the Russian social democrats, alone of all European marxists, had accepted as an item of their programme the 'dictatorship of the proletariat'. Marx had used this phrase almost casually, on isolated occasions, to designate the temporary form which the struggle of the proletariat with its opponents would take immediately after its seizure of power. He had never defined or elaborated the shape which he thought a revolutionary government would assume in practice. But, since in Marx's conception the proletarian revolution was to take place at a moment when the vast exploited majority finally rose against a small minority of exploiters, it was plain that this dictatorship would be temporary and short-lived. Moreover, since the seizure of power by the proletariat would inaugurate the advent of the classless society, and since the state existed only as a device for preventing class conflict from erupting into violence, it followed, in marxist analysis, that the state must begin to wither away progressively from the moment that the proletariat had seized and consolidated its power. On the very eve of the bolshevik revolution Lenin still fully accepted this analysis. In his *State and Revolution*, written in August and September 1917 while he was in hiding—a work written with care and much thought, and a statement of principles to which he attached the utmost importance—Lenin fully accepted the classical marxist analysis. 'The proletarian state', he wrote, 'will begin to wither away immediately after its victory, since in a society without class contradictions, the state is unnecessary and impossible.' True, it would not, as the anarchists demanded, simply be abolished overnight. But neither, according to Lenin, would it resemble, while it lasted, the state which it had overthrown, with its police and other machinery of repression. Supported as it would be by the overwhelming mass of the population, it would enforce its will 'almost without any special machinery'.[2] These words, it should be emphasized, were not part of the demagogy with which the Bolsheviks captured the support of the masses between March and November 1917, since *State and Revolution* was not published until the spring of 1918. By the time Lenin's words were published, the *Vecheka* had been active for several months, and not even the most sanguine marxist could have discerned any signs of the state beginning to wither away. When the question of 'withering away' came up in March 1918, at the Seventh Party Congress, Lenin now impatiently brushed it aside. 'One may well wonder when the state will begin to wither away. . . . To proclaim this withering away in advance is to violate historical perspective.' It was Bukharin, the Left Communist, who had raised the question. Many years passed before the question was raised again. The Left Communists, the Democratic Centralists, the Workers' Opposition,—all accepted the need for the terror, the *Vecheka*, the unbridled powers of the executive. The reason was not, perhaps, far to seek. The Bolsheviks, so far from winning over the great majority of the country after they had seized power, as doctrine demanded, remained a small, unpopular minority, ruling by force. Their survival in sole power depended upon the state and the apparatus which they had created, and few Communists were prepared to question the necessity for this survival.

Thus, so far as one of the most fundamental departures from marxist theory was concerned, the realities of power operated to dictate its acceptance, and without much discussion at that. The same proved to be the case with some other crucial questions of marxist theory which did cause some division within the communist party during the civil war. The Left Communists were opposed to Lenin not only on the

<hr>

[2] *Lenin*, Vol. XXI, pp. 388, 431-2.

question of peace, but also on fundamental questions of economics and politics. But, when once Lenin's peace policy appeared to be justified in practice, their opposition on questions of theory faded away. The Democratic Centralists, who opposed a fairly reasoned alternative to Lenin's doctrine of party organization, capitulated at the Tenth Party Congress in March 1921 without firing a shot. Yet both these groups included some of the best intellectuals in the party. The main struggles on questions of theory—on the New Economic Policy, on socialism in one country, on the nature and meaning of the October Revolution, on the withering away of the state, on dialectical materialism—all lay ahead. But by the time these debates began to develop, in 1923 and in the succeeding years, questions of theory had largely become a screen or an instrument for a struggle to capture, or resist, the party apparatus among the men who had in 1921 helped to create it.

Indeed, so little did questions of doctrine animate the Russian Communists for some time after the October Revolution, that the biggest departure from marxism of all passed unnoticed. The main opposition within the communist party, the Workers' Opposition and the general discontent loosely linked with it, only came to a head at the end of 1920, with the virtual end of the civil war. This was not surprising. Until then the Soviet régime had been engaged in a life and death struggle for survival, of which the issue was at no time certain. The common danger created unity, and discontent with such matters as over-centralization, or interference in trade union affairs was assuaged by the faith that these were temporary, if necessary evils, which would be put right when the danger had been averted. The failure to analyse the theoretical implications of policy was understandable during the civil war, while the existence of the new state was in danger. But the blindness to questions of theory continued after the civil war, when the Soviet state was no longer in peril from outside attack, but the communist monopoly of power was threatened from the inside. When in March 1921 the foundation of the future state structure was laid, it became apparent that no one within the communist party had grasped the theoretical issues which were at stake, perhaps not even Lenin. For what now took place was no less than a reversal in practice of the very basis of marxist teaching, that the political machine is the mere reflection or superstructure of the economic structure. Henceforward, political power was to control the economic form of society.

The coup d'état of November 1917 had been accepted as a proletarian revolution, cutting short the democratic phase— that is, accepted as such by the Communists; the Mensheviks, who continued to believe that the October Revolution, in spite of appearances, remained in essence a bourgeois, democratic revolution, nonetheless accepted its 'historical necessity'. The first impact of Lenin's unorthodox decision to seize power had thrown his followers into confusion. But the confusion did not last long. The unexpected failure of their opponents to rally and overthrow the new communist government was probably as powerful an advocate for the correctness of Lenin's decision as any theoretical doctrine. So long as war communism remained the official policy, the virtual one party state which existed in the country after the peace of Brest-Litovsk might have appeared to many to be justified as the correct political super-structure for the putting into effect of extreme socialist policies. But by the spring of 1921 war communism had failed. It was now to be replaced by an economic system in which there would be room for private capitalist enterprise and interests. Marxist logic therefore demanded that the political machine corresponding to such an economic system should be composed of parties representing the interests of the various classes which were now to be tolerated, in a state which was no longer regarded even in theory as a one class state. Lenin himself had conceded this theoretical necessity in 1905, when he had argued that so long as the revolution had not emerged from the democratic, and therefore multi-class stage, government should take the form of a coalition dictatorship of the peasantry and the proletariat. Yet, in 1921 no serious opinion within the communist party was prepared to challenge the monopoly of all political power by their own proletarian party, though many Communists were ready to criticize the abuses which proceeded from the monopoly. In this respect the simple mutineers at Kronstadt, who at all events demanded political freedom for all workers' and peasants' parties, may be said to have proved themselves better marxists than the Communists.

The question can be looked at from another aspect in which marxist theory plays no part. The Bolsheviks had never proclaimed the one party state as their avowed policy before the revolution. The seizure of power had been ostensibly accomplished in the name of the soviets in which several parties were represented. When Lenin's decision to govern alone became apparent immediately after the October Revolution it even provoked a short-lived crisis inside the bolshevik ranks. For some years to come the fiction that the Communists were but one party among many was maintained. The suppression of the socialists was, with the exception of the short period between June and November 1918, invariably bolstered by charges such as 'counter-revolution', or speculation: it was not action openly taken against political opponents. The communist policy of defaming the political integrity of all socialists dates from this time. Up to 1921 it was not difficult for the Communists to justify to themselves their decision to take, and keep, power alone. The socialists had after all failed to achieve between March and November 1917 a solid and efficient government, and had then repudiated the Bolsheviks, who were at any rate prepared to take the responsibility for decisive action. The peace with Germany had been bitterly opposed by Mensheviks and Socialist Revolutionaries alike. Was it not logical that the Communists should take upon themselves the burden of government alone? The Socialist Revolutionaries had for a time even sided with the anti-bolshevik forces in the civil war. But all these factors had ceased to exist in 1921. The socialist parties inside Russia, or those of them who still had an opportunity of voicing their views, were vying with one another in their loyalty to the ideals of the revolution as such, while condemning the excesses of the Communists. There was not the remotest threat of any right wing or counter-revolutionary restoration. Long after 1921, though deprived of all political power and though many of their number were in prison or exiled, the intelligentsia and the middle-class continued to serve the Soviet state. The emigré socialists and *Kadety* even developed a whole philosophy of collaboration with the Communists in order to build up Russia, and many of them returned to implement what they considered to be their duty. There was opposition inside Russia, to be sure.

But as the programme of the Kronstadt insurgents, which was typical of this opposition, shows, it was opposition not to Soviet government but to the Communists' monopoly of power, and to their party's illegal methods of preserving it. Those, and there are many,[3] who justify the Communists' elimination of their socialist opponents in 1921 by the necessity of safeguarding the 'revolution' from its enemies ignore two essential facts: first, that enmity against the Communists was not enmity against the revolution, i.e, the Soviet form of government, but against the methods of communist rule in the name of that revolution. It was therefore not only an enmity of the Communists' own creation, but one which it was in their power to remove without danger to the revolution, though with undoubted risk to their own monopoly of power. To be sure, Lenin and the Communists identified 'the revolution' with themselves. But it was an identification made by them alone, which did not correspond to facts. Secondly, that a large number, perhaps even the majority, of the conscious proletariat, were in early 1921 menshevik or menshevik sympathizers. The revolutionary nature of this party's policy, which accorded political freedom to workers and peasants alone, and advocated large scale nationalization of industry and state control of foreign trade, cannot be conjured away, as is normally done by apologists of Lenin's policy, by describing it as 'bourgeois'. The socialists were not eliminated in 1921 because they were counter-revolutionary. They were described as counter-revolutionary in order to justify their elimination.

The fate of the socialists was sealed when it became apparent that in their criticism of communist methods they were

[3] See e.g. *Deutscher*, p. 226, 'It was true enough that concern for the revolution compelled Bolshevism to take the road chosen by the tenth congress . . '; *Carr*, *I*, p. 183. The latter concludes that the demise of the legal opposition 'cannot fairly be laid at the door of one party. If it was true that the Bolshevik régime was not prepared after the first few months to tolerate an organized opposition, it was equally true that no opposition party was prepared to remain within legal limits. The premise of dictatorship was common to both sides of the argument.' This judgment ignores not only the Mensheviks, but most of the Socialist Revolutionaries as well. The premise of dictatorship was certainly common to both sides in Lenin's 'argument' with Denikin. But what relation to fact does such an assertion bear in the case of Martov and the Mensheviks, whose policy was founded upon the need to 'remain within legal limits'? Or in the case of the Samara Socialist Revolutionaries, who gave up the fight for fear it might assist the victory of a right wing dictatorship? The charge that the Mensheviks were not prepared to remain within legal limits is part of the Bolsheviks' case; it does not survive an examination of the facts.

speaking much the same language as the many malcontents inside the communist party. The realization of the extent of the support which the Kronstadt mutineers could muster, even inside the communist party within the naval garrison, had come as a grave shock. But different considerations applied to the Workers' Opposition. There was no vestige in their programme of any quarrel with the communist leaders for their treatment of socialist opponents, or of the peasantry. It was a mixture of the early syndicalism which the Communists had abandoned, utopianism, and nostalgia for the lost enthusiasm of the first months. They combined with it some well-founded criticism of the abuses of bureaucracy and of excessive party discipline and control. The communist leaders may have been right in seeing in the existence of this critical group a potential party split. The moral case for the Workers' Opposition was perhaps not very strong. They demanded freedom for themselves, but had no thought of conceding it to others. When they complained of control by the centre over the communist committees in the trade-unions, they did not pause to think that those same communist committees for which they demanded more freedom of action did not hesitate to impose their will on a trade union membership, some fourteen times their number, which was bitterly opposed to them. They accepted the state of affairs in which a party of a few hundred thousand could impose its will by force on millions of workers who did not support them. But they did not realize that if a minority party is to survive in sole power against the will of the great majority, it can only do so if it maintains the strictest discipline and control by its leaders over its own members. Once again the Kronstadt mutineers proved themselves more mature politicians than the Workers' Opposition.

But if the communist leaders were right in sensing in the Workers' Opposition a danger of a party split, they were wrong in attempting to identify the views of this opposition with menshevism. It is true that one of the fundamental differences between bolshevism and menshevism, which had even preceded the formal split in 1903, had been disagreement on the value of the spontaneous effort of the masses. The Mensheviks, following Plekhanov, and Lavrov before him, believed that the revolution must be the work of the masses themselves. Lenin had replaced this view by the doctrine that, left to themselves, the masses will be content with palliative reforms, and must therefore be led on to revolution by a party of professional revolutionaries. This difference of view was reflected in the rival formulas put forward for incorporation in the party statute by Lenin and Martov at the Second Congress in 1903 —Lenin's, confining membership to those who 'personally participate in one of the party organizations', i.e. put themselves under party discipline; and Martov's, extending it much more widely to all who 'co-operate' with the party 'under the direction of one of its organizations'. The Mensheviks were concerned with the relations between the social democratic party and the proletariat as a whole, or, in other words, with the nature of and, more important, the degree of leadership which the party of the proletariat should exercise over that proletariat. It was in this context that, in opposition to Lenin, they claimed that a greater degree of initiative should be left to the workers themselves as distinct from the party which claimed to speak in their name. But the Workers' Opposition were concerned with an entirely different question, the relation of the party at a low level to the party at a higher level. They were not concerned with the workers outside that party, who formed the majority. It is true that in their demands for less restriction on the freedom of local party and trade union committees, for example, the Workers' Opposition may have appeared at times to be speaking the same language as the Mensheviks. But the Mensheviks wanted free elections in the trade unions, which would have put socialist, but not communist majorities into power. The Workers' Opposition did not seek to alter the rigged elections which ensured communist majorities, but merely sought to safeguard the local trade union committee or cell from being replaced by central nominees. It was also true that Mensheviks and Workers' Opposition shared in common a somewhat romantic faith in the superiority of the proletariat actually engaged in manual labour over the professional party bureaucrat, or the intellectual. But in basic political aims the two were poles apart.

The balance sheet of political support was not an encouraging one for the communist party in March 1921. Among the peasantry it had lost most, if not all, the support or at least neutrality which had once played an important part in achieving victory both in November 1917 and in the civil war. Even among the proletariat dislike of the Communists had grown. With it grew the popularity of the socialist parties, notably of the Mensheviks. No communist leader could have had any doubt, and some, such as Zinoviev, openly admitted, that in any free election to any soviet, or trade union committee, in March 1921 the number of communist candidates elected would have been small. It was true that much of this unpopularity was due to privations brought about by the civil war. But it was also true that much of it was due to the revolt of the Russian people against the unfairness, the violence, and the illegality with which the Communists suppressed all who did not accept their rule without question. The Kronstadt revolt proved this beyond any doubt. In these circumstances there were only two policies open to Lenin. Either to resign himself to his failure to win over the majority, to moderate the policy by which his monopoly of power had been secured and to accept the consequent loss of that monopoly. Or, to preserve his monopoly of political power at all costs, and at the same time make the task of preserving it easier by removing, at the price of sacrificing communist doctrine, some of the economic causes of discontent. He chose the second course. But it was plain that this policy could only be successfully achieved by a disciplined party, united, if necessary by force, for the difficult task which now confronted it. There could be no room for party democracy. The trade union discussion, which had revealed the personal rivalries dividing the party as well as the wide divergence of view on fundamental questions of policy, had proved that. The views of the Democratic Centralists, of Preobrazhensky or Krestinsky, of Shlyapnikov or Kollontay, suffered from the contradiction that they stood for two incompatible aims: *both* a democratic communist party, *and* the exclusion of all other parties from power. It was this circumstance more than any other which determined their quick collapse at the Tenth Party Congress.

Lenin easily steered his policy to victory at this congress. He was still the outstanding figure in the party, much as he had been in 1917. There was no rival leader within sight who could have succeeded in rallying the discontented inside the party around himself and in raising a revolt against Lenin, even if there had been anyone, which there was not, who had the courage to assume such a rôle. The only possible candidate would have been Trotsky. But Trotsky was much too close in outlook to Lenin on the vital question of communist monopoly of power to have thought of such a course. Moreover, his personal popularity was already seriously impaired in 1921 by policies associated with his name. Nor is there the slightest reason to suppose that he ever contemplated such a move for a moment. The Workers' Opposition lacked any leaders of note, the intellectual Democratic Centralists had no thought of struggle, and certainly no stomach for it. It was therefore easy for Lenin to carry the leaders of his party with him, in spite of the misgivings which some of them uttered, and perhaps many more felt. It is plain that in 1921, as in 1917, many followed Lenin without completely realizing where he was leading them. The full significance of his policy then may have been no more apparent than had been the full significance of the seizure of power. In November 1917 a number of bolshevik leaders cavilled when they discovered that what they had believed to be seizure of power by the soviets was in reality seizure of power by the bolshevik party. In 1921 those who followed Lenin believed that what was being achieved was the consolidation of the power of the communist party. Many of them were to rebel once again, in 1923, when they discovered that what had really taken place was the consolidation in power of the central party apparatus. But it was then too late.

Thus once again, in 1921 as in 1917, the personal qualities and influence of Lenin proved the decisive factor. In 1917 the political immaturity and inexperience of the Russian parties had played into the hands of anyone both resolute enough to seize power, and untroubled by the doubts and hesitancies which beset the more scrupulous. After 1918 Lenin's democratic opponents had no armed forces at their disposal. Their sole hope of overthrowing the Communists might have been in alliance with the White Armies. The overwhelming majority of them had not been prepared to accept such an alliance for fear that the only outcome would be the downfall of the revolution, and the restoration of the monarchy. The population, distracted by hardships of every kind, was able to achieve no more than a peasant guerrilla war and the Kronstadt revolt. In 1921 the fate of the country lay in the hands of Lenin. He had a chance of burying past enmities and of carrying the vast majority of the country with him in an attempt to build up ruined Russia on the basis of co-operation and legal order, and not of the dictatorship of an unpopular minority. It is difficult to escape the conclusion that a greater man than Lenin would have seized this chance. But Lenin's genius lay in the technique of grasping and holding power. He was a great revolutionary, but not a statesman. His conviction that he and his followers alone held the secret of successful rule in their hands was, to a large extent, the product of the struggle by which he had achieved his position. But from his fateful decision in the spring of 1921 flowed all the consequences of the one party dictatorship which became apparent in the subsequent years of Soviet history.

Two main consequences derived from Lenin's political policy of 1921, both of enormous importance for the future history of Soviet Russia. The first was the emergence of what Engels has so well described as the 'conventional hypocrisy'. During the civil war there was at any rate some justification for the view that 'he who is not with us is against us'. In the heat of battle it was possible for the Communists to see in those socialists who were fighting against them enemies of the revolution, without seeming to do undue violence to truth. After 1921, the lumping together of Mensheviks, Workers' Opposition, serious theoretical critics, and malcontents inside the communist party as counter-revolutionaries was a falsification, and everyone knew it. The acceptance of this official lie by almost the entire leadership of the communist party inevitably led to the result that whoever among them was strong enough to exploit it in his own interest had the rest of them at his mercy. What is the difference between the attempt by Lenin to expel Shlyapnikov, in 1921, and the expulsion of Trotsky six years later, if both can be justified by the same argument—that the stability of the dictatorship is the supreme law? But this, in turn, leads to the second main consequence of Lenin's policy. For, who has the power to decide by what faction the stability of the régime is to be best served? Clearly, he who manipulates the apparatus of the party, and can thereby ensure both the necessary majorities at the centre and implicit obedience to central orders throughout the country. The malignant figure of the General Secretary, Stalin, has become only too familiar in its portrayal by disappointed oppositionists, defeated by the apparatus which he controlled. But it was Lenin, with their support, who equipped him with the weapons, and started him upon his path.

APPENDIX A

SOME USEFUL DATES

1917

15 March.	Abdication of Nicholas II.
	Provisional Government formed.
11–14 April.	Petrograd Bolshevik Party Conference.
15–16 April.	All-Russian Bolshevik Party Conference.
16 April.	Lenin arrives in Petrograd.
3–5 May.	Demonstrations in Petrograd against the Provisional Government.
7–12 May.	Seventh All-Russian Conference of the Russian Social-Democratic Labour Party (Bolsheviks).
17 May.	Trotsky arrives in Russia.
18 May.	First coalition government formed.
16 June.	Opening of First All-Russian Congress of Soviets.
16–18 July.	Attempted rising in Petrograd.
8–16 August.	Sixth Congress of the Russian Social Democratic Labour Party (Bolsheviks).
6 September.	General Kornilov starts movement of troops on Petrograd.
10 September.	Collapse of Kornilov's movement.
27 September–5 October.	Democratic Conference in Petrograd.
20 October.	Council of the Republic (Pre-Parliament) opens in Petrograd.
23 October.	Bolshevik Central Committee votes for armed insurrection.
7 November.	Provisional Government arrested. Second All-Russian Congress of Soviets opens in Petrograd.
19–28 November.	First Conference of the Left Socialist Revolutionaries.
25 November.	Elections to the Constituent Assembly.
3 December.	Preliminary armistice negotiations with the Central Powers.
15 December.	Armistice signed with Central Powers.
19 December.	*Vecheka* set up.

1918

7–14 January.	First All-Russian Congress of Trade Unions.
18 January.	Opening of Constituent Assembly.
19 January.	Closing of the Constituent Assembly.
23–31 January.	Third All-Russian Congress of Soviets.
3 February.	Special Bolshevik Party Conference.
10 February.	Negotiations broken off with Central Powers.
18 February.	German advance resumed.
23 February.	Bolshevik Central Committee votes acceptance of German proposed peace terms.
3 March.	Peace Treaty of Brest-Litovsk signed.

363

6–8 March.	Seventh Congress of the Russian Social Democratic Labour Party (Bolsheviks).
14–18 March.	Fourth All-Russian Congress of Soviets.
21–27 May.	All-Russian Menshevik Conference in Moscow.
25 May–4 June.	First Congress of Councils of National Economy.
26 May.	Eighth Conference of the Socialist Revolutionaries.
26 May.	Czechoslovaks seize a number of towns in Siberia. Start of Civil War.
8 June.	Samara captured by Czechs. Anti-bolshevik governments set up in Samara and in Omsk.
4–10 July.	Fifth All-Russian Congress of Soviets.
6 July.	Assassination of von Mirbach. Revolt of the Left Socialist Revolutionaries.
10 July.	Constitution of the R.S.F.S.R. adopted.
2 August.	Anti-bolshevik government set up in Archangel.
30 August.	Attempt on Lenin's life. Uritsky assassinated.
8–23 September.	Anti-bolshevik State Conference at Ufa. All-Russian Provisional Government formed.
6–9 November.	Sixth All-Russian Congress of Soviets.
18 November.	All-Russian Provisional Government overthrown. Admiral Kolchak becomes Supreme Ruler.
27 December–1 January 1919.	All-Russian Menshevik Conference in Moscow.

1919

16–25 January.	Second All-Russian Congress of Trade Unions.
2–7 March.	First Congress of the Third (Communist) International.
18–23 March.	Eighth Communist Party Congress.
18–20 June.	Ninth Socialist Revolutionary Conference in Moscow.
2–4 December.	Eighth All-Russian Conference of the Communist Party.
5–9 December.	Seventh All-Russian Congress of Soviets.

1920

29 March–4 April.	Ninth Communist Party Congress.
6–15 April.	Third All-Russian Congress of Trade Unions.
21 July–6 August.	Second Congress of the Third (Communist) International.
8 September.	Tenth Socialist Revolutionary Conference.
22–25 September.	Ninth All-Russian Communist Party Conference.
2–9 November.	All-Russian Trade Union Conference.
14 November.	Wrangel evacuates Crimea. Virtual end of Civil War.
7 December.	Split in Communist Central Committee on question of *Tsektran*.
9 December.	Water Transport representatives resign from *Tsektran*.
22–29 December.	Eighth All-Russian Congress of Soviets.
30 December.	Trade union discussion opens.

1921

12 January.	Communist Central Committee votes on the election of delegates to the Tenth Congress by 'Platforms'.
13 February.	Kropotkin's funeral.
1–17 March.	Kronstadt Revolt.
8–16 March.	Tenth Communist Party Congress.
16 March.	Central Executive Committee decrees replacement of requisitioning of food by a tax in kind (N.E.P.).
	Anglo-Soviet Trade Agreement signed.
17–25 May.	Fourth All-Russian Congress of Trade Unions.
26–28 May.	Tenth All-Russian Communist Party Conference.
22 June–12 July.	Third Congress of the Third (Communist) International.
19–22 December.	Eleventh All-Russian Communist Party Conference.

1922

27 March–2 April.	Eleventh Communist Party Congress.
4 April.	Stalin's election as General Secretary to the party announced in *Pravda*.
26 May.	Lenin's first stroke.
8 June.	Trial of Socialist Revolutionary leaders opens.

APPENDIX B

LIST OF THE MORE IMPORTANT LEFT COMMUNISTS IN 1918

Abramovich, R.*
Antonov, N. (Luikn)
Arkady, (Krumin)
Baryshnikov, V.
Bela-Kun, K.
Bobinsky, S. I.
Bogolepov, D.
Boky, G.
Bronsky, M.
Bubnov, A.
Bukharin, N. I.
Fenigshtein, Ya. (Doletsky)
Inessa (Armand)
Ivanov, Vladimir.
Kossior, S.
Kollontay, A.
Kritsman, L.
Kuybyshev, V.
Lensky, Yu.
Lomov, A. (Oppokov)
Lukina N. (Bukharina)
Min'kov, I.
Muralov, N.
Myasnikov, V. G.

Osinsky, V. (Obolensky)
Pokrovsky, M.
Preobrazhensky, E.
Pyatakov, G.
Radek, K.
Ravich, S.
Safarov, G.
Sapronov, T.
Saveliev, M. (I. Vetrov)
Shternberg, P.
Skvortsov-Stepanov, I. I.
Smirnov, V. M.
Sol'ts, A.
Sorin, Vl.
Spunde, A.
Stukov, In.
Unshlikht, I.
Uritsky, M.
Usievich, G.
Vardin-Mgeladze, I.
Vyborgskaya, A.
Vasiliev, M. (Saratov)
Yakovleva, V. N.
Yaroslavsky, Em.
Zul', B. G.

* Not the Menshevik leader of the same name.

APPENDIX C

MEMBERS OF CENTRAL ORGANS OF
THE RUSSIAN COMMUNIST PARTY 1917–22

CENTRAL COMMITTEE

(The order of names up to the Eighth Congress is in accordance with the number of votes cast for the candidates.)

Elected at the Seventh All-Russian Conference, 7–12 May 1917:

V. Lenin, G. Zinoviev, J. Stalin, L. Kamenev, P. Milyutin, V. Nogin, Ya. Sverdlov, I. Smilga, G. Fedorov.

Candidate members: I. Teodorovich, A. Bubnov, N. Glebov-Avilov, A. Pravdin.

Elected at the Sixth Congress, 8–16 August 1917:

V. Lenin, G. Zinoviev, L. Kamenev, L. Trotsky, V. Nogin, A. Kollontay, J. Stalin, Ya. Sverdlov, A. Rykov, N. Bukharin, A. Sergeev (Artem), M. Uritsky, V. Milyutin, Ya. Berzin, A. Bubnov, F. Dzerzhinsky, N. Krestinsky, M. Muranov, I. Smilga, G. Sokol'nikov, S. Shaumyan.

Candidate members: G. Lomov, A. Ioffe, E. Preobrazhensky, N. Skrypnik.

Elected at the Seventh Congress, 6–8 March 1918:

V. Lenin, L. Trotsky, Ya. Sverdlov, G. Zinoviev, N. Bukharin, G. Sokol'nikov, J. Stalin, N. Krestinsky, I. Smilga, E. Stasova, M. Lashevich, V. Schmidt, F. Dzerzhinsky, M. Vladimirsky, A. Sergeev (Artem).

Candidate members: A. Ioffe, A. Kiselev, Ya. Berzin, M. Uritsky, P. Stuchka, G. Petrovsky, G. Lomov, A. Shlyapnikov.

Elected at the Eighth Congress, 18–23 March 1918:

A. Beloborodov, N. Bukharin, F. Dzerzhinsky, G. Evdokimov, G. Zinoviev, M. Kalinin, L. Kamenev, N. Krestinsky, V. Lenin, M. Muranov, K. Radek, Ch. Rakovsky, L. Serebryakov, I. Smilga, J. Stalin, E. Stasova, P. Stuchka, M. Tomsky, L. Trotsky.

Candidate members: A. Sergeev (Artem), A. Bubnov, M. Vladimirsky, K. Danishevsky, A. Mitskevich, I. N. Smirnov, V. Schmidt, E. Yaroslavsky.

Elected at the Ninth Congress, 29 March—5 April, 1920:

A. Andreev, A. Sergeev (Artem), N. Bukharin, F. Dzerzhinsky, G. Zinoviev, M. Kalinin, L. Kamenev, N. Krestinsky, V. Lenin, E. Preobrazhensky, K. Radek, Ch. Rakovsky, Ya. Rudzutsk, A. Rykov, L. Serebryakov, I. Smirnov, J. Stalin, M. Tomsky, L. Trotsky.

Candidate members: G. Petrovsky, E. Yaroslavsky, M. Muranov, V. Milyutin, P. Stuchka, V. Nogin, S. Gusev, I. Pyatnitsky, A. Beloborodov, P. Zalutsky, V. Molotov, I. Smilga.

Elected at the Tenth Congress, 8–16 March 1921:

A. Sergeev (Artem), N. Bukharin, K. Voroshilov, F. Dzerzhinsky, G. Zinoviev, M. Kalinin, L. Kamenev, N. Komarov, I. Kutuzov, V. Lenin, V. M. Mikhaylov, V. Molotov, G. Ordzhonikidze, G. Petrovsky, K. Radek, Ch. Rakovsky, Ya. Rudzutak, A. Rykov, J. Stalin, M. Tomsky, L. Trotsky, I. Tuntul, M. Frunze, A. Shlyapnikov, E. Yaroslavsky.

Candidate members: V. Chubar', S. Kirov, V. Schmidt, I. Zelensky, N. Uglanov, G. Pyatakov, G. Safarov, P. Zalutsky, V. Milyutin, V. Kuybyshev, S. Gusev, V. Obolensky (Osinsky), I. Smirnov, A. Kiselev, D. Sulimov.

Elected at the Eleventh Congress, 27 March–2 April, 1922:

A. Andreev, N. Bukharin, K. Voroshilov, F. Dzerzhinsky, I. Zelensky, G. Zinoviev, M. Kalinin, L. Kamenev, I. Korotkov, V. Kuybyshev, V. Lenin, V. Molotov, G. Ordzhonikidze, G. Petrovsky, K. Radek, Ch. Rakovsky, Ya. Rudzutak, A. Rykov, T. Sapronov, A. Smirnov, G. Sokol'-nikov, J. Stalin, M. Tomsky, L. Trotsky, M. Frunze, V. Chubar', E. Yaroslavsky.

Candidate members: A. Bubnov, A. Badaev, S. Gusev, S. Kirov, N. Komarov, A. Kiselev, T. Krivoy, N. Lebedev, I. Pepse, S. Lobov, D. Manuilsky, V. Mikhaylov, A. Mikoyan, A. Rakhimbaev, G. Pyatakov, G. Safarov, I. Smilga, D. Sulimov, V. Schmidt.

SECRETARIAT

1919: Krestinsky.
1920: Krestinsky, Preobrazhensky, Serebryakov.
1921: Molotov, Yaroslavsky, Mikhaylov.
1922: Stalin, Molotov, Kuybyshev.

ORGANIZATION BUREAU

1919: Stalin, Krestinsky, Serebryakov, Beloborodov, Stasova.
1920: Stalin, Rykov, Krestinsky, Serebryakov, Preobrazhensky.
   Candidates: Dzerzhinsky, Tomsky.
1921: Molotov, Yaroslavsky, Mikhaylov, Komarov, Stalin, Rykov, Tomsky.
   Candidates: Dzerzhinsky, Rudzutak, Kalinin.

POLITICAL BUREAU

1919: Lenin, Stalin, Trotsky, Kamenev, Bukharin.
1921: Lenin, Stalin, Trotsky, Kamenev, Zinoviev.

Of this total of 82:—

3 are still active in politics.

4 are believed to be retired, but not disgraced.

14 died a natural death, so far as is known.

14 were sentenced to death, or to long terms of imprisonment, and have not been heard of since. (Among them one executed by anti-bolsheviks during the civil war).

3 committed suicide.

3 were assassinated (of them one by anti-bolsheviks).

The remainder, forming exactly half of the total, have not been heard of for many years and when last heard of were engaged in, or suspected of being engaged in, oppositionist activity. They must be presumed dead, imprisoned, or disgraced.

APPENDIX D

BIBLIOGRAPHY

GENERAL WORKS

ALEKSANDROV (no initials. Pseudonym for Mikhel'son): *Kto upravlyaet Rossiey: bol'shevistskiy partiynopravitel'stvennyy apparat i 'stalinizm'*. *Istoriko-dogmaticheskiy analiz*. Berlin. n.d. (The best analysis of the party apparatus though not always completely accurate.)

ALEKSEEV, S. A. (editor). *Revolyutsiya i grazhdanskaya voyna v opisaniyakh belogvardeytsev. Fevral'skaya revolyutsiya.* 2nd edition: Moscow, Leningrad, 1926.

ANET, CLAUDE. *La révolution russe*. 4 vols. Paris, 1919.

ANTONOV-OVSEENKO, V. 'Stroitel'stvo krasnoy armii v revolyutsii', in *Za pyat' let.*, *1917–22, sbornik Ts. K.R.K.P. (b)*, Moscow, 1922, p. 145.

ANTONOV-SARATOVSKY, V. P. *Pod styagom proletarskoy bor'by*, tom 1. Moscow, Leningrad, 1925. [*Antonov-Saratovsky.*]

—— (editor). *Sovety v epokhu voennogo kommunizma.* Sbornik dokumentov, 2 vols. Moscow, Leningrad, 1928.

ARGUNOV, A. *Mezhdu dvumya bol'shevizmami*, Paris, 1919.

ARONSON, GRIGORIY. *Na zare krasnogo terrora.* (*Prilozhenie. Iz materialov Krasnoy Knigi V. Ch.K. Rasskazy V. Ch.K. o samoy sebe*). Berlin, 1929.

ARSHINOV, P. *Istoriya makhnovskogo dvizheniya* (1918–21 gg.). Berlin, 1923.

ASTROV, N. I., ZEELER, V. F., MILYUKOV, P. N., OBOLENSKY, Prince, V. A., SMIRNOV, S. A., ELYASHEV, L. E. (editors). *Pamyati pogibshikh.* Paris, 1929.

ASTROV, N. I., KOKOSHKIN, TH. TH, MUROMTSEV, S. A., NOVGORODTSEV, P. I., and SHAKHOVSKOY, PRINCE D. I. (editors). *Zakonodatel'nye proekty i predlozheniya partii narodnoy svobody (1905–7 gg.).* St. Petersburg, 1907.

AVDEEV, N. *Revolyutsiya 1917 goda.* (*Khronika sobytiy.*) Vol. I, January to April; Vol. II, April to May. Moscow, 1923.

BALABANOFF, ANGELICA. *My Life as a Rebel*, London, 1938.

BARMINE, Alexander. *One Who Survived.* New York, 1945.

BATSELL, W. R. *Soviet Rule in Russia.* New York, 1929.

BAYKOV, ALEXANDER. *The Development of the Soviet Economic System.* Cambridge, 1946.

BEBEL, AUGUST. *Nicht stehendes Heer sondern Volkswehr.* Stuttgart, 1898.

BERKMAN, ALEXANDER. *Die Kronstadt Rebellion.* Berlin, 1923.

—— *The Bolshevik Myth.* (Diary 1920–2.) London, 1925.

BLOK, ALEKSANDR. *Polnoe sobranie stikhotvoreniy v dvukh tomakh.* Edited by V. Orlova. 2 vols. Leningrad, 1946.

BOLDYREV, V. G. *Direktoriya, Kolchak, Interventy. Vospominaniya (Iz tsikla 'Shest' Let' 1917–22 gg.).* Edited by V. D. Vegman. Novonikolaevsk, 1925.

Bol'shaya Sovetskaya Entsiklopediya. Vols. 1–46, 50–65. Moscow, 1926–39.

Bol'sheviki i krestyanstvo, n.p. 1921. (A socialist revolutionary pamphlet.)

Bol'sheviki u vlasti. Moscow, 1918. (A collection of articles by socialist revolutionary writers on the results of the October Revolution.)

Bol'sheviki v period podgotovki: khronika sobytiy. Moscow, 1947.
Bol'shevizatsiya petrogradskogo garnizona: sbornik materialov i dokumentov.
Leningrad, 1932.
BONCH-BRUEVICH, V. *Na boevykh postakh fevral'skoy i oktyabr'skoy revolyutsiy.*
Moscow, 1930.
BOSH, EVGENIYA. *God bor'by.* Moscow, Leningrad, 1925.
Der Briefwechsel zwischen Friedrich Engels und Karl Marx. Herausgegeben
von A. Bebel und Ed. Bernstein. 4 vols. Stuttgart, 1913.
BRUSILOV, A. A. *Moi vospominaniya.* Moscow, Leningrad, 1929.
BUBNOV, A. S. *VKP(b).* Moscow, Leningrad, 1931.
BUBNOV, A. S., KAMENEV, S. S., TUKHACHEVSKY, M. K., and EIDEMAN,
R. P. (editors). *Grazhdanskaya voyna.* 3 vols. Moscow, 1930.
[*Grazhdanskaya voyna.*]
BUKHARIN, N. *Ekonomika perekhodnogo perioda. Obshchaya teoriya transformat-
sionnogo protsessa.* Moscow, 1920.
—— *Imperialism and World Economy.* With an introduction by V. I.
Lenin, London, 1930.
—— *Ot diktatury imperializma k diktature proletariata.* Petrograd, 1918.
BUKHARIN, N., and PREOBRAZHENSKY, E. *The ABC of Communism.*
London, 1922.
BUNYAN, JAMES, and FISHER, H. H. *The Bolshevik Revolution 1917–1918.*
Documents and Materials. Stanford, California, and Oxford, 1934.
[*B. & F.*]
BUNYAN, JAMES. *Intervention, Civil War and Communism in Russia.* April–
December, 1918. Documents and Materials. Baltimore and Oxford,
1936. [*Bunyan.*]
BURTSEV, V. L. *Prestupleniya i nakazanie bol'shevikov.* Paris, n.d.
CARR, EDWARD HALLETT. *A History of Soviet Russia. The Bolshevik Revolu-
tion, 1917–1923.* Vol. I. London, 1950. Vol. II, 1952, Vol. III,
1953.
CHAADAEVA, O. N. (editor). *Soldatskie pis'ma 1917 goda.* Moscow,
Leningrad, 1927.
CHAMBERLIN, W. H. *The Russian Revolution, 1917–1921.* 2 vols. London,
1935. (The best history of the period.)
CHERNOV, V. (TCHERNOV). *Mes tribulations en Russie soviétique.* Traduit
par V.O. Paris, 1921.
—— *Pered burey,* New York, 1953.
—— *The Great Russian Revolution.* Translated and abridged by Philip E.
Mosley. Yale University Press, 1936.
CHICHERIN, G. V. *Vneshnyaya politika sovetskoy Rossii za dva goda. Ocherk
sostavlennyy k dvukhletney godovshchine rabochekrestyanskoy revolyutsii.* Mos-
cow, 1920.
CILIGA, ANTON. *The Russian Enigma.* (English version by Fernand G.
Renier and Anne Cliff.) London, 1940.
—— *The Kronstadt Revolt.* Freedom Press, London, 1942.
*The Communist International between the Fifth and the Sixth World Congresses—
1924–1928.* London, 1928.
CUMMING, C. K., and PETTIT, WALTER, W. (editors). *Russian-American
Relations.* March 1917–March 1920. Documents and Papers. New
York, 1920.
DALIN, D. *Posle voyn i revolyutsiy.* Berlin, 1922.
DAN, F. I. *Dva goda skitaniy* (1919–21). Berlin, 1922. (Most valuable
on menshevik activity during this period.)

DAN, F. I. *Proiskhozhdenie bol'shevizma.* New York, 1946.
—— *Die Sozialdemokratie Russlands nach dem Jahre 1908*—see Martov.
DENIKIN, GENERAL A. I. *Ocherki russkoy smuty.* Vol. II, 1922. Vol. III, Berlin, 1924.
DENNIS, A. L. P. *The Foreign Policies of Soviet Russia.* London, 1924.
DEUTSCHER, ISAAC. *Stalin. A Political Biography.* Oxford, 1949. [*Deutscher.*]
—— *Soviet Trade Unions—Their Place in Soviet Labour Policy.* London, 1950.
DIMANSHTEIN, S. (editor). *Natsional'naya politika sovetskoy vlasti za dva goda.* Moscow, 1920.
DOBB, MAURICE. *Soviet Economic Development since 1917.* London, 1948.
Dokumenty velikoy proletarskoy revolyutsii. I tom. *Iz protokolov i perepiski voennorevolyutsionnogo komiteta Petrogradskogo soveta 1917, goda.* Moscow, 1938. [*Dokumenty.*]
DRAGOMANOV, M. P. (editor). *Pis'ma K. D. Kavelina i I. S. Turgeneva k A.I. Gertsenu.* Geneva, 1892.
DRAGOMIRETSKY, V. S. *Chekhoslovaki v Rossii 1912–1920.* Paris/Prague, 1928.
ENGELS, FRIEDRICH. *Fridrikh Engel's o Rossii.* 1. *Otvet P. N. Tkachevu, 1875 g.* 2. *Posleslovie k nemu, 1894.* (Translated by Vera Zasulich, with a preface by G. V. Plekhanov.) Geneva, 1894.
—— *Der deutsche Bauernkrieg,* Ed. Fr. Mehring. Berlin, 1920.
—— *Herr Eugen Dühring's Revolution in Science (Anti-Dühring).* (Translated by Emile Burns.) London, 1936.
ERMANSKY, O. A. *Iz perezhitogo* (1887–1925 g.). Moscow, Leningrad, 1927.
ESENIN, SERGEY. *Stikhotvoreniya,* 1910–25. *Pod redaktsiey i so vstupitel'noy statiey Georgiya Ivanova.* Paris, 1950.
FAINSOD, MERLE. *International Socialism and the World War.* Harvard University Press, 1935.
FARBMAN, MICHAEL S. *Bolshevism in Retreat.* London, 1923.
FEDOTOFF-WHITE, D. *The Growth of the Red Army.* Princeton, 1944. (The best account of the Red Army and its development.)
FERIN, V. R. *Severnye partorganizatsii v grazhdanskoy voyne.* Archangel, 1939.
FISCHER, LOUIS. *The Soviets in World Affairs.* A History of Relations between the Soviet Union and the Rest of the World. 2 vols. London, 1930.
—— *Men and Politics.* An Autobiography. London, 1941.
FISCHER, RUTH. *Stalin and German Communism.* A Study in the Origins of the State Party. London, 1948.
FLECHTHEIM, OSSIP K. *Die Kommunistische Partei Deutschland in der Weimar Republik.* Berlin, 1948.
FRUNZE, M. V. *Sobranie sochineniy.* Edited by A. S. Bubnov. 3 vols. Moscow, Leningrad, 1926–9.
GANKIN, O. H., and FISHER, H. H. *The Bolsheviks and the World War. The Origin of the Third International.* Stanford, 1940. [*G. & F.*]
GARDENIN, YU (CHERNOV, V. M.). *Voyna i 'tret'a sila'. Sbornik statey.* Geneva, 1915.
—— *Chuzhimi putyami.* Geneva, 1916.
GERONIMUS, A. *Partiya i krasnaya armiya. Istoricheskiy ocherk.* Moscow, Leningrad, 1928.

GOLDMAN, EMMA. *My Disillusionment in Russia.* London, 1925.
Goneniya na anarkhizm v Sovetskoy Rossii. Published by the Anarchist Group in Germany. Berlin, 1922.
GORKY, M., MOLOTOV, V., and others (editors). *Istoriya grazhdanskoy voyny v SSSR.* Vol. II. *Velikaya proletarskaya revolyutsiya oktyabr'-noyabr' 1917 goda.* Moscow, 1943.
GORTER, HERMAN. *Offener Brief an den Genossen Lenin.* Eine Antwort auf Lenins Broschüre: Radikalismus, eine Kinderkrankheit des Kommunismus. Verlag KAPD, Berlin, n.d. (Written in July–August 1921.)
GRAVE, B. B. *Burzhuaziya nakanune fevral'skoy revolyutsii.* Moscow, Leningrad, 1927.
Grazhdanskaya voyna. See BUBNOV, A. S.
Grazhdanskaya voyna na Volge v 1918 g. Sbornik pervyy. Prague, 1930.
GRISHIN, P. P. *Men'sheviki i oktyabr'skaya revolyutsiya.* Moscow, Leningrad, 1932.
GUINS, G. K. *Sibir', soyuzniki i Kolchak.* 2 vols. Pekin, 1921.
GUL', ROMAN. *Dzerzhinsky-Menzhinsky-Peters-Latsis-Yagoda.* Paris, 1936.
GUSEV, S. *Grazhdanskaya voyna i krasnaya armiya. Sbornik voenno-teoreticheskikh i voennopoliticheskikh statey (1918–24).* Moscow, Leningrad, 1925.
HARD, WILLIAM. *Raymond Robins' Own Story.* New York and London, 1920.
HELFFERICH, KARL. *Der Weltkrieg,* 3 vols. Berlin, 1919.
HOFFMAN, MAX. *War Diaries and Other Papers.* Translated from the German by Eric Sutton. 2 vols. London, 1939.
HUNT, R. N. CAREW. *The Theory and Practice of Communism.* An Introduction. London, 1950.
IL'IN ZHENEVSKY, A. F. *Ot fevralya k zakhvatu vlasti.* Leningrad, n.d.
—— *Bol'sheviki u vlasti, vospominaniya o 1918 gode.* Leningrad, 1929.
IOFFE, A. *Krakh men'shevizma* (with a preface by L. Trotsky). Petrograd, 1917.
Istoriya vsesoyuznoy kommunisticheskoy partii (bol'shevikov). Kratkiy kurs. Moscow, 1942. (Officially approved by the Central Committee in 1938.) [*Istoriya VKPb.*]
IVANOVICH, ST. *Krasnaya armiya.* Paris, 1931.
IVANOV, GEORGIY. *Peterburgskie zimy.* New York, 1952.
IVANOV-RAZUMNIK (pseudonym for R. V. Ivanov). *Istoriya russkoy obshchestvennoy mysli.* 4th edition, 2 vols. St. Petersburg, 1914.
—— *Pisatel'skie sud'by.* New York, 1951.
JASNY, NAUM. *The Socialized Agriculture of the USSR.* Plans and Performance. Stanford, 1949.
KACHOWSKAJA, IRÈNE. *Souvenirs d'une révolutionnaire.* (4th edition) Paris, 1926. (Translated from the Russian manuscript by M. Livane and Joe Newman.)
Kak bol'sheviki torguyut Rossiey, n.p. 1921. (socialist revolutionary pamphlet.)
Kak tambovskie krestyane boryatsya za svobodu. n.p. 1921. (socialist revolutionary pamphlet.)
KAKURIN, N. E., and MELIKOV, V.A. *Voyna s belopolyakami 1920 g.* (Contains a full appendix of documents indispensable on the Polish war of 1920.)
KAKURIN, N. E. (editor). *Razlozhenie armii v 1917 godu.* Moscow, Leningrad, 1925.

KAMENEV, S. S. (editor). *Fronty krasnoy armii i flota. Sbornik statey k Syezdu Sovetov pod redaktsiey i s predisloviem Glavnokomanduyushchego vsemi vooruzhennymi silami Respubliki tov.S. S. Kameneva*, Moscow, 1920.

KAMKOV, B. *Kto takie levye sotsialisty-revolyutsionery?* Petrograd, 1918.

—— *Organicheskiy nedug.* (in *Teoriya i praktika sovetskogo stroya, vypusk pervyy*) Berlin, n.d. (Written in Moscow in January 1919.)

KAPLAN, S. N. *Lavrov. Sistematicheskaya khrestomatiya.* (Edited by A. Z. Steinberg.)

KAUTSKY, KARL. *Terrorismus und Kommunismus.* Berlin, 1919.

KEDROV, M. S. *Bez bol'shevistskogo rukovodstva.* (*Iz istorii interventsii na Murmane. Ocherki.*) Leningrad, 1930.

KEELING, H. V. *Bolshevism. Mr. Keeling's Five Years in Russia.* London, 1919.

KERENSKY, A. *Izdaleka. Sbornik statey (1920–21 g).* Paris, 1922.

—— *The Catastrophe, Kerensky's Own Story of the Russian Revolution.* New York, London, 1927.

—— *Delo Kornilova.* Moscow, 1918.

KLIMUSHKIN, P. D. *Bor'ba za demokratiyu na Volge.* (In *Grazhdanskaya voyna na Volge v 1918 g. Sbornik pervyy*, pp. 38–102.)

KOLESNIKOV, B. *Professional'noe dvizhenie i kontrrevolyutsia. Ocherki iz istorii professional'nogo dvizheniya na Ukraine.* Kharkov, 1923.

KOLLONTAY, ALEKSANDRA. *Komu nuzhna voyna?* Kharkov, 1917.

—— *Workers' Opposition in Russia.* London (The Dreadnought Publishers), n.d. (written early in 1921).

KOLOKOL'KIN V. *Sotsial'nye korni oppositsionnogo bloka.* Leningrad, Moscow, 1927.

KORNATOVSKY, N. (editor). *Kronshtadtskiy myatezh. Sbornik statey, vospominaniy i dokumentov.* Leningrad, 1931.

KOSTOMAROV, D. (editor). *Oktyabr' v Moskve. Materialy i dokumenty.* Moscow, Leningrad, 1932. [*Kostomarov.*]

—— (editor). *Dokumenty velikoy proletarskoy revolyutsii.* Glavnoe arkhivnoe upravlenie M.V.D., SSSR, Vol. II, Moscow, 1948. [*Kostomarov-Dokumenty.*]

KOZHEVNIKOV, M. V. *Istoriya sovetskogo suda.* Moscow, 1948.

Krasnaya kniga Vecheka. MAKINTSIAN, L. (editor) 2 vols. Moscow, 1920. (Very rare. Quoted from a typescript copy in the Hoover War Library.) [*Krasnaya Kniga.*]

KRASSIN, LUBOV. *Leonid Krassin: his life and Work.* London, 1929.

Kreml' za reshetkoy (Podpol'naya Rossiya). Berlin, 1922. (Letters of A. A. Izmailovich and M. A. Spiridonova from prison, and other materials on the Left Socialist Revolutionaries).

KRITSMAN, L. *Geroicheskiy period velikoy russkoy revolyutsii.* 2nd edition. Moscow, Leningrad, 1926. (An excellent and objective analysis of war communism.)

KRUPSKAYA, N. D. *Memories of Lenin.* Translated by E. Verney from the Russian second edition. Moscow, 1930, 2 vols. London, n.d.

KRYLENKO, N. V. *Za pyat' let. 1918–1922 gg. Obvinitel'nye rechi.* Moscow, 1923.

KUBANIN, M. *Makhnovshchina.* Leningrad, n.d.

KUZNETSOV, V. *Iz vospominaniy politrabotnika.* Moscow, Leningrad, 1930.

LATSIS, M.Ya. *Chrezvychaynye kommissii po bor'be s kontr-revolyutsiey.* Moscow, 1921.

LAVROV, P. L. *Istoricheskiya pis'ma.* 2nd edition. Geneva, 1891.

LAZITCH, BRANKO. *Lénine et la III Internationale.* Préface de Raymond Aron. Paris, 1950.

Lenin v pervye mesyatsy sovetskoy vlasti. *Sbornik statey i vospominaniy.* Moscow, 1933.

LENIN, V. I. *Sobranie sochineniy.* 20 vols. Moscow. 1920–6.
[*Lenin (1).*]

—— *Sochineniya.* 30 vols. 3rd edition, 1935–7. (The best edition. All references are to this edition, unless otherwise indicated.)
[*Lenin.*]

—— *Sochineniya.* 35 vols. 4th edition. Moscow, 1942–50.
[*Lenin (4).*]

LIBERMAN, SIMON. *Building Lenin's Russia.* Chicago, 1945.

LOCKHART, R. H. BRUCE. *Memoirs of a British Agent.* London, 1932.

LOZOVSKY, A. L. *Profsoyuzy i oktyabr'skaya revolyutsia.* In *Za pyat' let 1917–1922. Sbornik Ts.K.R.K.P.*, Moscow, 1922 (pp. 190–201.)

LUDENDORFF, ERICH. *Meine Kriegserinnerungen, 1914–1918.* Berlin, 1919.

LUNACHARSKY, A. *Ideologiya nakanune oktyabrya.* In *Za pyat' let, 1917–1922. Sbornik Ts. K.R.K.P.*, Moscow, 1922.

LUXEMBURG, ROSA. *Die Russische Revolution.* Edited by Paul Levi. Berlin, 1922.

LYUBIMOV, I. N. *Revolyutsiya 1917 goda. Khronika sobytiy.* Vol. VI. (October–December). Moscow, Leningrad, 1930.

MAISKY, I. *Demokraticheskaya kontr-revolyutsiya.* Moscow, Petrograd, 1923.

MAKHNO, NESTOR. *Russkaya revolyutsiya na Ukraine (ot marta 1917 g. po aprel' 1918 god). Kniga I,* Paris, 1929; *Kniga II, Pod udarami kontrrevolyutsii (aprel' 1918 god)* Paris, 1936; *Kniga III, Ukrainskaya revolyutsiya iul'-dekabr' 1918 god.* Paris, 1937.

MAL'CHEVSKY, I. S. (editor). *Vserossiyskoe uchreditel'noe sobranie.* Moscow, Leningrad, 1930.

MARTOV, Yu.O. (L.), MASLOV, P. and POTRESOV, A. (editors). *Obshchestvennoe dvizhenie v Rossii v nachale XX-go veka.* Vols. I, II and III. St. Petersburg, 1909.

MARTOV, YU.O. *Bol'shevizm v Rossii i v Internatsionale. Rech' proiznesennaya na syezde Nezavisimoy Sotsialisticheskoy Partii Germanii v Galle (15-go oktyabrya 1920 goda.)* Berlin, 1923.

—— (L.). *Ob odnom 'nedostoynom' postupke (Otvet Leninu, Lyadovu i ko).* Geneva, May 1904.

—— (L). *Spasiteli ili uprazdniteli? (kto i kak razrushal R.S.-D.R.P.).* Paris, 1911.

—— (L). (editor). *Voprosy sotsial-demokraticheskoy politiki. Vypusk I. Oborona revolyutsii i sotsial-demokratiya. Sbornik statey.* Petrograd, Moscow, 1920.

—— (L). *Doloy smertnuyu kazn'.* Berlin, 1923. (Reprint of a pamphlet published in 1918 in Moscow.)

—— (Martov, J.). *Geschichte der russischen Sozialdemokratie mit einem Nachtrag von Th. Dan: Die Sozialdemokratie Russlands nach dem Jahre 1908.* Autorisierte Übersetzung von Alexander Stein. Berlin, 1926.
[*Martov, Geschichte.*]

Materialy po peresmotru partiynoy programmy. (Collection of articles by members of the Moscow *Oblast'* Bureau: V. Milyutin, V. Sokol'nikov, A. Lomov and V. Smirnov.) Moscow, 1917.

MAUTNER, WILHELM. *Der Bolschewismus. Voraussetzungen, Geschichte, Theorie, zugleich eine Untersuchung seines Verhältnisses zum Marxismus.* Berlin, Stuttgart, Leipzig, 1920.

MAVOR, JAMES. *The Russian Revolution.* London, 1928.
MAXIMOFF, G. P. *The Guillotine at Work.* Twenty Years of Terror in Russia. (Data and Documents.) Chicago, 1940.
MAYNARD, MAJOR-GENERAL SIR C. *The Murmansk Venture.* London, n.d.
MEL'GUNOV, S. P. *N.V. Chaykovsky v gody grazhdanskoy voyny.* (*Materialy dlya istorii russkoy obshchestvennosti, 1917–24 gg.*). Paris, 1929.
—— *Tragediya Admirala Kolchaka. Iz istorii grazhdanskoy voyny na Volge, Urale i v Sibiri.* 3 vols. Belgrade, 1930–1.
—— *Zolotoy nemetskiy klyuch bol'shevikov.* Paris, 1940.
—— *Kak bol'sheviki zakhvatili vlast'. Oktyabr'skiy perevorot 1917 goda.* Paris, 1953.
METT, IDA. *La Commune de Cronstadt.* Crépuscule sanglant des Soviets. Spartacus, Paris, 1949.
MIKHAYLOV, G. *Sovetskoe predstavitel'stvo i izbiratel'noe pravo.* Moscow, 1922.
MILONOV, YU.K. (editor) *Professional'nye soyuzy SSSR v proshlom i nastoyashchem, 1905–1917–1927.* Moscow, Leningrad, 1927.
MILYUKOV, P. N. *Istoriya vtoroy russkoy revolyutsii,* Vol. I. (in three parts). Sofia, 1921. [*Milyukov-Istoriya.*]
—— *Rossiya na perelome,* Vols. I. and II. *Proiskhozhdenie i ukreplenie bol'shevistskoy diktatury,* Paris, 1927. [*Milyukov.*]
MILYUTIN, V. P. *Istoriya ekonomicheskogo razvitiya SSSR.* (1917–27). Moscow, Leningrad, 1927.
MONKHOUSE, ALLAN. *Moscow, 1911–1933.* London, 1933.
MOORE, BARRINGTON, Jr. *Soviet Politics.* The Dilemma of Power. The Role of Ideas in Social Change. Harvard University Press, 1950.
MOSKALEV, M. *Russkoe byuro TsK bol'shevistskoy partii 1912-mart 1917.* Moscow, 1947.
MYASNIKOV, A. *Bespartiynaya konferentsiya.* Moscow, 1919.
MYASNIKOV, G. I. *Diskussionnyy material.* (A collection of articles and speeches, published for party members only.) Moscow, 1921.
—— *Ocherednoy Obman.* Paris, 1931.
Narodovlastie. Sbornik statey chlenov uchreditel'nogo sobraniya fraktsii sotsialistov revolyutsionerov. Moscow, 1918.
NOULENS, JOSEPH. *Mon Ambassade en Russie Soviétique 1917–1919.* 2 vols. Paris, 1933.
NOVGORODTSEV, P. *Ob obshchestvennom ideale. Vypusk I.* 3rd edition. Berlin, 1921.
Oktyabr'skie dni v Moskve i rayonakh. Moscow, 1922.
OLDENBOURG, SERGE. *Le coup d'état bolchéviste: 20 octobre–3 décémbre 1917.* Recueil de documents traduits et annotés par S.O. Paris, 1929.
ORDZHONIKIDZE, G. K. *Izbrannye stat'i i rechi 1911–1937.* Moscow, 1939.
ORDZHONIKIDZE, ZINAIDA. *Put' bol'shevika. Stranitsy iz vospominaniy o Sergo Ordzhonikidze.* Moscow, 1939.
OSINSKY, N. (Obolensky). *Gosudarstvennoe regulirovanie krestyanskogo khozyaystva.* Moscow, 1920.
OVSYANNIKOV, N. (editor). *Oktyabr'skoe vosstanie v Moskve. Sbornik dokumentov, statey i vospominaniy.* Moscow, 1922.
PANNEKOEK, ANTON. *Weltrevolution und kommunistische Taktik.* Vienna, 1920.
PARES, BERNARD. *The Fall of the Russian Monarchy.* A study of the evidence. London, 1939.
PAZHITNOV, K. A. *Razvitie sotsialisticheskikh idey v Rossii.* Vol. I. Kharkov, 1913.

PETRICHENKO (no initials). *Pravda o kronshtadtskikh sobytiyakh* n.p.—n.d.

PILSUDSKI, JOSEPH. *Année 1920.*—édition complète avec le texte de l'ouvrage de M. Toukhatchevski 'La marche au delà de la Vistule' et les notes critiques du Bureau Historique Militaire de Varsovie; traduit du polonais. Paris, 1929.

PIONTKOVSKY, S. A. (editor). *Sovety v oktyabre. Sbornik dokumentov.* Moscow, 1928.

Pis'ma P. B. Aksel'roda i Yu. O. Martova. Berlin, 1924.

PLAMENATZ, JOHN P. *German Marxism and Russian Communism,* London, 1954.

Platforma Shlyapnikova i Medvedeva. Moscow, 1927.

PLATONOV, A. P. *Fevral' i oktyabr' v chernomorskom flote.* Sebastopol, 1932.

PLEKHANOV, G. V. *Sochineniya.* 12 vols. Moscow, Petrograd, 1923–4.

—— *God na rodine.* 2 vols. Paris, 1921.

POKROVSKY, M. N. (editor). *Ocherki po istorii oktyabr'skoy revolyutsii.* Vol. II. Moscow, Leningrad, 1927. Contents: Genkina, E. B.: 'Fevral'-skiy perevorot'; Yugov, M. S.: 'Sovety v pervyy period revolyutsii'; Lidak, O. A.: 'Iul'skie sobytiya 1917 goda'; Rubinshtein, N. L. 'Vneshnyaya politika kerenshchiny'.

—— *Oktyabr'skaya revolyutsiya—sbornik statey, 1917–27.* Moscow, 1929.

POPOV, N. *Outline History of the Communist Party of the Soviet Union,* parts 1 and 2; English translation, printed in the U.S.S.R., of the 16th Russian edition. London, 1935.

Po sovetskoy Rossii. Moscow, 1918. (A collection of reports of the Military Inspectorate.)

POSTNIKOV, S. P. *Bibliografiya russkoy revolyutsii i grazhdanskoy voyny, 1917–1921. Iz kataloga biblioteki R.Z.I. Arkhiva.* Prague, 1938.

Pravda o Kronshtadte. Published by *Volya Rossii,* Prague, 1921. (With an appendix containing Nos. 1–14 of *Izvestiya vremennogo revolyutsionnogo komiteta matrosov, krasnoarmeytsev i rabochikh goroda Kronshtadta.*)

PREOBRAZHENSKY, E. *Trekhletie oktyabr'skoy revolyutsii.* Moscow, 1920.

Proekt ustava rossiyskoy kommunisticheskoy partii (bol'shevikov); s prilozheniem tsirkularov Tsentral'nogo Komiteta R.K.P. Moscow, 1920.

PROKOPOVICZ, S. N. *Russlands Volkswirtschaft unter den Sowjets.* Zurich, New York, 1944.

PUKHOV, A. S. *Kronshtadtskiy myatezh v 1921 g.* (The most complete Soviet account.) Leningrad, 1931.

PUKHOV, G. S. *Kak vooruzhalsya Petrograd.* Moscow, 1933.

PUTNA, V. *K Visle i obratno.* Moscow, 1927.

PYATNITSKY, OSIP. *Zapiski bol'shevika. Vospominaniya (1896–1917 gg).* Leningrad, 1925.

RADKEY, OLIVER HENRY. *The Election of the Russian Constituent Assembly of 1917.* Harvard University Press, 1950.

RAKITNIKOVA, INNA. *Kak russkoe krestyanstvo borolos' za uchreditel'noe sobranie. Doklad mezhdunarodnomu sotsialisticheskomu byuro. S predisloviem I. Rubanovicha.* Paris, 1918.

RANSOME, ARTHUR. *Six weeks in Russia in 1919.* London, 1919.

REED, JOHN. *Ten Days that Shook the World.* New York, 1922.

REICHENBACH, BERNHARD. *Zur Geschichte der Kommunistischen Arbeiter-Partei Deutschlands;* in *Archiv fur die Geschichte des Sozialismus und der Arbeiterbewegung.* Vol. XIII, Leipzig, 1928 (pp. 117–40).

RíOS, FERNANDO DE LOS. *Mi viaje a la Rusia sovietista.* Segunda edición. Madrid, 1922.

ROLLIN, HENRY. *La révolution russe. Ses origines—ses résultats.* 3 vols. Paris, 1931.

ROBINSON, GEROID TANQUERAY. *Rural Russia under the Old Regime.* A History of the Landlord-Peasant World, and a Prologue to the Peasant Revolution of 1917. New York, 1949.

ROSENBERG, ARTHUR. *A History of Bolshevism from Marx to the First Five Year Plan.* (Translated from the German by I. F. D. Morrow.)

ROSMER, ALFRED. *Le Mouvement ouvrier pendant la guerre.* De l'union sacrée à Zimmerwald. Paris, 1936.

—— *Moscou sous Lénine. Les origines du Communisme.* Préface par Albert Camus. Paris, 1953.

RUBINSHTEIN, N. *Bol'sheviki i uchreditel'noe sobranie.* Moscow, 1938.

RUSSELL, BERTRAND. *The Practice and Theory of Bolshevism.* London, 1920.

Russie Socialiste, La. (Evènements de juillet 1918). Geneva, 1918. (Published by the Left Socialist Revolutionaries.)

RYABINSKY, K. *Revolyutsiya 1917 goda (Khronika sobytiy).* Vol. V (October). Moscow, Leningrad, 1926.

RYAZANOV, D. *Zadachi profsoyuzov do i v epokhu diktatury proletariata.* Moscow, Leningrad, 1921.

SAKHAROV, LIEUT.-GEN. K. V. *Belaya Sibir'.* Munich, 1923.

SAVELIEV, M. A. (editor). *Protokoly tsentral'nogo komiteta R.S.-D. R.P. avgust 1917—fevral' 1918.* Moscow, Leningrad, 1929.

SAVINKOV, BORIS (Ropshin, V.). *Kon' voronoy.* Paris, 1923.

—— *Bor'ba s bol'shevikami.* Warsaw, 1920.

—— *Memoirs of a Terrorist.* Translated by Joseph Shaplen. With a foreword and an epilogue. New York, 1931.

SCHWARZ, SALOMON. *Lénine et le mouvement syndical.* Paris, 1935.

SEMENOV, G. (pseudonum for Vasiliev). *Voennaya i boevaya rabota partii sotsialistov-revolyutsionerov za 1917–19 gg.* Berlin, 1922.

SERGE, VICTOR. *L'An I de la révolution russe.* Paris, 1930.

SHEPIKHIN, S. A., GENERAL. *Ural'skoe kazach'e voysko v bor'be s bol'shevikami. Istoricheskiy material dlya izsledovaniya perioda grazhdanskikh voyn v Rossii.* (Unpublished manuscript.)

SHLYAPNIKOV, A. *Semnadtsaty god.* 4 vols. Leningrad, Moscow (1923, 1925, 1927, 1931).

SHUB, DAVID. *Lenin.* New York, 1948.

SLEPKOV, A. *Kronshtadtskiy myatezh.* (*K sed'moy godovshchine.*) Moscow, Leningrad, 1928.

Smena Vekh. Sbornik statey Yu. V. Klyuchnikova, N. V. Ustryalova, S. S. Lukianova, A. V. Bobrishcheva-Pushkina, S. S. Chakhetina i Yu. N. Potekhina. Iul' 1921 g. 2nd edition. Prague, 1922.

SMILGA, I. T. *Na povorote. Zametki k X-mu syezdu partii.* Moscow, 1921.

—— *Ocherednye voprosy stroitel'stva krasnoy armii.* *K desyatomu syezdu R.K.P.* Moscow, 1921.

SOLOMON, G. A. *Sredi krasnykh vozhdey. Lichno perezhitoe i vidennoe na sovetskoy sluzhbe.* 2 vols. Paris, 1930.

SORIN, V. *Partiya i oppozitsiya.* Vol. I. *Fraktsiya levykh kommunistov.* Leningrad, Moscow, 1925.

SOROKIN, PITIRIM. *Leaves from a Russian Diary.* London, n.d.

SOUVARINE, BORIS. *Staline.* Aperçu historique du bolchévisme. Paris, 1935. (The French edition contains a most valuable bibliography omitted in the English translation.)

378 THE ORIGIN OF THE COMMUNIST AUTOCRACY

SOYUZ S-R MAKSIMALISTOV. *Trudovaya sovetskaya respublika.* Moscow, 1918.
—— *O rabochem kontrole.* Moscow, 1918.
STALIN, I. V. *Problems of Leninism.* English translation of 11th Russian
    edition. Foreign Languages Publishing House, Moscow, 1947.
—— *Sochineniya,* Moscow, 1946 (in course of publication).
                                                                 [*Stalin.*]
—— *Ob oppozitsii.* Moscow, Leningrad, 1928.
—— *Na putyakh k oktyabryu.* Moscow, Leningrad, 1924.
STEINBERG. A. *The Left-Social-Revolutionaries and the October Revolution.* (A
    manuscript essay in the British Library of Political Science by the
    daughter of the Commissar of Justice.)
STEINBERG, I. Z. *Ot fevralya po oktyabr' 1917 god.* Berlin, n.d. (written
    1918–19).
—— *Nravstvennyy lik revolyutsii.* Berlin, 1923.
—— *Als ich Volkskommissar war.* Episoden aus der russischen Oktober-
    revolution. Munich, 1929.
—— *Spiridonova, Revolutionary Terrorist.* Translated and edited by Gwenda
    David and Eric Mosbacher. London, 1935.
STEPUN, FEDOR. *Vergangenes und Unvergängliches.* Aus meinem Leben.
    Dritter Teil 1917–22. Munich, 1950.
STRUVE, PETR. *Obshchestvennoe dvizhenie pri Aleksandre II (1865–1881).*
    Istoricheskie ocherki. Paris, 1905.
—— *Patriotica. Politika, kul'tura, religiya, sotsializm. Sbornik statey za piat' let.*
    (1905–1910 gg.). St. Petersburg, 1911.
—— *Razmyshleniya o russkoy revolyutsii.* Sofia, 1921.
SUKHANOV, N. *Zapiski o revolyutsii.* 7 vols. Berlin, St. Petersburg,
    Moscow, 1923.
SVERDLOV, YA. M. *Izbrannye stat'i i rechi 1917–1919.* Leningrad, 1939.
TASHKAROV, P. *V. I. Lenin i L. B. Kamenev o strategii i taktike partii v 1917*
    godu. Moscow, Leningrad, 1927.
THUN, A. *Istoriya revolyutsionnago dvizheniya v Rossii.* Translated from the
    German and edited by L. E. Shishko. Geneva, 1903.
TKACHEV, P. N. *Izbrannye sochineniya.* Edited by B. P. Koz'min. Vols.
    1–4, Moscow, 1932.
TOWSTER, JULIAN. *Political Power in the U.S.S.R. 1917–1947.* Oxford,
    New York, 1948.
TROTSKY, L. *De la révolution d'octobre à la paix de Brest-Litovsk.* Geneva,
    1918.
—— *O zadachakh profsoyuzov. Doklad prochitannyy na sobranii 30 dekabrya*
    1920 goda. Moscow, 1921.
—— *The Defence of Terrorism.* (Terrorism and Communism.) With a
    preface by H. N. Brailsford, London, 1921.
—— *Sochineniya.* Tom III, chast' 1: *Ot fevralya do oktyabrya.* Moscow,
    Leningrad, n.d. Tom XIII: *Kommunisticheskiy internatsional,* Moscow,
    Leningrad, 1926. Tom XV: *Khozyaystvennoe stroitel'stvo sovetskoy*
    respubliki. Moscow, Leningrad, 1927.
—— *1905.* 3rd edition, Moscow, Leningrad, 1924.
—— *1917. Uroki oktyabrya.* Berlin, 1924.
—— *Kak vooruzhalas' revolyutsiya.* 3 vols. Moscow, 1923–5.
                                                         [*Trotsky, KVR.*]
—— *Lenin.* Authorized translation, London, 1925.
—— *The Real Situation in Russia.* Translated by Max Eastman. London,
    n.d.

TROTSKY, L. (Leon). *Ma Vie.* 3 vols. Paris, 1930. (Authorized translation from the Russian.) [*Trotsky, Ma Vie.*]

—— *Permanentnaya revolyutsiya.* Berlin, 1930.

—— *Stalinskaya shkola fal'sifikatsii.* Berlin, 1932.
[*Trotsky, Stalinskaya shkola.*]

—— *The History of the Russian Revolution.* Translated by Max Eastman. 3 vols. London, 1932.
[*Trotsky, History.*]

—— *The Suppressed Testament of Lenin.* The complete original text; with two explanatory articles by Leon Trotsky. New York, n.d.

—— *Stalin.* Translated from the Russian by Charles Malamuth. London, 1947.

TUKHACHEVSKY, M. *Voyna klassov. Stat'i 1919–20 g. n.p.*

—— (Toukhachevski). *La marche au delà de la Vistule.* Conférences faites au cours de complément de l'Académie Militaire de Moscou du 7 au 10 février, 1923. Reprinted in Pilsudski, *L'Année 1920*, pp. 203–55 (in a French translation made from the Polish translation from the Russian.)

U.S. Department of State. *Papers relating to the Foreign Relations of the United States, 1918. Russia.* 3 vols. Washington, 1931–2. [U.S. *Foreign Relations.*]

USTINOV, G. *Krushenie partii levykh es-erov.* Moscow, 1918.

VALENTINOV, N. *Vstrechi s Leninym.* New York, 1953.

VANDERVELDE, EMILE ET WAUTERS, ARTHUR. *Le procés des social-révolutionnaires à Moscou.* Brussels, 1922.

VARDIN, I. *Ot melko-burzhuaznoy kontr-revolyutsii k restavratsii kapitalizma.* (*Partiya men'shevikov posle oktyabrya.*) In *Za pyat' let, 1917–22 Sbornik, Ts. K.R.K.P.* Moscow, 1922.
[*Vardin in Za 5 Let.*]

—— *Revolyutsiya i men'shevizm.* Moscow, Leningrad, 1925.
[*Vardin.*]

VARNECK, ELENA, and FISHER, H. H. *The Testimony of Kolchak and other Siberian Materials.* Stanford, 1935.

VENTURI, FRANCO. *Il populismo russo.* 2 vols. Turin, 1952.

VIKTOROV-TOPOROV, V. *La première année de la révolution russe mars 1917 —mars 1918.* Faits, documents, appréciations, Berlin, 1919.

VLADIMIROVA, VERA. *Revolyutsiya 1917 goda.* (*Khronika sobytiy*). Vol. III, (June–July), Vol. IV, (August–September). Moscow, Leningrad, 1923–4. [*Vladimirova.*]

—— *Kontr-revolyutsiya v 1917 g.* (*Kornilovshchina*). Moscow, 1924.
[*Vladimirova, Kontr-revolyutsiya.*]

—— *God sluzhby 'sotsialistov' kapitalistam.* Ocherki po istorii kontr-revolyutsii v 1918 godu. Moscow, Leningrad, 1927.
[*Vladimirova, God sluzhby.*]

VLADIMIRSKY, M. *Organizatsiya sovetskoy vlasti na mestakh.* Moscow, 1919.

—— *Sovety, ispolkomy i syezdy sovetov.* Moscow, Vypusk I, 1920; Vypusk II, 1921.

Voyna. Sbornik statey. Paris, 1915. (A collection of articles by Plekhanov, Leo Deutsch, Aleksinsky, Ida Aksel'rod and others.)

VOLINE (pseudonym for V. M. EICHENBAUM). *La révolution inconnue (1917–1921).* Documentation inédite sur la révolution russe. Paris, n.d.

VORONOVICH, N. *Zapiski predsedatelya soveta soldatskikh deputatov.* (In *Arkhiv grazhdanskoy voyny, vypusk II.*) Berlin, n.d.

Voroshilov, K. *Lenin, Stalin, i krasnaya armiya. Stat'i i rechi.* Moscow, 1934.
Vyshinsky, A. Y. *The Law of the Soviet State.* (Translated by H. W. Babb.) New York, 1948.
Wetter, Gustavo, A. *Il materialismo dialettico sovietico.* Turin, 1948.
Wheeler-Bennett, John W. *Brest-Litovsk. The Forgotten Peace,* March 1918. London, 1939.
Wolfe, Bertram D. *Three who made a Revolution.* A biographical history. New York, 1948.
Wollenberg, Erich. *The Red Army.* A Study of the Growth of Soviet Imperialism. London, 1940. (Translated from the German by Claud W. Sykes.)
Yaroslavsky, Em. *Tret'ya sila.* Moscow, 1932.
—— *Istoriya VKP(b),* Vol. IV. Moscow, Leningrad, 1929.
[*Yaroslavsky.*]
—— *Kratkie ocherki po istorii VKP(b),* 2 vols. Moscow, Leningrad, 1926, 1928. [*Yaroslavsky, Kratkie ocherki.*]
—— *Anarkhizm v Rossii.* Moscow, 1939.
Zagorsky, S. *La république des soviets.* Bilan économique, Paris, 1921.
Zaytsev, Svyashchennik Kiril. *Pravoslavnaya Tserkov' v sovetskoy Rossii.* Chast' pervaya: *Vremya Patriarkha Tikhona.* Shanghai, 1947.
Zenzinov, Vladimir. *Iz zhizni revolyutsionera.* Paris, 1919.
—— (editor.) *Gosudarstvennyy perevorot admirala Kolchaka v Omske 18 noyabrya 1918 goda. Sbornik dokumentov.* Paris, 1919.
[*Zenzinov, Gos. perevorot.*]
—— *Perezhitoe,* New York, 1953.
Zinoviev, G. *G. V. Plekhanov. (vmesto rechi na mogile).* Petrograd, 1918.
—— *Bespartiynyy ili kommunist.* Moscow, 1919.
—— *N. Lenin, Vladimir Il'ich Ulyanov. Ocherk zhizni i deyatel'nosti.* Moscow, 1919.
—— *Spor o professional'nykh soyuzakh. (Doklad v Peterburge.)* Petrograd, 1921.
—— (editor). *Partiya i soyuzy. (K diskussii o roli i zadachakh profsoyuzov.)* Petrograd, 1921.
—— *Sochineniya.* 16 vols. Leningrad, 1924–6.
Zinoviev, G., and Trotsky, L. *O myatezhe levykh S-rov.* Petrograd, 1918.
Zorky, M. (editor). *Rabochaya oppozitsiya. Materialy i dokumenty 1920–6 gg.* Moscow, Leningrad, 1926.

OFFICIAL REPORTS, etc.

Boris Savinkov pered voennoy kollegiey verkhovnogo suda S.S.S.R. Polnyy otchet po stenogramme suda. Moscow, 1924.
[*Boris Savinkov.*]
British Labour Delegation to Russia 1920: Report. London 1920.
[*B.L.D. Report.*]
Bulletin of the IV Congress of the Communist International. Nos. 1 to 32. Moscow, 1922. [*Komintern IV.*]
Chetvertyy chrezvychaynyy syezd sovetov rabochikh, krestyanskikh, soldatskikh i kazach'ikh deputatov, 15–16 marta 1918 g. Moscow, 1920.
Chetvertyy vserossiyskiy syezd professional'nykh soyuzov (17–25 maya 1921 goda). Stenograficheskiy otchet. Moscow, 1921.
[*Vs. Syezd prof. IV.*]

APPENDIX D   381

Desyatyy syezd rossiyskoy kommunisticheskoy partii. Stenografcheskiy otchet, Moscow, 1921.

Devyatyy vserossiyskiy syezd sovetov rabochikh, krestyanskikh, krasnoarmeyskikh i kazach'ikh deputatov, (22–27 dekabrya, 1921 goda). Stenografcheskiy otchet. Moscow, 1922.   [*Vs. Syezd IX.*]

Dixième Congrès International Socialiste et Ouvrier tenu à Genève du 31 juillet au 5 aout 1920. Compte rendu. Brussels, 1921.
                                                        [*Dixième Congrès.*]

Obvinitel'noe zaklyuchenie po delu tsentral'nogo komiteta . . . partii sotsialistov-revolyutsionerov po obvineniyu ikh v vooruzhennoy bor'be protiv sovetskoy vlasti, etc. Moscow, 1922.   [*Obvinitel'noe zaklyuchenie.*]

Otchety o deyatel'nosti tsentral'nogo komiteta R.K.P.(b-ov) s VIII do X syezda. Perepechatany iz 'Izvestiy Ts.K.R.P'. Moscow, 1921.
                                                                [*Otchety.*]

Partiya sotsialistov-revolyutsionerov: Devyatyy sovet partii i ego rezolyutsii (Iun' 1919, Moskva). Paris, 1920.   [*PSR IX Sovet.*]

Partiynoe soveshchanie R. S.–D. R.P. 27 dekabrya 1918 g.–1 yanvarya 1919 g. (Rezolyutsii). Moscow, 1919.

Pervyy legal'nyy peterburgskiy komitet bol'shevikov v 1917 godu. Sbornik materialov i protokolov zasedaniy peterburgskogo komiteta RSDRP(b). . . . Za 1917 god. Moscow, Leningrad, 1927.
                                                        [*Pervyy leg. komitet.*]

Pervyy vserossiyskiy syezd sovetov R.i.S.D. Edited by V. N. Rakhmetov. 2 vols. Moscow, Leningrad, 1930.   [*Vs. syezd I.*]

Po sovetskoy Rossii (Vypuski vysshey voennoy inspektsii raboche-krestyanskoy krasnoy armii). Vypusk pervyy. Moscow, 1918.

Postanovleniya 7-go vserossiyskogo syezda sovetov. Moscow, 1920.

Postanovleniya i rezolyutsii 8-go vserossiyskogo syezda rabochikh, krestyanskikh, soldatskikh i kazach'ikh deputatov (23–29 dekabrya 1920 goda). Moscow, 1921.

Programma i organizatsionnyy ustav partii sotsialistov-revolyutsionerov utverzhdennye na pervom partiynom syezde, n.p. 1906.

Programma partii revolyutsionnogo kommunizma. Moscow, n.d. (Adopted 26 October 1919.)

Protokoly kongressov kommunisticheskogo internatsionala: Vtoroy kongress kominterna iul'-avgust 1920 g. Moscow, 1934.
                                                            [*Komintern II.*]

Protokoly pervago syezda partii sotsialistov-revolyutsionerov. n.p. 1906.

Protokoly pervoy obshchepartiynoy konferentsii P. S.–R. Avgust, 1908. Paris, 1908.

Protokoly syezdov i konferentsiy vsesoyuznoy kommunisticheskoy partii (b). Shestoy syezd R.S.D.R.P. (b). Moscow, 1934.
                                                            [*Protokoly VI.*]

Protokoly syezdov i konferentsiy vsesoyuznoy kommunisticheskoy partii (b): Sed'-maya aprel'skaya vserossiyskaya i petrogradskaya obshchegorodskaya konferentsiya R.S.D.R.P. (b). Moscow, 1934.
                                                        [*Protokoly VII Konf.*]

Protokoly syezdov i konferentsiy vsesoyuznoy kommunisticheskoy partii (b). Sed'moy syezd R.K.P. (b) mart 1918 g. Moscow, Leningrad, 1928.
                                                            [*Protokoly VII.*]

Protokoly syezdov i konferentsiy vsesoyuznoy kommunisticheskoy partii (b). Vos'moy syezd R.K.P. (b). Moscow, 1933.
                                                            [*Protokoly VIII.*]

Protokoly syezdov i konferentsiy vsesoyuznoy kommunisticheskoy partii (b). Devyatyy syezd R.K.P. (b). Moscow, 1933.

[*Protokoly IX.*]
Protokoly syezdov i konferentsiy vsesoyuznoy kommunisticheskoy partii (b). Desyatyy syezd R.K.P. (b) mart 1921 g. Moscow, 1933.

[*Protokoly X.*]
Protokoly syezdov i konferentsiy vsesoyuznoy kommunisticheskoy partii (b). Odinnadtsatyy syezd R.K.P. (b) mart-aprel' 1922 g. Moscow, 1936.

[*Protokoly XI.*]
Protokoly tsentral'nogo komiteta R.K.P. (b) reprinted in *Proletarskaya revolyutsiya:*—August—September, 1917: No. 8–9 (67–68), 1927, pp. 321–351; September—October 1917: No. 10 (69), 1927, pp. 246–98; November 1917: No. 11 (70), 1927, pp. 202–14; 17–24 February 1918: No. 2. (73), 1928, pp. 132–69.

Protokoly zasedaniy TSIK i byuro TSIK soveta rabochikh, i soldatskikh deputatov I-go sozyva posle oktyabrya. In *Krasnyy Arkhiv* Vol. X. 1925, pp. 95–137.

Protokoly zasedaniy vserossiyskago tsentral'nago ispolnitel'nago komiteta sovetov rabochikh, soldatskikh, krestyanskikh i kazach'ikh deputatov 2-go Sozyva. Moscow, 1918.

[*Protokoly VTSIK II.*]
Protokoly zasedaniy vserossiyskago tsentral'nago ispolnitel'nago komiteta 4-go sozyva. Stenograficheskiy otchet. Moscow, 1920.

[*Protokoly VTSIK IV.*]
Protsess kontr-revolyutsionnoy organizatsii men'shevikov. Moscow, 1931.

[*Protsess (Mensh).*]
Protsess partii sotsialistov-revolyutsionerov. Rechi gosudarstvennykh obviniteley. Moscow, 1922.

Pyatyy sozyv vserossiyskogo tsentral'nogo ispol'nitel'nogo komiteta. Stenograficheskiy otchet. Moscow. 1919.

[*Protokoly VTSIK V.*]
Pyatyy vserossiyskiy syezd sovetov rabochikh, krestyanskikh, soldatskikh i kazach'ikh deputatov. Stenograficheskiy otchet. Moscow, 1918.

[*Vs. syezd V.*]
Raboche-krestyanskaya krasnaya armiya rossiyskoy sotsialisticheskoy federativnoy sovetskoy respubliki. Kniga 1-aya (information up to June 1918). *Kniga 2-aya* (information up to December 1918). Kiev, 1918. (Printed by the General Staff of the Volunteer Army.)

Report (Political and Economic) of the Committee to Collect Information on Russia. (Command Paper 1240 of 1921.)

Report of Court Proceedings in the case of the Anti-Soviet Trotskyite Centre, etc. Moscow January 23–30, 1937, in the case of Y. L. Pyatakov, K. B. Radek, etc. Verbatim Report. Moscow, 1937.

Report of Court Proceedings in the Case of the Anti-Soviet Bloc of Rights and Trotskyites. Moscow, 1938. [*Report (Bukharin, etc.).*]

Report of Court Proceedings: The Case of the Trotskyite-Zinovievite Terrorist Centre. Moscow, 1936.

Rezolyutsii i postanovleniya III-go vserossiyskogo syezda professional'nykh soyuzov. S predisloviem A. Lozovskogo. Moscow, 1920.

Rezolyutsii vtorogo vserossiyskogo syezda sovetov narodnogo khozyaystva. Moscow, 1919.

Sbornik dokladov i rezolyutsiy pervogo vserossiyskogo syezda partii revolyutsionnogo kommunizma. n.d. n.p.

The Second and Third Internationals and the Vienna Unions: Official Report of the Conference between the Executives held at the Reichstag, Berlin, on the 2nd April, 1922 and following days. London, 1922.

Sed'moy syezd rossiyskoy kommunisticheskoy partii. Stenograficheskiy otchet, 6–8 marta 1918 g. Moscow, Leningrad, 1923.

[*Sed'moy Syezd.*]

Sed'moy vserossiyskiy syezd sovetov rabochikh, krestyanskikh, krasnoarmeyskikh i kazach'ikh deputatov. Stenograficheskiy otchet. Moscow, 1920.

[*Vs. Syezd VII.*]

I–IV Sessii vserossiyskogo tsentral'nogo ispolnitel'nogo komiteta VIII sozyva. (31 Dec. 1920, 19–20 March 1921, 30–31 May 1921, 5–7 October 1921). Moscow, 1922. [*Protokoly VTSIK VIII.*]

Shestoy vserossiyskiy chrezvychaynyy syezd rab. kr. kaz. i. krasnoarm. deput. Stenograficheskiy otchet. 6–9 noyabrya 1918 g. Moscow, 1919.

[*Vs. syezd VI.*]

Sobranie uzakoneniy i rasporyazheniy rabochego i krestyanskogo pravitel'stva (R.S.F.S.R.) 1917–22. [*S.U.R.*]

Sistematicheskiy sbornik vazhneyshikh dekretov 1917–1920. Moscow, 1920.

[*Sist. sbornik.*]

Spravochnik partiynogo rabotnika., sostavleno sekretariatom Ts.K.R.P. Moscow, 1921; and ditto, Vypusk II, Moscow, 1922.

[*Spravochnik I. Spravochnik II.*]

Stenograficheskie otchety moskovskogo soveta rabochikh i krasnoarmeyskikh deputatov (for 1919 and 1920). Moscow, 1920, 1921.

[*Sten. mosk. soveta.*]

Tretiy vsemirnyy kongress kommunisticheskogo internatsionala. Stenograficheskiy otchet. Petrograd, 1922.

[*Komintern III.*]

Tretiy vserossiyskiy syezd sovetov rabochikh, soldatskikh i krestyanskikh deputatov. Petrograd, 1918. (A short summary of the proceedings.)

[*Vs. syezd III.*]

Tretiy vserossiyskiy syezd professional'nykh soyuzov 6–15 aprelya 1920 goda. Stenograficheskiy otchet. Chast' 1-ya (plenumy). Moscow, 1921.

[*Vs. Syezd prof. III.*]

Trudy I vserossiyskogo syezda sovetov narodnogo khozyaystva 25 maya—4 iyunya 1918 g. Stenograficheskiy otchet. Moscow, 1918.

[*Trudy I. VSNKh.*]

Trudy II vserossiyskogo syezda sovetov narodnogo khozyaystva. Stenograficheskiy otchet. Moscow, n.d.

[*Trudy II VSNKh.*]

Ufimskoe gosudarstvennoe soveshchanie. Official protocols. Edited by A. Izyumov in *Russkiy Istoricheskiy Arkhiv.* 1929. pp. 59–280.

Unabhängige Sozialdemokratische Partei: Protokoll über die Verhandlungen des ausserordentlichen Parteitages in Halle vom 12 bis 17 Oktober 1920. Berlin, n.d. [*USPD Protokoll.*]

VKP(b) i voennoe delo v rezolyutsiyakh syezdov i konferentsiy VKP(b). Second edition. Moscow, 1928.

Vos'moy syezd sovetov. Ezhednevnyy byulleten' syezda. Nos. 1 to 8, December 1920. Moscow.

Vos'moy vserossiyskiy syezd sovetov rabochikh, krestyanskikh, krasnoarmeyskikh i kazach'ikh deputatov. Stenograficheskiy otchet. 22–29 dekabrya, 1920 goda. Moscow, 1921.

[*Vs. Syezd VIII.*]

Vsesoyuznaya kommunisticheskaya partiya (b) v rezolyutsiyakh i resheniyakh syezdov, konferentsiy i plenumov Ts.K. (1898–1932). Chast' I. 1898–1924. Moscow, 1932. [*VKP(b) v rez.*]
Vtoroy ocherednoy syezd rossiyskoy sots. dem. rabochey partii. Geneva, n.d.
Vtoroy vserossiyskiy syezd professional'nykh soyuzov 16–25 yanvarya 1919 goda. Stenograficheskiy otchet. Chast' 1-ya (plenumy). Moscow, 1921.
[*Vs. syezd prof. II.*]
Vtoroy vserossiyskiy syezd sovetov rabochikh i soldatskikh deputatov. Moscow, Leningrad, 1928. With an introduction by Ya. A. Yakovlev.
[*Vs. syezd. II.*]

NEWSPAPERS, PERIODICALS AND BROADSHEETS

(Only the date of first publication is given, except where otherwise indicated.)

Anarkhicheskie organizatsii. Moscow, 8 February 1921.
Arkhiv russkoy revolyutsii. Berlin, 1921.
Bol'shevik. Moscow, 1924– .
Byloe. Monthly. 1900–6, Paris; 1907, St. Petersburg; 1917–27, Petrograd (Leningrad). (Founded by Burtsev.)
Byulleten' oppozitsii. Paris, 1929– .
(The) Communist Review. Monthly. London, May 1921–
Diskussionnyy listok. Moscow (2 issues in 1920–21).
Ekonomist. Vestnik XI otdela russkogo tekhnicheskogo obshchestva. No. 1 1922– .
Europäische Gespräche. Hamburger Monatshefte für Auswärtige Politik. Stuttgart, Berlin and Leipzig, 1923– .
Ezhenedel'nik chrezvychaynykh kommissiy. (Six numbers published in Moscow in 1918.)
Istorik marksist. Moscow, 1926– (irregular).
Izvestiya, Petrograd, Moscow, 1917– .
Izvestiya tsentral'nogo komiteta rossiyskoy kommunisticheskoy partii (bol'shevikov). 28 May 1919 to October 1929 (when it was replaced by a fortnightly *Partiynoe stroitel'stvo*). [*Izvestiya Ts.K.*]
Kommunist. Petrograd, Moscow, March–June, 1918.
Kommunisticheskiy internatsional. (The Russian version of the organ of ECCI published in Russian, French, German and English. January 1919–).
Krasnaya letopis'. Leningrad, 1921– .
Krasnyy arkhiv. Moscow, 1920– .
Leninskiy sbornik. Moscow, Leningrad, 1924– .
Maksimalist. Weekly organ of the Union of S.R. Maximalists (monthly in 1918).
Mysl'. (Weekly), Kharkov, 1918–19.
Narodnoe khozyaystvo. Monthly, published by the Supreme Council of National Economy. Moscow, 1918– .
Novaya zarya. (Weekly); *Organ komiteta tsentral'noy oblasti R.S.–D.R.P.* Nos. 1–6, April–June, 1918, Moscow.
Novaya zhizn' (daily), Petrograd, 1917–18.
Novyy luch. Organ Byuro Ts.K. i P.K. R.S.–D.R.P. (daily). Petrograd, 2 December 1917—26 May 1918.
Novyy zhurnal. Quarterly. New York, 1942– .
Osvobozhdenie. Edited by P. Struve. Stuttgart, 1902–5.

Partiya levykh sotsialistov revolyutsionerov (internatsionalistov). Otvet fraktsii
levykh s-r petrogradskomu sovetu na zapros ot 14-go fevralya. Leaflet, n.d.
Partiya revolyutsionnogo kommunizma. Kak dolzhno byt' organizovano narodnoe
khozyaystvo pri vlasti trudyashchikhsya. Moscow, n.d. (Brought back
by the British Labour Delegation in 1920, now in the British Museum.)
Broadsheet.
Partiya revolyutsionnogo kommunizma. Zemel'nyy vopros. Moscow, n.d. (Broad-
sheet. Not later than May 1920. Brought back by the British
Labour Delegation.)
Portiynyya Izvestiya. Fortnightly journal of the Central Committee of the
R.S.–D.R.P. Last number, No. 8, appeared in Moscow on 10 January
1918.
Petrogradskaya pravda. Petrograd, 1918– .
Politics. New York, 1944– .
Pravda. March 1917– . Petrograd, Moscow.
Proletarskaya revolyutsiya. Leningrad, Moscow, 1921– .
Revolyutsionnaya Rossiya. Tallinn, 25 December 1920– .
Révolution prolétarienne. Revue mensuelle syndicaliste communiste. Paris,
1925– .
Rossiya (later *Velikaya Rossiya*) (daily). Edited by V. Shul'gin. Ekaterin-
odar, August, 1918– .
Russkiy istoricheskiy arkhiv. Izdanie russkogo zagranichnogo istoricheskogo
arkhiva v Prage. Sbornik pervyy. Prague, 1929.
Sotsialisticheskiy vestnik. Organ zagranichnoy delegatsii R.S.–D.R.P. (Fort-
nightly.) Berlin, 1st February 1921– .
[*Sots. vestnik.*]
Sovremennyya zapiski. Paris, 1920– .
Vestnik truda. Ezhemesyachnyy organ vserossiyskogo tsentral'nogo soveta professional'
nykh soyuzov. Moscow. (Nos. 1 and 2, October and December 1920.)
Voennoe delo. Moscow, 1918– .
Vozrozhdenie. Literaturno-politicheskiya tetradi. (Edited by S. P. Mel'-
gunov.) Paris, 1949– .
Workers' Dreadnought. London, 1921– .
Zarya. Organ sotsial-demokraticheskoy mysli. (Fortnightly.). Berlin, No. 1,
April, 1922– .
Znamya. (Fortnightly.) Edited by R. V. Ivanov-Razumnik, V. E.
Trutovskiy, O. L. Chizhikov, I. Z. Shteinberg. (Two issues early
1919. Reappeared in April 1920, for a few issues.)

SELECTED ARTICLES

'Agrarnoe dvizhenie v 1917 godu'. *Krasnyy arkhiv.*, Vol. 14. 1926,
pp. 182–226.
ASCHER, ABRAHAM. 'The Kornilov Affair.' *Russian Review.* October
1953, pp. 235–52.
BAEVSKY, D. 'Leninskaya i kamenevskaya otsenka revolyutsii 1917 g.'
Proletarskaya revolyutsiya, No. 12 (71), 1927, pp. 3–52.
BOLDIN, N. I. 'Men'sheviki v kronshtadtskom myatezhe', *Krasnaya
letopis'*, No. 3 (42), 1931, pp. 5–31.
BOSH, E. 'Oblastnoy komitet yugo-zapadnogo kraya 1917 g.' *Proletars-
kaya revolyutsiya.* No. 5 (28), 1924, pp. 128–49.
BRONIN, YA. 'Platforma tov. Bukharina v profsoyuznoy diskussii.'
Proletarskaya revolyutsiya, No. 12 (95), 1929, pp. 13–35.

BUKHARIN, N. I. 'Iz rechi tov. Bukharina na vechere vospominaniy v 1921 g.' *Proletarskaya revolyutsiya*, No. 10, 1922, pp. 316–22.

CILIGA, ANTON. 'A talk with Lenin in Stalin's Prison.' *Politics*. Vol. III. No. 7, August, 1946, pp. 234–41.

DOBROVOL'SKY, S. 'Bor'ba za vozrozhdenie Rossii v severnoy oblasti.' *Arkhiv russkoy revolyutsii*, Vol. III, pp. 5–146.

'Doklad i preniya po voprosu o leninskikh zamechaniyakh na knigu Bukharina "Ekonomika perekhodnogo perioda", etc.' *Proletarskaya revolyutsiya*. No. 12 (95), 1929, pp. 176–87.

'Dokumenty po istorii chernomorskogo flota v marte-iyune, 1918 g.' *Arkhiv russkoy revolyutsii*, Vol. XIV, 1924, pp. 151–221.

FLEROVSKY, I. 'Myatezh mobilizovannykh matrosov v Peterburge 14 oktyabrya 1918 g'. *Proletarskaya revolyutsiya*, No. 8 (55), 1926, pp. 218–37.

GERONIMUS, A. 'Osnovnye momenty razvitiya partiyno-politicheskogo apparata krasnoy armii v 1918–1920 gg.' *Grazhdanskaya voyna*, Vol. II, pp. 110–27.

'K istorii moskovskogo voenno-revolyutsionnogo komiteta'. *Krasnyy arkhiv*, Vol. LIV–LV, 1932, pp. 80–161.

KORNATOVSKY, N. A. 'Lenin i Trotsky v bor'be s interventami na Murmane.' *Krasnaya letopis'*. No. 3 (36), 1930, pp. 5–63.

KUZ'MIN, A. 'V petrogradskoy gubernii v 1917–1918 gg.' *Krasnaya letopis'*. No. 3 (27), 1928, pp. 227–53.

LUTOVINOV, YU. 'Udarnost' i zadachi profsoyuzov.' *Vestnik truda*, No. 2, December 1920, pp. 11–14.

MINTS, I. and EIDEMAN, R. 'Rasstanovka boevykh sil kontrrevolyutsii nakanune oktyabrya.' *Istorik marksist*. No. 1 (39), 1934, pp. 53 ff.

'Moskovskiy voenno-revolyutsionnyy komitet.' *Krasnyy arkhiv*. Vol. XXIII, 1927, pp. 63–148.

'Nakanune peremiriya.' *Krasnyy arkhiv*, Vol. XXIII, 1927, pp. 195–249.

PODVOYSKIY, N. I. 'Voennaya organizatsiya R.K.P.(b).' *Krasnaya letopis'*, Nos. 6–7, 1928.

'Pozitsiya Ts. K. partii v oktyabr'skie dni 1917 g.' *Proletarskaya revolyutsiya*, No. 10, 1922, pp. 459–70.

PUKHOV, A. S. 'V Petrograde nakanune kronshtadtskogo vosstaniya v 1921 g.' *Krasnaya letopis'*. No. 4 (37), 1930, pp. 77–122.

—— 'Kronshtadt i baltiyskiy flot pered myatezhem 1920 goda.' *Krasnaya letopis'*. No. 6 (39), 1930, pp. 149–212.

—— 'Kronshtadt vo vlasti vragov revolyutsii.' *Krasnaya letopis'*, No. 1 (40), 1931, pp. 5–80.

PUKHOV, G. S. 'Stroitel'stvo krasnoy armii v Petrograde i okruge.' *Krasnaya letopis'*. No. 6 (33), 1929, pp. 91–114; No. 34, 1930, pp. 47–76.

RABINOVICH, S. E. 'Vserossiyskaya konferentsiya bol'shevistkikh voennykh organizatsiy, 1917 goda.' *Krasnaya letopis'*, No. 5 (38), 1930, pp. 105–32.

—— 'Delegaty 10-go syezda R.K.P.(b) pod Kronshtadtom v 1921 godu.' *Krasnaya letopis'*, No. 2 (41), pp. 22–55.

RAKHMETOV, V. 'K istorii yanvarskikh tezisov Lenina.' *Proletarskaya revolyutsiya*, No. 5 (88), 1929, pp. 3–16.

RASKOL'NIKOV, F. 'Tragediya chernomorskogo flota 1918 g.' *Proletarskaya revolyutsiya*, No. 2 (37), 1925, pp. 170–85.

SAPOZHNIKOV, N. 'Izhevsko-votkinskoe vosstanie', *Proletarskaya revolyutsiya*, Nos. 8–9 (31–2), 1924, pp. 5–42.

SELIVANOV, V. 'Pervyy vserossiyskiy syezd voennogo flota.' *Krasnaya letopis'*. No. 1 (28), 1929, pp. 89–112.

SERGE, VICTOR. 'The Danger was Within.' 1. 'War Communism.' *Politics*, March, 1945, pp. 74–8: 2. 'Kronstadt,' *ibid.*, April, 1945, pp. 107–11: 3. 'Vignettes of NEP', *ibid.*, June, 1945, pp. 176–80. (All forming Chapter IV of his Memoirs.)

SIDEROV A. 'Ekonomicheskaya programma oktyabrya i diskussiya s levymi kommunistami o zadachakh sotsialisticheskogo stroitel'stva.' *Proletarskaya revolyutsiya*, No. 6 (89), 1929, pp. 26–75; No. 11 (94), 1929, pp. 11–66.

SMILG-BENARIO, M. 'Na sovetskoy sluzhbe.' *Arkhiv russkoy revolyutsii*, Vol. III, 1921, pp. 147–89.

SOKOLOV, B. 'Padenie severnoy oblasti.' *Arkhiv russkoy revolyutsii*, Vol. IX, pp. 5–90, 1927.

—— 'Zashchita uchreditel'nogo sobraniya.' *Arkhiv russkoy revolyutsii*, Vol. XIII, pp. 36–70, 1931.

STANCHINSKY, A. 'Vserossiyskaya aprel'skaya partiynaya konferentsiya 1917 goda.' *Proletarskaya revolyutsiya*, No. 4 (63), 1927, pp. 11–66.

STRUVE, PETR. 'Moi vstrechi i stolknoveniya s Leninym.' *Vozrozhdenie*, No. 9, 1950, pp. 113–21; No. 10, 1950, pp. 109–18.

—— 'M.V. Chelnokov i D.N. Shipov.' (Glava iz moikh vospominaniy.) *Novyy zhurnal*, No. XII, 1949, pp. 240–5.

STUPOCHENKO, L. 'Brestskie dni.' *Proletarskaya revolyutsiya*. No. 4 (16), 1923, pp. 94–111.

TOLSTOV, V. 'Pervoe vystuplenie Plekhanova i Lenina po ikh vozvrashchenii iz-za granitzy v aprele 1917 g.' *Krasnaya letopis'*. No. 3 (18), 1926, pp. 70–5.

VALENTINOV, N. 'Tragediya G. V. Plekhanova.' *Novyy zhurnal*, No. XX, 1948, pp. 270–93.

VLADIMIROVA, V. 'Levye esery v 1917–1918 g.' *Proletarskaya revolyutsiya*, No. 4 (63), 1927, p. 101.

'Vospominaniya ob oktyabr'skom perevorote.' *Proletarskaya revolyutsiya* No. 10, 1922, pp. 43–93.

INDEX

18096665R00234

Printed in Great Britain
by Amazon